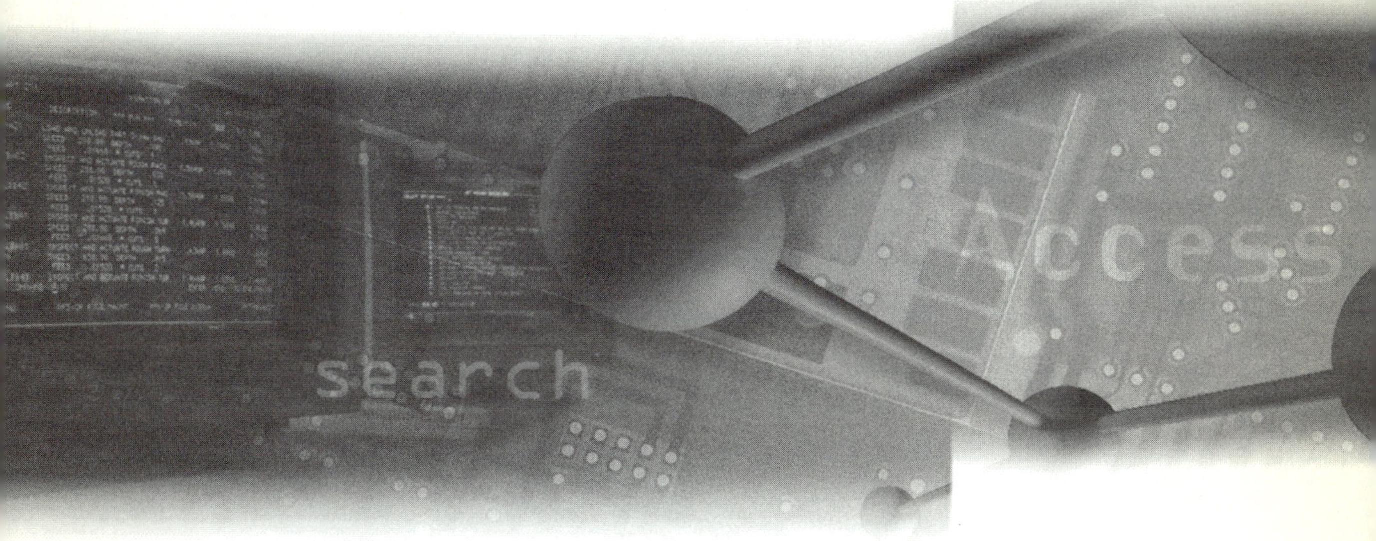

Client/Server Programming With Access & SQL Server

Windows 95/NT

VENTANA

Leo Sanin
Renzhong Chen

Client/Server Programming With Access & SQL Server

The Integrated Guide for Programmers & Developers

Windows 95/NT

Client/Server Programming With Access & SQL Server

Library of Congress Catalog Card Number: 97-061133

First Edition 9 8 7 6 5 4 3 2 1

Printed in the United States of America

Ventana Communications Group
P.O. Box 13964
Research Triangle Park, NC 27709-3964
919.544.9404
FAX 919.544.9472
http://www.vmedia.com

Ventana Communications Group is a division of International Thomson Publishing.

Limits of Liability & Disclaimer of Warranty

The authors and publisher of this book have used their best efforts in preparing the book and the programs contained in it. These efforts include the development, research, and testing of the theories and programs to determine their effectiveness. The authors and publisher make no warranty of any kind, expressed or implied, with regard to these programs or the documentation contained in this book.

The authors and publisher shall not be liable in the event of incidental or consequential damages in connection with, or arising out of, the furnishing, performance or use of the programs, associated instructions and/or claims of productivity gains.

Trademarks

Trademarked names appear throughout this book and on the accompanying compact disk, if applicable. Rather than list the names and entities that own the trademarks or insert a trademark symbol with each mention of the trademarked name, the publisher states that it is using the names only for editorial purposes and to the benefit of the trademark owner with no intention of infringing upon that trademark.

President
Michael E. Moran

Vice President of Content Development
Karen A. Bluestein

Director of Acquisitions and Development
Robert Kern

Editorial Operations Manager
Kerry L. B. Foster

Production Manager
John Cotterman

Brand Manager
Jamie Jaeger Fiocco

Art Director
Marcia Webb

Creative Services Manager
Diane Lennox

Acquisitions Editor
Neweleen A. Trebnik

Project Editor
Judith F. Wilson

Development Editor
Michelle Corbin Nichols

Copy Editor
Judy Flynn

CD-ROM Specialist
Ginny Phelps

Technical Reviewer
Russ Mullen

Desktop Publisher
Kristin Miller

Proofreader
Amity Brown

Indexer
Lynn Brown

Interior Designer
Patrick Berry

Cover Illustrator
Lisa Gill

About the Authors

Leo Sanin has more than 16 years of experience working as a systems programmer, applications developer, project leader, and database administrator. He is a Microsoft Certified Systems Engineer specializing in Data Warehousing based on Microsoft SQL Server. For the past three years he has been working for the Commonwealth of Massachusetts as a database administrator. He coauthored several articles on networks and database management systems in computer journals in the USSR and participated in industry conferences.

Renzhong Chen entered the computer industry after graduating from Stanford University with a master's degree in electrical engineering. He has had considerable research and technical writing experience and has authored or coauthored publications in several academic journals. He works for the Commonwealth of Massachusetts as a systems analyst.

Acknowledgments

First, we owe much to both of our families, who have been understanding and supportive through our sometimes hectic schedules. Special thanks to Leo's parents and his wife, as well as the Byrd family, who have been like family to Renzhong all these years.

Our gratitude to the various editors at Ventana who worked with us on this book. Their thorough professionalism and competence helped to guide us through what was for us new waters. Thanks also to our agent, Laura Belt, without whose help this book would not have been possible.

We are fortunate to have a group of able and kind colleagues at the Commonwealth. Working with them allowed us to better understand the needs of developers and programmers.

Thanks to Gabriel Gagliano for being a supportive friend and for providing valuable suggestions.

—L.S. and R.C.

Contents

Introduction

Modern enterprise computing hinges on the concept of sharing: the sharing of information, the sharing of resources, and the sharing of processing power. Advances in network technology have allowed multiple computers to simultaneously participate in a single, complex computing environment. Computer networks now often support highly heterogeneous environments, with computers of all types running a variety of software to accomplish a wide spectrum of tasks.

As more and more computers are brought into a network to work together, it is important to organize them into a logical architecture so that each computer's role and function is clearly delineated. There have been several well-recognized computing models over time. The past half-decade saw the client/server model firmly established and widely accepted in all corners of the computing industry. The client/server architecture divides information processing between front-end (client) components and back-end (server) components. By distributing the workload between front- and back-end modules, client/server computing gives a system a great deal of flexibility as well as high performance.

The client/server architecture is especially useful for database systems. There are a number of database software products on the market that can play the role of either the client or server component. Many of these database software products conform to the relational data model, which is a framework for organizing data and which offers efficient, powerful, and formalized tools for structuring and manipulating data.

Microsoft SQL Server and Microsoft Access have emerged as a potent combination that sets the trend to converge toward the client/server architecture. Together, they form a powerful tool for relational database programming in a multiuser environment. The relational data model and the client/server architecture constitute the twin pillars of the combined Access/SQL Server system. SQL Server offers high performance, manageability, and security in the role of a back-end processor, while Access for Windows 95 serves as a user-friendly and flexible front-end interface.

Microsoft Access is a personal relational database management system (RDBMS) that combines powerful RDBMS capabilities with intuitive user control. It's designed to be run on each client workstation. The ability of Access to work with different data sources and provide a user-friendly graphical user interface (GUI) makes it an ideal product for a front-end component in a database system. Since its introduction, Microsoft Access has garnered an extensive user base.

Microsoft SQL Server is a multiuser, high-performance RDBMS that runs in the Windows NT operating system. It's designed to be run centrally on a server computer. Using Transact-SQL, a high-level database language, SQL Server performs standard DBMS functions such as data manipulation, security, integrity check, and backup/recovery. SQL Server is specifically designed to be used as the server component in the client/server environment. It is capable of controlling very large amounts of data; it can simultaneously processes multiple data requests from client software and return only the data that has been requested; it also performs selective data locking so that multiple users can work on different parts of the same set of data at the same time.

Although both Microsoft Access and Microsoft SQL Server have been available for some years, for many programmers and developers, the full potential of the two as a whole has yet to be realized. Access and SQL Server form a unique programming environment, one which has its own idiosyncrasies, nuances, and bag of tricks. This book treats the SQL Server/Access environment as one integrated system instead of two disparate bodies and takes a close look at some of the fine points of client/server programming with Access and SQL Server.

Who Needs This Book?

This book is intended for those who have had at least a little exposure to Access or SQL Server. With the immense popularity of Access, we expect this book to be of some help to readers who have used Access, done some good things in it, and now would like to expand and improve their applications with SQL Server.

However, this book is by no means intended to be an exhaustive study of SQL Server and Access. In fact, there is no lack of good books on those subjects. This book stresses the interaction between Access and SQL Server, which covers a small, albeit very interesting, subset of the two products' total capabilities. We hope this book will give you enough tools and insight to initiate yourself to the full potential of the combined Access/SQL Server system.

What's Inside?

This book contains 10 chapters and four appendices. The following is an overview of all the modules of the book.

Chapter 1: The Basics of Client/Server Computing explains client/server computing in the context of other computing models. Networking protocols are introduced in discussions about the OSI model. The respective roles of Access and SQL Server in a client/server environment are discussed.

Chapter 2: The Relational Data Model presents the basic theory of the relational data model. Normalization, integrity rules, and relationships are discussed as part of the relational model.

Chapter 3: Client Component: Microsoft Access stresses the distinction between running Access in the file server configuration and running Access in the client/server configuration. Data access object (DAO) reference and Visual Basic for Applications, (will be referred to as Visual Basic throughout the book) which will be used extensively later in the book, are introduced here. Updatable queries, a unique and powerful feature of Access, are discussed, too.

Chapter 4: Server Component: Microsoft SQL Server for Windows NT provides an introduction to the Windows NT Server as an operating system of choice for SQL Server. Chapter 4 then delves into Microsoft SQL Server for Windows NT Database Management System as well as the basics of database administration and database design in SQL Server.

Chapter 5: Introduction to Open Database Connectivity presents ODBC as the intercommunications component in the client/server model. The ODBC architecture is outlined. Topics include ODBC drivers, data sources, ODBC API, and how the Jet database engine makes ODBC calls. ODBC-related performance issues are discussed here, too.

Chapter 6: Manipulating Data in The Client/Server Architecture is concerned with the non-dynamic transfer of data into or out of an Access/SQL Server system. Access/SQL Server's interaction with several types of systems are covered: mainframe legacy systems, other client/server applications (built in a different relational database system, for example), and file server-type databases (such as dBase). The Import/Export utility and replication in Access are also discussed.

Chapter 7: Accessing Data Using Linked Tables examines how to dynamically access SQL Server data from Access by using linked tables. The mechanics of linking SQL Server tables, including the use of the Upsizing Wizard, is presented. Much attention is paid to the non-ideal situations in which linked tables don't behave like local tables.

Chapter 8: Accessing Data Using SQL Pass-Through Queries is about how to dynamically access SQL Server data from Access by using pass-through queries. Pass-through queries are introduced and compared with ordinary queries. Examples of SQL Server stored procedures, which can be called from pass-through queries, are given. Techniques are detailed to manipulate pass-through queries in Visual Basic code.

Chapter 9: Optimization & Tuning is the bag-of-tricks chapter of the book. It contains a diverse selection of useful and interesting techniques for improving system performance, facilitating database maintenance, and optimizing database system layout.

Chapter 10: Security discusses Access and SQL Server security separately at first. Several possible security implementations involving both Access and SQL Server are then presented. Considerable emphasis is given to security implementation in Visual Basic code.

Appendix A: About the Companion CD ROM contains instructions on how to use and install the this book's Companion CD-ROM.

Appendix B: Access Run-Time Error is a collection of Access error codes and their explanations.

Appendix C: Transact-SQL Reference provides reference material on some of the most useful Transact-SQL statements.

Appendix D: Visual Basic Language Reference brings together some useful Visual Basic commands, constants, and constructs.

About the Companion CD-ROM

This book comes with a CD-ROM, which contains the following:

- An SQL Server database that you can load into your local SQL Server as an example database. This database is to be used in conjunction with the Access applications included in the CD-ROM.
- A number of Access applications (.mdb files), each illustrating a set of functionalities discussed in the book.
- Several handy SQL Server tools for such tasks as database administration and performance analysis.
- CuteFTP, an FTP tool.

For detailed information on how to use and install the CD-ROM, refer to Appendix A.

Conventions

The acronym SQL, which stands for *Structured Query Language*, is used extensively in this book. In spoken English, SQL is either pronounced as *sequel* or spelled out as S-Q-L. We have adopted the latter of these two conventions in this book, so that we use "an SQL statement" rather than "a SQL statement."

Throughout this book, when an important term is first introduced in a chapter, it is placed in italics.

We use the symbol | to specify a menu command. For example, File | Open Database refers to the Open Database command under the File menu in the menu bar.

The object-manipulation language know as Access Basic in previous versions of Microsoft Access (Access 1.x and Access 2.0) has been renamed to Visual Basic in Access for Windows 95, although the language itself has largely stayed the same. Don't confuse the Visual Basic language used in Access with Microsoft Visual Basic, which is a closely related but independent software product. When we refer to Microsoft Visual Basic as an independent entity in the text, we always provide sufficient context to make clear that it is distinct from Access. When used alone, Visual Basic always refers to the language that's part of Access.

Moving On

As database developers who use SQL Server and Access extensively, we have often been frustrated by the lack of a book that gives an in-depth, systematic treatment on the unique Access/SQL Server hybrid programming environment. Sure, there are plenty of books that discuss either Access or SQL Server, but they usually don't address even some of the frequently encountered problems unique to the Access/SQL environment. At times answers and insight were so hard to come by, that we felt as if we were fighting a lonely battle in the dark.

Hence the impetus behind this book. As we have come to gain a good grasp on the Access/SQL Server environment, we'd like to share some of our knowledge and experience with you. We truly hope this book will help you clear some of the same obstacles that had so frustrated us.

Happy programming!

Leo Sanin & Renzhong Chen

chapter 1

The Basics of Client/Server Computing

Client/server computing is one of a number of network computing models that take advantage of the ability to work with multiple computers in the same system. As its name suggests, client/server computing splits data processing between a client component and a server component. In this book, we'll consider client/server computing in the context of relational database design using Microsoft Access and Microsoft SQL Server. Before we can delve into the fine details of Access and SQL Server, however, we must first answer a number of important questions:

- What technologies enable multiple computers to process and share information in a network?
- What is client/server computing, and how is it different from other methods of computing for networked computers?
- Why is client/server so widely accepted?
- How do Access and SQL Server fit into the client/server architecture?
- Why bother using Access and SQL Server when Access alone does so much?

To those of you who have had some exposure to Access but who are new to the client/server architecture, the last question is an especially relevant one. Access is a powerful and popular tool, and many people have been able to accomplish a great deal with it. So it seems only natural to question the wisdom of adding an extra element to an already successful system.

The OSI Model

Computer networks can be classified into two broad categories: *local area networks* (LAN) and *wide area networks* (WAN). A LAN is a communications network that enables data exchange between devices within a small geographic area. (Here, devices mostly refer to computers and peripheral devices such as printers.) A WAN usually consists of a collection of LANs and spreads over a much larger geographical area, sometimes even spanning the globe.

Networks are commonly discussed in the framework of the *Open Systems Interconnect* (OSI) model. Like many other technologies in the computer industry, network communications didn't have a uniform protocol at the beginning. Companies such as IBM, DEC, and Honeywell had incompatible standards for connecting computers, so products from different companies could not communicate with each other. In 1978, the *International Standards Organization* (ISO), an internationally recognized body responsible for creating worldwide uniform standards in science and technology, introduced the several-layer Open Systems Interconnect (OSI) model to facilitate data communication among disparate equipment from different vendors. Figure 1-1 shows the conceptual layout of the OSI model.

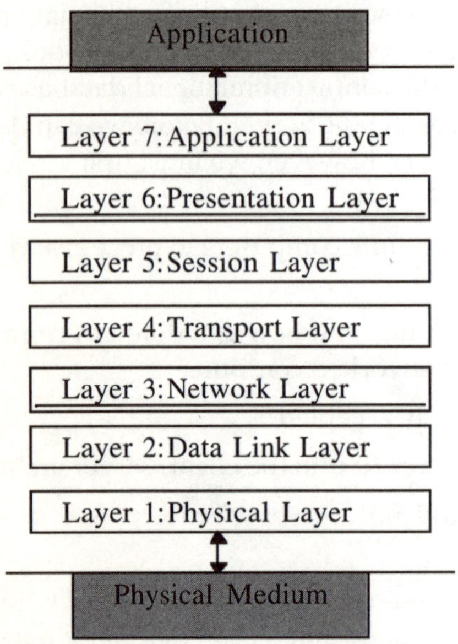

Figure 1-1: Conceptual layout of the seven-layer OSI model.

In the OSI model, each layer performs a specific set of network functions and builds on its immediate predecessor, resulting in progressively higher-level functionality through the seven layers. Guidelines have been defined for implementing interfaces between layers.

Ideally, a networking product would perform functions assigned to one of the layers in the OSI model, and different products from various vendors may be interchanged for the same layer without affecting the rest of the network. In practice, however, this is not always the case. Many vendors offer products that span multiple OSI layers, do not conform to the OSI model, or simply don't fit into any of the layers.

Physical Layer

The physical layer is the lowest layer in the OSI model. It deals with how electrical or optical signals are generated, transmitted, and received in a physical medium. The most common standard at this layer is RS-232C. Other standards include RS-449 and X.21, which is commonly used in Europe. This layer consists of four major components involved in the processing of signals:

- Transmission format, which can be either digital or analog.
- Physical transmission medium, which refers to whether bits of data are transmitted as electrical or optical signals.
- Data encoding, which specifies what signal patterns represent ones and zeroes and the synchronization between sending and receiving devices.
- Physical medium attachment, which deals with wiring and pin layouts connectors.

Data Link Layer

Networks transfer data in "chunks," or packets, of a certain size. The data link layer forms data packets, manages their movement at each node in the network, and adds the appropriate addresses of the source and destination nodes. In PC-based LANs, it is at this layer that protocols like Token Ring and Ethernet are implemented. These functions are often performed by *network interface cards* (NICs) installed in computers.

Network Layer

The network layer performs data routing (i.e., determining the physical path data packets take) based on the network conditions, priority of data packets, and other factors. This layer usually doesn't have a great deal of importance in

LANs since every node communicates directly with all other nodes in a LAN; hence, data packets don't need to go through intermediate nodes to reach their final destinations. In WANs, however, intermediate routing is often needed, and the network layer software usually resides on special switching nodes that are part of the network.

Transport Layer

The transport layer makes sure that messages are delivered in the order in which they were sent. Typically, it also guarantees that there is no loss or error in the delivery of messages. The size and complexity of a transport protocol depend on the type of service it can get from the network layer or data link layer. The common protocols that exist at this layer include Transmission Control Protocol/Internet Protocol (TCP/IP) and Sequenced Packet Exchange/Internet Packet Exchange (SPX/IPX).

At the transport layer and above, computers communicate with each other using high-level source-to-destination addressing specified in message headers and control messages. This contrasts sharply with the lower layers, in which only immediate neighboring nodes can communicate with each other.

Session Layer

The session layer is responsible for establishing virtual connections between processes running on different computers. Each such connection is called a *session*. This layer is usually the interface to the network for programmers. It handles such functions as name recognition, administration, and security in a network. NetBIOS Extended User Interface (NETBEUI) is a commonly used protocol for the session layer.

Presentation Layer

The presentation layer is responsible for translating one data format into another. At the sending computer, the presentation layer transforms the format sent by the application layer into a common format. At the receiving computer, the presentation layer translates the common format to a format chosen by the application layer. Terminal emulation is performed at this layer.

It is in this layer that the network operating system (NOS) software resides. This software offers network services and provides the application layer with independence from lower-level details. Often, however, many applications bypass the NOS to interact directly with the session or transport layer for greater control over network resources.

Application Layer

The application layer serves as the user interface through which network resources can be accessed. The application layer offers the following functions:

- Resource sharing (e.g., the sharing of printers)
- Remote file access
- Remote printer access
- Inter-process communication support
- Remote procedure call support
- Network management
- Directory services
- Electronic messaging, including e-mail messaging

Inter-Process Communication

With *inter-process communication* (IPC), two different processes, such as applications, on different computers have the ability to communicate. In a PC local area network, IPC is provided by the network operating system (NOS). IPC is especially important to client/server computing because the client application running on a client computer must be able to communicate with the server application on the server computer.

IPC is implemented at various OSI levels, including the presentation, session, and transport layers. Different levels of implementation offer trade-offs between system transparency and flexibility. High-level implementations hide much of the underlying complexity; lower-level implementations offer more control and flexibility.

Models of Computing

A network is a very structured system with distinct modules running at different levels performing various tasks that ultimately allow computers to communicate with each other. Placing multiple computers in a single networked environment leads to computing possibilities not found with stand-alone, isolated computers. There are a number of ways in which computers can work together. These are referred to as *computing models.*

Conceptual Models vs. Physical Layout

Before we take a detailed look at the classification of computing models, we must be very clear about an important point: such classifications concern the conceptual ways in which computing tasks are performed. They do not necessarily correspond to the physical layout of computers in a network.

Today's computer networks are often heterogeneous, meaning that they are composed of many client computers, mainframes, file servers, and so on. To complete a specific computing task, however, only some of these computers are likely to be involved. It is the way in which the subset of involved computers interact with one another that defines the type of computing model for that computing task.

Classifying Computer Systems

Computers are machines that electronically manipulate and process binary streams of data, or information. One way to classify computer systems is based on their power to process information. Traditionally, computers have been grouped into three broad categories: mainframes, minicomputers, and microcomputers, listed here in descending order by their respective processing prowess and corresponding cost.

Mainframes include the likes of Cray supercomputers, IBM 3090s, and DEC Vax machines. Workstations, including those produced by Sun Microsystems and Silicon Graphics, belong to the minicomputer category. The ubiquitous PCs are usually considered microcomputers. Of course, the rapid advances in semiconductor technology and microprocessor design have made some supposed microcomputers so powerful and at the same time so inexpensive that the boundaries between the categories are becoming increasingly indistinct.

So far, our discussion of the classification of computer systems emphasizes the processing power of single computers. If we expand the definition of a computer system to include any collection of one or more computers, then we must consider the sharing of the system's collective processing power. Depending on how this collective processing power is used by end users, we can classify computer systems into four types: single processing, shared processing, file server computing, and client/server processing computing.

Pre-Client/Server Computing Models

Client/server computing is a relatively new computing model. Single processing, shared processing, and file server processing were widely used long before client/server computing.

Single Processing

In this case, a computer is used by one user. The computer has exclusive access to its own system's resources, including central processing unit (CPU) time, memory, and data. The typical home PC is a good example of a single-processing system, where the all the needs of the user, including the processing, storage, and retrieval of data, the user interface, and peripheral matters such as printing, are taken care of by that one PC.

A single-processing system can actually comprise more than one computer. For example, two PCs connected by a LAN can exchange data between them; one of them functions as a server, sending files to the other computer at its request. As long as the server only has to deal with one user at a time, these two computers remain a single-processing system. Figure 1-2 illustrates the concept of single processing.

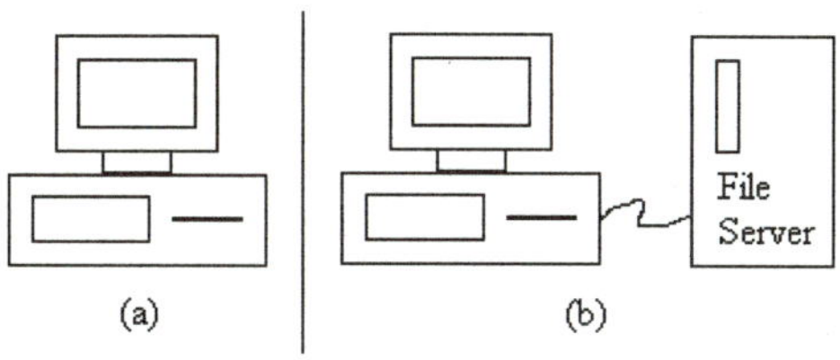

Figure 1-2: (a) Single processing—the one-computer configuration; and (b) single processing with an extra server.

The chief advantage of single-processing computing is that it is simple. The scale of a single-processing system is typically quite small, and it does not use complex protocols and algorithms for intercomputer communications. As a result, such a system is relatively inexpensive. In addition, since each computer constitutes an isolated environment, customizing that computing environment is often much easier than in other computing environments.

On the other hand, if information and computer resources are to be shared at all by a group of people, this approach to computing becomes very unwieldy. Just try to imagine distributing something like a corporate policy file to everyone in a company using floppy drives through the good old "sneaker net"! It is clear that something else is needed for computing in a complex environment.

Shared Processing

Whereas in single processing each computer is used by one user only, shared processing is designed to allow multiple users to use one machine at the same time. This form of computing belongs mostly in the realm of mainframes. Typically, multiple terminals are connected to a mainframe computer. When users log in to the mainframes through these terminals, they each open up a "session" with the mainframe and are presented with an interface through which they enter commands, run programs, and send and receive data (see Figure 1-3 for an illustration of these concepts). Of course, the sessions run independently of one another so that different users logged on to the mainframe do not interfere with other users' work. The mainframe makes sure of that by keeping track of all the current users and sessions.

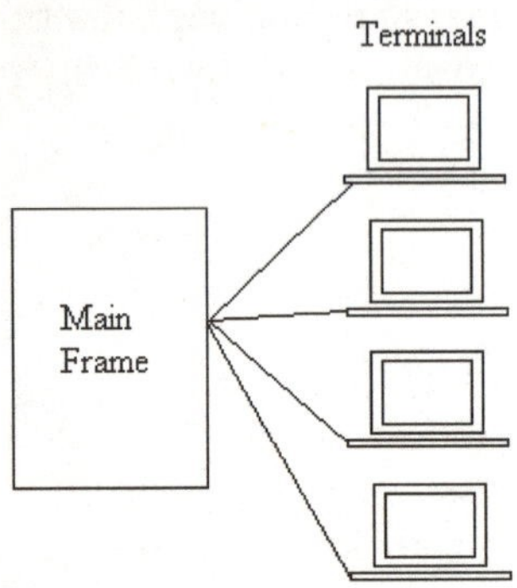

Figure 1-3: Shared processing based on a mainframe computer.

Originally, mainframe terminals were simple interfacing devices specifically designed to do one thing: communicate with their companion mainframes. Usually they consisted of not much more than a monitor and a keyboard and did not possess any processing power. They were therefore called "dummy terminals." Today, the role of the terminals is more often taken up by PCs running software packages called *terminal emulators.* Although the PCs have their own CPUs and are perfectly capable of processing data on their own, terminal emulators rarely use that processing power.

Shared processing is a highly centralized computing method. Not only does all the processing happen in the CPU of the mainframe, but all memory used for the processing and all data in the system come from the mainframe, too. And herein lies the chief strength of shared processing: since data resides in the same place, it is equally accessible to all users, and any changes in data are almost instantaneously available to all users. Without having to worry about transferring data between different platforms or about making sure several copies of the same data are consistent with one another, it becomes relatively easy to manage and impose security on the data. In addition, mainframes can handle large volumes of data with high performance. All these attributes lead to the extensive use of mainframes in mission-critical applications such as those used by the military and various financial professions.

Mainframes are powerful and complex machines. Many of them have several CPUs and very large amounts of memory. However, what makes mainframes so desirable also underlies their weaknesses. Complex systems are expensive, and mainframes are no exception. Furthermore, the typical application development cycle for mainframes is much longer than in other systems, and maintaining mainframes can also be costly and labor intensive. These shortcomings limit the prevalent use of mainframe-based shared processing in today's corporate enterprise computing.

File Server Computing

So far, we have looked at two computing models in which there is no sharing of resources among different computers. In single processing, each computer is used by one user only; even when there is a server, the very definition of single processing requires that the server only "talk" to one user. In shared processing, all the processing takes place on only one computer, albeit a very powerful one, so there is no possible interaction between several computers.

The file server architecture, on the other hand, is a form of *distributed computing* in which both data and computing resources are shared between two or more computers.

File server computing is based on two types of component systems: file servers and clients (or workstations). File server computing is sometimes referred to as client-based computing: all the data processing is done on workstations, and file servers merely hold shared data and answer requests from clients to perform certain simple tasks. These tasks include transferring files between workstations and file servers and issuing instructions to peripheral devices (such as printers, plotters, and so on), say, to print a file. When a central file server is present in a LAN, computers on the same network can share data as well as expensive peripheral devices such as laser printers (see the diagram in Figure 1-4, which illustrates the architecture).

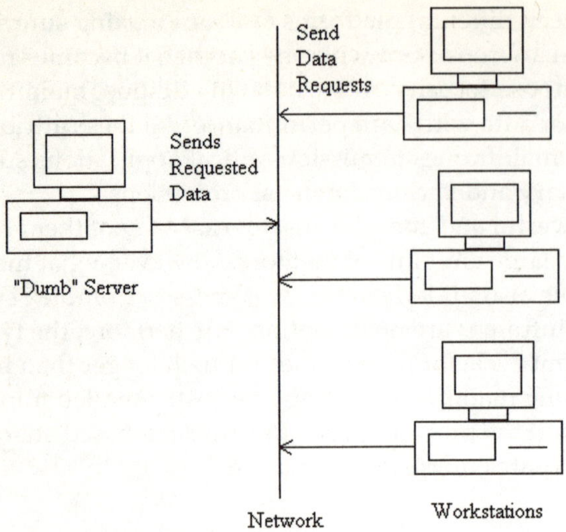

Figure 1-4: A file server computing system. Note that the main difference between this and the single-processing system shown in Figure 1-2(b) is that the file server is shared by several client computers (workstations).

File server computing is not very different from the single processing model in that information processing is done by non-server computers. However, file server computing does have an important advantage over single processing: it enables data and peripheral resource sharing. Compared with mainframe-based shared processing architecture, file server computing is simpler and therefore less costly to implement and maintain.

There are several important limitations to the file server architecture. One has to do with the way file servers manage file transfers over the LAN. When a workstation on the LAN requests a file from a file server, the file server simply ships a copy of the file in its entirety to the workstation by using the LAN's network software. Since all data processing takes place at the workstation level, the file server is not aware of the content of the file and is therefore incapable of intelligently responding to data requests. As file servers blindly ship out entire files without knowing their content, more data may be transferred over the LAN than is needed.

This is an especially relevant issue with database systems. A user, for example, may only need to make some changes to one record in a database, but because the file server cannot selectively send data to the user's workstation, the user must have all the records in the database downloaded to his or her workstation and find the record of interest. Only then can he or she start to make changes to that record. The first step in this process, the downloading of the entire database file, is not only unnecessary, but it could also congest the LAN traffic as well as decrease the overall performance of the database system.

Another problem with file server computing has to do with data sharing. After successfully sending a copy of a file to a workstation, a file server places a lock on the original file so that no other computer can access it until the first workstation is finished with it. Since file servers treat each file as one entity and do not deal with the content of the file, they can't selectively lock pieces of data in the file. File servers prevent any user from accessing a file if one user already has it open, even if the user is using a small part of the file. This means that different users can't update the same data file simultaneously. In a multiuser environment, this could lead to great inconvenience.

Client/Server Computing

Client/server computing arose in response to the limitations of the previous computing architectures. Client/server computing is also a form of distributed computing and comprises three components: the client component, the server component, and an intercommunications component that connects the two; all of these components operate across a network. Although both the file server and client/server models belong to the class of distributed computing, client/server computing improves on file server architecture by dividing data processing between the client and server components. In other words, the server component in the client/server architecture is granted "intelligence" and is capable of performing complex processing functions.

Computers that function as either clients or servers run either client or server applications (or, sometimes, front-end or back-end applications), respectively. These applications are usually full-featured, powerful, complex software packages that can operate independently. The intercommunications component serves as a sophisticated communications tool between the client and server. It runs on both the client and server sides and performs a plethora of functions, from transporting data to translating between different formats, all to make the interface between the client and server seamless. Figure 1-5 shows the skeletal structure of client/server computing.

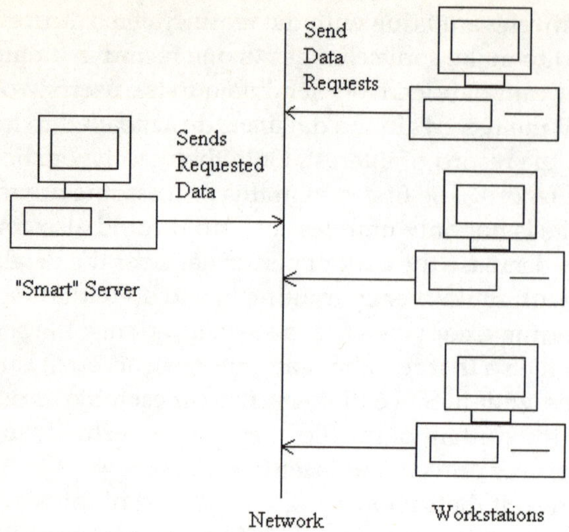

Figure 1-5: The structure of client/server computing. Note that the main difference between this architecture and file server computing illustrated in Figure 1-4 is that processing is split between the client and server components.

This client in the client/server architecture functions in very much the same way as the one in the file server architecture. It provides an end-user interface, often a graphical user interface (GUI), or an object-oriented user interface (OOUI). The client is not intended to have direct access to a great deal of data; instead, it sends requests for data to the server whenever the need arises. It has some form of distributed system management (DSM) so that it possesses multiuser capabilities of its own.

The server in the client/server architecture is aware of the contents of the files that it holds and is therefore an intelligent server. It can selectively lock data in a file as well as return across the LAN only the data required to answer the client requests. It is also capable of understanding high-level requests (i.e., requests written in a high-level language) for data manipulation. The server is often a very powerful computer with a great deal of processing power, memory, and disk storage space. It keeps track of all the concurrent users in a multiuser environment. To facilitate data sharing and security implementation, data in a client/server system mostly resides on the server.

The intercommunications element must be present on both the client and server machines for them to communicate properly. The intercommunications component can be further broken down into four functional categories: transport stacks, network operating systems (NOSes), distributed system management (DSM), and service-specific software. Transport stacks and NOSes provide the basic communications foundation for the entire intercommunications package. DSM runs on every node in a client/server network; it requires its own intercommunication layer on top of the NOS to carry messages between managing stations and managed stations. And of course, the function and selection of service-specific software depends on the application model.

The modular nature of client/server computing holds the key to its desirability. Because processing can be accomplished at either the client or the server level, it is often viable to develop applications in this environment in various ways. As a result, within a given client/server environment, different methods of processing configurations can be substituted for and balanced against one another to achieve the optimal result.

The modular characteristic of client/server computing extends beyond the possible operations that a given combination of front- and back-end applications allows. At the hardware level, various computers can take on the role of either a client or server. At the software level, a proliferation of often functionally similar software products designed with the client/server environment in mind offers users and developers the freedom to substitute one client or server software product for another without losing much continuity.

With such a wide spectrum of choices and flexibility, there are many benefits to client/server computing:

- **Data Accessibility.** Since the server component holds most of the data in a centralized location, multiple users can access and work on the data simultaneously. Data access can be done through LANs as well as wide area networks (WANs) and different client software.
- **System Administration (SA).** From a systems administrator's perspective, the client/server environment is very manageable. Since data is centralized, data management can be centralized. This means that all the SA functions, including security, data integrity, and backup/recovery, can be enforced with relative convenience on the server. There is no need to "uniformize" and synchronize data across distinct multiple hardware and software platforms, so maintenance labor can be kept relatively low.
- **Performance.** As mentioned earlier, because of the multiple hardware, software, and processing choices available for building a client/server system, there is a great deal that can be "tweaked" to achieve the optimal result. This book will show examples in which the superior performance of the client/server architecture clearly shines through.

- **Scalability.** Because of the modular nature of client/server computing, the main components of a client/server system may be replaced without adversely affecting the rest of the system. For example, it is possible to upgrade the server to a more powerful machine with no visible changes to the end user. This ability to change component system makes client/server systems especially receptive to new technologies in both hardware and software.
- **System Interoperability.** Client/server computing not only allows one component to be changed, it also makes it possible for different types of component systems—be it the client, network, or server—to work together. A good example is a system in which multiple client software coexist and work in conjunction with the same server.
- **Cost.** The cost of a client/server system is generally higher than its file server counterpart. However, because of all the advantages we have just discussed, the client/server system tends to be more cost effective. In addition, cost effectiveness in client/server computing can be maximized by choosing economical hardware or software component systems to replace more expensive ones.

Access & SQL Server as a Client/Server System

Over the past few years, Microsoft Access and Microsoft SQL Server have emerged as a formidable combination for relational database programming in a multiuser, client/server programming environment. Access acts as a user-friendly and flexible front-end application, while SQL Server offers high performance, manageability, and security in the role of a back-end processor.

SQL Server as The Server

Microsoft SQL Server is a multiuser, high-performance relational database management system (RDBMS) that runs in the Windows NT operating system. SQL stands for *structured query language*, a high-level database language approved as the standard relational query language by the American National Standards Institute (ANSI) and widely used in many DBMSes. An enhanced version of SQL, called Transact-SQL, is used by SQL Server to perform standard DBMS functions such as data manipulation, security, integrity check, and backup/recovery.

SQL Server is specifically designed for the client/server environment. It assumes the role of the back-end, or server, component in this architecture. Since the server component is supposed to control most of the data in a client/server system, SQL Server is capable of managing very large amounts of data (on the order of several gigabytes for each database it controls). SQL Server communicates with client software, processes data requests, and returns only data that has been requested. SQL Server also performs selective data locking so that multiple users can work on different parts of the same set of data at the same time.

SQL Server relies on the client component to provide user-interface and application-processing functions (e.g., structuring work flow in a multistep business process). SQL Server can pair with any of several commercially available front-end, or client, software products through an intercommunications standard called Open Database Connectivity (ODBC). One of the most popular client products is, of course, Access. Access sends requests for data, written in the form of Transact-SQL statements, through ODBC to SQL Server; SQL Server then returns to Access the requested data, assuming the requests meet security and data integrity requirements.

Although SQL Server often runs on a single dedicated high-performance computer, it doesn't have to. SQL Server is a software package that doesn't require specialized hardware, so it can run in different hardware configurations, which gives it a large measure of flexibility. In fact, SQL Server can be installed on the same machine as its client counterpart, and several SQL Servers may run on dedicated computers in the same LAN.

To access SQL Server directly (instead of from a client application), you need several administrative and utility tools from the Microsoft SQL Server 6.5 program group, which is available after the installation of the Server software. The tools include the SQL Enterprise Manager, SQL Server Manager, ISQL/W, and so on. Through them, you can design your database, monitor server activities, or perform administrative functions.

Figure 1-6 contains an example of the Server Manager window of SQL Enterprise Manager. There are a total of three SQL 6.50 Servers in this case, each for one of three departments in a company: SALES, MARKETING, and MIS. Under MARKETING, there are four categories of objects: Database Devices, Backup Devices, Databases, and Logins. This example illustrates the typical structure of an SQL Server database.

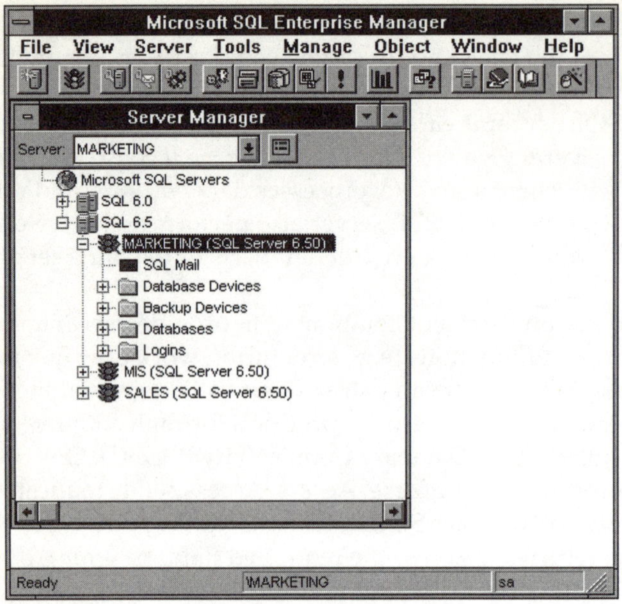

Figure 1-6: The Server Manager window.

You will find a detailed discussion on SQL Server in Chapter 4.

Access as The Client

By itself, Access is a full-featured relational database management system (RDBMS). If you have had any exposure to Access, you probably already have an appreciation for the convenience provided by its forms, reports, and the QBE (query by example) grid. Underneath this user-friendly graphical interface, however, is a formal and powerful data system based on the SQL database language. In addition, Access provides Visual Basic, a fourth-generation language for advanced operational control and complex data manipulation. Chapter 3 provides a detailed discussion on several aspects of Access that are especially relevant to client/server programming with SQL Server.

Its data processing power notwithstanding, we are mainly interested in using Access as the client component in a client/server architecture. Since the version of SQL used by Access is very similar in syntax and functionality to Transact-SQL, and since both SQL Server and Access come from the same vendor and have much in common, Access is particularly well suited as a front end to SQL Server.

When Access is run by itself, all data in a database system is stored in *.MDB files on local drives or network file servers; in a client/server system, by contrast, data resides mostly on SQL Server. The *.MDB files hold pointers to SQL Server for data access. In its capacity as the client component, Access mostly performs such functions as presenting data, furnishing user interfaces, exercising process sequence control, and forming dynamic data requests to SQL Server.

The last of these functions, constructing and submitting data requests, is especially important for the client/server architecture. (We are not talking here about importing data from SQL Server into Access and then storing the data in *.MDB files—such downloaded data doesn't automatically reflect changes in the original data on SQL Server.) There are only two methods for Access to get data from SQL Server dynamically: either through linked tables (covered in Chapter 7) or through passthrough queries (covered in Chapter 8). In either case, the principle is to transport as little data as possible over the network. This way, LAN traffic can be minimized, no time will be wasted in transporting unnecessary data, and the performance of applications can be maximized.

Consider, for example, a simple Access/SQL Server application for a magazine publisher. The publisher would like to select a customer by pointing and clicking and then see subscription information about the customer. Let's say two tables, Customers and Subscriptions, are already stored in SQL Server. Also suppose that the finished Access application has a main screen that contains a drop-down box listing all of the customers by name. As soon as a name is chosen, all subscription information related to the consumer shows up on the same screen. In this scenario, the main screen, the drop-down box, and the operation of this simple screen are all controlled by Access, the front end of the system.

Of course, in the same example, Access also has to fill the drop-down box with customers' names and the screen with subscription information. To do so, it must try to retrieve data from SQL Server by making data requests. In the case of the subscription information, instead of sending the whole subscription table to Access for processing, only information related to the chosen customer should be sent.

ODBC as the Intercommunications Layer

The intercommunications layer between Access and SQL Server is based on Open Database Connectivity (ODBC), a common programming interface among DBMSes that support SQL. ODBC was designed by a computer industry consortium led by Microsoft, and its purpose was to allow DBMSes from different vendors to communicate with each other and to make data access among DBMSes seamless.

ODBC consists of a set of functions, collectively referred to as an *application programming interface* (API), that is called every time a data request is made. The API functions can be used in a variety of computing environments to shield programmers from the complexities of the underlying hardware platforms and operating and network systems.

The ODBC architecture consists of three layers:

- **Application layer.** Uses ODBC API to submit SQL statements and retrieve results.
- **ODBC Driver Manager layer.** Loads and unloads ODBC Drivers and passes API commands to the appropriate Drivers.
- **ODBC Driver layer.** Processes ODBC API calls, submits SQL requests to a specific database, and returns results to the application.

Figure 1-7 illustrates the ODBC architecture. Note that although only SQL Server and Oracle drivers are shown, there are numerous other types of ODBC drivers.

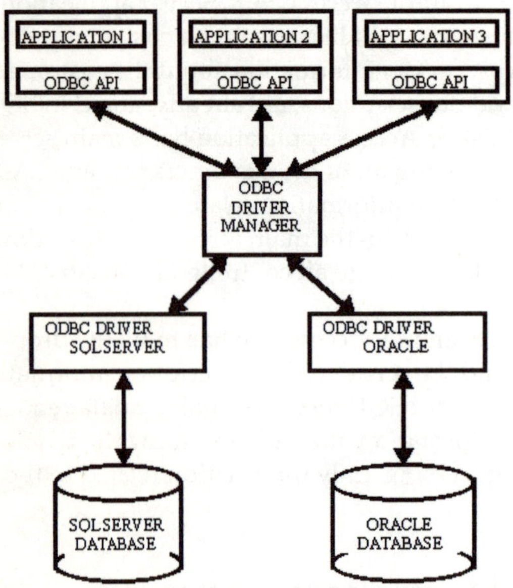

Figure 1-7: The ODBC architecture.

The following is an actual ODBC API call made by Access to SQL Server when it tries to open a linked SQL Server named Test1. It first tries to retrieve the unique record identifier column, RowID, and then retrieves the rest of the columns. As you can see, the syntax used here is similar to Access SQL and Transact SQL:

```
SQLExecDirect: SELECT "dbo"."Test1"."RowID" FROM "dbo"."test1"
SQLExecDirect: SELECT "A","B","RowID"  FROM "dbo"."Test1"
```

By going through such records of API calls, you can gain a better understanding of what is taking place behind the scenes between Access and SQL Server. Chapter 5 will cover this and other ODBC-related issues in detail.

Multi-Layer Client/Server Systems

Access and SQL Server constitute a two-tier client/server database environment. The two-tier architecture is by far the most often adopted configuration in client/server systems. You should be aware, however, that there are derivatives of this basic configuration that have come to play an increasingly important role in client/server computing.

In recent years, some three-layer client/server systems have been successfully implemented. At the core of the three-tier concept is the realization that a business system must provide three types of main services:

- Presentation services, which include maintaining the graphical user interface and generating what users see on the monitor.
- Application services, which include executing applications and controlling program flow.
- Database services, which simply refer to the management of underlying databases.

In the three-layer client/server configuration, different computers are used to provide the three different services. Depending on whether they provide presentation, application, or database services, the computers are referred to as presentation servers, application servers, and database servers, respectively. There may be multiple servers within each functional category in a system. Users can access several application servers at the same time, and the application server can in turn access multiple database servers simultaneously.

A three-tier architecture spreads out the computing load even more than the two-tier configuration. Because of the modular nature of its component systems, a three-tier client/server system can have many possible overall hardware configurations. Various front- and back-end computers can be tried and matched to optimize cost-efficiency. For instance, specialized application servers can be installed for a bottle-neck function to maximize the performance of the entire system.

The R/3 system from SAP AG is an example of a multi-tier client/server software package. This system can also be configured to implement centralized processing (like a mainframe) or two-tier client/server computing.

Moving On

The client/server architecture was designed in response to possibilities created by the now-prevalent multiuser computing environment. At this point, it should be clear to you what client/server computing is, why it is gaining widespread acceptance in the world of computing, and how Access and SQL Server fit into the general model of client/server computing.

Client/server programming is not about just learning component programs; it's about bringing together largely disparate systems to harness the power inherent in the architecture. You must understand how to use the hybrid nature of the architecture and learn to distribute the workload between the front and back ends in a balanced way so as to optimize the outcome. That takes time, thinking, and most of all, tweaking. It's the finesse involved in client/server database design that we now set out to convey to you in this book.

Next, we will examine Access and SQL Server in the context of relational database theory.

chapter 2

The Relational Data Model

Loosely defined, a database is a collection of data, or information, about real-world *entities* such as objects and events. A database has two fundamental utilities. On one hand, it is a repository for data; on the other hand, it must possess an internal organization that makes information about the data it holds available. In this sense, a database is to data what a library is to books. A library not only holds books, it also structures and arranges the books so that they can be accessed. Similarly, a database must have an internal structure that reflects a certain order in the data.

The data in a database can be viewed at two levels. The internal organization of a database is implemented at a very low level. It concerns how information, in the form of bits (1 or 0) of data, is stored and arranged on physical devices such as hard disk drives. This view is referred to as the *physical view* of data. Of course, the end users of a database cannot be concerned with information at such a low level. They perceive and deal with data in higher-level "chunks," which is the *conceptual view*. It is the responsibility of a *database management system* (DBMS) to translate between the conceptual view and the physical view.

A DBMS is a software system that manages the storage of and access to data in databases. It is responsible for mapping high-level data requests to low-level requests for data at a physical level. It manages data through administering security, data integrity, and data backup/recovery. Every DBMS must have one high-level language (similar to human language) for users to convey conceptual requests about data. By mapping the conceptual view to the physical view of data, a DBMS can provide data to end users regardless of how the data is physically stored. Almost every DBMS strives to achieve physical data independence.

At the conceptual level, a DBMS relies on one of several well-defined *data models* to organize data. The *relational data model* is one such model. It applies abstract mathematical theory to real-world data and defines specific relational rules to structure data; it also includes tools to create, manipulate, and maintain data.

The relational model is widely employed in today's DBMSes. Both SQL Server and Access are full-featured *relational database management systems* (RDBMSes) in that they largely conform to the requirements imposed by the standard relational data model. They both use *Structured Query Language* (SQL, often pronounced "sequel") as the high-level data-access language requisite in all DBMSes (there are some important differences between Transact-SQL, the "flavor" of SQL used in SQL Server, and Access SQL, and they will be discussed later in Chapter 8).

Although Access and SQL Server are capable of performing many similar relational data functions, they assume different roles in a client/server environment. As we discussed in Chapter 1, SQL Server is designed to be the back-end, or server, component: it holds the majority of data, does most of the heavy-duty data processing, and offers a higher and more comprehensive level of data security, integrity, and backup/recovery than Access does. Access is more suited for the front-end, or client, component: it has a more user-friendly *graphical user interface* (GUI) for application development than SQL Server has, it is capable of presenting data in a sophisticated manner through the use of forms and reports, and most importantly, it is responsible for constructing dynamic data requests to send to SQL Server for processing.

Data Models

A user perceives and deals with data in a database using the conceptual view. In turn, any conceptual view is based on one of several data models. A data model defines a method for data organization, and it specifies relationships and integrity rules in a database. In addition to databases, DBMSes can be based on a data model. There have been three widely used data models: hierarchical, network, and relational models.

The Hierarchical Model

As its name suggests, the hierarchical model is based on the idea of a hierarchy, something that we can grasp almost intuitively. The hierarchical model is often presented in the form of a tree. One familiar example is the organizational tree of a company: chief executive officer, vice presidents, divisions, departments, project groups, and employees. Another example is the directory structure in DOS. There are multiple directories in the root directory of a computer; each directory can have subdirectories, which may have their own sub-directories, and so on. Figure 2-1 illustrates such a structure.

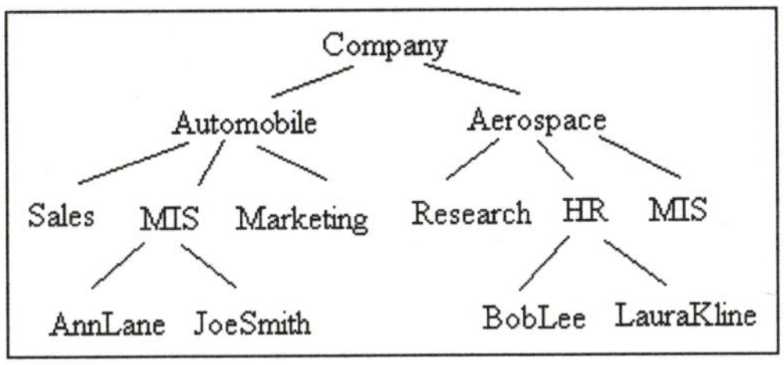

Figure 2-1: A hierarchical data model—the network directory structure for the employees of an imaginary corporation.

In this model, every entity has one to two immediate neighbors, which can be either superior or subordinate to the first entity. Therefore, every entity exists in the context of its superiors and/or subordinates. All entities, with the exception of the one at the top of the tree, must be defined in terms of the hierarchical tree "branch" passing through it. Without the context provided by its superior, an entity will have no meaning.

Let's say you want to create a database of organizational information based on Figure 2-1. Note there is an MIS department under the Aerospace division, and there is also an MIS department under the Automobile division. It would be meaningless to refer to an MIS department without specifying the corporation-division-department sequence.

There are a few restrictive rules governing the construction of a hierarchical model. First, going down the tree, the branches in the hierarchy can only diverge and are not allowed to converge. As a result, a child element can be related to only one parent element. For example, an employee whose time is split between two departments cannot have a line joining him to two departments at the same time. The second restriction prevents any subordinate entity from being related to any entity more than one level up the hierarchy. For example, an employee cannot be directly related to any division.

The Network Model

To ease some of the inflexibility inherent in the hierarchical model, the network model was created. Derived from the hierarchical model, the network model is very similar in that the basic structure of superiors and subordinates is retained. Two main differences between the two models are that (1) the network model allows a child entity to have more than one parent entity, and (2) the network model also allows a child entity to be connected directly to a "grandparent" element, a superior element that is one level removed from the child element.

These two rules lead to a "messier" visual representation than the hierarchical model. Gone is the neat treelike, increasingly diverging structure; instead, there are crisscrossing lines connecting elements at different levels. Such a diagram gives rise to the name *network model*. Figure 2-2 represents part of a database system that catalogs an imaginary company's organizational structure.

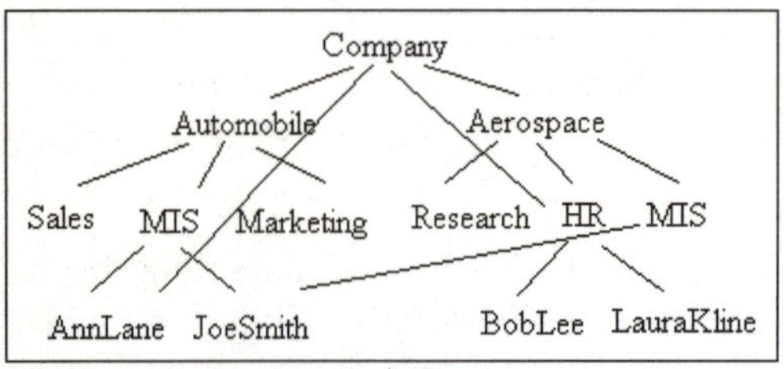

Figure 2-2: A network data model.

The Shortcoming in Hierarchical & Network Models

Both the hierarchical and network models have one critical shortcoming: each data entity exists in the context of others. As a result, every reference to an entity must specify all its superiors (or the branch of the hierarchical tree that leads to the element). This may not sound like a serious problem until you develop an application using the data in a hierarchical model. Let's take, for example, a simple DOS batch file that runs in the directory structure illustrated in Figure 2-1:

```
type q:\users\auto\mis\joesmith\test
```

This batch command displays the content of the file named test in the personal directory of Joe Smith, who is in project group one, of the development department of the automobile division of the imaginary company. Now if Joe Smith is moved to the company's aerospace division, all his files are moved to:

```
users\aero\mis\joesmith,
```

This batch program would fail when run because the data that the batch command refers to is no longer where the pointer (the path in this case) says it is.

This example shows that in a hierarchical or network model, pointers to physical locations of data must be hard-coded into an application. When relationships change, such pointers in the application programs must be changed. This example contains only one line of code referring to one physical location; just imagine an application that refers to dozens, or even hundreds, of pieces of data whose physical locations may keep shifting! It will place a severe limitation on physical data independence.

The Relational Model

The relational data model is deeply rooted in two branches of mathematics—set theory, which studies the mathematical properties of sets, and predicate calculus, which deals with the construction of mathematical propositions through the manipulation of symbols. Traditionally, these were well-developed but highly theoretical fields that did not see much use outside of the circle of mathematical specialists.

In 1969, E. F. Codd, a mathematician and researcher at IBM at the time, published a paper entitled "A Relational Model of Data for Large Shared Data Banks," in which he applied set theory and predicate calculus to the realm of real-life data. He realized that if he could establish rules and restrictions to "mold" data to fit the mathematical concepts of set theory, then precisely defined and well-known mathematical operations can be carried out to manipulate and process the data. Codd's paper became the defining work for the relational data model.

Unlike their counterparts in hierarchical and network models, entities in a relational model are not organized in a superior-subordinate structure. All data about the entities are contained in tables. These tables sit on the same conceptual plane, and any table can reference other tables through the use of keys and relationships.

Components of Relational Databases

The basic elements of the relational data model include *tables*, *keys*, and *relationships*. The concept of a table appeals to us intuitively—after all, we encounter tables in familiar forms such as tax tables and tables of contents all the time in daily life. Although bearing some resemblance to these real-life examples of tables, tables as defined in the relational model are quite different and must meet some quite stringent requirements. When constructed according to the relational model, tables contain keys, which are columns used to map data from one table to another. A relationship defines the structure of the mapping. The ability to reference data through the use of keys (instead of through extra imbedded pointers) is one of the distinguishing characteristics of the relational model.

Tables

At the center of Codd's relational model is the idea that all data in a database should be organized into tables, which are the conceptual equivalent of sets as described in set theory. Data-manipulation procedures, derived from set operations, can be run on the tables to yield resultant tables. Each table holds information about one, and only one, real-world entity set. For example, one table can describe all the items in a company's inventory, and another table can describe all the company's employees, but obviously a table should not be allowed to describe both the inventory and employees.

Three types of tables are used in relational databases:

- **Base Tables.** These tables are created by some data definition language command. Data in base tables do not come from any source internal to a database; instead, data must be entered into base tables manually or through some batch data transfer process. Data in these tables are stored "permanently" in relation to the databases themselves.
- **Derived Tables.** These tables are derived from base tables through some type of relational data-manipulation language command. For example, temporary tables are derived tables.
- **Views.** Views are not real, physical tables. They are virtual tables (such as views in SQL Server) derived from base tables through some type of relational data-manipulation language command and can be treated just like real tables.

A table is composed of a predefined number of columns and a changeable number of rows. Each column in a table draws values from a domain, which is simply a collection of permissible values. For the mathematically inclined, the term *domain* is used here in a way that is somewhat similar to the way *domain and range* is used in the context of mathematical functions and mappings; in lay language, domain just means a set of values that are allowable under some rules and on which certain predefined operations can be performed. For example, a column named Gender_Code might be based on a domain consisting of the letters M and F.

Codd stipulated that each row in a table must be unique; in other words, there must not be two identical rows in the same table. This is a very important property of the relational model, for if duplicate rows were allowed in a table, then there would be no way for a program to uniquely reference a certain row in a table, thus creating an inherent problem for programming.

Coining of Terms

Here is an interesting historical side note. Codd did not actually use the terms *table, row,* and *column* in his original paper; in their place, he employed the more formal words *relation, tuple,* and *attribute.* In fact, it is the use of the word *relations* in this context that led to the coining of the term *relational data model.*

To purge any trace of hierarchical structure from the relational model, Codd specified a few more properties for tables:

- There is no inherent ordering among the tables in a database.
- Within a table, there is no inherent ordering of rows.
- Within a table, there is no inherent ordering of columns.

The last two properties mean that the operations on tables in the relational model should not depend on a specific ordering of columns or rows. In short, all tables and fields are equal in the sense that none of them has to exist in the context of others and that none is higher or lower than others in the overall data structure.

Primary Keys

Tables can contain multiple rows of data, and the rows are identified and referenced through the use of keys. You guarantee uniqueness for a table, which is a requirement for relational data in tables, by designating a primary key—a column or a combination of columns whose values uniquely identify the rows in a table.

Each table can have only one primary key, even though several columns or combinations of columns may contain unique values. All columns (or combinations of columns) in a table with unique values are referred to as *candidate keys,* from which the primary key is chosen. All other candidate key columns are referred to as *alternate keys.* Keys can be simple or composite. A *simple key* is a key made up of one column, whereas a *composite key* is made up of two or more columns.

Choosing Among Candidate Keys

Since there may be multiple candidate keys in a table, you must make a decision as to which candidate key is to be the primary key. There is no general rule that can be applied here; you have to use your own judgment in many cases. Some rules of thumb are:

- Choose the column(s) least likely to change.
- Choose as few columns as possible.
- Choose columns that are familiar to users, if possible.

SSN	LastName	FirstName	Address	City	State	Zip	Dept_Code
123456789	Smith	John	1 Pine St.	Boston	MA	01345	06
987654321	Williams	Jennifer	81 Fermat Av.	Imaville	MA	01355	01
876834974	Anderson	Susan	3 Cauchy St	Landtown	MA	01345	03
789309358	Sikorski	Ivan	17 Gauss Lane	Ginsville	MA	01523	01
580983475	Smith	John	7 Wiles Pl	Moreburg	MA	03452	01
890974019	Carry	Anne	8 Euc Sq	Caninvale	MA	09873	02

Table 2-1: An employees table.

Let's take a look at the example of an employee's table for a company. Candidate keys for Table 2-1 might include SSN (employee social security number), (LastName + FirstName), (Address+City+State), and (Address + ZipCode). You can rule out the last three candidates because addresses can change fairly frequently. The name composite key can be eliminated easily, too: there are two John Smith's. In fact, even if there were no duplicate names, you should avoid using names as unique keys unless there is no better choice.

For Table 2-1, the best choice for the primary key is clearly the SSN column, because people's social security numbers rarely change, there are no duplicates (at least under ordinary circumstances), and every employee must have a social security number. In many situations, it is best to use an alphanumeric or integer whole number (e.g., employee ID, order ID, and so on) as a primary key instead of a descriptive text column so that the key will not be affected by misspellings and name changes. Furthermore, real numbers are always stored in a computer with some degree of approximation, so two seemingly identical real numbers could have different low decimal digits. Therefore, real numbers should not be used as primary keys.

Counter/Identity Columns

Both Access and SQL Server allow you to have automatically generated, sequentially incrementing integer columns in your tables. In Access, they are called *counter columns;* in SQL Server, they are referred to as *identity columns.* They could function as primary keys, especially if you simply do not have good candidate keys and there is no existing identification number. They also come in handy when you need to keep the rows in the order in which they were entered. For example, after a user manually enters data into a table and closes it, he or she may wish to return to the table and compare the records in the table against the his or her original records on paper. Using a counter/identity column, each row in the table will have a unique, incrementing number assigned to it. With these numbers, you can sort the rows from the table in the same order as the original records on paper.

However, it is best not to use counter/identity columns as primary keys. Because the counter columns are machine-generated, you have little control over their actual values. In fact, the only way you can affect the generation of counter/identity columns is by controlling the order in which the rows are entered into the table. Once you have a large table that uses a counter column as the primary key, it will be almost impossible for you to identically renumber the rows when you need to (such as if the table is accidentally deleted) unless you know the exact order in which the rows were entered and there was absolutely no break in the counter/identity sequence of the original table. Furthermore, since both Microsoft Access and SQL Server support only integer counter/identity values, a counter/identity column would be unsuitable if your system requires an alphanumeric primary key.

Foreign Keys

The power of a relational database lies in the fact that rows (or records) in one table can be matched to records in other tables through the use of keys; therefore, primary keys would be largely useless if not used for cross-referencing between tables. Primary keys are referenced through foreign keys. A foreign key is a column in a table used to reference a primary key in another table. Take, for example, Table 2-2, which defines all the departments corresponding to the company in Figure 2-1.

Dept_Code	Dept_Name	Contact_First_Name	Contact_Last_Name	Phone
01	Research	Anna	Burgin	271-8883
02	Sales	Clarence	Dillon	271-8881
03	Marketing	Elliot	Freeman	271-8882
04	Legal	Gail	Healy	271-8884
05	MIS	Ilene	Jordan	271-8885
06	Security	Keith	Landon	271-8889

Table 2-2: A table of departments corresponding to Figure 2-1.

Note that the Dept_Code column appears in both the employees and the departments tables. In the departments table, Dept_Code functions as the primary key; in the employees table, however, this field is used as a foreign key.

You must make sure that both foreign keys and their corresponding primary keys share a common meaning and draw their values from the same domain. Access and SQL Server will only force the matching of data types (i.e., text, datetime, and so on) between a foreign key and its associated primary key. However, if both zip_code and phone_number are text (or char on SQL Server) columns, as they should be, Access and SQL will not prevent you from joining them in a relationship even though it makes no sense. It is your responsibility to ensure that such a join does not take place. Joining and relationships are explained in the next section.

Relationships

Once tables and keys have been established, you have the tools to deal with the relationships in a database. In the relational data model, a relationship is defined strictly between two tables, and it delineates the schema by which primary and foreign keys are mapped. When an explicit relationship has been made between two tables, they are said to be joined. There are three types of relationships between tables: one-to-one, one-to-many, or many-to-many.

One-to-One Relationships

Two tables are joined in a one-to-one relationship if every row in the first table can be mapped to at most one row in the second table, and every row in the second table can be mapped to at most one row in the first table. Note that according to this definition, each row may have zero or one associated row in another table. Tables that are related in a one-to-one relationship should always have the same primary key, which will serve as the join column.

Imagine the relationship between a table of current husbands and another of current wives (Figure 2-3). Of course, we have to restrict the system to include only lawfully married spouses; that is, no one is married to more than one person at the same time. Then, by definition, the two tables have to be related in a one-to-one relationship. Some kind of a unique "marriage ID" (which could be a composite of spouse names, marrying authority's name, wedding date, place, and so on) can serve as the primary key in both tables as well as the joining column.

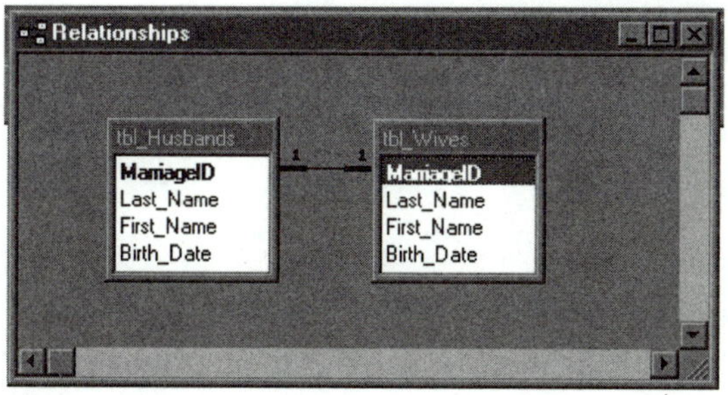

Figure 2-3: The one-to-one relationship between tbl_husbands and tbl_wives. All spouses in the tables are assumed to be monogamous. Note the line connecting the tables representing a one-to-one relationship.

Although the current wives/current husbands example is real, it is nonetheless a bit forced. True one-to-one relationships can often be found in the study of mathematical functions and sets; in the real world, however, it is quite hard to find many entities that fit the one-to-one model exactly. In relational databases, this type of relationship is sometimes employed to get around some limitations of a DBMS, such as the 255-column-per-table limit in Access and 250-column limit in SQL Server.

Tables containing more than 250 columns may be hard to find, but they do have real uses. One possible example is a table that holds the service records for all patients under the long-term care of a service organization. Each row contains the daily service indicators for a patient during an entire fiscal year, with one column for each day: if a patient receives service on a certain day, the corresponding column is checked off. So there needs to be 366 columns (accounting for leap years), and each column can have one of two possible values: service or no service. Because of the limit on the maximum number of columns a table can have, you may wish to split the table into two, with each half recording half a year's service records (Figure 2-4). Both halves will have a unique Patient_ID as the primary key. You can join the tables together on Patient_ID for both data entry and retrieval.

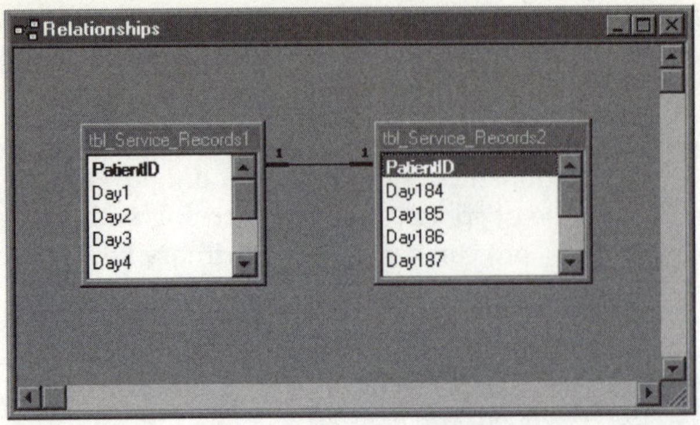

Figure 2-4: A one-to-one relationship used to break up an original table (tbl_Service_Records, which contains a large number of columns) into two tables: tbl_Service_Records1 and tbl_Service_Records2.

One-to-Many Relationships

The one-to-many relationship is the relationship most often encountered in database design. Two tables are related in a one-to-many relationship if for every row in the first table, there can be from zero to a theoretically infinite number of rows in the second table, but for every row in the second table, there is exactly one row in the first table. For example, Figure 2-5 shows two tables—tbl_Parents and tbl_Children. Each pair of biological parents (considered as one entity uniquely identified by a ParentsID, which may be combination of, for example, the pair's social security numbers, etc.) may have no children, one child, or several children; at the meantime, every child must have one and only one pair of parents. Because of this obvious example, the one-to-many relationship is sometimes referred to as the *parent-child relationship*.

One-to-many relationships are also used to link base tables to information stored in lookup tables. For example, tblPatient might have a short one-letter DischargeDiagnosis code, which can be linked to a lookup table, tlkpDiagCode, to get more complete Diagnosis descriptions (stored in the column DiagnosisName).

In this case, tlkpDiagCode is related to tblPatient in a one-to-many relationship (i.e., one row in the lookup table can be used in zero or more rows in the patient table).

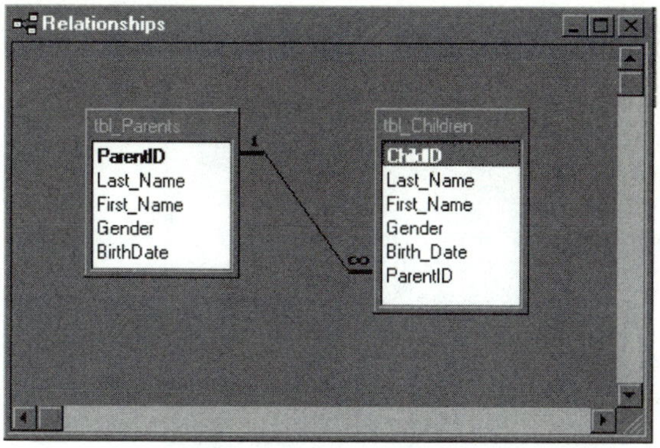

Figure 2-5: Tbl_Parents and tbl_Children are related in a one-to-many relationship because there may be multiple children for each pair of parents. Note the line that represents the one-to-many relationship connecting the tables.

Many-to-Many Relationships

Two tables are related in a many-to-many relationship if for every row in the first table, there can be zero to many rows in the second table; and for every row in the second table, there can be zero to many rows in the first table. Many-to-many relationships cannot be directly modeled in relational DBMSes; instead, they have to use an intermediate table that breaks a many-to-many relationship into multiple one-to-many relationships.

Suppose there is a table of health care providers that offer service programs to patients who are listed in a patients table. Each provider may offer services to many patients, and each patient may receive services from multiple providers. So the relationship between tbl_Patients and tbl_Providers must be a many-to-many one. Clearly, it is not possible to construct a relationship between these two tables using the tables alone—try it, and you will see why. Instead, you must create a third table, tbl_Patients_Providers, which contains all the patient-provider combinations. There is a one-to-many relationship between tbl_Patients and tbl_Patients_Providers, and there is another one-to-many relationship between tbl_Providers and tbl_Patients_Providers. These two relationships now replace the original many-to-many relationship between tbl_Patients and tbl_Providers. This example is illustrated in Figure 2-6.

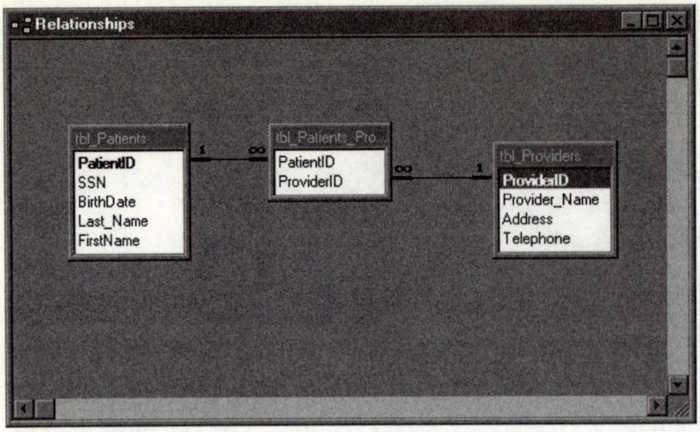

Figure 2-6: The many-to-many relationship between tbl_Patients and tbl_Providers is broken down into two one-to-many relationships with the aid of an intermediate table, tbl_Patients_Providers.

Relationships: Access vs. SQL Server

In SQL Server, you cannot explicitly declare the relationships among tables; instead, relationships in SQL Server manifest themselves implicitly in query joins, triggers, and defaults.

In an Access database, on the other hand, you can define the relationships among tables in the Relationships window, which you can open by choosing Tools | Relationships from the menu bar or by clicking the Relationships button in the Database window's toolbar. Note that Figures 2-3 through 2-6 all come from the Access Relationships window.

In the Relationships window, relationships among tables are specified graphically by join lines connecting fields in different tables. In the relational model, tables cross-reference each other through the use of primary and foreign keys, so you typically connect the primary key (in bold) in one table to a corresponding foreign key in another table. In the Relationships window, you can add new tables (or copies of existing tables) by clicking the Add Table button in the toolbar and then choosing the appropriate tables. You can create a new relationship by dragging one field to another in the Relationships window, or you can edit an existing relationship by double-clicking a join line. In either case, the Relationships dialog box will pop up, as shown in Figure 2-7.

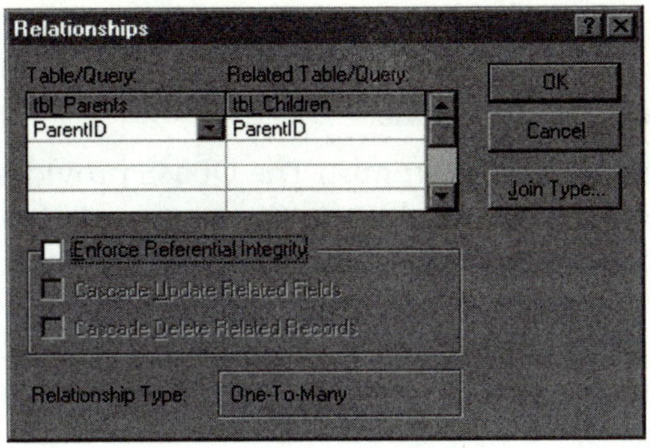

Figure 2-7: The Relationships dialog box.

If you proceed to check the Enforce Referential Integrity check box (and referential integrity is the main reason why you want to explicitly declare relationships in Access), a one-to-many join line automatically appears in the Relationships window, with the "one" side always ending on the primary key. Therefore, if referential integrity is enforced, all join lines specify one-to-many relationships. Referential integrity will be discussed later in the chapter.

In the Relationships dialog box, you can choose to change the join type between the tables by clicking the Join Type button. There are three types of joins, and they will be discussed in detail in the context of the Structured Query Language (SQL) in Chapter 8. What's important for the discussion here is that, whereas relationships are used for enforcing referential integrity, join types are meaningful only in the construction of queries. Specifying a join type does not affect a relationship at all; it simply sets the default join type for any query that may involve the two related tables. This default can be overridden in the construction of the actual query.

Codd's "Twelve" Rules

Codd defined a number of rules to test whether a data system can be considered relational. Even though there are thirteen rules, they are commonly referred to as Codd's Twelve Rules, with the extra rule being Rule 0:

- **Rule 0**—A relational DBMS must be able to manage databases entirely through its relational capabilities. In other words, a truly relational system may not perform non-relational operations.
- **Rule 1—The Information Rule.** All information in a relational database (including table and column names) is represented explicitly as values in tables.

- **Rule 2—Guaranteed Access.** Every value in a relational data base is guaranteed to be accessible by using a combination of the table name, primary key value, and column name.
- **Rule 3—Systematic Null Value Support.** The DBMS provides systematic (i.e., independent of data type) support for the treatment of null values (unknown or missing data). The DBMS must use special indicators—which are different from the number zero, a character string comprising blank spaces, or an empty character string—to signify missing information. The DBMS must also support functions that deal with such null indicators.
- **Rule 4—Dynamic, Online Relational Catalog.** The system catalog, which contains information about a database, is also a relational database based on the same database model as other data managed by the DBMS. The description of the database and its contents are represented at the logical level as regular tables and can therefore be queried using the same database language as that used to query ordinary data.
- **Rule 5—Comprehensive Data Sub-language.** The DBMS must support at least one language whose statements are expressible as character strings according to some well-defined syntax, and which is comprehensive in that it supports data definition, data manipulation, integrity rules, security authorization, and transactions (e.g., Begin, Commit, and Rollback).
- **Rule 6—View Updating Rule.** A view is a logical representation of one or more base tables. It is sometimes possible to alter (i.e., insert into, delete from, or update) base tables through views; sometimes it is not possible. An RDBMS should automatically be able to determine, at the time of creating a view, whether you can use a view to update its underlying base tables.
- **Rule 7—Bulk Insertion, Update, and Deletion.** The DBMS is able to perform not only bulk retrievals, but also bulk inserts, updates, and deletes. In other words, the DBMS must be able to process many records simultaneously.
- **Rule 8—Physical Data Independence.** Application programs and ad-hoc programs remain logically unaffected when changes are made to physical access methods or storage structures. Changes may include changing fields from fixed to variable length, changing the order of rows in a table, adding or removing indexes, and moving tables or entire databases to different physical drives.

- **Rule 9—Logical Data Independence.** Application programs and ad-hoc programs remain logically unaffected when changes that theoretically should not interfere with the operation of the programs are made to the structure of base tables. Changes may include adding columns to a base table.
- **Rule 10—Integrity Independence.** The database language must be able to define integrity rules, which are stored in the online catalog (as opposed to the application database) and cannot be bypassed.
- **Rule 11—Distribution Independence.** Application programs and ad-hoc programs remain logically unaffected when data is first distributed (if the originally installed DBMS manages non-distributed data only) or when it is redistributed (if the originally installed DBMS manages distributed data). In other words, when moving data from one computer to another, data independence should still hold.
- **Rule 12—Non-Subversion.** It must not be possible to bypass the integrity rules defined through the database language by using lower-level languages. In addition to the database language that's built for batch (or multiple-row) processing, many RDMSes provide a low-level, fourth-generation language that deals with one row at a time. No matter what such low-level language is, it should not be possible to change the integrity rules already in place in the online system catalog.

These rules can be applied to databases as well as DBMSes to gauge how well they adhere to the relational principles. We will leave it to the interested reader to determine how well today's DBMSes measure up to these standards. (Hint: You probably will not find one that completely satisfies all the rules. Try Rule 6, for example.)

Normalization

In every discipline, students are taught that "good form" is extremely important for optimal results. Athletes must learn the correct moves; musician are told to practice fundamental techniques in the right way; mathematicians go to great length to achieve "rigor;" and so on. The field of relational database design is no exception. In order to create a solid foundation for a database, there are some very basic questions that need to be answered:

- How many tables are needed in a database? What data should each table hold?
- What's the best way to construct each table so as to make the database robust (i.e., internally consistent and error-free)?
- How should the relationships among tables be structured?

To answer these questions, a set of rules have been compiled that are generally accepted as the guiding principles of relational database design. The process of applying these rules is called *normalization*, and each of the rules is called a *normal form*. Normal forms are used to ensure that various types of anomalies and inconsistencies don't occur in databases.

Anomalies

If the proper normal forms aren't followed, various undesirable side effects can occur in a database. These side effects are commonly referred to as *anomalies*. There are three types of anomalies:

- **Insertion anomalies.** These occur when you can't add a row into a table.
- **Deletion anomalies.** These occur when you can't delete a row from a table, when the row you delete contains an important piece of information, or when the row you delete is the last one in the table that contains this piece of information.
- **Update anomalies.** These occur when there is unnecessary redundancy in the data.

Normal Forms

The normal forms are a series of rules that you apply to your database. Each higher form is based on the previous one; when applied in sequence, the forms progressively make the database more efficient. There are six normal forms:

- First Normal Form
- Second Normal Form
- Third Normal Form
- Boyce-Codd Normal Form
- Fourth Normal Form
- Fifth Normal Form

First Normal Form

The First Normal Form (1NF) dictates the following:

- Columns can contain only scalar values, not arrays.
- There can be only one value per column-row position (or field) in a table.
- There can be no repeating groups.

Arrays are sets or lists consisting of multiple values. Proper names of people can be viewed as arrays since each name consists of a salutation/title, first name, middle initial, and last name (e.g., Mr. William C. Johnson). According to the 1NF, you should not have the entire proper name in a column; instead, the first names, middle initials, last names, and titles/salutations should all be placed in different columns. Another example of arrays is coordinates on the surface of the earth. Each coordinate is given four values: longitude, latitude, south/north hemisphere designation, and east/west hemisphere designation. Table 2-3 violates the 1NF because all four coordinates are stored in the same column.

City_Code	City_Name	Coordinates
SATO250	Sato	(East-135, North-40)
DRMV832	Dreamville	(West-90, North-38)
CLDC342	Cloudcity	(West-120, South-15)
MBNB39	Mbonba	(East-30, South-30)

Table 2-3: A table of the global coordinates of some imaginary places. This table violates the First Normal Form because the Coordinates column contains multiple values.

Obviously, the Coordinates column in Table 2-3 can be further broken down into four smaller elements. When a column value cannot be broken down into more elemental components, it is considered atomic (the word *atomic* comes from the Greek *atomos*, meaning indivisible). What the 1NF requires is that all column values be atomic. The significance of this requirement is fairly easy to understand. If multiple values are stored in a single column, referencing and manipulating each component value becomes more difficult than otherwise. In Table 2-3, for example, to see whether Sato or Dreamville is closer to the equator, you would have to extract the coordinate components (south/north designation and the latitude values) from the Coordinates strings before any real comparison can be done.

The 1NF also prohibits repeating groups in tables. Table 2-4 shows a table that contains repeating groups. Each patient is given one row in the table, and all of a patient's relatives are listed in the same row, even though the exact number of relatives is indeterminate.

PatientID	RelativeID1	Relationship1	RelativeID2	Relationship2
2490974	GGP001	Father	GGP002	Guardian
0803484	PDE001	Brother	PDE002	Uncle
9847092	AGE001	Sister	AGE002	Cousin
4895098	IOD001	Son	IOD002	Grandmother
3448748	HWK001	Guardian	HWK002	Mother

Table 2-4: A table of the relatives of patients. It violates the First Normal Form because the RelativeID-Relationship column structure is repeated.

The main problem with Table 2-4 is that the number of relatives for each patient is not known beforehand. If there are more than two relatives to be recorded for a patient, the number of columns would have to increased. This in itself is not problematic. But how many columns should you add? You can increase the column count to 100, and this would probably satisfy almost all conditions. But there would be great deal of space wasted. You can add just a few columns at a time. But if more columns are needed in the future, you would have to add columns again. Furthermore, since all relatives of patients are in different columns, any query that attempts to take a look at all the relatives would have to involve all the columns. Therefore, if there is a change in the columns, such queries would have to be rewritten, making programming content-dependent.

The proper way to structure the same table is shown in Table 2-5. Instead of listing all the relatives of a patient in the same row, each row now only includes only a patient ID and one relative of the patient. The primary key is the PatientID-RelativeID combination.

PatientID	RelativeID	Relationship
2490974	GGP001	Father
2490974	GGP002	Guardian
2490974	GGP003	Mother
2490974	GGP004	Sister
0803484	PDE001	Brother
0803484	PDE002	Uncle
9847092	AGE001	Sister
9847092	AGE002	Cousin
4895098	IOD001	Son

PatientID	RelativeID	Relationship
4895098	IOD002	Grandmother
4895098	IOD003	Wife
3448748	HWK001	Guardian
3448748	HWK002	Mother

Table 2-5: A table of the relatives of patients that conforms to the First Normal Form.

Second Normal Form

A table is in Second Normal Form (2NF) if it is in the 1NF and every column that is not a part of the primary key is functionally dependent on the entire primary key. Let's take a look at an example. Table 2-6 is very similar to Table 2-5.

PatientID	RelativeID	Relationship	Patient_Telephone
2490974	GGP001	Father	123-1324
2490974	GGP002	Guardian	123-1324
2490974	GGP003	Mother	123-1324
2490974	GGP004	Sister	123-1324
0803484	PDE001	Brother	789-3421
0803484	PDE002	Uncle	789-3421
9847092	AGE001	Sister	421-5968
9847092	AGE002	Cousin	421-5968
4895098	IOD001	Son	849-3421
4895098	IOD002	Grandmother	849-3421
4895098	IOD003	Wife	849-3421
3448748	HWK001	Guardian	543-3485
3448748	HWK002	Mother	543-3485

Table 2-6: This table is not in 2NF because Patient_Telephone is not functionally dependent on the entire primary key, which consists of PatientID and RelativeID. The Patient_Telephone column is fully dependent on Patient_ID alone.

The primary key in tbl_Patients_Relatives (Table 2-6) is the combination of PatientID and RelativeID. It is clear that the table conforms to the 1NF, so to determine if it satisfies 2NF, you have to find out if all other columns in it depend fully on both PatientID and RelativeID; that is, you need to decide whether the following conditions are true:

- PatientID + RelativeID (implies→Relationship; and
- PatientID + RelativeID (implies→Patient_Telephone

However, in tbl_Patients_Relatives, only the following are true:

- PatientID + RelativeID (implies→Relationship; and
- PatientID (implies→Patient_Telephone

In other words, Patient_Telephone depends only on PatientID and not on the composite primary key consisting of both PatientID and RelativeID. Therefore, Table 2-6 is not in the 2NF.

You can turn Table 2-6 into the 2NF by breaking it into two normalized tables. This process is called *decomposition*. The Patient_Telephone column really doesn't belong in tbl_Patients_Relatives because patients' telephone numbers have nothing to do with the patients' relatives and should be associated with patients only. So to decompose Table 2-6, you simply need to remove Patient_Telephone from the original table, place it in another table, say tbl_Patient_Info, and put the rest of the information in tbl_Patients_Relatives, using PatientID as the joining column between tbl_Patients_Relatives and tbl_Patient_Info. The two resultant tables are shown in Table 2-7.

a *Tbl_Patients_Relatives*

PatientID	RelativeID	Relationship
2490974	GGP001	Father
2490974	GGP002	Guardian
2490974	GGP003	Mother
2490974	GGP004	Sister
0803484	PDE001	Brother
0803484	PDE002	Uncle
9847092	AGE001	Sister
9847092	AGE002	Cousin
4895098	IOD001	Son
4895098	IOD002	Grandmother
4895098	IOD003	Wife
3448748	HWK001	Guardian
3448748	HWK002	Mother

b Tbl_Patient_Info

PatientID	Patient_Telephone
2490974	123-1324
0803484	789-3421
9847092	421-5968
4895098	849-3421
3448748	543-3485

Table 2-7: The tables tbl_Patients_Relatives and tbl_Patient_Info are in the Second Normal Form.

Third Normal Form

A table is in Third Normal Form (3NF) if it is in 2NF and if all of its columns that are not part of the primary key are mutually independent. The 3NF is concerned with the removal of *transitive dependencies* in tables. A transitive dependency is of the form:

```
Primary Key (implies →Column1 (implies →Column2
```

Here, Column2 depends on Column1 but not directly on the primary key; this kind of dependency is forbidden by the 3NF. Let's take a look at an example in which an interdependency occurs. The tbl_Employees_Directory table in Table 2-8 contains the directory of some employees in a company.

EmployeeID	First_Name	Last_Name	Department	Dept_Address
8934	Anna	Burgin	Research	1 Fermat St.
3049	Clarence	Dillon	Research	1 Fermat St.
4589	Elliot	Freeman	Research	1 Fermat St.
7623	Gail	Healy	MIS	3 Gauss Lane
6103	Ilene	Jordan	MIS	3 Gauss Lane
0327	Keith	Landon	MIS	3 Gauss Lane
4503	Michael	Neopreen	Plastics	6 Wiles Place

Table 2-8: Tbl_Employees_Directory, which violates the Third Normal Form because Dept_Address depends on Department, which is not part of the primary key.

The primary key in tbl_Employees_Directory is EmployeeID. The columns First_Name, Last_Name, and Department are all directly associated with EmployeeID, the primary key. The last column, Dept_Address, however, contains the addresses of the departments and therefore is determined by Department, which is not part of the primary key. In short, the following holds true in this table:

```
EmployeeID (implies →Department (implies →Dept_Address
```

which is a case of transitive dependency, so the tbl_Employees_Directory table is not in the 3NF.

To make the table conform to the 3NF, you need to decompose the table in a fashion similar to the way Table 2-7 was decomposed. Simply take the Dept_Address column out of tbl_Employees_Directory and put it into another table, say, tbl_Department_Info, which in turn has Department as its primary key. The resultant tables are shown in Table 2-9.

a *Tbl_Employees_Directory*

EmployeeID	First_Name	Last_Name	Department
8934	Anna	Burgin	Research
3049	Clarence	Dillon	Research
4589	Elliot	Freeman	Research
7623	Gail	Healy	MIS
6103	Ilene	Jordan	MIS
0327	Keith	Landon	MIS
4503	Michael	Neopreen	Plastics

b *Tbl_Department_Info*

Department	Dept_Address
Research	1 Fermat St.
MIS	3 Gauss Lane
Plastics	6 Wiles Place

Table 2-9: The tables tbl_Employees_Directory and tbl_Department_Info are in the Third Normal Form.

Another example of a transitive dependency is a column that is calculated from another column. Suppose there is an employees table containing the Annual_Salary column. In the same table, you could create another column, Pay_Check_Amount, to hold the employees' paycheck amounts, and it would equal Annual_Salary/26 (assuming a biweekly pay schedule). However, this table wouldn't be in the 3NF. It's better to leave this column out of the table and make the calculation elsewhere, such as in a query. This avoids the problem of having to update Pay_Check_Amount every time Annual_Salary is changed.

Transitive dependencies could result in various insertion, update, or delete anomalies. For insertion anomalies, take for example the not yet normalized tbl_Employees_Directory in Table 2-8. Suppose a new department has just been created, but the company hasn't hired anyone for this new department. An error would occur you attempted to add data into the table because there is no EmployeeID associated with the department. Since EmployeeID is the primary key, you can't add a new row into the table with EmployeeID being null. In the normalized form in Table 2-9, on the other hand, you can simply add the new department into tbl_Department_Info without any problem. Since there is no one in the new department yet, you don't have to do anything to tbl_Employees_Directory.

A deletion anomaly can occur to the non-normalized tbl_Employees_Directory in Table 2-8 if, for example, Michael Neopreen leaves the company and his record is deleted from the employees table. Because Michael Neopreen is the only member of the Plastics department, all information associated with the Plastics department will be wiped out even though the department itself has not been eliminated. In the normalized form in Table 2-9, on the other hand, you can simply delete Michael Neopreen's row from tbl_Emloyees_Directory without removing information about the Plastics department in tbl_Department_Info.

An update anomaly could occur to the non-normalized tbl_Employees_Directory in Table 2-8 if the MIS department moves to another address. You would have to update three fields in the table even though only one piece of information about a department is changed. In the normalized form in Table 2-9, on the other hand, you only need to change one field, namely Dept_Address for the MIS department.

Boyce-Codd Normal Form

The Boyce-Codd Normal Form (BCNF) is an extension to the 3NF for the special case where:

- There are at least two candidate keys in the table (as we said earlier in the chapter, candidate keys are keys in a table that meet the requirements for being the primary key).
- All the candidate keys are composite keys.
- There is an overlapping column in the candidate keys.

When a table satisfies all these conditions, the 3NF can't eliminate all forms of transitive dependency. For a table to be in the BCNF, it must be in the 3NF, and all columns in all its candidate keys must be functionally independent. Table 2-10 shows a sample table that violates the BCNF. The tbl_First_Quarter_Overtime table lists by month the amount of overtime employees in a company have accumulated in the first quarter of the year. In this company, each employee has a different telephone extension, so either the EmployeeID column or the Extension column can uniquely identify employees.

EmployeeID	Extension	Month	Overtime_Hours
8934	9089	January	2
8934	9089	February	1.5
8934	9089	March	2
7623	8607	January	0
7623	8607	February	3
7623	8607	March	3
4503	3869	January	2
4503	3869	February	8
4503	3869	March	0

Table 2-10: Here, tbl_First_Quarter_Overtime shows the number of overtime hours each employee worked in the first quarter of a year. It violates the Boyce-Codd Normal Form.

There are two candidate keys in tbl_First_Quarter_Overtime: (EmployeeID + Month) and (Extension + Month). There is clearly no interdependency among non-key columns since there is only one such column—Overtime_Hours. Therefore, the table is in the 3NF. However, there is a functional dependency between EmployeeID and SSN. As a result, the following transitive dependency still exists in the table:

```
EmployeeID (implies →Extension
                        +          (implies →Dept_Address
                      Month
```

Due to the interdependency between key columns, the table is not in the BCNF.

To normalize the table, you need to resort again to the technique of decomposition. Simply break the Extension column out of tbl_First_Quarter_Overtime, place it in another table, tbl_Employee_Phone_Extensions, for example, and use the EmployeeID as the linking column between the two normalized tables. This is shown in Table 2-11.

a *Tbl_First_Quarter_Overtime.*

EmployeeID	Month	Overtime_Hours
8934	January	2
8934	February	1.5
8934	March	2
7623	January	0
7623	February	3
7623	March	3
4503	January	2
4503	February	8
4503	March	0

b *Tbl_Employee_Phone_Extensions*

EmployeeID	SSN
8934	498479089
7623	170498607
4503	094049869

Table 2-11: The tables tbl_First_Quarter_Overtime and tbl_Employee_Phone_Extensions are in the Boyce-Codd Normal Form.

Anomalies could occur if the BCNF is not followed. Insertion anomalies can happen to tbl_First_Quarter_Overtime in Table 2-10 at the beginning of the first quarter when no one has had any overtime for the months in the quarter. In this case, there is no way to enter employee telephone extensions into tbl_First_Quarter_Overtime because no month value can be entered into the Month column, which does not allow nulls. If the table is the only place where employees' telephone extensions are stored (and if not, then there is data redundancy in the database, which is to be avoided, too), then you can enter employees' telephone extensions only if the employees have valid overtime records. In the normalized form in Table 2-11, on the other hand, an employee's extension can be recorded without any restrictions imposed by the overtime records of the employee.

Deletion anomalies can take place if an employee becomes a salaried employee and, as a result, is removed from the overtime table. Assuming that tbl_First_Quarter_Overtime is the only place in the database where the employee's telephone extension is stored (if not, then there is data redundancy in the database, which is to be avoided, too), then his or her telephone extension will be lost. This problem obviously doesn't exist in the normalized tables in Table 2-11 because the telephone extension numbers are stored separately from overtime data.

Update anomalies can take place if an employee's extension number is changed. Since there can be multiple overtime records in tbl_First_Quarter_Overtime for different months, multiple changes may be necessary. In the normalized tables in Table 2-11, only one change to the tbl_Employee_Phone_Extensions table is needed to record the extension change.

Fourth Normal Form

A table is in the Fourth Normal Form (4NF) if it satisfies the 3NF and if there is only one multivalued dependency per table. Multivalued dependency occurs when there is a many-to-many relationship between two columns in a table. It is best to illustrate the concept of multivalued dependency with the example in Table 2-12.

AuthorID	BookTitle	Editor
Smith023	Monkeys Are From Asteroids	Lisa
Smith023	How to Exercise	Catherine
Smith023	How to Exercise	John
Williams153	Monkeys Are From Asteroids	John
Williams153	AP Programming	Elaine
Johnson823	Dogs Are From Hale-Bopp	Lisa
Johnson823	Monkeys Are From Asteroids	Silvia
Johnson823	Monkeys Are From Asteroids	Silvia

Table 2-12: The tbl_Books_Info table violates the Fourth Normal Form. There is no functional dependency between the BookTitle and Editor columns.

Suppose there is no functional dependency between AuthorID and Editor in tbl_Books_Info in Table 2-12; in other words, let's assume that editors are assigned to authors instead of books. Since each author may have written multiple books and one book may have several authors, there is a many-to-many relationship between AuthorID and BookTitle; similarly, there is a many-to-many relationship between AuthorID and Editor (several editors may be assigned to work with the same author, and one editor may be assigned to work with several authors). Each of these two relationships constitutes a multivalued dependency, so there are two multivalued dependencies in the table. Hence the table violates the 4NF. To normalize the table, you need to break it up into two tables, as shown in Table 2-13.

a *Tbl_Author_Books*

AuthorID	BookTitle
Smith023	Monkeys Are From Asteroids
Smith023	How to Exercise
Williams153	Monkeys Are From Asteroids
Williams153	AP Programming
Johnson823	Dogs Are From Hale-Bopp
Johnson823	Monkeys Are From Asteroids

b Tbl_Author_Editors

AuthorID	Editor
Smith023	Lisa
Smith023	Catherine
Smith023	John
Williams153	John
Williams153	Elaine
Johnson823	Lisa
Johnson823	Silvia

Table 2-13: The tables tbl_Author_Books and tbl_Author_Editors conform to the Fourth Normal Form.

Insertion anomalies can easily happen with the non-normalized table in Table 2-12. It should be clear that all three columns form the primary key of the tbl_Books_Info table. This means that none of the columns can contain null values. Now let's say the author Johnson823 has another editor assigned to him (Elliot, for example) without writing another book. In order to add this editor to the table under the name Johnson823, a book name must then be chosen, either *Dogs Are From Hale-Bopp* or *Monkeys Are From Asteroids*, making the data in the table arbitrary. In the normalized tables in Table 2-13, on the other hand, you simply need to add an extra record to tbl_Author_Editors, with Johnson823 in the AuthorID column and Elliot in the Editor column.

Deletion anomalies can happen to tbl_Books_Info in Table 2-12 if, for example, the author Williams153 no longer has Elaine as one of his editors. Again, since the Editor column is part of the primary key and can't be null, the only way to remove the Williams153-Elaine record is to delete the entire Williams153-AP Programming-Elaine record. This would mean the book *AP Programming* would be deleted from the database even though the book should still be under Williams153's name. In the normalized tables in Table 2-13, books are insulated from editors, and such deletion anomalies will consequently not occur.

Update anomalies can occur if the title *How to Exercise* changes to something else. In the non-normalized tbl_Books_Info table, two updates are needed, whereas in the normalized tbl_Author_Books table, only one update needs to be effected. In short, data not normalized to the 4NF can cause inefficiencies.

Fifth Normal Form or Project-Joint Normal Form

A table is in Fifth Normal Form (PJNF, or Project-Joint Normal Form) if it is in the 4NF and if its decomposed tables can be joined to reconstruct the original table. This normal form goes one step beyond the 4NF and deals with join dependencies among decomposed tables. Let's look at an example.

AuthorID	BookTitle	Editor
Smith023	Monkeys Are From Asteroids	Lisa
Smith023	How to Exercise	Catherine
Smith023	How to Exercise	John
Williams153	Monkeys Are From Asteroids	John

Table 2-14: Tbl_Books_Info.

Table 2-14 shows tbl_Books_Info, which is similar to, but smaller than, tbl_Books_Info in Table 2-12. It can be decomposed to the tables in Table 2-15.

a *Tbl_Author_Books*

AuthorID	BookTitle
Smith023	Monkeys Are From Asteroids
Smith023	How to Exercise
Williams153	Monkeys Are From Asteroids

b *Tbl_Author_Editors*

AuthorID	Editor
Smith023	Lisa
Smith023	Catherine
Smith023	John
Williams153	John

Table 2-15: Tbl_Author_Books and tbl_Author_ Editors are decomposed tables based on tbl_Books_Info in Table 2-14.

If you join the tables in Table 2-15, you will get tbl_Reconstructed, as shown in Table 2-16. If you compare tbl_Reconstructed against the original tbl_Books_Info in Table 2-14, you can see that there are three spurious rows in the reconstructed table (marked →). Therefore, tbl_Books_Info in Table 2-14 does not conform to the PJNF.

	AuthorID	BookTitle	Editor
	Smith023	Monkeys Are From Asteroids	Lisa
→	Smith023	Monkeys Are From Asteroids	Catherine
→	Smith023	Monkeys Are From Asteroids	John
→	Smith023	How to Exercise	Lisa
	Smith023	How to Exercise	Catherine
	Smith023	How to Exercise	John
	Williams153	Monkeys Are From Asteroids	John

Table 2-16: Tbl_Reconstructed.

As is the case with the other normal forms, not following the PJNF can lead to various anomalies. Since a detailed discussion of the PJNF can become a bit involved, we will not delve more deeply into it here.

Normalization vs. Denormalization

The normal forms should be taken as general guidelines for structuring data in a database. When used with good judgment and common sense, they can produce very good results. However, they are by no means dogma. Sometimes it's necessary to break the rules of normalization and create a database that is deliberately less normal than it otherwise could be. You may want to do so to achieve better performance, reduce system complexity, or make data entry easier for your users. If you do break the rules and decide to denormalize you database, it's important that you follow these guidelines:

- You should first normalize your database (to 3NF or higher), and then denormalize it if you have a good reason to do so. Don't automatically assume that the denormalized database will perform better. If your users demand that you denormalize the database to simplify data-entry, first try to base data-entry forms on updatable queries while keeping the base tables fully normalized (see Chapter 3 for a detailed discussion on updatable queries).
- Be aware of the trade-offs this decision entails. Weigh how much performance your database can gain or how much simpler certain queries can become against the amount of extra code you have to write. You should document all the changes to be made and make plenty of backups.
- Create the necessary adjustments in your database to avoid anomalies. In most cases, when you denormalize, you need to create additional application code to avoid insertion, update, or deletion anomalies that a normalized system would avoid.

As an example for the last point, consider Table 2-6. You may choose to keep the Patient_Telephone column in the table so that Table 2-6 doesn't need to be joined with another table when Patient_Telephone is needed as part of the output of a SELECT query. To avoid the action query-related anomalies on Table 2-6, you have to create a procedure which calls a query to refresh the values in the Patient_Telephone column in Table 2-6 based on another reference table containing the telephone numbers of patients. Every time that reference table is updated, the procedure is automatically triggered, and Table 2-6 will contain the most up-to-date telephone numbers of patients.

Integrity Rules

One of the basic functions of a database is to organize and structure its data so that the data is internally consistent. In more informal terms, this means that a database should be able to prevent the occurrence of bad data, data conflicts, and unmatched data. Integrity rules are made to enforce all these things and therefore are a very important aspect of relational database design. There are two types of integrity rules: general and database specific. General rules apply to all databases and emphasize the technical aspect of database design, while database-specific rules are often content related and involve business rules that are outside the realm of relational theory itself. General integrity rules can be further broken down to two subcategories: entity integrity and referential integrity.

Entity Integrity

The entity integrity rule is very simple: It says that primary keys cannot contain null values. The reason for this rule should be obvious. You can't uniquely identify or reference a row in a table if the primary key of that table can be null. It's important to note that this rule applies to both simple and composite keys. For composite keys, none of the individual columns can be null. In both SQL Server and Access, the entity integrity rules are automatically enforced: No component of a primary key can be null.

Referential Integrity

The referential integrity rule says that the database must not contain any unmatched foreign key values. This implies that:

- A row may not be added to a table with a foreign key unless the referenced value exists in the referenced table.
- If the value in a table that's referenced by a foreign key is changed (or the entire row is deleted), the rows in the table with the foreign key must not be "orphaned."

In general, there are three options available when a referenced primary key value changes or a row is deleted. The options are:

- **Disallow.** The change is completely disallowed.
- **Cascade.** For updates, the change is cascaded to all dependent tables. For deletions, the rows in all dependent tables are deleted.
- **Nullify.** For deletions, the dependent foreign key values are set to Null.

Microsoft Access lets you disallow or allow cascade referential integrity updates and deletions in the Edit Relationships dialog box (shown in Figure 2-8), although nullify is not an option in Access. To open the Edit Relationships dialog box, choose Relationships | Edit Relationship from the menu bar in the Relationships window. You simply need to specify what you want in the Edit Relationships dialog box, and the Access Jet Database Engine does the rest for you. In SQL Server, however, all referential integrity rules must be implemented through the use of triggers and defaults.

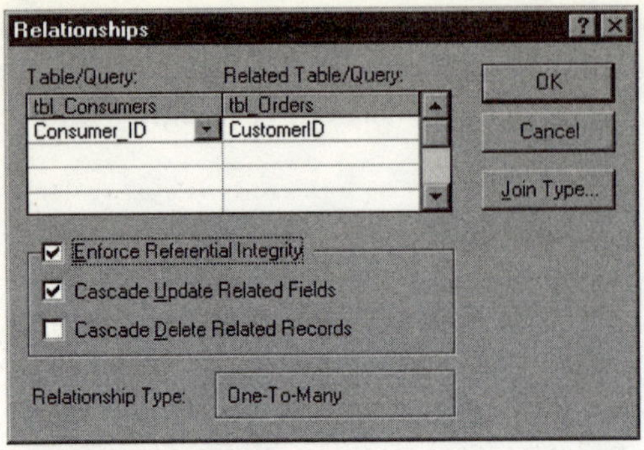

Figure 2-8. Specifying a relationship with referential integrity between the tbl_Customers and tbl_Orders tables using the Edit Relationships dialog box. Updates of CustomerId in tbl_Customers will be cascaded to tbl_Orders. Deletions of rows in tbl_Customers will be disallowed if rows in tbl_Orders would be orphaned.

Note that when you wish to implement referential integrity in Microsoft Access, you must perform one additional step outside of the Edit Relationships dialog box: In table design, you must set the Required property for the foreign key column to Yes. Otherwise, Access will allow your users to enter a null foreign key value, thus violating strict referential integrity.

Database-Specific Integrity Rules

All integrity constraints that do not fall under entity integrity or referential integrity are referred to as *database-specific rules* or *business rules*. These rules reflect the business process being modeled by a database and are specific to the database. Although database-specific integrity rules lack generality in the context of relational database design, they are vital for the operation of the database they apply to.

The main purpose of database-specific integrity rules is to prevent bad data from being entered into a database. Human error, lack of communication between different business organizations, and misunderstanding of business rules could all result in erroneous or inconsistent data being entered into a database. Such bad input data will inevitably lead to bad output data. For example, a health care provider may have the following business rules that need to be implemented in a database:

- Services cannot be provided to deceased patients.
- One patient cannot be listed as simultaneously enrolling in more than one hospital stay.

- A patient's birth date must not be a future date.
- A patient's birth date cannot be more than 130 years from the current date.
- Certain services cannot be provided to a patient without the consent of the patient's doctor.
- The length of a service must be within a certain limit.
- The total bill for a patient within a certain period may not exceed a certain limit.
- A patient may receive certain services only if he or she is Medicaid-eligible.

Business rules are often far more difficult to implement than general relational rules. You have to learn a whole new set of constraints for each new database. These constraints can be very complex, and each one of them could take considerable time and energy to implement. In addition, some rules may conflict with others, in which case you may need to go back to the drawing board and rebuild the entire business model.

Moving On

Our discussion of the basics of the relational model in this chapter is by no means an in-depth treatment of the subject. The purpose of this chapter is to take you one step beyond what you already know about relational databases. The theory provided here is meant to formalize some of the things you already know intuitively.

The benefits of a database that has been designed according to the relational model are numerous. Some of the benefits are:

- Data entry, updates, and deletions will be efficient.
- Data retrieval, summarization, and reporting will also be efficient.
- Since the database follows a well-formulated model, it behaves predictably.
- Since much of the information is stored in the database rather than in the application, the database is somewhat self-documenting.
- Changes to the database schema are easy to make.

With this foundation laid, we will proceed to discuss the inner workings of SQL Server and Access in the next two chapters.

chapter 3

Client Component: Microsoft Access

Microsoft Access is a multiuser desktop relational database management system (RDBMS). It is multiuser because the same Access database can be opened at the same time by several users on a LAN; it is desktop oriented because the Access Jet database engine runs on each user's computer even though the database being used may be in a shared network drive.

One distinguishing characteristic of Access is that it combines powerful RDBMS capabilities with intuitive user control. This is done through a cleverly designed graphical user interface (GUI), which presents complex underlying functionalities with an easy-to-understand graphical depiction. The QBE (query by example) grid is such an example: A query is difficult to read while in the form of an SQL statement, shown in Figure 3-1, but it becomes eminently lucid when represented graphically in the QBE grid, shown in Figure 3-2.

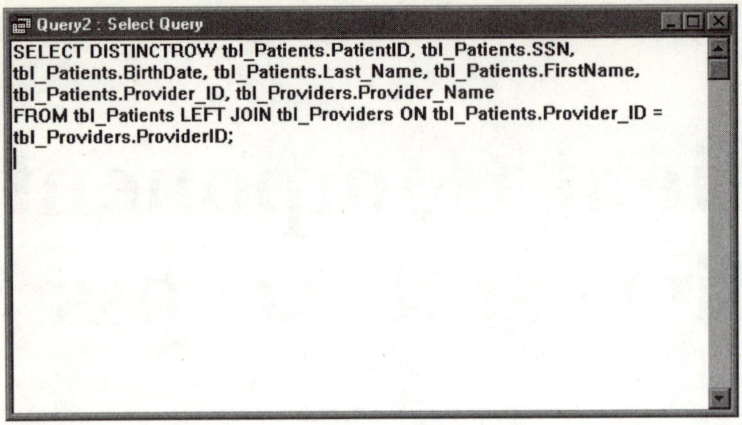

Figure 3-1: An SQL statement used in a SELECT query.

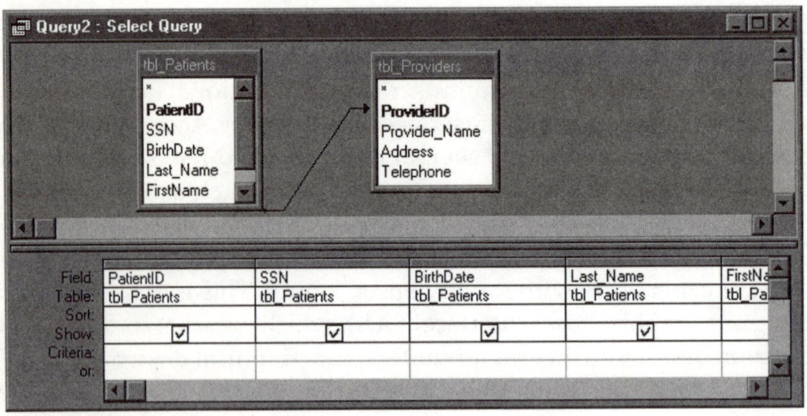

Figure 3-2: The same query with the SQL statement shown in Figure 3-1 represented in the QBE grid.

However, the GUI does have limits in its expressive power—for example, it's not possible to represent sub-queries graphically. In certain cases, there can be more than meets the eye to what the GUI presents. In this chapter, we will look under the Access GUI to gain a better understanding of the inner workings of Access. In particular, considerable attention will be paid to those aspects of Access that pertain to the client/server architecture.

Operational Modes of Access

As discussed in Chapter 1, Access can be run in either a file-server mode or a client/server mode. To an end user of an Access application which configuration is in actual use should ideally make no difference in the appearance and operation of the application. This is a design philosophy of Access; when working with a foreign data source, Access strives to make external data calls transparent. To the designer of a database, however, the particular configuration that the database is in must be clear. To take full advantage of the client/server architecture, and to maximize the efficiency of the database, the designer has to know precisely where data resides and where processing takes place.

Unlike most other desktop DBMSes, Access uses only one file for each database. This file always has a default filename extension of .MDB and contains both data structures (i.e., definitions for tables, queries, forms, etc.) and data. The actual amount of data held in an MDB file is determined by whether the database is in a file-server or client/server configuration.

The File-Server Configuration

In the file-server configuration, an MDB file residing on a file server holds all the data for an application. Data held in Access MDB files will be referred to as *local data* in this book. Of course, in this context, *local* means that the data is exclusively in Access format; it doesn't necessarily mean that it is in any individual workstation's hard drive.

In a LAN, an MDB file residing in a shared network drive can be accessed by multiple workstations that run Access independently. When one workstation needs data in a table, as in the query shown in Figure 3-3, the file server transfers a copy of the entire table over the LAN to the workstation before any processing, which in this case is the SELECT query, is done.

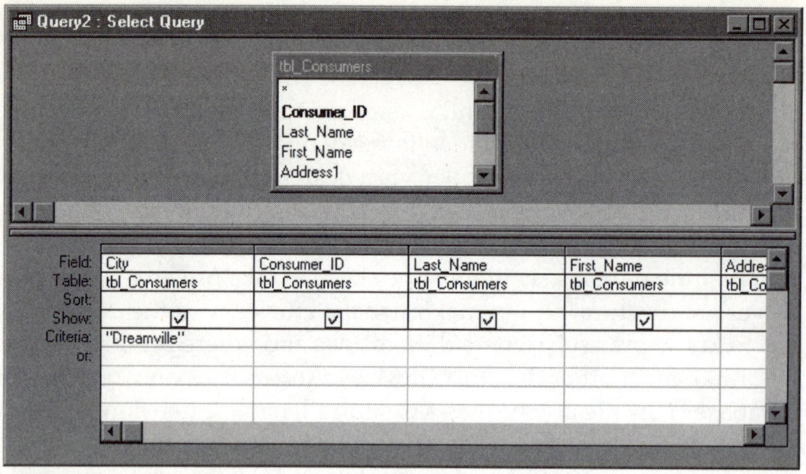

Figure 3-3: A simple Access query that selects all consumers who live in Dreamville from tbl_Consumers.

This example illustrates the limitations of running Access in a file-server architecture: it could put excessive strains on LANs. Imagine that the tbl_Consumers table contains tens of thousands of records. Running the query in Figure 3-3 could cause megabytes of data to be transferred over a LAN to a workstation, even though there may only be a few requested records corresponding to consumers who live in Dreamville. This not only wastes network resources but also slows down the query.

The Client/Server Configuration

Access is capable of working with different database servers from several vendors, including Microsoft, IBM, and Oracle. We will, of course, examine SQL Server as the back-end component to Access. There are two ways for Access to access data in SQL Server: through linked tables (called attached tables in Access 2.0) or through pass-through queries.

The goal of using Access and SQL Server in a client/server configuration is to minimize local processing as well as data flow in the network.

Linked Tables

A linked SQL Server table can be treated in very much the same way as a local table; it is represented by a table icon in the tables window, you can base a form or report on it, and you can run queries on it. The same query shown in Figure 3-3 will operate quite differently if the table used is a linked SQL Server table, even though the QBE grid definition of the query will appear exactly the same, as shown in Figure 3-4.

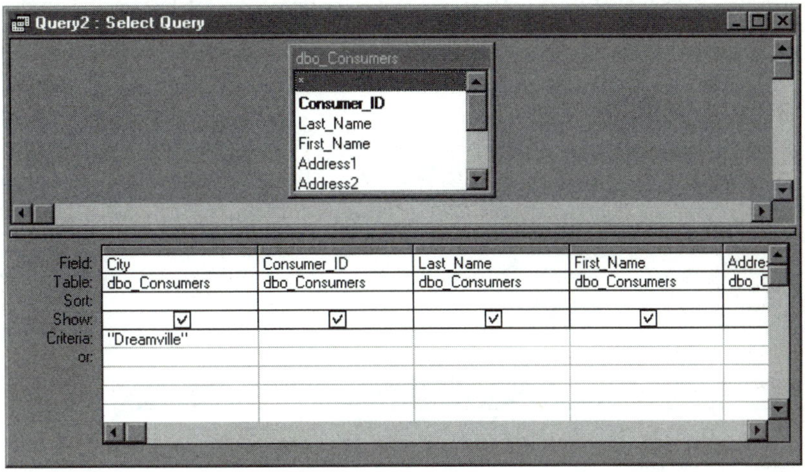

Figure 3-4: The query from Figure 3-3 now operates on a linked SQL Server table, dbo_Consumers.

When you run the query in Figure 3-4, the Access Jet database engine first constructs a data request that calls ODBC functions:

```
SQLExecDirect: SELECT "dbo"."Consumers"."Consumer_ID" FROM "dbo"."Consumers"

SQLExecDirect: SELECT "Consumer_ID","City"  FROM "dbo"."Consumers" WHERE
```

The Jet engine then sends this request to the SQL Server on which the Consumers table resides. SQL Server interprets it as a Transact-SQL statement:

```
SELECT Consumer_ID, City
FROM Consumer
WHERE City = 'Dreamville'
```

SQL Server then processes the query accordingly and sends back to your workstation only those consumer records whose City column is equal to 'Dreamville.'

Note that in this whole process, the content of the table is never sent in its entirety to your workstation; instead, only a limited number of rows are transferred. This means that no time is wasted on the transfer of unneeded data, and consequently, the query runs much faster.

The preceding example is only a very simple one intended to delineate the usual processes that take place when you run an Access query on a linked SQL

Server table. You should be aware that the presence of a linked table in an Access query does not guarantee that the query will be run on SQL Server. There are cases in which the Access Jet engine will force entire SQL Server tables to be sent to a workstation for local processing. Chapter 7 provides a detailed discussion on working with linked tables and Access queries on linked tables.

Pass-Through Queries

To run the query in Figure 3-4, it has to go through ODBC as an intermediate layer between Access and SQL Server. Instead of relying on the ODBC layer to translate an Access query into a Transact-SQL query, you can send an SQL statement directly to SQL Server. You can do this via a *pass-through query*, which contains either a Transact-SQL statement or a call on SQL Server procedures, as shown in Figure 3-5.

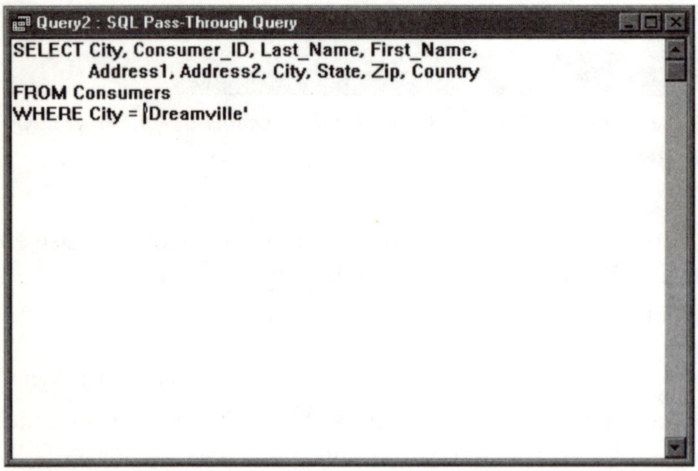

Figure 3-5: A pass-through query that performs the same task as the query in Figure 3-4.

You can specify in the properties section of the pass-through query a data source (i.e., a specific SQL Server database) to which this query will be sent. When you run this query, the Transact-SQL statement is sent directly to the SQL Server of choice. After SQL Server processes the query, it returns the resultant data back to your workstation. Again, only the data that meets the query criteria is returned through the LAN to your workstation, but the ODBC layer has been circumvented in running the pass-through query.

A pass-through query can contain more than SQL statements. You can write a *stored procedure* on SQL Server, which is an executable program written in Transact-SQL that is very much like a DOS batch file, and compile and store it on SQL Server. You can then invoke the stored procedure from a pass-through query. Pass-through queries and stored procedures will be discussed in detail in Chapter 8.

The Access Object Model

You are probably no stranger to the concept of objects in Access. When you open up a database such as that shown in Figure 3-6, all the things you can see in the database window, including tables, queries, forms, reports, macros, and modules, are *database objects*.

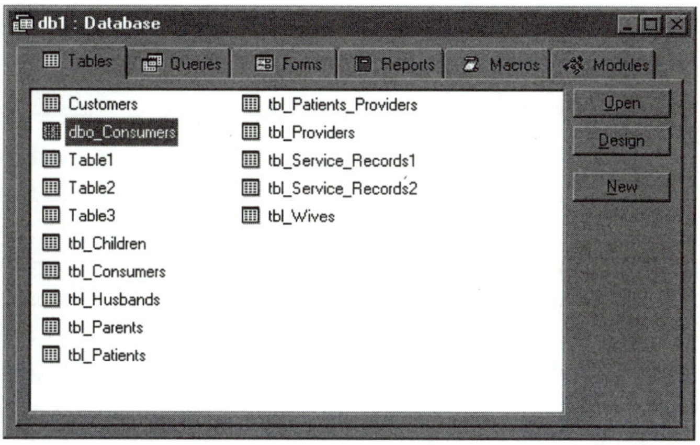

Figure 3-6: The database window contains GUI objects such as tables, queries, forms, reports, macros, and modules. They don't always mean the same thing as objects that can be manipulated in VBA code.

Database objects, however, can't be referenced directly for data access in Visual Basic for Applications (VBA) code because a database object can be the abstract aggregate of several possible VBA objects. For example, when you open a table in the design view, you are looking at a graphical representation of a *TableDef* object, which holds information about the structure of the table, including column definitions and defaults. When you open the table in the datasheet view, you are really viewing a *Recordset* object, which is the structure Access uses to hold data in a computer's memory, in a spreadsheet format. In this section, we are going to examine the system of objects used in VBA to organize and manipulate data.

An end user of Access applications doesn't need to know the object model at all. On the other hand, if you want to create an application of some complexity (especially one that uses VBA), you need to have a fairly good understanding of the Access object model. The proper use of some objects, such as recordsets, can be crucial in achieving high performance in a client/server system.

Chapters later in this book will make extensive use of VBA, in which the Access object model plays a pivotal role. For example, to build an SQL pass-through query that dynamically passes parameters to SQL Server, you must write VBA code to manipulate data access objects, such as the Database object and the QueryDef object, as well as the methods and properties associated with these objects. Chapter 8 will illustrate the use of VBA procedures for constructing pass-through queries. As another example, consider the Recordset object, which is used to retrieve data from tables or queries. The proper use of the Recordset object on linked SQL Server tables can lead to improved speed of data retrieval from SQL Server. Performance issues related to the Recordset object will be discussed in Chapter 9.

Access' Architecture

In order to understand how objects are organized in Access databases, we must go one step further to examine how Access divides DBMS functions among its constituent parts.

Access as a software product is driven by two principle components, the *application engine* and the *Jet database engine*, in very much the same way cars are driven by automobile engines. The application engine provides the programming environment and user interface. The Jet database engine directly handles data.

The typical end user sees and works with the application engine but does not directly interact with the Jet database engine. The Jet database engine is a quite distinct module—it is shared by several Microsoft applications and even has its own version number that's distinct from Access's. You can think of Microsoft Access as an RDBMS built on the Jet database engine as a data manager.

Objects & Collections

Each engine used by Access controls a distinct set of objects, as shown in Figure 3-7. The objects created by the application engine are simply referred to as *Microsoft Access objects*, and the objects defined by the Jet database engine are called *data access objects* (*DAOs*). Such a distinction is necessary because the Jet database engine is really a software component shared by several products, one of which is Microsoft Access. As a result, the objects defined and manipulated by the Jet database engine are not unique to Access and should be distinguished from the indigenous Access objects.

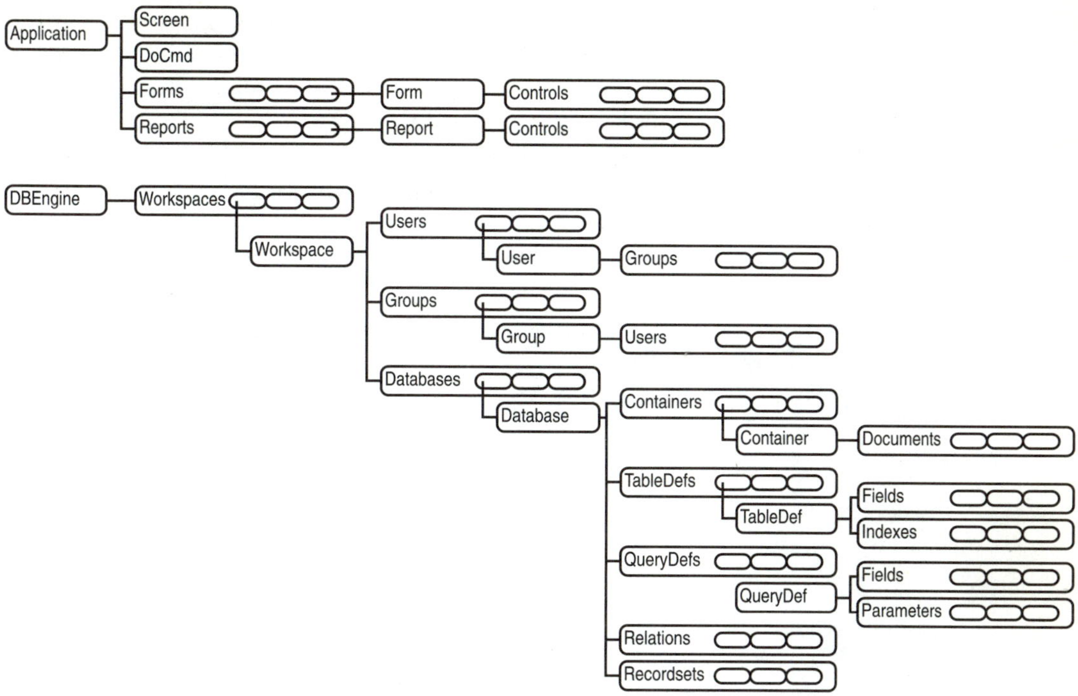

Figure 3-7: The architecture of Access.

All the objects used by Access are organized into a hierarchical system of containment: each higher level is said to contain its subordinate objects. For example, the DBEngine object contains all Workspace objects. To refer to any object, the entire path in the hierarchy leading to the object must be specified. For example, the currently open Access session is referred to as:

```
DBEngine.Workspaces(0)
```

The meaning of the (0) will be discussed later in the VBA section.

Most objects in this model are grouped into collections. A *collection* is a type of object, except that a collection may contain only objects of the same type, while an object can contain objects and collections of different types. For example, the TableDefs collection may contain only TableDef objects, but each TableDef object contains fields and indexes, two distinct classes of objects. Note that the name of a collection is always plural.

Properties & Methods

In addition to being able to contain subordinate objects and collections, each object or collection also has associated with it two sets of important attributes: *properties* and *methods*.

Properties are relatively easy to understand: the width, height, and record source of a form are all properties of the form; the number of TableDef objects contained in a TableDefs collection is a property of that TableDefs collection; the SQL statement in a query is a property, too.

Each property has a one-word name, such as Width, Height, RecordSource, Count, or SQL. Some properties can be read and changed in the properties window of an object. Figure 3-8 shows a few properties of a form. You can also access properties through VBA code by referring to their property names.

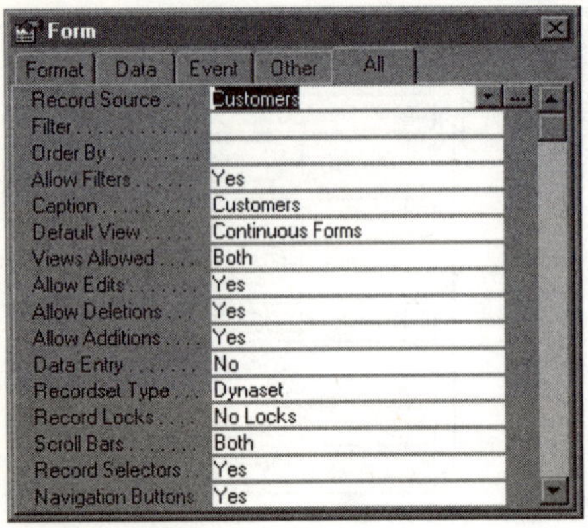

Figure 3-8: All items shown in the properties window here correspond to specific properties of a form. For example, the Record Source line shows the property called RecordSource.

A method is an action associated with an object. To use an analogy in grammar, you can think of methods as verbs and objects as nouns. A method should always be used with an object, and the method performs a specific function related to the object. Each object or collection can use only a distinct repertoire of methods. For example, a Database object can use the CreateQueryDef method to create a new query in the database specified by the Database object. Methods can only be invoked in VBA code and will be discussed in greater detail in the VBA section later in this chapter.

The Application Engine

Although it is a distinct component of the Access architecture, the application engine is not isolated from the Jet database engine. The application engine relies on the Jet database engine for data-related information.

When you open up a database, the application engine obtains from the Jet database engine a list of all the tables, queries, forms, reports, macros, and modules in the database and displays them in the database window. Once the database is open, the application engine determines which menu bars and toolbars are to be shown, assembles and displays forms and reports based on data supplied by the Jet database engine, and keeps track of the active objects in the Access window.

The application engine controls the Application object, the Screen object, the Forms collection, and the Reports collection.

The Application Object

The Application object refers to the entire Microsoft Access program. Strictly speaking, the Application object contains all Access objects and collections (i.e., those not controlled by the Jet database engine), including the Screen object, the DoCmd object, the Forms collection, and the Reports collection.

However, when referring to these subordinate objects and collections within Access, you don't have to invoke the Application object. In other words, even though the following are perfectly valid references to those objects and collections:

```
Application.Screen
Application.DoCmd
Application.Forms
Application.Reports
```

if these reference are made in Access, you can actually remove the prefix of *Application* and independently refer to them as:

```
Screen
DoCmd
Forms
Reports
```

Since the Application object is database independent, you can use it to alter a user account's general environmental settings. For example, you can use the SetOption method of the Application object to disable a user's built-in toolbars:

```
    Application.SetOption "Built-in Toolbars Available", False
```

Unless this option is re-enabled, the user won't see the built-in toolbars in any database he or she opens. We will revisit this example in Chapter 10 in the context of security.

Two other properties of the Application object come in handy sometimes. You can use the CurrentObjectName property to extract the name of the active object and the CurrentObjectType property to determine whether the current object is a table, query, form, report, macro, or module.

The Application object has yet another interesting use: You can use it to work with Access objects from another software program. For example, you can create a new instance of the Application object from within Microsoft Excel and use the OpenCurrentDatabase method of the Application object to open an existing Access database. Or you can use the NewCurrentDatabase method of the Application object to create a new database. You can then proceed to manipulate the objects in the database via method and properties associated with the Application object.

The DoCmd Object

The DoCmd object is new to Microsoft Access for Windows 95. It is intended to replace the DoCmd statement from earlier versions of Microsoft Access. The actions that were used as arguments to the DoCmd statement are now methods of the DoCmd object. For example, this line of code in Access 2.0:

```
DoCmd OpenForm "Orders"
```

becomes the following in Access for Windows 95:

```
DoCmd.OpenForm "Orders"
```

When you convert an existing Microsoft Access 2.0 database into Access for Windows 95, all DoCmd statements and their associated actions will be automatically converted to DoCmd methods and appropriate arguments.

The Screen Object

The screen object has no methods and only four properties: ActiveControl, ActiveForm, ActiveReport, and PreviousControl. Using these properties, you can reference the control, form, or report that currently has the focus, or the control that previously had the focus, without knowing the actual name of object you refer to. If you try to refer to the active control, form, or report when there is no currently active form, report, and control, Access will return a run-time error.

The act of referring to the Screen object doesn't make a form, report, or control active. To make a form, report, or control active, you must use the SelectObject method of the DoCmd object.

The Forms Collection

The Forms collection consists of all the active (i.e., open) forms. There are no methods available to the Forms collection, and the only property of the collection is Count, which is always equal to the number of open forms.

Obviously, you have to open a form before you can reference any of its controls or attributes. To reference any active form, you must use the Forms collection as the top of the hierarchy, in this format:

```
Forms![Form_Name]
```

Alternatively, you can replace this with the Access *keyword:*

```
Me
```

which represents the form in VBA code if the code is part of the form itself.

The Reports Collection

The Reports collection consists of all the active (i.e., open) reports. Just like the Forms collection, there are no methods available to the Reports collection, and the only property of the collection is Count, which is equal to the number of open reports.

The Reports collection contains Report objects. To reference any report, you must use the Reports collection as the top of the hierarchy, in this format:

```
Reports![Report_Name]
```

Again, you can replace this line by using the keyword:

```
Me
```

which can represent the report in VBA code if the code is part of the report itself.

The Controls Collection

Each form or report object contains a Controls collection, to which all the controls on that form or report belong.

You refer to a control or a property of a control in an expression by using an *identifier*. There are two types of identifiers: implicit or explicit. An explicit identifier explicitly refers to the name of the Controls collection to which a control belongs; an implicit identifier does not include the collection name. For example, to refer to the value of the Author_ID control on the Authors form, you can use any the following implicit identifiers:

- Forms!Authors!Author_ID
- Forms!Authors![Author_ID], which is especially useful if the control name contains spaces (for example, "Author ID").
- Forms!Authors!("Author_ID")
- Forms!Authors(0), which refers to the control's index in the Controls collection. (Here we assume the control Author_ID is the first in the Controls collection.)

Or you can refer to them explicitly by including the name of the Controls collection in the identifier:

- Forms!Authors.Controls!Author_ID

- Forms!Authors.Controls![Author ID]
- Forms!Authors.Controls!("Author_ID")
- Forms!Authors.Controls(0)

Controls In Subforms & Subreports

To refer to a property of a subform or subreport, you must type a full identifier for the form or report with the Form or Report property of a subform or subreport control. For example, a main form, Patients, has on it a subform control called DoctorsSubformControl, which points to a Doctors subform. The following identifier refers to the Visible property of the Doctors subform:

```
Forms![Patients]![DoctorsSubformControl].Form.Visible
```

In this example:

- Forms![Patients]![DoctorsSubformControl] refers to the subform control that points to the subform. It's important to remember that the subform control is a control object on the main form; it's not the subform itself.
- Forms![Patients]![DoctorsSubformControl].Form refers to the subform itself. You must specify the Form property to refer to the subform itself or one of its properties.

In contrast, to refer to the value of a control on a subform or subreport, or to refer to one of the control's properties, you don't have to use the Form or Report property. For example, the following identifier refers to the Visible property of the DoctorName control on the Doctors subform:

```
Forms![Patients]![DoctorsSubformControl]![DoctorName].Visible
```

Each Control object is described by a particular intrinsic constant. For example, the intrinsic constant acTextBox is associated with a text box control, and acCommandButton is associated with a command button. You can use the ControlType property of an existing control to determine what type of control it is. However, you don't have to know the specific type of a control in order to use it in code. You can simply represent it with a variable of data type Control.

The Jet Database Engine

A database engine is a component of a DBMS that directly interacts with data. Microsoft added the term *jet* to the name of their database engine to convey a sense of speed and power. The Microsoft Jet database engine is often abbreviated to *Jet engine* or *Jet* in common usage.

The Jet engine is shared among several Microsoft software products: Microsoft Access, Microsoft VBA, Microsoft C++, and Microsoft Excel. However, it can't be purchased as a stand-alone product.

The objects that are defined by the Jet database engine are *data access objects* (*DAOs*).

The DBEngine Object

The DBEngine object is at the top the DAO hierarchy. All other DAOs are members of DBEngine, so references to all other DAOs must include the DBEngine as part of the object identifier.

The DBEngine object is closely related to the DBEngine property of the Application object. From another Microsoft program, such as VBA or Microsoft Excel, you can control Access by using the DBEngine property of the Application object to return a reference to the DBEngine object. All DAOs are then accessible through the DBEngine object.

The Workspaces Collection

A Workspace object defines a session for a user. When you start Access, the first thing the Jet database engine does is create a Workspaces collection and a default Workspace object within that collection.

The Workspace object holds information about the current user. If you can start Access without being prompted for a password, the UserName property of the default Workspace object is set to "Admin" (and the password is assumed to be ""). On the other hand, if you have to log in when you start Access, the UserName Property of the default Workspace object is set to the name under which you log in.

You can use the DefaultWorkspaceClone method to create a new Workspace object without requiring the user to log in again. For example, if you need to conduct two sets of transactions simultaneously in separate workspaces, you can use the DefaultWorkspaceClone method to create a second Workspace object with the same username and password so that the user is not prompted for this information again.

The Workspace object is often used for user/group administration and security implementation. For example, using the CreateGroup and CreateUser method of the Workspace object, you can create new users and groups.

The Users Collection

The Users collection is a member of the Workspace object and contains User objects. Each User object corresponds to an actual user defined in the current Access system. The only default User object (which exists before any new user is created and which can't be deleted) has a username of Admin. The User objects are used almost exclusively for the purpose of implementing database security and assigning object-level permissions to individual users. See Chapter 10 for details on the use of User objects in Access security.

A User object has a Name property that you can use in setting permissions for a Container or Document object (i.e., a database object such as a table, query, form, report, macro, or module) to individual users. For example, you can assign the value of a User object's Name property to the UserName property of a Container or Document object. You can then set the Permissions property of the Container or Document object to establish permissions for the user defined by the UserName property. Or you can read the Permissions property to determine existing permissions for that user.

The Groups Collection

The Groups collection is a member of the Workspace object and contains Group objects. Each Group object corresponds to an actual user group defined in the current Access system. There are two default Group objects (which exist before any new group is created and which can't be deleted), and they are named Admins (note the *s*) and Users. The Group objects are used almost exclusively for the purpose of implementing database security and assigning object-level permissions to user groups.

A Group object has a Name property that you can use in setting permissions for a Container or Document object (i.e., a database object such as a table, query, form, report, macro, or module) to user groups. For example, you can assign the value of a Group object's Name property to the UserName property of a Container or Document object. You can then set the Permissions property of the Container or Document object to establish permissions for the group of users defined by the UserName property. Or you can read the Permissions property to determine existing permissions for that group.

The Databases Collection

The Databases collection is a member of the Workspace object and contains all open Database objects.

You can use the OpenDatabase method of the Workspace object to open a database other than the currently open database. However, you can only open the new database in VBA, and you can't make two database objects appear in the Access window. Therefore, you can't go back and forth between two databases the same way you can with two documents in Microsoft Word. Chapter 9 will discuss a technique for switching between Access databases.

A database object contains five collections: Containers, TableDefs, QueryDefs, Relations, and Recordsets.

The Containers Collection

There are two types of Container objects: those defined by Microsoft Access and those defined by the Jet database engine. The Containers collection encompasses both types.

The Jet database engine Container objects include:

Container Name	Contains Information About
Databases	Containing database
Tables	Saved tables and queries
Relationships	Saved relationships

The following four Container objects are defined by Microsoft Access:

Container Name	Contains Information About
Forms	Saved forms
Modules	Saved modules
Reports	Saved reports
Scripts	Saved macros

The Container objects defined by Microsoft Access are Microsoft Access database objects, not data access objects. These Container objects provide the Jet database engine with information about Microsoft Access objects. The Jet database engine uses this information to implement security on Microsoft Access database objects in the same way it does for data access objects.

The Documents collection of a Container object contains Document objects representing the individual objects of the type described by the Container object. For example, the Reports Container object has a Documents collection that may include a Document object corresponding to a report named Services.

You can use Container objects to establish and enforce permissions for Microsoft Access database objects. To set permissions for a Container object, set the UserName property of the Container object to the name of an existing User or Group object. Then set the Permissions property for the Container object.

You should be careful not to confuse the particular types of Container objects with the collection types of the same name. The Forms and Reports Container objects contain Documents collections, which include individual Document objects representing each saved form or report. The Forms and Reports collections refer only to open forms or reports.

The TableDefs Collection

The TableDefs collection includes all TableDef objects. A TableDef allows you to manipulate the definition of a table, including the type of each column, the default value of the column, and so on. A TableDef object contains a Fields collection and an Indexes collection.

Using VBA, you can accomplish the following with TableDef objects:

- Read or write the Connect and SourceTableName property settings for attached tables, and use the RefreshLink method to update connections to linked tables.
- Read (or write, if the Updatable property is set to True) the ValidationRule and ValidationText property settings to find (or specify) validation conditions.
- Use the OpenRecordset method to create a table-, dynaset-, or snapshot-type Recordset object based on the table definition.
- Use the CreateTableDef method to create a new TableDef object.

The QueryDefs Collection

The QueryDefs collection includes all QueryDef objects. A QueryDef object corresponds to a stored query definition in a database. You can think of a saved query as a compiled SQL statement. A QueryDef object contains a Parameters collection and a Fields collection.

You can use the properties of a QueryDef object to define a query. These are some of the things you can do with a QueryDef object:

- Check and modify the SQL property setting, set its parameters, and then run the query.
- Set or check the Type property to determine whether the query will select records from an existing table, make a new table, insert records from one table into another table, delete records, or update records.
- Retrieve data from an ODBC data source such as an SQL Server database by setting the ODBCTimeout and Connect properties and, if the query isn't a select query, setting the ReturnsRecords property to False.

The Relations Collection

The Relations collection contains all the Relation objects in a database. Each Relation object defines the relationship between two tables and contains a Fields collection to hold information about the primary and foreign keys in a relationship.

You can use the CreateRelation method of the Database object to create a

Relation object that specifies the two involved tables and the primary key in the primary table. You can then define the foreign key in the foreign table by adding a field to the Fields collection and making that field point to the foreign key. Remember that although you can perform all this manually in the Access Relationships window, doing it programmatically allows dynamic processing.

The Recordsets Collection

A Recordset object represents the records in a base table or the records that result from running a query. The Recordsets collection contains all open Recordset objects in a Database object. Recordsets are extremely important objects because they are the only structures through which you can manipulate data in VBA.

There are three types of Recordset objects corresponding to the following sets of data you can create in Access:

- **Table.** A recordset based on an Access base table. You can use a table-type recordset to update or delete records in a table or add records to a table. However, you can't create a table-type recordset on a linked SQL Server table. Also, you can't base a table-type recordset on an SQL statement (such as a SELECT query).
- **Dynaset.** A recordset based on a query whose resultant records can be updated. A dynaset-type recordset can contain fields from one or more base tables. The underlying table(s) for a dynaset-type recordset can be either local or foreign (such as linked SQL Server tables). A dynaset-type recordset cannot be based on an SQL pass-through query because the result of a pass-through query is not updatable.
- **Snapshot.** A recordset based on a query whose resultant records cannot be updated. A snapshot-type recordset, which is used strictly for data retrieval and record browsing, is simply a static picture of a set of records. Hence its name. You can use it to generate a report or find a record.

When you open a new Recordset object using the OpenRecordset method, the type of the Recordset is determined by the type of the object that the recordset is based on (i.e., QueryDef, Recordset, or TableDef objects) and the options you select. The type argument for the OpenRecordset method determines the type of Recordset objects you can open for a given base object.

A new Recordset is automatically added to the Recordsets collection when you open the object, and it's automatically deleted when you close it. You can declare an object variable as a Recordset, and you can have more than one object variable that refers to the same tables or queries. You can also have one or more Recordset objects that refer to some or all fields and some or all records in one or more tables or queries.

In a multiuser database, more than one user can open a dynaset-type Recordset object referring to the same records. Because a dynaset is dynamic, when one user changes a record, other users have immediate access to the changed data. However, if one user adds a record, the change isn't reflected for any of the other users until they use the Requery method on the recordset. If a user deletes a record, other users are notified when they try to access it.

In Access, to maintain data integrity, dynaset- and table-type Recordset objects are locked during Edit and Update operations so that only one user can update a particular record at a time. Not all fields can be updated in all dynaset-type recordsets. To determine whether you can update a particular field, check the Updatable property setting of the Field object.

Introduction to VBA

Access Basic, the programming language used in Microsoft Access versions 1.0 and 2.0, has been replaced by VBA in Microsoft Access for Windows 95. VBA is almost identical to Access Basic, and with only a few exceptions, Microsoft Access automatically converts Access Basic code into VBA when you convert your database. Appendix D contains a useful selection of reference material on VBA.

Where to Use VBA

VBA code can be invoked in a variety of places in Access, such as the immediate window, in macros and queries, or event procedures and reports.

The Immediate Window

The immediate window is the most direct and convenient place to test a function or subroutine. This will be discussed in detail in "The VBA Development Environment" later in this chapter.

Macros

Figure 3-9 shows how a VBA function is called from a macro.

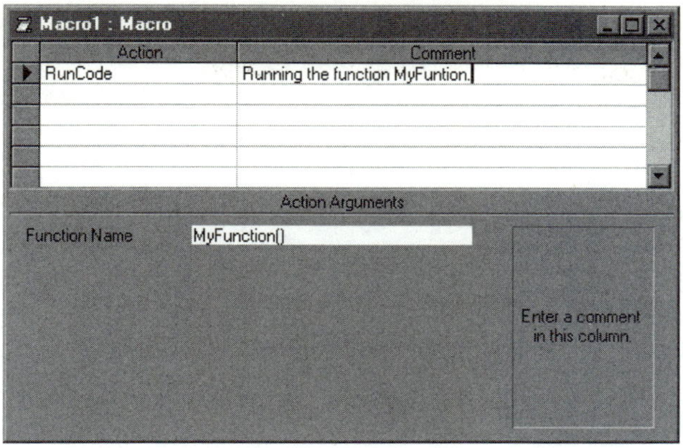

Figure 3-9: This macro calls the function MyFunction.

Queries

A function can be used to fill a column in a query, as shown in Figure 3-10. In this example, the function ComplexCriteria() returns a value of either TRUE or FALSE based on the value of BirthDate. The function could, for instance, perform some highly convoluted logical operation involving BirthDate that's too complicated for a simple expression. The query selects a row only if the value returned by the function ComplexCriteria(BirthDate) is TRUE.

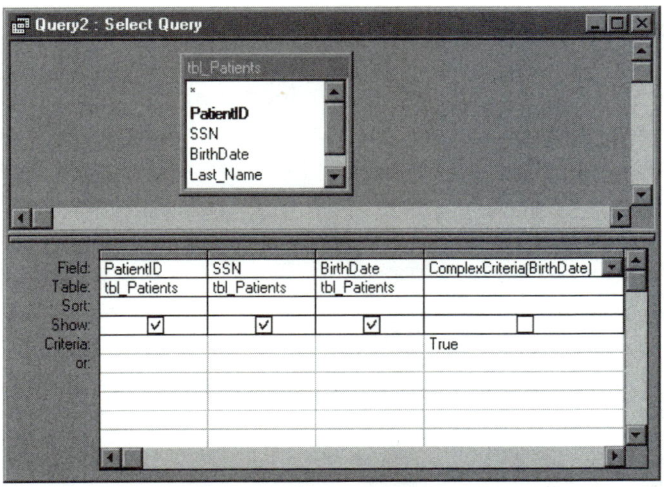

Figure 3-10: The value returned by the function ComplexCriteria() is compared with a selection criterion to determine if a row should be selected.

Alternatively, a function can be used to supply a criterion in a query, as in Figure 3-11. This is useful when, say, a global variable needs to be returned by a function and used as the criterion. In fact, this is the only way in which a global variable can be used as a criterion in a query.

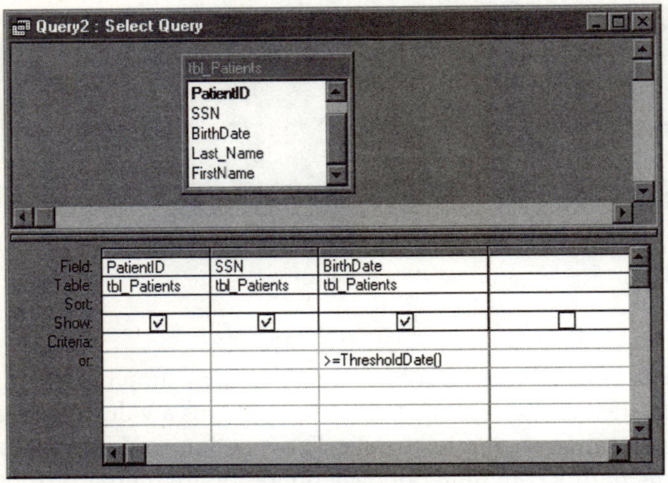

Figure 3-11: The value returned by the function ThresholdDate() provides the selection criterion.

Event Procedures in Forms & Reports

An *event procedure* is a function or subroutine triggered when something is done to a form, a report, or an object contained in a form (such as a command button). For example, an "On Open" event procedure is run right before a form is opened, and an "On Click" event procedure is run when a command button is clicked.

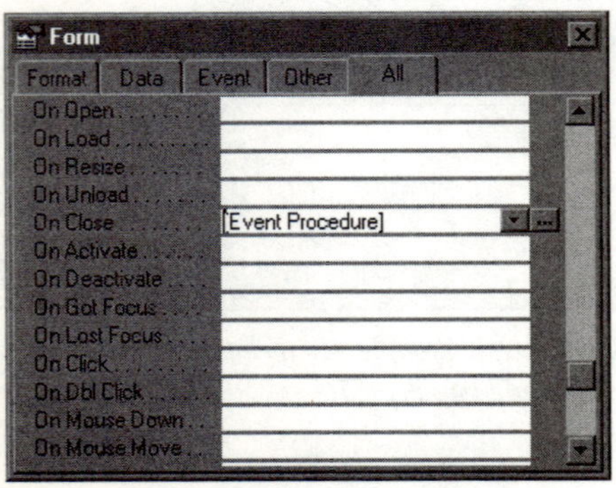

Figure 3-12: A VBA subroutine will be run right before this form is closed.

Functions vs. Subroutines

A procedure is simply a program. There are two types of VBA procedures: functions (or function procedures) and subroutines (or sub procedures). These types of procedures are similar in that both can accept parameters, both use the same VBA syntax, and both are developed in the same programming environment.

There are several important differences, though. A function can return a value, but a subroutine can't. A function can be run anywhere in Access (in another function or subroutine or from a form, report, query, and macro), but a subroutine can only be called in a function or subroutine or as event procedures in a form or report. Subroutines can't be used in queries or macros.

VBA vs. Macros

You have probably used macros in Access. Although they are very easy to use and powerful, macros have some pronounced limitations. For example, using macros alone, you can't construct a pass-through query to be sent to SQL Server that contains dynamically changed query parameters. Also, the ability of macros to trap errors is very limited.

By comparison, VBA code is far more powerful and flexible. In addition to full parameter-passing and error-trapping abilities, you can start new sessions of Access, create virtual objects to represent database objects, manipulate real data through these virtual objects, process data row by row, and implement entire processes, all in VBA code. You can also interact with other Microsoft Windows applications through dynamic data exchange (DDE). In addition, you can do most of these things with macros, with the following exceptions:

- Run the AUTOEXEC macro automatically when you start a database.
- Use the AUTOKEY macro to map keystrokes to certain actions.
- Set customized menus and submenus for forms.

The VBA Development Environment

In Microsoft Access, all VBA functions and subroutines are stored in modules. Modules, the Module window, and the Debug window constitute the development environment for VBA.

Types of Modules

Although you execute functions and subroutines by their names, you can't save them individually by their own names. Instead, all VBA procedures are collected in modules, and you can give the modules different names and save them independently. There are two types of modules: stand-alone module objects or modules that are part of a form or object.

Module objects are displayed in the Modules window, as shown in Figure 3-13. Each such module object may contain several functions and subroutines.

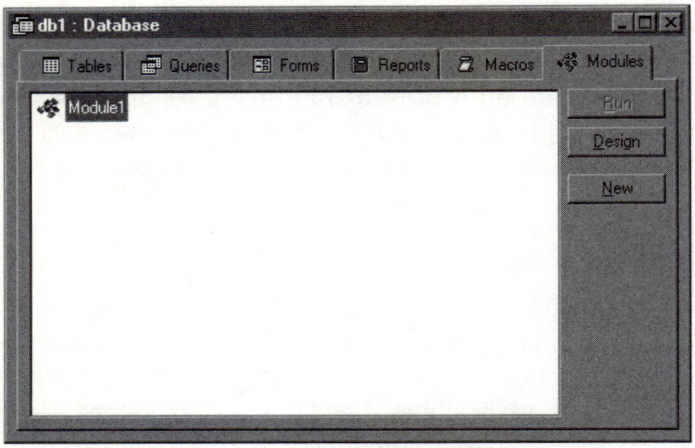

Figure 3-13: A Module object is shown in the Database window.

In addition to the Module objects in a database, each form or report has associated with it a module, which contains all event procedures for that form or report.

You can access both types of modules through the Module window. Don't confuse the Modules window, which is the Database window with the Modules tab selected (Figure 3-13), with the Module window, which is where you type in VBA code (Figure 3-14 and Figure 3-15).

The Module Window

The Module window is where you actually create and edit VBA procedures. When you select the Modules tab in the Database window and then click the New button, you get the Module window for a new, stand-alone module object.

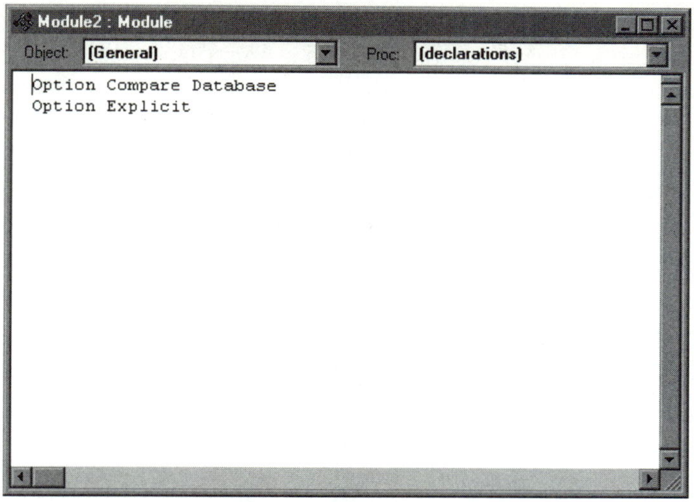

Figure 3-14: The Module window of a new module object.

The Module window for a module that's part of a report or form is slightly different from that of a stand-alone module object. To get to the Module window, open a form or report in design view, and then click the Code button in the toolbar. The Module window of a module associated with a form is shown in Figure 3-15. Note that the Object drop-down menu already contains all the already-defined objects in the form, and the Proc drop-down menu lists all the possible events associated with the selected object.

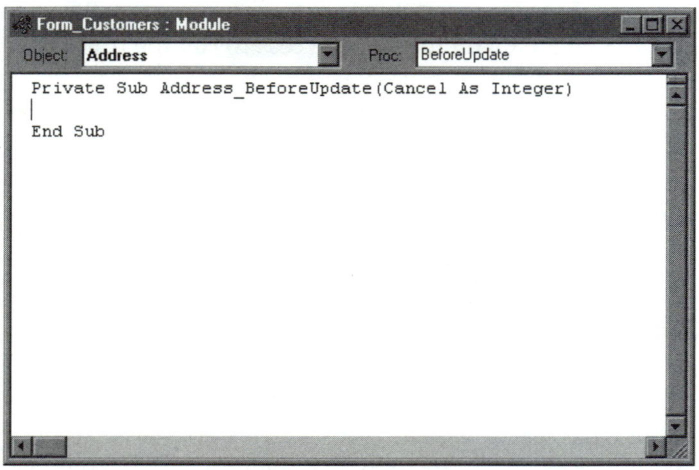

Figure 3-15: The Module window of a form module.

The Debug Window

The Debug window in Microsoft Access 95 is an indispensable tool for working with modules. The Debug window consists of two panes: an Immediate pane and a Watch pane. The Watch pane is visible only if you have set a watch expression.

To view the Debug window, open a module, and click the Debug Window button on the toolbar. You can also open the Debug window by pressing Ctrl+G when working in the module editor. Figure 3-16 shows the Debug window.

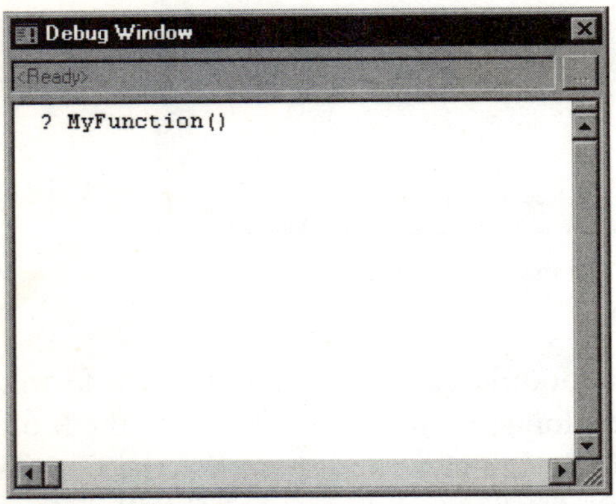

Figure 3-16: The Immediate pane of the Debug window.

You can run any subroutine or function procedure, including event procedures, in the Immediate pane. For example, after you type in the line in Figure 3-16, simply press Enter, and the function, MyFunction(), will be run. Note that the ? is a special character that tells Access to run the function following it in the Immediate pane.

To run an event procedure in a form module from the Debug window, you must specify the name of the form. You must also verify that the form is open in Form view. The following example runs the event procedure for a command button named ShowPatientInfo on an Employees form:

```
? Frm_Patients.ShowPatientInfo_Click()
```

A watch expression is an expression you specify to be monitored in the Debug window. When execution of your code is suspended, you can observe the values of the watch expressions you selected in the Watch pane of the Debug window. You can also perform an instant watch to see the value of an expression that hasn't been specified as a watch expression. The Watch pane enables you to view the value of an expression or a variable while code is running. To set a watch expression, choose Add Watch from the Tools menu.

The Debug window automatically provides status information about your code. When no code is running, the status bar at the top of the Debug window displays <Ready>. Once code begins executing, the status bar displays the name of the current database, the module in which the procedure that is executing resides, and the name of the procedure itself.

Referencing DAOs

In order to manipulate objects in VBA, you must first be able to reference the objects correctly. VBA uses the hierarchical data object model to reference data access objects. In discussions earlier in this chapter, we touched on some methods of referencing objects. There are three general rules for referencing an object within a collection:

- CollectionName![ObjectName]. For example: Reports![My Report].
- CollectionName!("ObjectName"). For example: Reports("My Report").
- CollectionName(IndexNumerOfObject). For example: Reports(3) refers to [My Report] if [My Report] happens to be the fourth open report in the database. Note that all such indices in collection start from 0 and always increment by 1.

Methods & Properties

Each object has a set of properties and methods associated with it. Always precede the properties and methods with a period. For example, the following line invokes the ShowToolbar method of the DoCmd object to show the toolbar for the Database window where appropriate:

```
DoCmd.ShowToolBar "Database", acToolbarWhereApprop
```

The following refers to the SQL property of a QueryDef object named MyQuery:

```
MyQuery.SQL
```

Building a Function

Now that you are familiar with the VBA development environment, let's build a simple, working function to illustrate what you can do with VBA.

Starting a New Function

In the Database window, click the Modules tab and then the New button to start a new Module window (shown in Figure 3-14). You are not in any procedure yet; instead, you are in the declarations section of the module, as shown in the Proc drop-down box at the top of the window. The Proc drop-down box will list all the procedures you store in this module.

Everything you do in the declarations section will affect the entire module. The Option statements configure the overall programming environment inside the module. For example, Option Explicit will force you to declare all variables you use in the module.

Now choose Insert | Procedure from the menu bar, and you get a dialog box. Enter **MyFunction** as the name, and click OK. Note that the scope of the function is set to Public (the default), meaning that MyFunction will be "visible" to procedures outside its own module and can be called anywhere in the application.

Now you are in the procedure section where an empty function has been created for you. The Proc drop-down box displays MyFunction, and you can switch to the declarations section or other procedures by choosing another item in the Proc drop-down box.

Entering & Compiling Code

We will first write a very simple function. Enter the following lines:

```
Debug.Print CurrentUser()
Debug.Print "Done!"
```

into the Module window. In VBA, the special object Debug has only one method, Print, which is used to output its argument to the Immediate pane of the Debug window.

You can't run this function yet because it hasn't been compiled. Compile the procedures in the module (in this case there is only one) by choosing Run | Compile Loaded Modules from the menu bar or by clicking the Compile Loaded Modules button in the toolbar. And now you are ready to run the function MyFunction().

Note that MyFunction() takes no input parameters. If MyFunction() accepted any input parameters, they would be placed between the parentheses. For example, if this function takes a string input parameter called MyInput, then the function will be defined as:

```
Public Function MyFunction(MyInput As String)
```

Testing the Procedure

To test this function, open the Debug window, and type the following line into it:

```
? MyFunction()
```

and then press Enter. The output of the function is displayed in the Debug window, as shown in Figure 3-17.

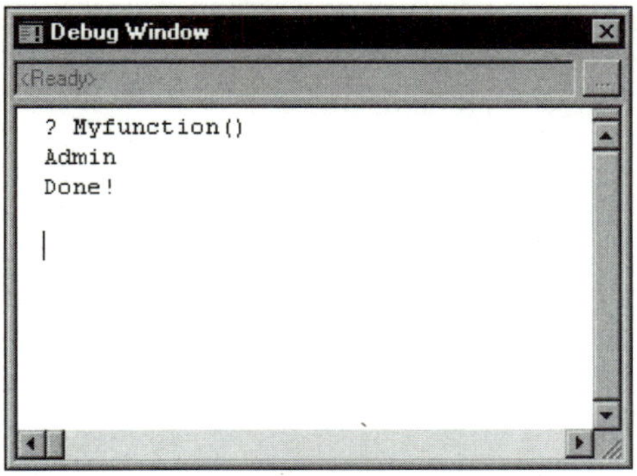

Figure 3-17: Testing MyFunction() in the Immediate pane of the Debug window.

To test MyFunction() again, bring the cursor to the right of MyFunction in the Debug window, and press Enter. Two more lines of output will be added to the Debug window.

Stepping Through Code

The function MyFunction() consists of several lines of code, each of which does something different. Instead of executing all of them together without pause, you can step through the code one line at a time and see the result of each line of code. This is a very useful feature for debugging a procedure.

In order to step through your code, you must specify a *break point* from which the stepping-through starts. To set a break point, go to a line of code at which you want the execution of the code suspended, and then press F9. That line will be highlighted. Press F9 again to cancel a break point.

Next, execute the function from the Debug window. You will notice that the execution of the function is suspended at the break point. To start stepping through the code, click either the Step Into button in the toolbar (or press F8) or the Step Over button in the toolbar (or press Shift+F8). The difference between Step Into and Step Over becomes relevant when another procedure is imbedded in the function; Step Over will allow you to treat the imbedded function as one step, and Step Into will allow you to step through the internal code of the imbedded procedure.

Building a Real Function

MyFunction() doesn't do anything useful. Now let's expand it to do something quite practical. The function looks like this:

```
Public Function MyFunction()

On Error GoTo Err_MyFunction                  '(1)

Dim I As Integer                              '(2)
Dim MyDB As Database, MyQuery As QueryDef     '(3)

Set MyDB = DBEngine(0)(0)                               '(4)

For I = 0 To MyDB.QueryDefs.Count - 1                   '(5)
   If MyDB.QueryDefs(I).Name = "qry_Test" Then '(6)
      MyDB.QueryDefs.Delete "qry_Test"                  '(7)
   End If                                     '(8)
Next I                                 '(9)

Set MyQuery = MyDB.CreateQueryDef("qry_Test")           '(10)
MyQuery.SQL = "SELECT * FROM tbl_Patients;" '(11)

DoCmd.OpenQuery "qry_Test"                              '(12)

Exit_MyFunction:                              '(13)
   Exit Function                              '(14)

Err_MyFunction:                        '(15)
   MsgBox Error$                              '(16)
   Resume Exit_MyFunction                               '(17)

End Function
```

Note that anything to the right of the ' (single quote) is considered a comment and not part of the code.

This function deletes any existing query called qry_Test, creates a new qry_Test that selects all records from the tbl_Patients table, and opens the query in the datasheet view. Here is what each line of code does in this function:

- **Line 1.** Along with Lines 13 through 17, constitutes the function's error-handling mechanism. If an error occurs during the execution of the MyFunction(), the normal flow of the function will be suspended, and the block of code with a label of Err_MyFunction will be executed.
- **Line 2.** Declares an integer variable, I. The statement Dim is the primary variable declaration statement in VBA.

- **Line 3.** Declares two object variables, MyDB and MyQuery, to represent a database and a query inside the function, respectively.
- **Line 4.** Assigns the currently open database to the object variable MyDB. If you want to assign a value to an object variable, you must use the Set statement. To assign values to other types of variables or object properties, you can simply use = without the Set statement.
- **Line 5.** Forms part of the For…Next flow-control statement. This For…Next loop goes through all the saved queries in the QueryDefs collection of the current database. Note that the index value of the queries starts from 0. The QueryDefs collection has a property called Count, which is equal to the number of saved queries in the collection.
- **Line 6.** Tests whether an existing query is named qry_Test. This is the start of an If…Then conditional statement.
- **Line 7.** Deletes a query if it is named qry_Test. Delete is a method of the QueryDefs collection.
- **Line 8.** Ends the conditional statement.
- **Line 9.** Increments I by 1 and goes back to the beginning of the For…Next loop. This flow-control block (Lines 5 through 9) deletes any existing query named qry_Test if it exists so that a new query with the same name can be created.
- **Line 10.** Creates a new query named qry_Test and assigns it to MyQuery, the object variable of the QueryDef type. You can manipulate the qry_Test query from within MyFunction() by using MyQuery.
- **Line 11.** Builds the query by assigning an SQL statement to the QueryDef object's SQL property. This query simply selects all rows and columns from the tbl_Patients table.
- **Line 12.** Opens the qry_Test query in datasheet view.
- **Line 13.** A label, to which other parts of the function can branch.
- **Line 14.** Exits the function.
- **Line 15.** Another branching label. If there is an error during the execution of the function, the flow of the function comes here.
- **Line 16.** Displays the error message(s).
- **Line 17.** Forces the function to branches of the label Exit_MyFunction.

Updatable Queries

By *updatable queries* we do not mean UPDATE queries, which directly change values in a table. Instead, the discussion on updatable queries has to do the ability to change data in a base table through the result of a query on the base table. This is a feature of Microsoft Access that is unmatched by most other DBMSes.

This section describes the rules governing query updatability.

Single-Table Query Updatability

A query based on a single table can select a subset of records or a subset of columns from that table. In the simplest case, the query returns all rows and all columns:

```
SELECT * FROM tbl_Patients
```

You can insert new rows into the query, delete rows from the query, and update any field in each row. You can also open up the query in datasheet view, freely browse the records, and make appropriate changes (within the constraints imposed by security restrictions, validation rules, and referential integrity requirements). All changes will be reflected in the underlying base table.

A query can also select and sort rows from the original table and remain updatable:

```
SELECT *
FROM tbl_Patients
WHERE tbl_Patients.City = "Boston"
ORDER BY tbl_Patients.Last_Name;
```

An updatable single-table query like this can be useful in a data entry situation in which you would like to present the rows to the user in a certain order or hide certain rows based on the selection criteria.

One thing to be aware of, however, is that the Jet database engine does not prevent the user from adding a new row through a query's result set that wouldn't have met the original selection criteria. For example, the preceding query selects only rows in which the City field is "Boston." The user could add a new row with the City field specified as "New York." Of course, when you run the query again, the newly created record will not show up.

Single-Table Query Updatability Restrictions

A query can select specific columns rather than selecting all columns with the asterisk (*) character:

```
SELECT
  Patients.Last_Name,
  Patients.Address,
  Patients.City,
  Patients.Zip_Code
FROM Patients;
```

You can use this technique to hide certain columns from users while still allowing them access to the information they need. The columns made available through a query like this are fully updatable. It may, however, be impossible to add a new row through this query. This restriction could happen if some fields (such as primary key fields or fields that are specified as *required*) that are excluded from the output cannot be null.

Another restriction is on remote ODBC tables, such as those from SQL Server. Any queries based on ODBC tables lacking a unique index are not updatable. Therefore, SQL Server tables must have a unique index on them in order for them to be updatable. Chapter 7 discusses this aspect in detail.

Multi-Table Query Updatability

The Access Jet database engine also supports updatable queries based on multi-table joins. This powerful feature allows you to combine data resulting from inner-join queries and outer-join queries.

Inner-Join Queries

Inner-join queries are also known as equal-join queries—a record is returned if and only if the primary and foreign keys are equal. There are two scenarios in this case: many-to-one joins and one-to-many joins.

The following example joins the tbl_Services table with the tbl_Patients table. In this query, tbl_Services is on the "many" (or child) side of the join, whereas tbl_Patients is on the "one" (or parent) side of the joint. The query emphasizes tbl_Services, the "many" side of the join, by selecting all rows and columns from tbl_Services while only looking up each consumer's Medicaid eligibility from tbl_Patients:

```
SELECT
  tbl_Services.*,
  tbl_Patients.Medicaid_Eligibility
FROM tbl_Patients INNER JOIN tbl_Services
ON tbl_Patients.PatientID = tbl_Services.PatientID;
```

Users can change data in any column from the tbl_Services table, including the PatientID field that links tbl_Services to tbl_Patients. If you change the value of PatientID in the output of the query through a form or the datasheet view, a new value of Medicaid_Eligibility will be automatically retrieved from tbl_Patients and displayed in the result set of the query (assuming the new PatientID value has a matching entry in the tbl_Patients table).

You can also change the values in columns retrieved from the lookup table. This may cause some confusion on the part of the users. A user who is under the impression that the change will affect only the current row may attempt to alter the value of Medicaid_Eligibility on one row of the result set created from this query. However, since the value is actually stored back in the tbl_Patients table, the value is changed for every row in the result set.

In the context of updatable queries, many-to-one and one-to-many joins are perfectly symmetrical—there is no real conceptual difference between the two. The distinction between the two lies in which base table the updatable query emphasizes. In the many-to-one case, most columns in the SELECT list come from the child table; in the one-to-many case, the parent-side table is at least as equally emphasized as the child side.

Just as we discussed earlier, when a value from the "one" side is altered, multiple rows in the query's result set may be affected. When a value from the "many" side is altered, only one row will be affected in the result set of the query.

Updatable multi-table joins may involve more than two tables. For example, the following query maps tbl_Patients to tbl_Services to tbl_Relatives:

```
SELECT
  tbl_Patients.PatientID,
  tbl_Patients.Date_of_Birth,
  tbl_Services.PatientID,
  tbl_Services.Start_Date,
  tbl_Relatives.Address
FROM (tbl_Patients INNER JOIN tbl_Services
     ON tbl_Patients.PatientID = tbl_Services.PatientID)
  INNER JOIN tbl_Relatives
    ON tbl_Services.PatientID = tbl_Relatives.PatientID;
```

Columns from all three of these joined tables are updatable in the result set.

When inserting a row into a result set based on a multi-table join, rows can be added to one, more than one, or all of the tables included in the join. Obviously, rows from the "many" side of the join are simply appended to the "many" table as needed. Rows from the "one" side of the join can be added as well if they do not violate referential integrity constraints.

The following query joins the tbl_Employees table (the "many" side) with the tbl_Departments table (the "one" side):

```
SELECT DISTINCTROW
  tbl_Employees.EmployeeID,
  tbl_Employees.Last_Name,
  tbl_Employees.First_Name,
  tbl_Departments.DepartmentID,
  tbl_Departments.Department_Name
FROM tbl_Employees INNER JOIN tbl_Departments
ON tbl_Employees.DepartmentID = tbl_Departments.DepartmentID;
```

If the user creates a new employee entry with a DepartmentID value that is already present in the tbl_Departments table, then only the tbl_Employees row is added. The corresponding Department_Name value is then retrieved from the tbl_Departments table for display in the record set.

If the user creates a new employee entry with a new DepartmentID, then a new department record will be automatically created in tbl_Departments. Note that you must have the primary key from the "one" table included in the join—in the preceding example, the presumed primary key DepartmentID from the tbl_Departments table is in the SELECT list.

Outer-Join Queries

An outer-join preserves all rows from one table in a join while selecting from another table only those rows that have matching values. For rows in which there is no match in one table, artificial NULL column values are supplied. Consider the following outer-join and its result:

```
SELECT
  tbl_Patients.Patient_Name,
  tbl_Patients.PatientID,
  tbl_Services.Service_Code,
  tbl_Services.Service_Name
FROM tbl_Patients LEFT JOIN tbl_Services
ON tbl_Patients.PatientID = tbl_Services.PatientID;
```

In this example, all records from the tbl_Patients table are selected even if some patients are not receiving any services. Let's say a patient, B.J., doesn't have any service. For him, the output row from the query will look something like this:

Patient_Name	Patient_ID	Service_Code	Service_Name
B.J.	893928		

In this case, you can fill in the blank fields to create a new service record for B.J.; the new record will inherit a Patient_ID value of 893928.

Multi-Table Query Updatability Restrictions

A query must satisfy several conditions for it to be fully updatable:

- Records from a child table cannot be orphaned.

  Any change to a multi-table query must not create "orphaned" records in the "many" side of the join. In other words, you cannot change the join column from the child table to a value that is nonexistent in the parent table.

- JOIN clauses must be used.

  You must specify an explicit INNER or OUTER JOIN between the tables. Joins created implicitly in the WHERE clause of the SELECT statement are not updatable. For example, the following join is not updatable:

  ```
  SELECT
    tbl_Services.PatientID,
    tbl_Services.Service_Code,
    tbl_Patients.Patient_ID,
    tbl_Patients.Patient_Name
  FROM tbl_Patients, tbl_Services
  WHERE tbl_Patients.PatientID = tbl_Services.PatientID;
  ```

  Queries with aggregated data in the SELECT list are not updatable.

  Summary (GROUP BY), UNION, DISTINCT, and crosstab queries are never updatable. Queries joined to one or more summary queries are not updatable even if you do not attempt to modify fields from an otherwise updatable table. However, a query may be updatable if all of its summary statements are solely used in a subquery and do not show up in the main SELECT list, as in the following example:

  ```
  SELECT DISTINCTROW tbl_Employees.*
  FROM tbl_Employees
  WHERE (tbl_Employees.Salary >
          (SELECT Avg(tbl_Employees.Salary)
           FROM tbl_Employees;));
  ```

  Columns from the tbl_Employees table are updatable.

- Primary key fields must be output in order to insert new records.

  To be able to insert new rows into a table in any query, all primary key columns must be present.

- Many-side fields may be non-updatable during updates to the "one" side.
  Let's say you have made a change to a column from the "one" side of a join, but for some reason, the change hasn't been written back into the one-side table. Now if you try to change the join key from the many-side table, Access tries to look up the new key in the one-side table and display this information in the same row. However, since doing so will lead to losing the unsaved changes on the "one" side, Access makes it impossible to change the join key from the many-side table until the change to the "one" side of the query is either canceled or committed.

Moving On

In this chapter, we didn't intend to teach you how to use Microsoft Access from the ground up; it is too vast a subject even for this whole book, let alone a chapter. Instead, we have assumed you are somewhat comfortable with Access and you want to glimpse under the cover of the Access GUI to get a feel for what Access is capable of doing as an RDBMS. For reference to some commonly used constructs in VBA, see Appendix D.

Next we will examine Access's back-end counterpart in the client/server architecture—SQL Server.

chapter 4

Server Component: Microsoft SQL Server for Windows NT

The Server component of the client/server applications described in this book is based on SQL Server 6.5 for Windows NT. This chapter provides an introduction to the Windows NT Server as an operating system of choice for the server components. We also discuss Microsoft SQL Server for Windows NT Database Management System (DBMS) and the basics of database administration and database design for MS SQL Server.

Windows NT Server as the Server Operating System

Windows NT Server is a 32-bit multipurpose network operating system that can be used for file and print services in addition to providing all the necessary architecture to run client/server applications. As discussed in Chapter 1, client/server computing generally means connecting a single-user client workstation to multiuser servers, with the workload of data querying or calculations generally performed by the server and the task of presenting data performed by the client workstation.

In the Windows NT environment, this idea is brought to the level of a single computer with its operating system divided into several processes, each of which performs a set of services. These processes communicate with each other and with their clients by exchanging messages. This approach results in a modular operating system. Each service is small, self-contained, and runs in its own protected, user-mode process; therefore, if a service fails, it won't take down the rest of the operating system. The modular structure of the operating system also makes it easier to utilize multiple processors on a single computer or even across multiple computers on a network.

Some of the features that make Windows NT Server an effective operating system for client/server applications are:

- **Preemptive multitasking.** Multitasking is the ability of an operating system to manage more than one process at the same time. Multitasking is preemptive if an operating system decides which process should be executed at any moment. Non-preemptive multitasking operating systems cannot interrupt a process that is running until the process voluntarily gives up control. Preemptive multitasking operating systems, on the other hand, will interrupt a running process if its time slice expires or if another process with higher priority becomes ready to run. Microsoft operating systems evolved from MS-DOS, which is a single-tasking environment, through Windows 3.1, a non-preemptive multitasking operating system, to Windows NT, which provides a true preemptive multitasking environment.
- **Threading.** In addition to preemptive multitasking, Windows NT is a multithreaded operating system. It allows every process to create its own subprocesses (threads), which participate in multitasking the same way the main processes do. In Windows NT, system resources are allocated on the processes level (as opposed to the thread level), and therefore, all of the threads in a process share the same memory, access token, and other resources. The use of multiple threads in preemptive multitasking environments helps to achieve decent response time even while some of the threads are engaged in some lengthy procedures. In a uniprocessor computer, however, only one thread can be executed at any particular moment. On a multiprocessor system, more than one processor may be running different threads in the same process, which is extremely important for running a powerful server component of a client/server application such as MS SQL Server.
- **Multiprocessing.** A multiprocessing operating system is capable of utilizing several processors (CPUs) in a computer. When an operating system assumes that all of the processors are equal, then it is a *symmetric multiprocessing* (SMP) system. In an SMP operating system, such as Windows NT, any process or a thread can be executed by any available CPU. An *asymmetric multiprocessing* (ASMP) system is one in which different processors perform different tasks; for example, one processor can be devoted to system processes only.

Microsoft SQL Server as the Server Database

Version 4.2 of SQL Server (the first version of SQL Server for Windows NT) was introduced by Microsoft in September 1993. The system was an immediate success, with customers taking delivery of 10,000 servers in the first three months of sales. Microsoft SQL Server has been recognized as Client/Server Product of the Year by *InfoWorld*, one of the 10 Best Products of 1993 and 1994 by *PC Week* Labs, and Database Server Product of the Year by *LAN Magazine*. It has been given the Readers' Choice award by the readers of *Byte*, *VARBusiness*, and *DataBased Advisor* magazines.

One of the most valuable features of Microsoft SQL Server 6 is its so-called Symmetric Server Architecture (SSA): high integration of internal database processes with Windows NT threads. The preemptive multitasking environment of Windows NT allows SQL Server to balance workload across multiple CPUs, minimize the affect of heavy calculations performed by some threads, and achieve greater fault isolation. SQL Server uses different threads to handle different tasks: support of each of the networks, database checkpoints, the "read-ahead manager" process, the "lazy writer" process, and so on. SQL Server also has a pool of "worker threads" that execute clients' requests. The Windows NT operating system schedules all these threads preemptively and selects an available CPU for each thread automatically.

Max Worker Threads and SMP Concurrency are two important SQL Server configuration parameters (see "Setting Up SQL Server Configuration Options" later in this chapter) that help you to achieve better SQL Server performance on a multiprocessor machine. Use the Max Worker Threads parameter to set up a number of the user connections at which SQL Server begins the actual thread pooling. The SMP Concurrency parameter controls the maximum number of CPUs that can be simultaneously utilized by SQL Server. When it is highly important to achieve the best SQL Server performance for the production system, the SMP Concurrency parameter should be set to Dedicated SMP Support, allowing SQL Server to grab all the available CPUs.

Introducing SQL Server Database Administration

SQL Setup application installs SQL Server software, including graphical tools, in a folder called Microsoft SQL Server 6.5 (Figure 4-1).

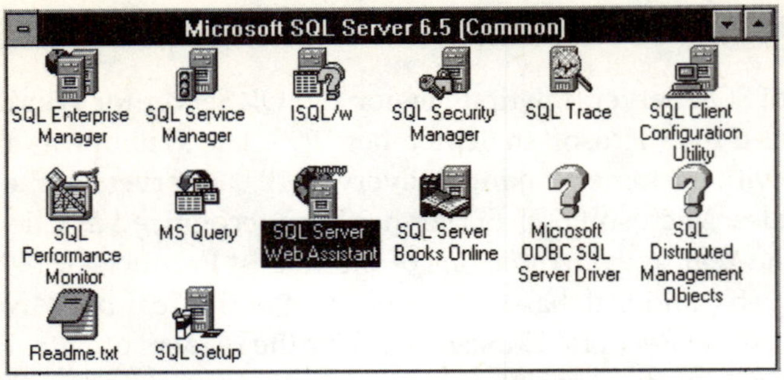

Figure 4-1: The Microsoft SQL Server 6.5 folder.

Graphical tools installed with the SQL Server software are:

- **SQL Setup.** Allows you to remove SQL Server, upgrade SQL Server software, rebuild the *master* database, or change various installation options (see "SQL Setup" later in this chapter).
- **SQL Client Configuration Utility.** Allows you to display the DB Library version currently installed on the system, set up the default Net Library, and set up server connection information on the client computer (see "SQL Client Configuration Utility" later in this chapter).
- **SQL Service Manager.** Allows you to start, stop, and pause SQL Server, SQL Executive, and MS DTC (see "SQL Service Manager" later in this chapter).
- **SQL Enterprise Manager.** Allows you to perform multiple functions of system administration and database design using graphical user interfaces (see "Microsoft SQL Enterprise Manager" later in this chapter).
- **SQL Trace.** Monitors and records SQL Server 6.5 database activity.
- **ISQL/w.** Allows you to run SQL queries. ISQL/w also provides the capability for query analyzing.
- **SQL Security Manager.** Allows you to manage user accounts for SQL Servers in the integrated security environment.
- **MS Query.** Provides a graphic query interface to relational databases.
- **SQL Server Web Assistant.** Allows you to generate standard HyperText Markup Language (HTML) files from SQL Server data.
- **SQL Performance Monitor.** Windows NT tool that allows you to monitor system activity. This particular instance of the Performance Monitor is integrated with SQL Server objects.

- **SQL Server Books Online.** Online SQL Server documentation.
- **Microsoft ODBC SQL Server Driver.** Online Help file on the Microsoft ODBC SQL Server Driver.
- **SQL Distributed Management Objects.** Online Help file on the Microsoft SQL Server Distributed Management Object Model.

SQL Setup

When executed for the first time, the SQL Setup installs the main SQL Server components: executables, DLLs and other files, SQL Server utilities, database device, and several databases (see "Managing Databases" later in this chapter). SQL Setup also creates an SQL Server 6.5 program group (or folder in Windows NT 4), the necessary Windows NT Registry entries, and three *Windows NT services*: MS SQLServer service, which performs all the database management functions; SQLExecutive service, which executes scheduling functions; and MSDTC service, which deals with distributed transactions.

Run SQL Setup any time after the installation is complete to change some of the SQL Server parameters, rebuild the master database, and upgrade or remove SQL Server files (see Figure 4-2).

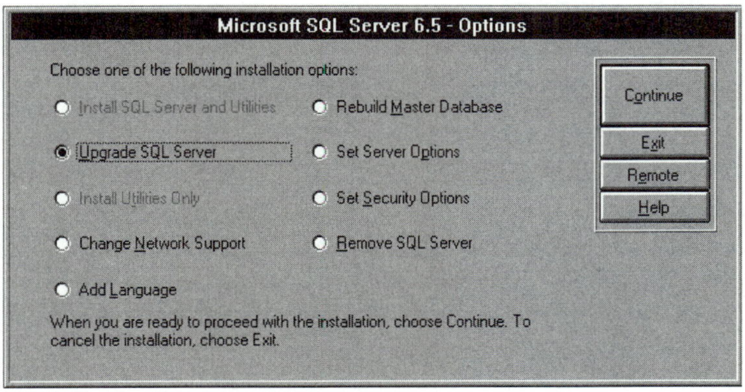

Figure 4-2: The SQL Setup Options window.

You can also perform some of these operations using SQL Enterprise Manager. For instance, the Set Security Options screen in SQL Setup is identical to the Security Options tab of the Server Configuration/Options window in the SQL Enterprise Manager (which is shown in Figure 4-25 later in this chapter). The same is true for the Set Server Options dialog in SQL Setup and the Server Options tab of the Server Configuration/Options window (see Figure 4-24).

To add or remove networks that are supported by your installation of SQL Server, use the Change Network Support function in SQL Setup (Figure 4-2). Once you have selected the option, click Continue and the Select Network Protocols window will appear (see Figure 4-3).

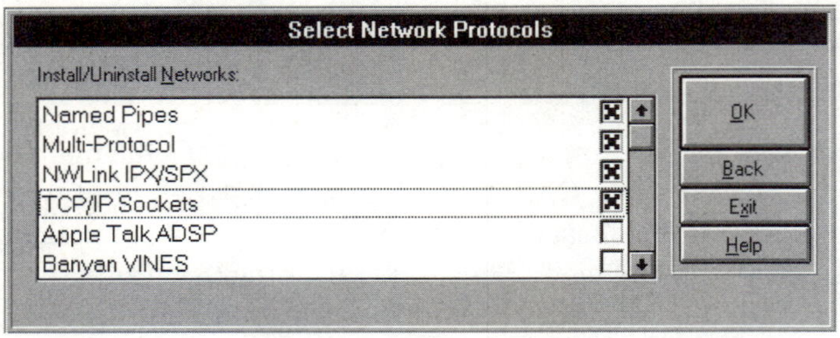

Figure 4-3: The SQL Setup Select Network Protocols window.

After you select the protocols, SQL Setup guides you through the sequence of dialog boxes, presenting you with the opportunity to change some of the network parameters. For example, to change the Novell Bindery Service name, type the new name in the Novell Bindery Service Name dialog box, and click on Continue (Figure 4-4).

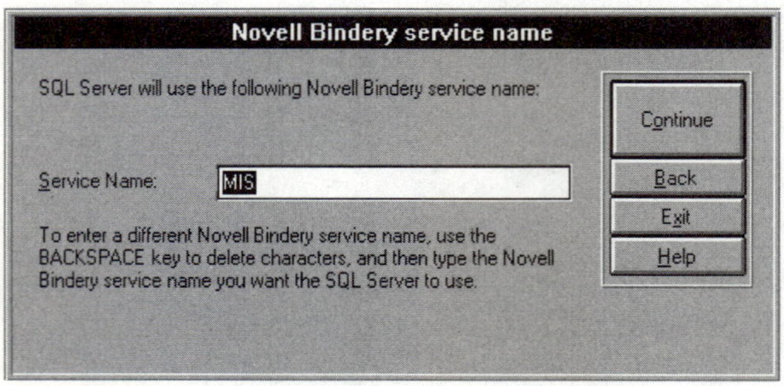

Figure 4-4: The SQL Setup Novell Bindery Service Name dialog box.

SQL Client Configuration Utility

Use the Client Configuration Utility to configure the DB Library and the Net Library parameters on your machine.

DB Library is a set of SQL-Server-specific API functions compiled into a .DLL file. To access SQL Server DBMS over the network, DB Library functions use network APIs provided by the network drivers (Net Libraries). A Net Library is a set of network and operating system functions compiled into a DLL file. Some of the commonly used Net Libraries are:

- **Novell Net Library for Windows 3.1.** DBMSSPX3.DLL
- **Novell Net Library for Win 95 and WinNT.** DBMSSPXN.DLL
- **TCP/IP Net Library for Win 95 and WinNT.** DBMSSOCN.DLL

To open the SQL Client Configuration Utility, double-click on its icon in the Microsoft SQL Server 6.5 folder. The DB Library tab of the SQL Client Configuration Utility window opens for you to configure the current version of the DB Library (Figure 4-5). Be careful to always use the correct version of DB Library to avoid multiple problems and unpredictable behavior. Normally, the two DB Library configuration parameters on this dialog should be left alone.

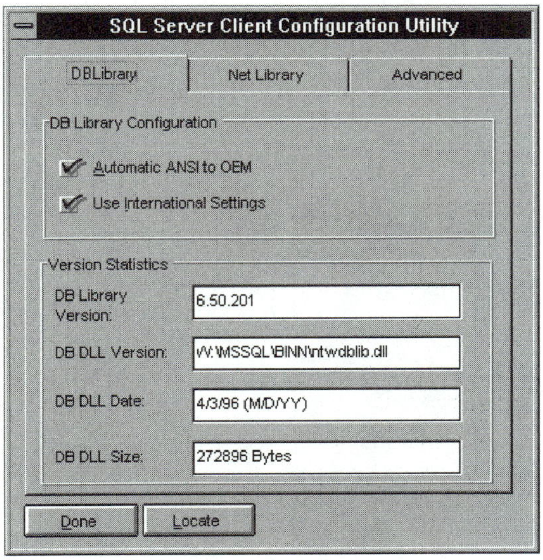

Figure 4-5: The DB Library tab of the SQL Server Client Configuration Utility window.

Use the Net Library tab of the SQL Server Client Configuration Utility window (Figure 4-6) to check for the current version of your Net Libraries and, more importantly, to set up the default Net Library on your machine (and therefore the default network for the client/server communications). Figure 4-6 shows NWLink IPX/SPX protocol (Novell network) set up as the default.

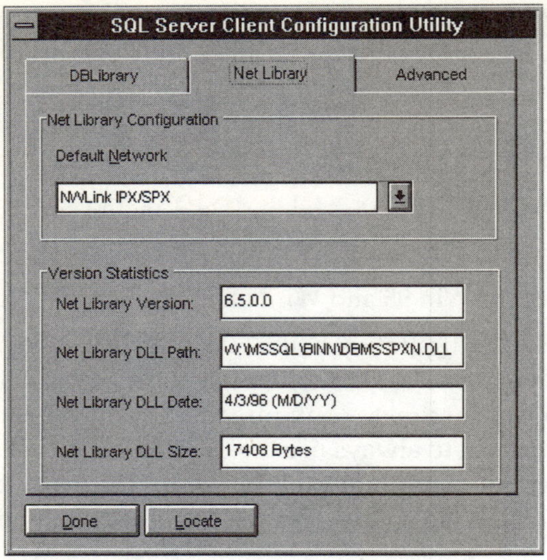

Figure 4-6: The Net Library tab of the SQL Server Client Configuration Utility window.

To assign a custom combination of the server name, Net Library, and a connection string (e.g. TCP/IP address), open the Advanced tab (Figure 4-7).

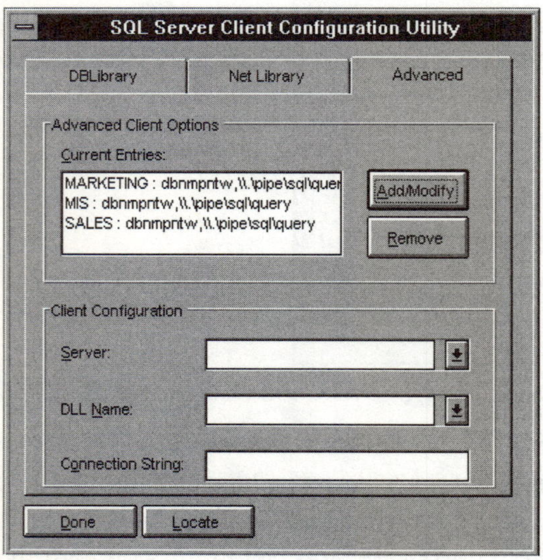

Figure 4-7: The Advanced tab of the SQL Server Client Configuration Utility window.

Finally, the Locate button on the bottom of the SQL Server Client Configuration Utility window initiates a search for all the copies of the DB Library and Net Library DLLs. The Client Configuration Utility displays DLLs found in the directories of your hard drive in the Locate Libraries window (Figure 4-8).

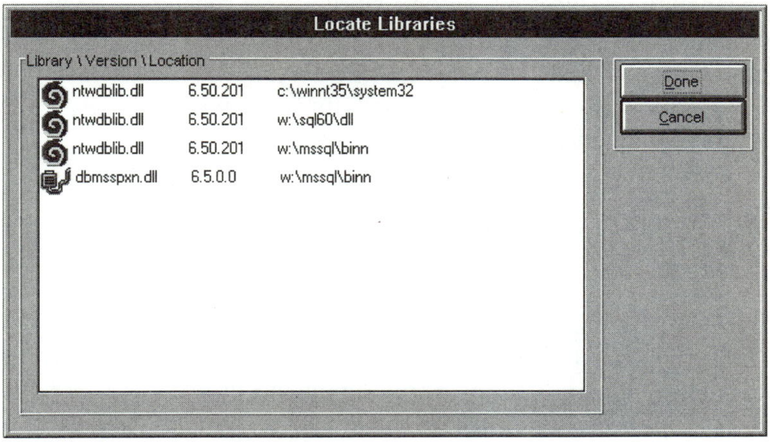

Figure 4-8: The Client Configuration Utility's Locate Libraries window.

SQL Service Manager

Use SQL Service Manager's graphical interface to start, pause, stop, and continue MS SQL Server, SQLExecutive, and MSDTC services (Figure 4-9).

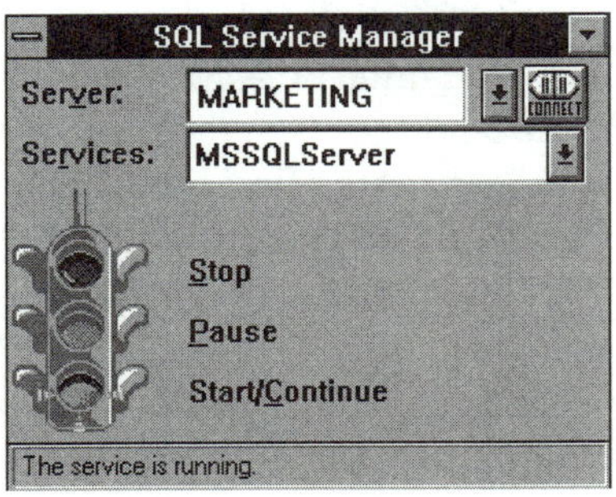

Figure 4-9: SQL Service Manager.

As a matter of fact, this utility will control any process that is set up as a Windows NT service if the appropriate entry is inserted into the Windows NT Registry. That is why some of the third-party products (e.g., SQL StorSQL Server backup/recovery interface) set themselves up as clients of the SQL Service Manager as a part their installation.

To manage services on remote Windows NT machines, select or enter the remote Windows NT Server name in the Server box, and then click the Connect button. SQL Service Manager connects you to the remote Windows NT Server and fills the Services box with the names of the SQL Server services that are registered on this remote computer.

TIP *The Server box appears only if the Remote Control option on the System menu is turned on.*

In the Services box, select MS SQL Server. The current state of the service is indicated by the light on the traffic signal and by the message on the status bar. To stop the service, click on the red light; to pause the service, click on the yellow light; to continue a paused service or start a stopped one, click on the green light.

Microsoft SQL Enterprise Manager

SQL Enterprise Manager is a set of powerful administration tools that allow you to manage multiple servers on the enterprise.

SQL Enterprise Manager is a 32-bit application installed by the SQL Setup application as a part of the SQL Server software on 32-bit operating systems (Windows NT and Windows 95). It is not installed and cannot work under Windows 3.1 or Windows 3.11. To start SQL Enterprise Manager, double-click its icon from the Microsoft SQL Server 6.5 folder.

When you start SQL Enterprise Manager for the first time, it asks you to register a server using the Register Server dialog (Figure 4-10).

In this chapter, we will use three SQL Servers: SALES, MARKETING, and MIS. We installed them and access them with the NWLink IPX/SPX protocol on the Novell network. The names were assigned using the Novell Bindery Service Name dialog box of the SQL Setup program (see Figure 4-4).

After all three servers have been registered, Enterprise Manager adds new icons to the Server Manager window (Figure 4-11).

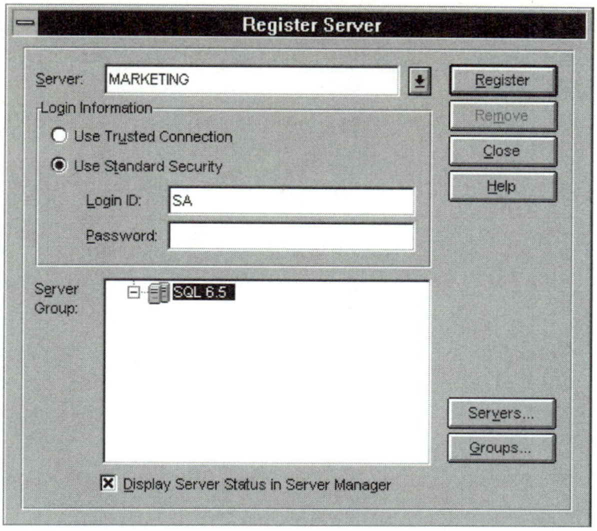

Figure 4-10: SQL Enterprise Manager's Register Server window.

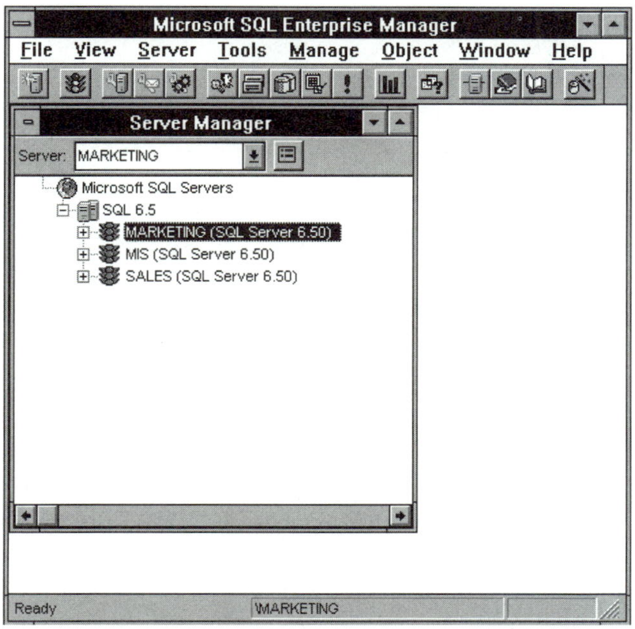

Figure 4-11: Server Manager window.

Use the Display Legend button in the Service Manager window to display the Server legend. The Server Legend window explains each icon in the Server Manager (Figure 4-12).

Figure 4-12: SQL Enterprise Manager's Server legend.

You do not need any special permission to use Enterprise Manager, but it is primarily a database administrator's tool, and therefore, the systems administrator's (SA) login is used in most cases. As an SA, you can access all objects and services in the SQL Server. If you are not using the SA login, you will be only allowed to see those objects you have permissions for, and you will not be able to perform some of the functions provided by the Enterprise Manager.

Use the SQL Enterprise Manager menus or toolbar buttons to administer SQL Server. Figure 4-13 lists the toolbar buttons from the SQL Server Enterprise Manager dialog (Figure 4-11 above shows them as part of the actual dialog). Because you use these toolbar buttons often, take some time to familiarize yourself with these buttons.

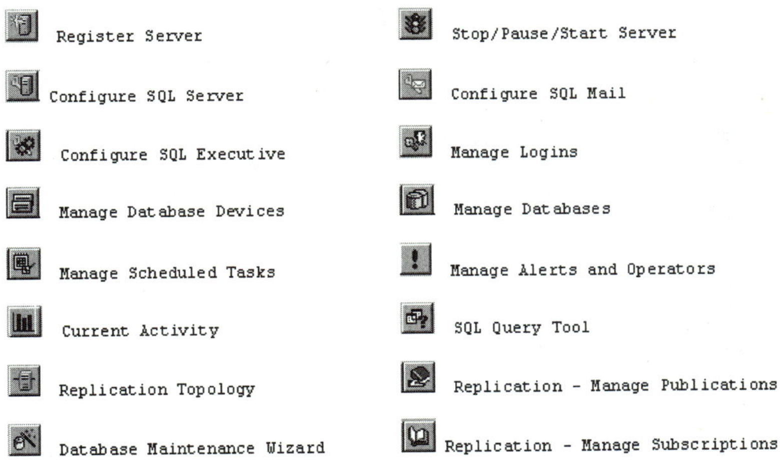

Figure 4-13: SQL Enterprise Manager's toolbar buttons.

In the Server Manager window (Figure 4-11), click on the + sign to the left of the MARKETING server icon to display the basic SQL Server components. They are arranged into four folders: Database Devices, Backup Devices, Databases, and Logins (Figure 4-14).

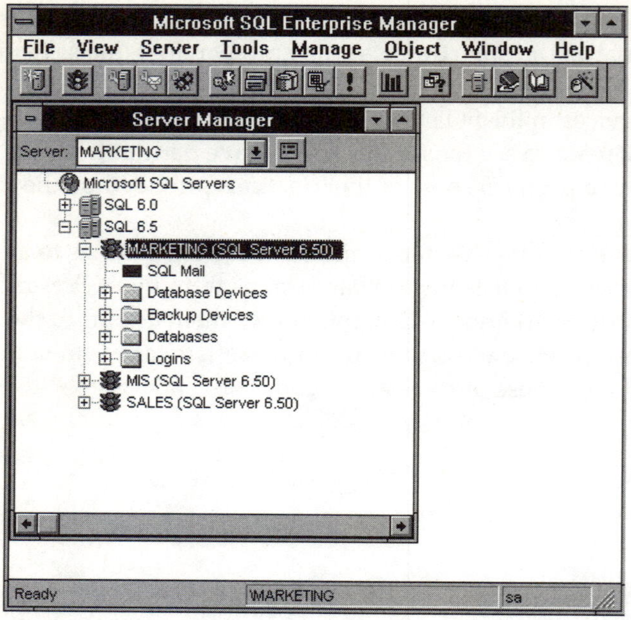

Figure 4-14: The SQL Server components are arranged into four folders, shown here in Server Manager.

Later in this chapter, we will show how easily and intuitively these SQL Server components can be administered using the Enterprise Manager.

SQL Query Tool

To execute ad hoc Transact-SQL queries, open another graphic tool provided by the SQL Enterprise Manager—the SQL Query Tool.

Structured Query Language (SQL) is a high-level language for relational database management systems and has been approved as the official relational query language standard by the American National Standards Institute (ANSI). As a data management programming language, SQL allows you to retrieve, add, and modify database objects and databases and perform other functions. You can also change the server configuration, modify database or session settings, and control data and access statements.

Transact-SQL is an enhanced version of SQL that is compliant with many ANSI standards. It also provides functions in addition to those that ANSI SQL provides. Transact-SQL statements are implemented by three main language categories:

- **Data Definition Language (DDL).** Refers to Transact-SQL statements that allow you to define databases and database objects and to manage their properties (e.g., CREATE TABLE, ALTER TABLE, CREATE VIEW, CREATE PROCEDURE statements).
- **Data Manipulation Language (DML).** Refers to Transact-SQL statements that allow you to manipulate database objects (e.g., SELECT, INSERT, UPDATE, DELETE statements).
- **Data Control Language (DCL).** Refers to Transact-SQL statements that permit access to database objects (e.g., GRANT and REVOKE statements).

In addition to being compliant with ANSI standards, Transact-SQL language includes powerful features such as declarative referential integrity (DRI) and server-based cursor support. See Appendix C for the definition of the most commonly used Transact-SQL statements.

Running Transact-SQL Queries

To open the SQL Query Tool window (Figure 4-15), click on the SQL Query Tool button on the SQL Enterprise Manager toolbar (see Figure 4-11).

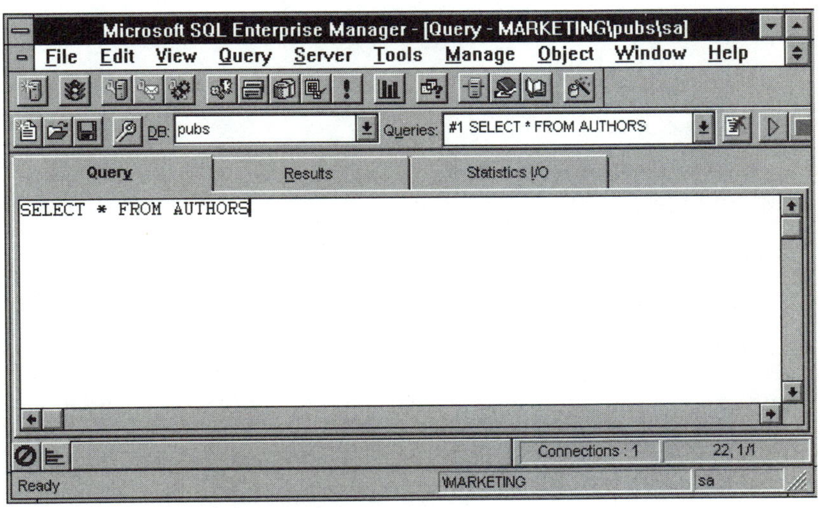

Figure 4-15: The SQL Query Tool window.

To execute a Transact-SQL query, type it in the Query tab of the SQL Query Tool window, and then click the Execute Query button (i.e., button with the green triangle). The query output will be returned in the Results tab. The SQL Query Tool also provides you with some statistics related to the query execution in the Statistics I/O tab.

Managing Databases

As a collection of user and system objects related to the same subject, a *database* is the central and, perhaps, the most important entity of the SQL Server DBMS. Using SQL Enterprise Manager, you can easily manage databases on any SQL Server of your enterprise.

To see the databases on the MARKETING server, open the Databases folder (Figure 4-16) from the Server Manager window.

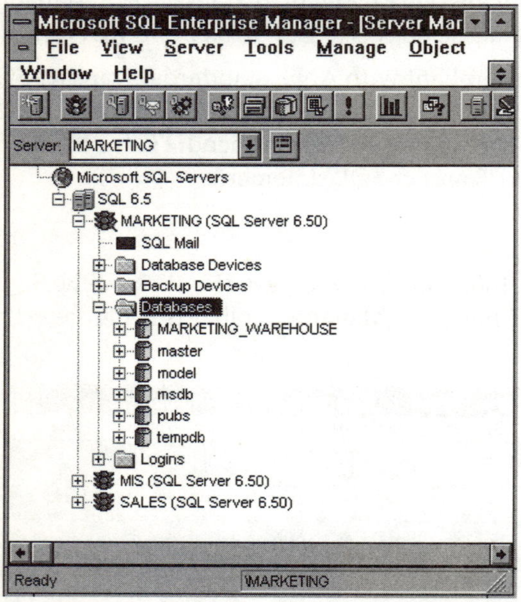

Figure 4-16: The databases folder on the MARKETING server.

We created the MARKETING_WAREHOUSE database to use for marketing applications, and the pubs database is a sample database supplied by Microsoft as a learning tool. All the other databases are part of the SQL Server Database Management System and can be found in any SQL Server:

- **Master database.** Contains information about user accounts, remote user accounts, remote servers, configurable environment variables, system error messages, databases, database devices and device usage, backup devices, and the active locks.

- **Model database.** The template on which new databases are based. Every time a new database is created, SQL Server uses the model database as a prototype and then extends it to the size requested for the new database.
- **Msdb database.** Used by SQL Executive to keep information about scheduled tasks.
- **Tempdb database.** A database where temporary tables and other temporary objects are created, even if a user who creates them is using another database.

SQL Enterprise Manager helps to perform a number of administrative functions on the databases. To open the Edit Database dialog (Figure 4-17), double-click on the name of a database in the Server Manager window.

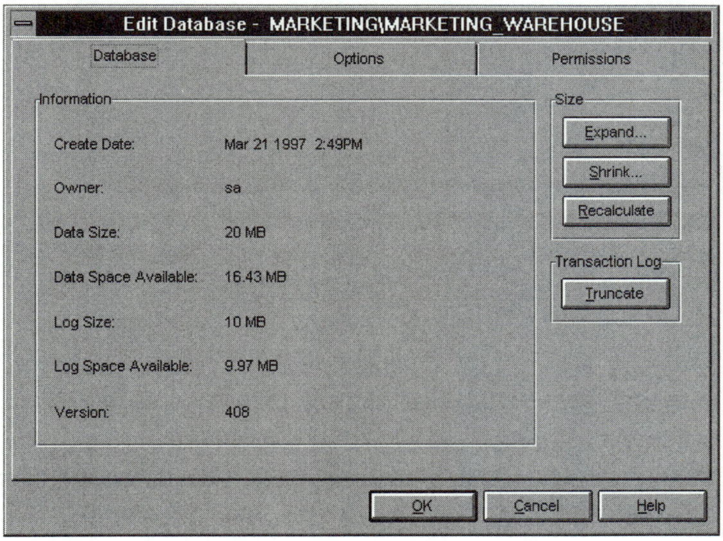

Figure 4-17: The Database tab of the Edit Database window.

Use the Database tab of this dialog to see some basic information about a database and perform some operations on the database (such as changing the database size or truncating the transaction log).

Use the Options tab (Figure 4-18) to fine-tune the performance of your database. Among other things you can:

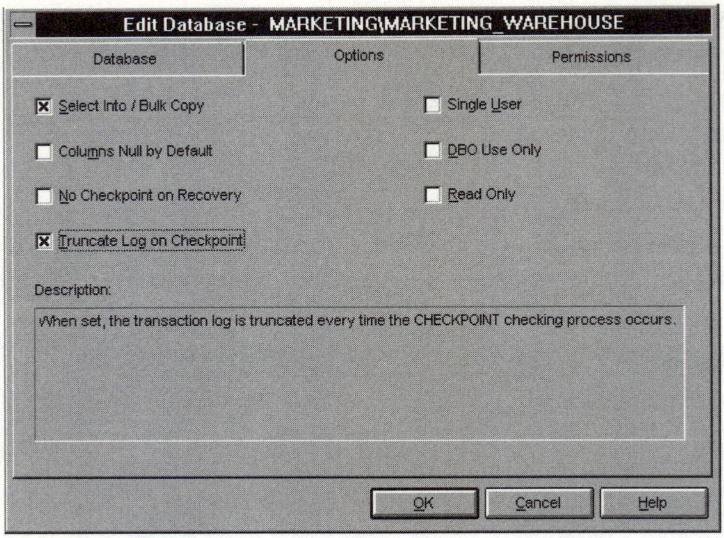

Figure 4-18: The Options tab of the Edit Database window.

- Enable non-logged operations to speed up data loading processes, or disable these operations to achieve greater database recoverability.
- Let everybody use the database, make it accessible for the DBO (database owner) only, or open it in the Single User mode.
- Prevent users from changing anything in the database by opening it as Read Only.

Finally, the Permissions tab of the Edit Database dialog window allows the System Adminstrator (SA) to set up or revoke permissions for the users/groups of the selected database (Figure 4-19).

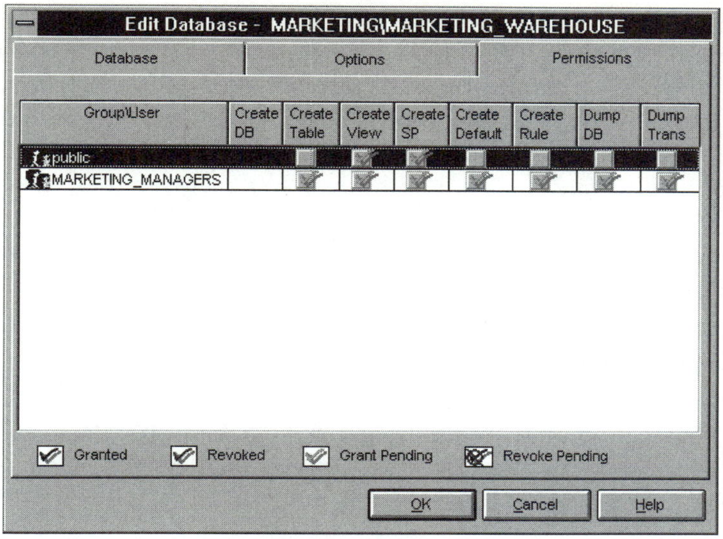

Figure 4-19: The Permissions tab of the Edit Database window.

Creating a New Database

To create a new database, open the New Database dialog (Figure 4-20). To open this dialog, right-click the "Databases" folder in the Server Manager window, and select the New Database option from the subsequent menu.

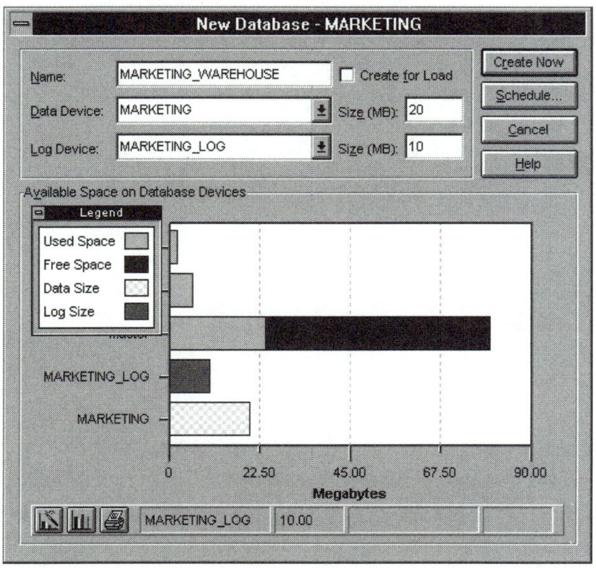

Figure 4-20: The New Database dialog.

Use the New Database dialog to type the name of a new database, select database devices for the data and log components of the new database, and specify the size of a chunk of each device that the database will occupy. Figure 4-20 shows how the database MARKETING_WAREHOUSE was created. After supplying all the necessary values in the dialog, click OK to create the new database. At this time, unless you checked the Create for Load check box in the dialog, SQL Server will initialize every allocation page in the new database, which can take from several minutes to several hours, depending on the database size.

Managing Groups & Users

To administer database users and groups, open the Groups/Users folder in the Server Manager window under the selected database. The database groups appear in the window. Open some of the group folders to see users in the groups (Figure 4-21).

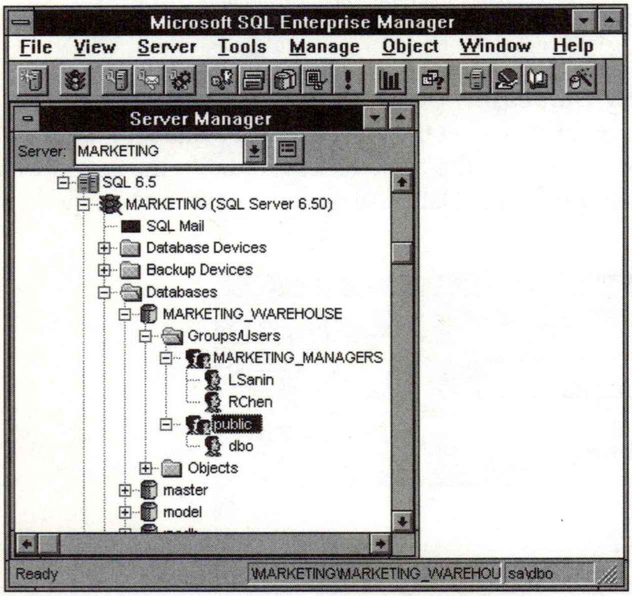

Figure 4-21: The Groups/Users folder.

To manage a group, double-click on the group name, and use the Manage Groups dialog to move database users in and out of the group (Figure 4-22).

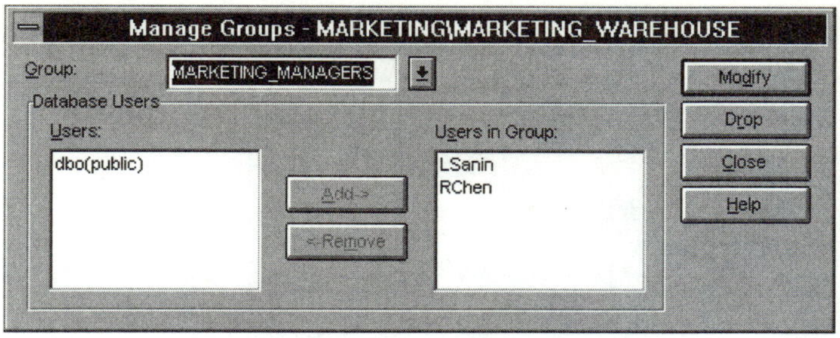

Figure 4-22: The Manage Groups dialog.

Similarly, double-click on the username to open the Manage Users dialog box, and use this dialog to change a group assignment for the user or to appoint an alias to a user (Figure 4-23).

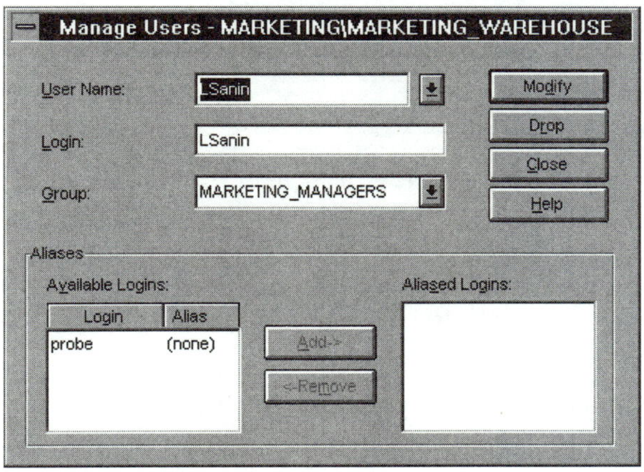

Figure 4-23: The Manage Users dialog box.

Setting Up SQL Server Configuration Options

For SQL Server configuration dialogs, click on the Configurations button on the SQL Enterprise Manager toolbar. The Server Configuration/Options window opens for you to adjust SQL Server configuration parameters.

Use the Configuration tab, one of the four tabs of the Server Configurations/Options window, to change some of the SQL Server configuration parameters (Figure 4-24).

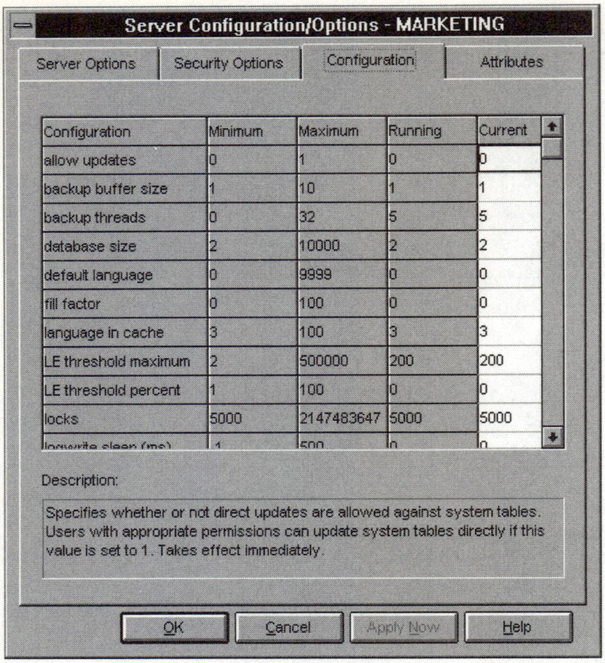

Figure 4-24: The Configuration tab of the Server Configurations/Options window.

Just as you can fine-tune your database using the database options (see Figure 4-18), you can use this tab to tune SQL Server as a whole. Some of the things that you can do in this dialog are:

- Allocate additional physical memory for the SQL Server.
- Increase the number of allowable user connections.
- Place the tempdb in RAM (physical memory).
- Change the number of CPUs that can be simultaneously used by SQL Server.

Use the Server Options tab of the Server Configuration/Options window to specify SQL Server directories, set up SQL Server and SQL Executive services to automatically start when the operating system boots, and integrate SQL Server with Windows NT Event Log and Performance Monitor (Figure 4-25).

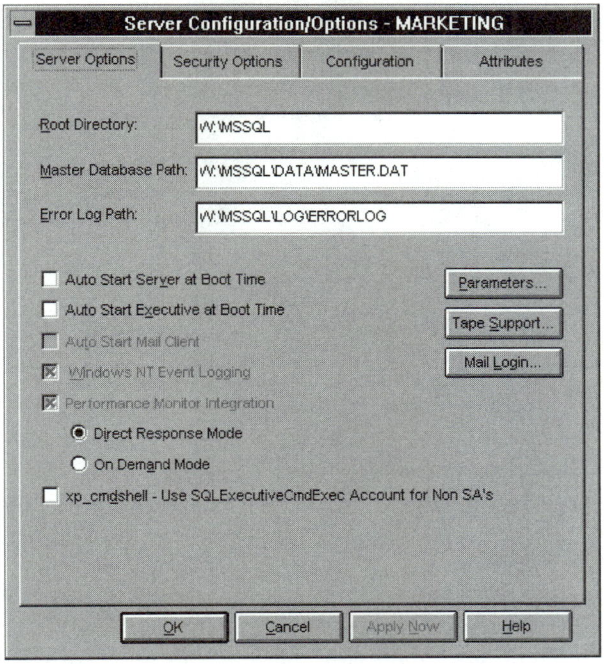

Figure 4-25: The Server Options tab of the Server Configuration/Options window.

Use the Security Options tab to choose one of the three available security modes: Standard, Windows NT Integrated, or Mixed (Figure 4-26).

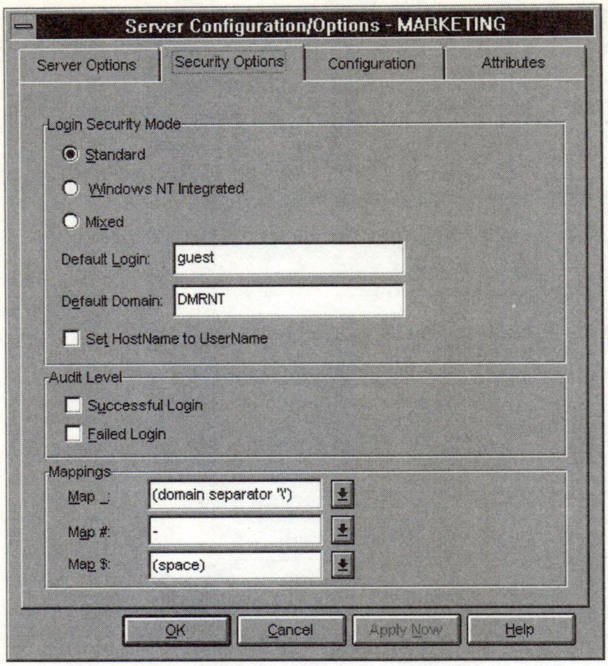

Figure 4-26: The Security Options tab of the Server Configuration/Options window.

By choosing the integrated security mode, you delegate almost all the responsibilities for maintaining SQL Server security to the Windows NT Security subsystem. This will work well, but only if all (or most) of your users connect to the SQL Server by Microsoft Network (Named Pipes protocol). If your users access SQL Server primarily by some other network software (e.g., NWLink or TCP/IP sockets), you have to use the standard security option.

Managing Logins

One of the most routine DBA functions is the management and maintenance of the SQL Server Logins. Naturally, it is very important to have a good set of tools to help you to perform these tasks both faster and without the great risk of ruining the production database by mistyping a single word. The Enterprise Manager provides this set of tools (although sometimes it feels like they could work a little faster).

To initiate the Manage Login dialog, click on the Manage Logins button of the SQL Enterprise Manager toolbar, and then select a login from the Login Name drop-down list (Figure 4-27).

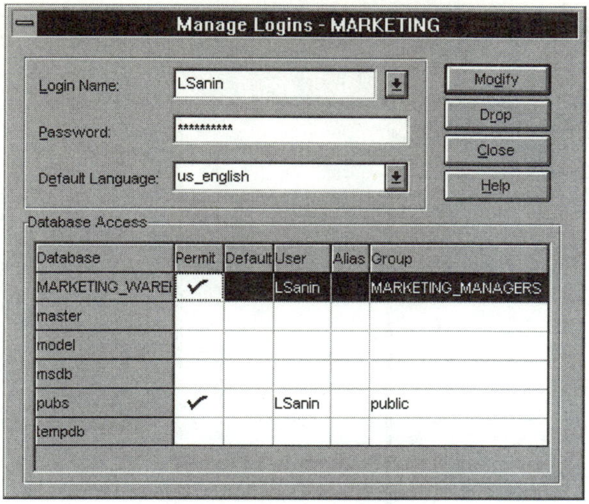

Figure 4-27: The Manage Logins dialog box.

Login LSanin, in this example, may use the MARKETING_WAREHOUSE and pubs databases. This login is mapped to the user LSanin in both of these databases, and the default database for this user is MARKETING_WAREHOUSE. In MARKETING_WAREHOUSE, LSanin is a member of a group called MARKETING_MANAGERS and in the master and pubs databases, he belongs to a group called public (which is the default group). Use this dialog to drop this login (if necessary) or to modify its properties.

There is an alternative way to look at the SQL Server Logins. To see all of them displayed in the Server Manager window, open the Logins folder (Figure 4-28).

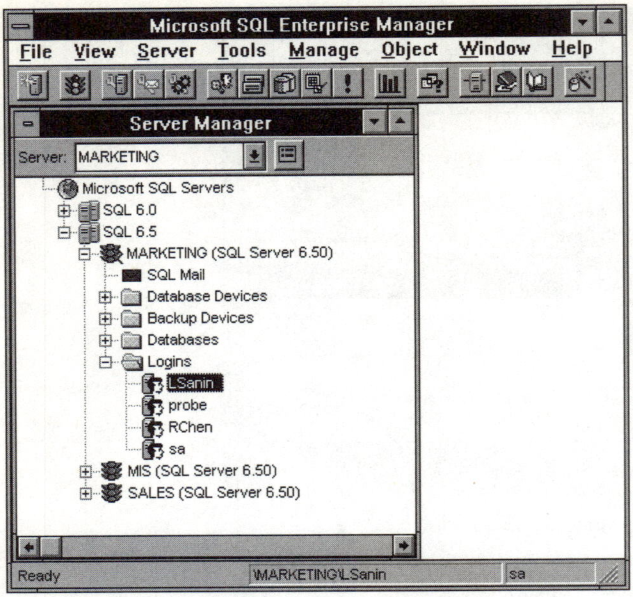

Figure 4-28: The Logins folder in the Server Manager window.

Double-click on any of the Login icons in the Server Manager window to open the Manage Logins window. Every user of an SQL Server database can assign a password to his or her login by using the system-stored procedure SP_PASSWORD or by using the Manage Logins dialog of the SQL Enterprise Manager (see Figure 4-27). SQL Server keeps passwords in the SYSLOGINS systems table of the master database. Passwords are encrypted so that even the systems administrator can not decipher them.

Managing Database Devices

SQL Server databases reside on *database devices.* A database device is basically just a Windows NT file created, initialized, and formatted by SQL Server. The database devices have logical names assigned to them within the SQL Server. These names and all the other relevant information about the database devices are kept in SYSDEVICES system table of the master database. Run this SQL query in your SQL Server:

```
USE MASTER
GO
SELECT NAME,PHYNAME FROM SYSDEVICES WHERE STATUS<>16
```

and the result may look similar to this:

```
NAME                           PHYNAME
------------------------------ ------------------------------
MARKETING                      W:\MSSQL\DATA\MARKETING.DAT
MARKETING_LOG                  W:\MSSQL\DATA\MARKETING_LOG.DAT
master                         W:\MSSQL\DATA\MASTER.DAT
MSDBData                       W:\MSSQL\DATA\MSDB.DAT
MSDBLog                        W:\MSSQL\DATA\MSDBLOG.DAT

(5 row(s) affected)
```

This query lists all the logical names of the database devices and the corresponding physical names of the operating system files. SQL Enterprise Manager offers another (and a much better) way to look at the database devices. Open the Database Devices folder in the Server Manager window to see the existing database devices (Figure 4-29).

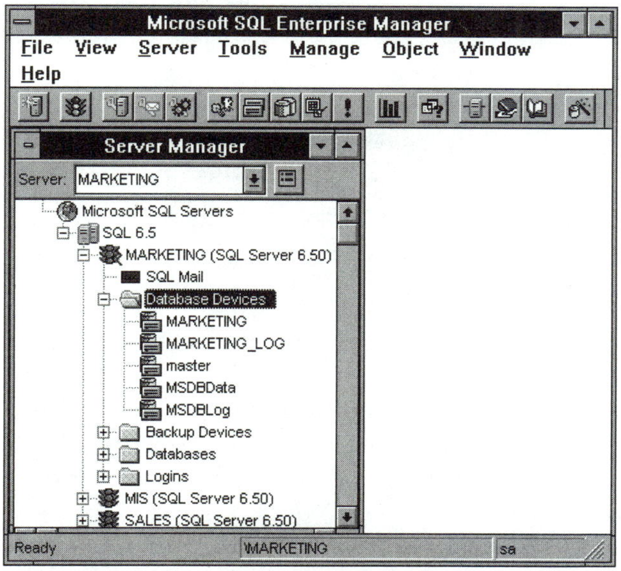

Figure 4-29: The Database Devices folder in the Server Manager window.

To manage database devices, right-click on a database device, and select one of the functions from the menu. You can add a new device, edit or delete an existing device, or mirror a device. The latter means that you actually assign two Windows NT files on separate physical drives for one database device; one file is an exact copy of the other at any moment, so that if a disk drive gets lost because of hardware failure, SQL Server will still be running by using the remaining copy of the lost device.

To open the Manage Database Devices dialog (Figure 4-30), right-click on the whole Database Devices folder, and then choose Edit from the menu. You can also click on the Manage Database Devices button on the SQL Enterprise Manager toolbar.

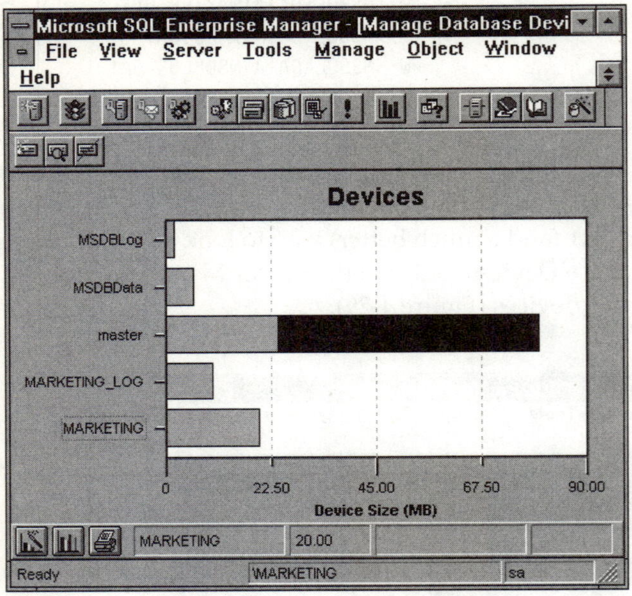

Figure 4-30: The Manage Database Devices dialog box.

To edit, delete, or create a new device, use the toolbar buttons in the top left corner of this dialog.

Click on the Create New Device button of the SQL Enterprise Manager toolbar to initiate the New Database Device dialog (Figure 4-31); then type logical and physical device names, and select a disk drive for the device and the device's size in megabytes.

Figure 4-31 shows how the database device MARKETING was created.

To change the parameters of an existing device, use a similar dialog called Edit Database Device (Figure 4-32).

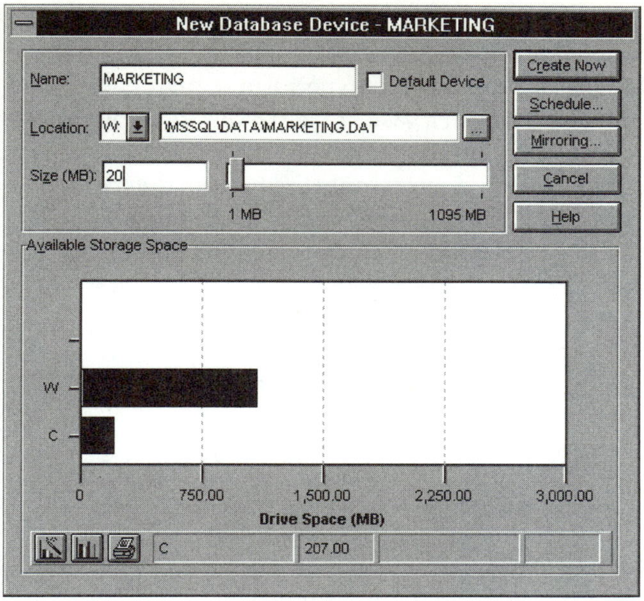

Figure 4-31: The New Database Device dialog box.

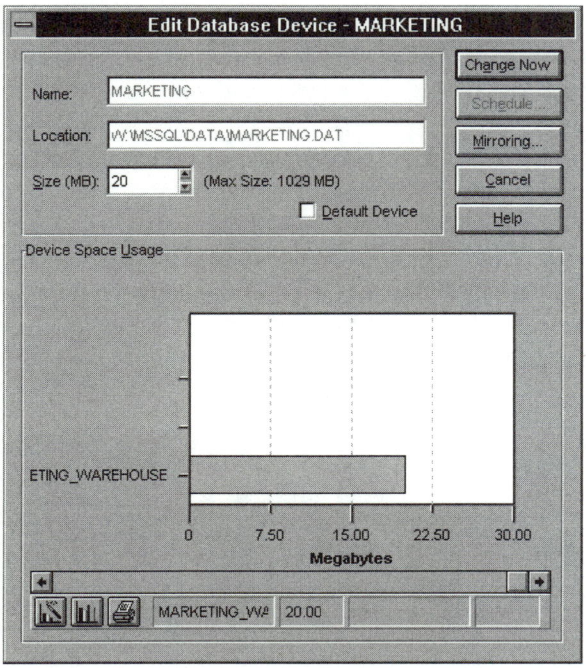

Figure 4-32: The Edit Database Device dialog box.

Managing Backups

Backup devices store backup copies of databases, tables, and transaction logs. It is convenient to use backup devices to perform regular backups so that you can recover your databases in a case of media failure. Information about the backup devices can be found in the SYSDEVICES table of the master database (same as with the database devices, only the backup device entries in the table have the value of STATUS column set to 16). To display the backup device entries in the SYSDEVICES table, run the following SQL script in the SQL Query Tool:

```
USE MASTER
GO
SELECT NAME,PHYNAME FROM SYSDEVICES WHERE STATUS=16
```

the result is:

```
NAME                           PHYNAME
------------------------------ ------------------------------
diskdump                       nul
diskettedumpa                  a:sqltable.dat
diskettedumpb                  b:sqltable.dat
Marketing_backup               W:\MSSQL\BACKUP\Marketing_backup.DAT

(4 row(s) affected)
```

A backup device can be a disk file, a tape, a diskette, or for integration with other applications, a named pipe (a virtual networking connection). SQL Enterprise Manager provides several ways to view information about the backup devices.

To list the backup devices on the server, open the Backup Devices folder in the Server Manager window. To browse information about the contents of the backup device, click on the + sign to the left of the device icon (Figure 4-33).

Look at the backup devices in the Server Manager window and note that all the backups made to the Marketing_backup device are listed here. Each entry includes a backup icon indicating the type of backup (whole database, transaction log, a table), the date of the backup, and the number of pages in the backup.

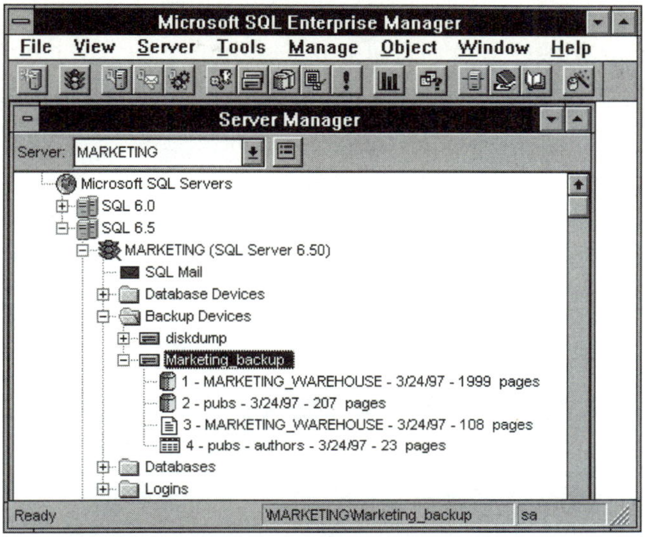

Figure 4-33: The Backup Devices folder.

Information about the backup devices can be also viewed in the Database Backup/Restore dialog. To open this dialog, select Database Backup/Restore from the Tools menu of the SQL Enterprise Manager (Figure 4-34).

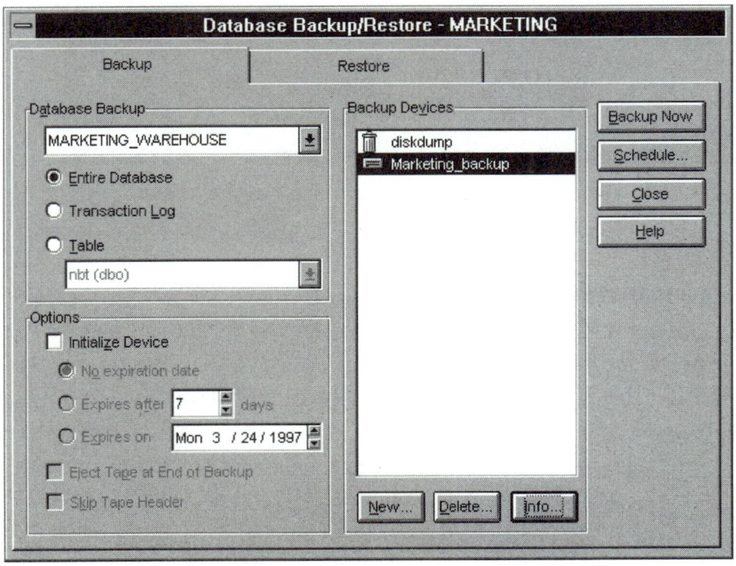

Figure 4-34: The Backup tab of the Database Backup/Restore window.

Use the Backup/Restore dialog to back up or restore the databases, transaction logs, or individual tables. To perform a backup, select the appropriate options on the Backup tab of the Database Backup/Restore window (e.g., full database backup, transaction log backup, table backup, or initialize/append backup device). Then click on the Backup Now button to start the backup or on the Schedule button to schedule it to run in the future.

To restore a database or a table or to apply a backed-up transaction log, open the Restore tab of the Database Backup/Restore dialog box (Figure 4-35), select a database and the appropriate backup options, and press the Restore Now button.

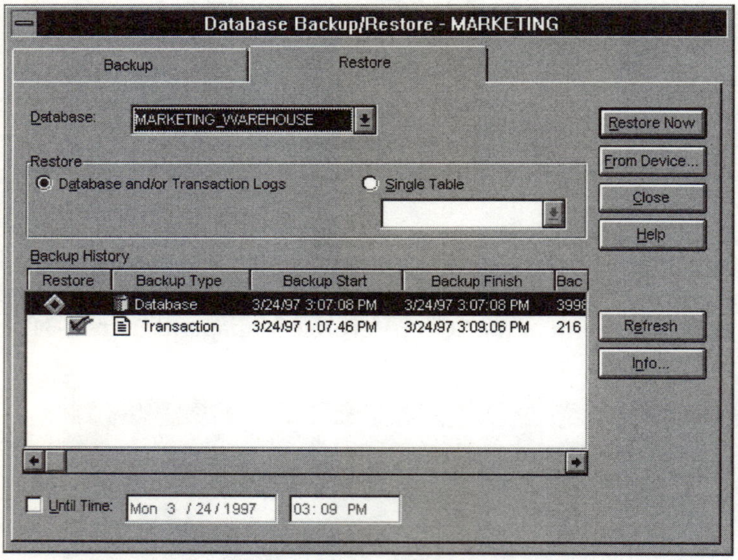

Figure 4-35: The Restore tab of the Database Backup/Restore window.

DataBase Consistency Checking

One of the most powerful DBA tools provided with SQL Server is a collection of programs used to verify the integrity of an SQL Server database—the set of DataBase Consistency Checker (DBCC) utilities. The DBCC command is a part of the Transact-SQL language; it does not have any graphical user interface, so you have to run it using the SQL Query Tool or another similar utility.

The general syntax of the DBCC statement is:

```
DBCC {
    CHECKALLOC [(database_name [, NOINDEX])] |
    CHECKCATALOG [(database_name)] |
    CHECKTABLE (table_name [, NOINDEX | index_id]) |
    CHECKDB [(database_name [, NOINDEX])] |
    CHECKIDENT [(table_name)] |
    DBREPAIR (database_name, DROPDB [, NOINIT]) |
    dllname (FREE) |
    INPUTBUFFER (spid) |
    MEMUSAGE |
    NEWALLOC [(database_name [, NOINDEX])] |
    OPENTRAN ({database_name} | {database_id})
        [WITH TABLERESULTS] |
    OUTPUTBUFFER (spid) |
    PERFMON |
    PINTABLE (database_id, table_id) |
    SHOW_STATISTICS (table_name, index_name) |
    SHOWCONTIG (table_id, [index_id]) |
    SHRINKDB (database_name [, new_size [, 'MASTEROVERRIDE']]) |
    SQLPERF ({IOSTATS | LRUSTATS | NETSTATS | RASTATS [, CLEAR]} |
        {THREADS} | {LOGSPACE}) |
    TEXTALL [({database_name | database_id}[, FULL | FAST])] |
    TEXTALLOC [({table_name | table_id}[, FULL | FAST])] |
    TRACEOFF (trace#) |
    TRACEON (trace#) |
    TRACESTATUS (trace# [, trace#...]) |
    UNPINTABLE (database_id, table_id) |
    UPDATEUSAGE ({0 | database_name} [, table_name [, index_id]]) |
    USEROPTIONS}
[WITH NO_INFOMSGS]
```

Microsoft's recommendation is to run a couple of these DBCC functions, namely DBCC CHECKDB and DBCC NEWALLOC, before every database backup just to make sure that a database you are backing up is not corrupted. Another useful DBCC function is DBCC MEMUSAGE. Use it to analyze memory allocation for the SQL Server, including data cache, procedure cache, and the size of the SQL Server executable code.

Monitoring Current Activity

Use the SQL Enterprise Manager's Current Activity window to view detailed information about active users, locks, and threads in SQL Server. You have to register in the Enterprise Manager as SA to be able to open the Current Activity window. To open it, click on the Current Activity button on the SQL Enterprise Manager toolbar. The Current Activity window has three tabs: User Activity, Detail Activity, and Object Locks.

The User Activity tab shows all the users' and systems' processes within the server. They are grouped by the logins and sorted alphabetically (Figure 4-36).

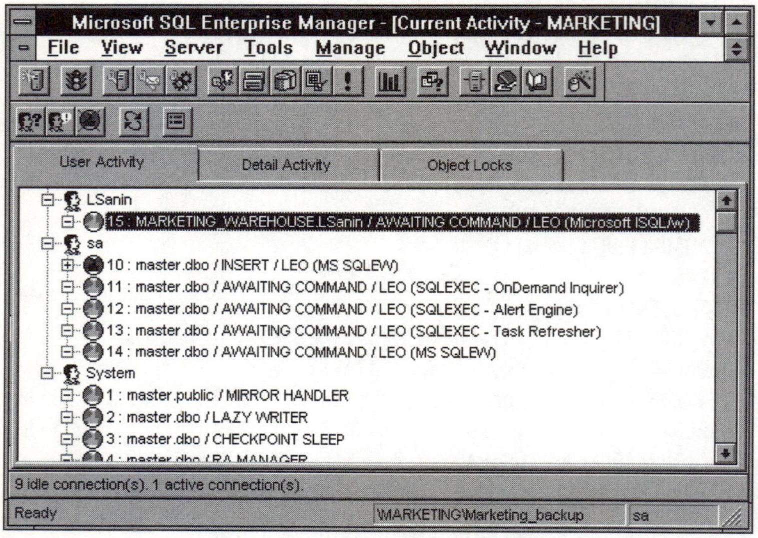

Figure 4-36: The User Activity tab of the Current Activity window.

Use the Toggle Legend button (the right-most button on the Current Activity window's toolbar) to display definitions of the activity icons (Figure 4-37).

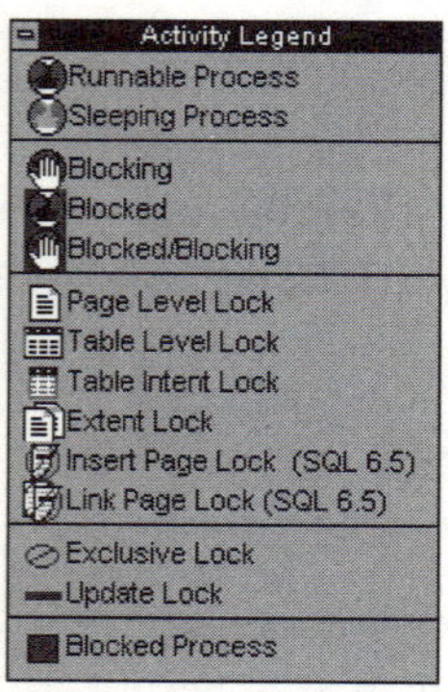

Figure 4-37: The Activity Legend.

Select a process, and click on the More Info button (the left-most button on the Current Activity window's toolbar) to see the last command executed by this process. In this example, the last Transact-SQL statement executed by the process with the PROCESS_ID=15 was SELECT * FROM AUTHORS (Figure 4-38).

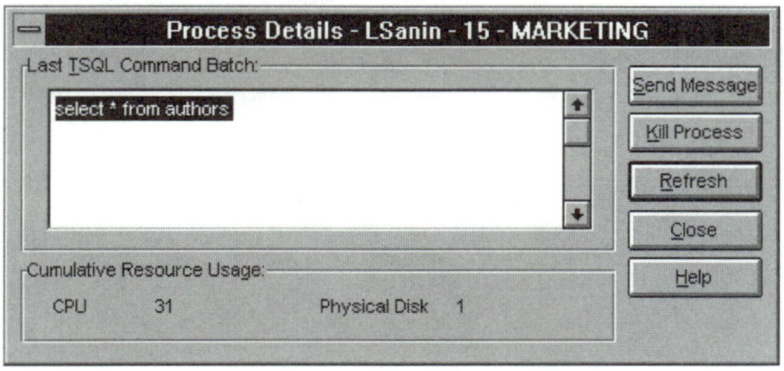

Figure 4-38: The Process Details dialog box shows the last command executed.

The Detail Activity tab shows all the same SQL Server processes the User Activity tab does, but it presents more details, including the number of physical I/Os and CPUs the process used (Figure 4-39).

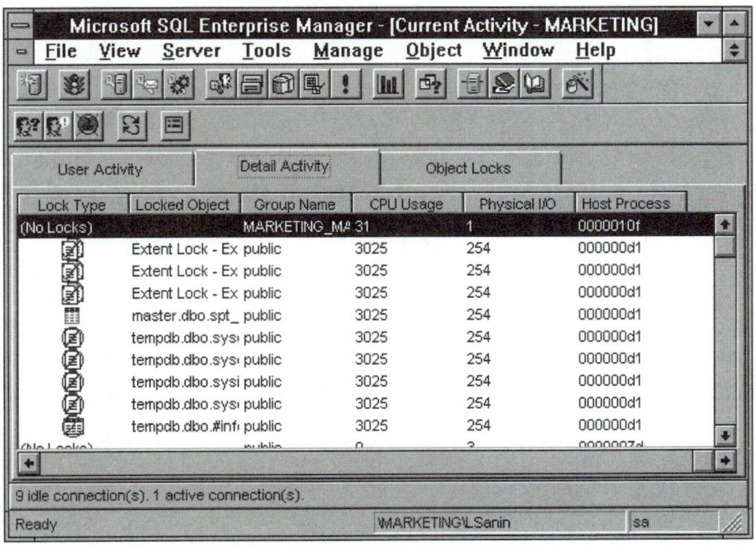

Figure 4-39: The Detail Activity tab of the Current Activity window.

Finally, open the Object Locks tab to view the locks on the SQL Server tables and the processes that cause these locks (Figure 4-40).

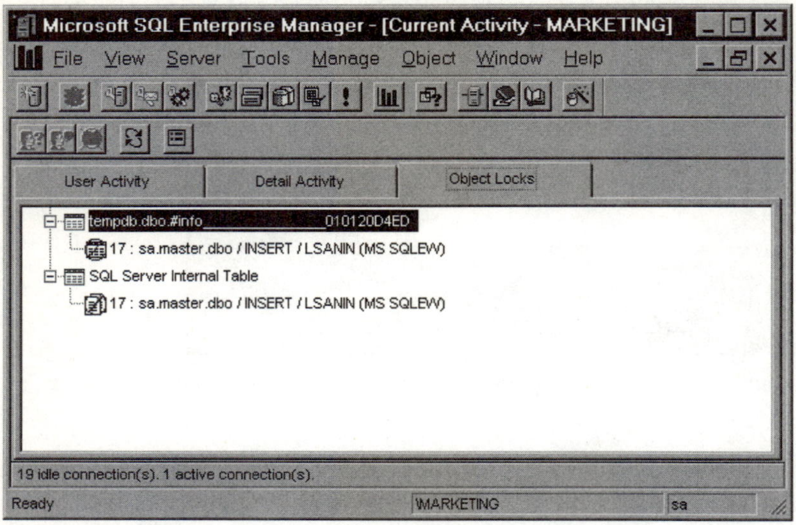

Figure 4-40: The Object Locks tab of the Current Activity window.

SQL Executive

SQL Executive is a part of the SQL Server for Windows NT DBMS. It provides the ability to schedule SQL Server tasks (e.g., database backups, Transact-SQL scripts, or transaction log dumps) and to manage alerts (automatic responses to SQL Server events). SQL Executive is implemented as a Windows NT service, and it can be started or stopped by SQL Service Manager. SQL Executive administration is integrated within the SQL Enterprise Manager. SQL Executive keeps its scheduling and alerts information in the msdb database.

Click on the Configure SQL Executive button on the SQL Enterprise Manager toolbar to open the Configure SQL Executive dialog box (Figure 4-41).

Adjust the parameters to optimize performance of the SQL Executive and its integration with other subsystems (e.g., Microsoft Mail).

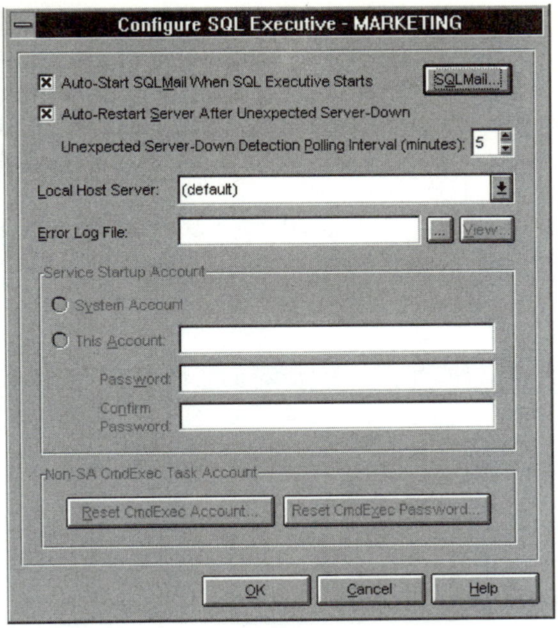

Figure 4-41: The Configure SQL Executive dialog box.

To manage task scheduling, press the Manage Scheduled Tasks button on the SQL Enterprise Manager toolbar. Use this window to create, edit, delete, and run scheduled tasks and view their history (Figure 4-42).

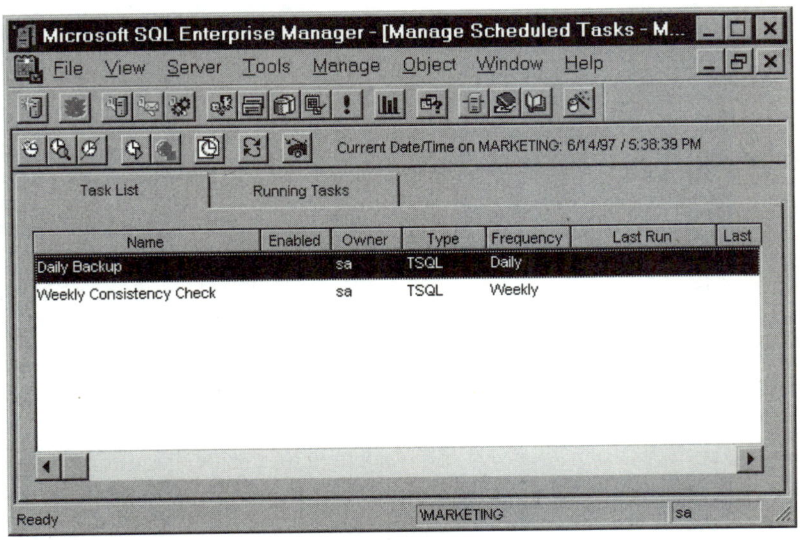

Figure 4-42: The Task Scheduling window.

In the example in Figure 4-42, only one scheduled task currently exists; it is called Database Consistency Check, and it is scheduled to run once a week.

Another function of SQL Executive is to provide a way to set automatic responses (alerts) on various SQL Server events. When an event occurs, SQL Executive executes a task assigned to this event and sends an e-mail and/or pager message to a specified person.

To monitor alerts, click on the Manage Alerts button on the SQL Enterprise Manager toolbar. Use the Manage Alerts window (Figure 4-43) to create, edit, and delete alerts.

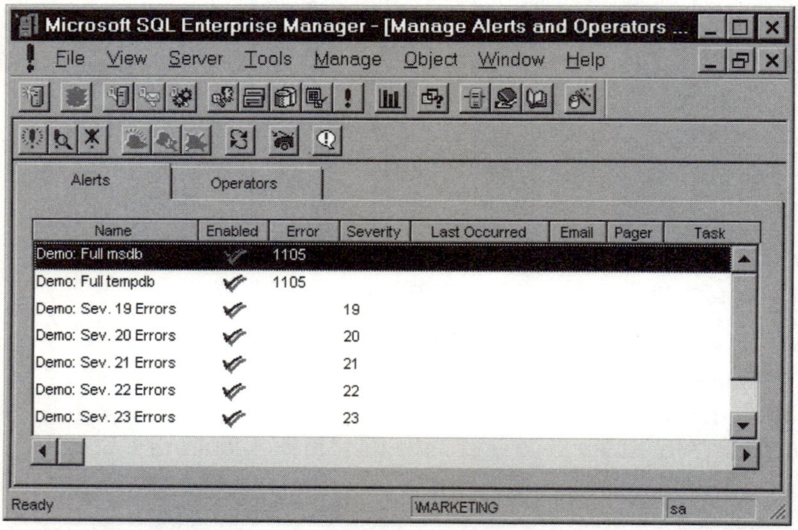

Figure 4-43: The Manage Alerts window.

Introducing SQL Server Database Design

While the basics of relational database design are described in Chapter 2, SQL Server offers a concrete implementation of the relational database model. SQL Enterprise Manager provides a set of graphical tools designed to improve the manageability of this implementation and to make it more intuitive.

An SQL Server database is a collection of the following objects: user and system tables, views, stored procedures, triggers, rules, defaults, constraints, and user defined datatypes.

The concepts of some of these objects (e.g., tables, triggers, rules, and constraints) were examined in Chapter 2. Use the Enterprise Manager's graphical tools to explore their practical implementation.

List the views and the stored procedures in a database by opening the appropriate folders, which are hidden in the Objects folder in the Server Manager (Figure 4-44).

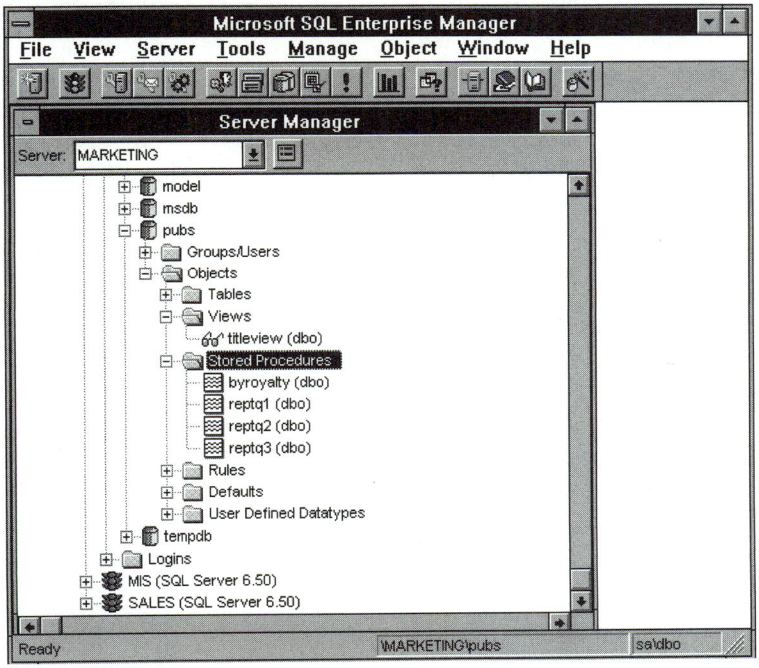

Figure 4-44: The Objects folder in the Server Manager.

To examine an individual object, use the Manage submenu, or as we always do in the Enterprise Manager, right-click on the object to bring up a menu (Figure 4-45).

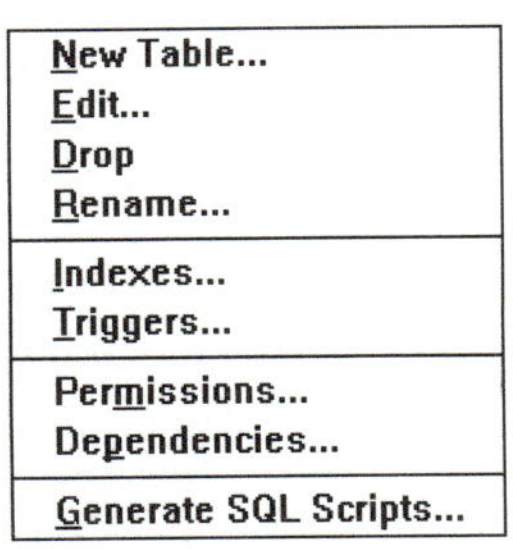

Figure 4-45: The Tables right-click menu.

User tables are the central objects of any relational database, and the Enterprise Manager provides an impressive set of tools to manage the user tables, their properties, and their relationships with other database objects. Look at the Manage Table dialog (Figure 4-46) to find some of the terms you will need to know to manage user tables; the terms should be familiar from the discussion in Chapter 2:

- Primary Key
- Foreign Keys
- Identity Property
- Unique Constraints
- Column Default Values
- Null Values

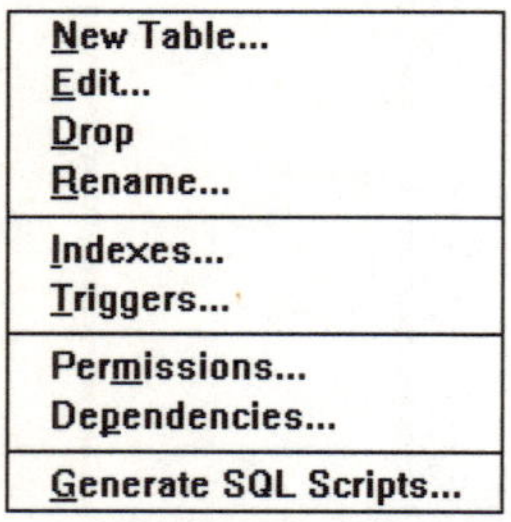

Figure 4-46: The Manage Tables dialog box.

Use these powerful tools to create or edit tables and to apply referential integrity constraints (which are also called *declarative referential integrity* or DRI) to them.

As discussed in Chapter 2, the value of a user table can often be significantly enhanced by creating indexes on the table columns. Use the Manage Indexes dialog (Figure 4-47) to create or edit the table indexes.

Choose an existing index on this dialog to examine the size of the underlying table, the size of the index, the distribution of the index's values, and other properties.

Use the Object Dependencies dialog to find all objects in a database that are related to the selected table (Figure 4-48). The objects listed in the dialog may have to be reexamined if you decide to drop or significantly change the selected table.

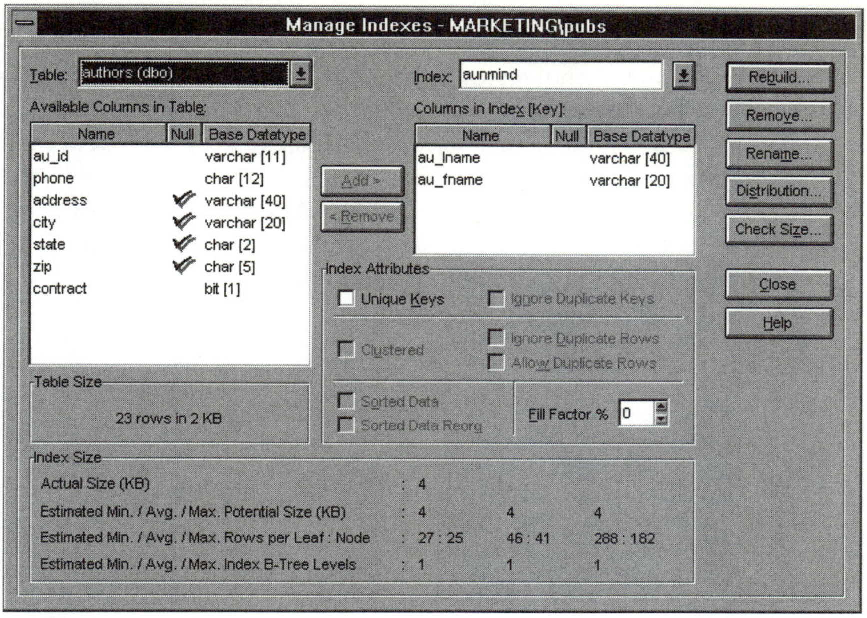

Figure 4-47: The Manage Indexes dialog box.

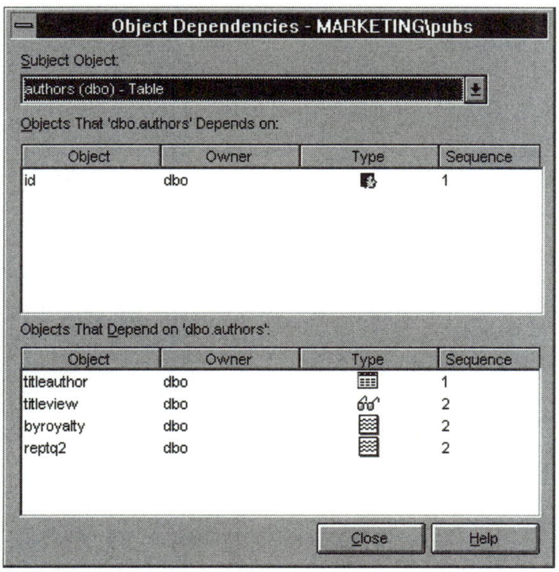

Figure 4-48: The Object Dependencies dialog box.

Moving On

There is obviously not enough space in this chapter to adequately describe all the database administration and design abilities that SQL Server tools can provide, nor is it the main subject of this book. Now, with better understanding of Microsoft Access and Microsoft SQL Server for Windows NT, it is time to move to the next part of the client/server architecture, the element that binds client and server component together—Microsoft Open Database Connectivity (ODBC), which is a database-independent connectivity API for Microsoft Windows-based applications.

chapter 5

Introduction to Open Database Connectivity

Open Database Connectivity (ODBC) is the database component of Microsoft's Windows Open Systems Architecture (WOSA), which enables Windows-based applications to be fully integrated with a wide range of enterprise systems running across multiple hardware and software platforms. In actuality, the Open System Architecture consists of several sets of standard commands or functions called application programming interfaces (APIs). These APIs could be used in a variety of computing environments without exposing programmers to the complexities of the underlying hardware platforms, operating and network systems, or manufacturers of back-end services. ODBC is, essentially, the WOSA's data access API, which allows Windows applications to access most of the popular database management systems. ODBC has become Microsoft's most successful effort in establishing an open interface for the Windows operating system.

According to the main concept of the client/server architecture, client workstations communicate with the server component across a network (e.g., Microsoft network, TCP/IP, or Novell NetWare). The ODBC SQL Server drivers enable applications to communicate with the SQL Server DBMS. The ODBC API functions are designed to establish connection, transmit and execute queries, and return query results. Other more specific functions are used to examine the status of a network connection and to extract error messages or information about a driver itself. Considering that even a short session of a client/server application calls dozens of these functions, it is no wonder that the overall performance of a client/server application can be dramatically improved by adjusting ODBC-related parameters.

Most of the error messages that you get during execution of your client/server Access application (and therefore most of the angry telephone calls that you answer) usually have something to do with failed ODBC functions. The ODBC error messages passed to you by MS Access can be highly convoluted: sometimes you get a half dozen messages for a single error that are much too specific; other times you might get a very generic message (i.e., "ODBC Failure") with no specifics whatsoever. To be able to optimize, successfully debug, and efficiently maintain your client/server application, you really need to have a clear knowledge and understanding of the ODBC component.

ODBC Architecture

The basic ODBC architecture consists of three layers:

- **Application layer.** Calls ODBC API functions to connect to the data source, submit SQL statements, and retrieve results.
- **ODBC Driver Manager layer.** Loads and unloads ODBC drivers and passes API commands to the appropriate drivers.
- **ODBC Driver layer.** Processes ODBC API calls, submits SQL requests to a specific database, and returns results to the application.

Figure 5-1 illustrates the structure of the ODBC layers.

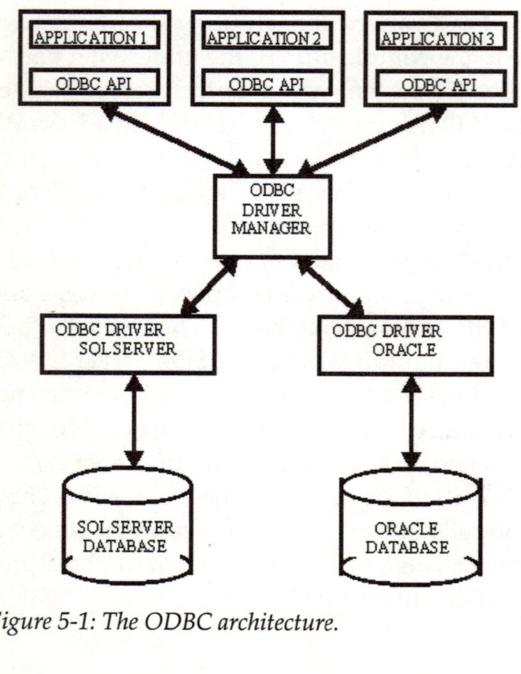

Figure 5-1: The ODBC architecture.

The first ODBC layer consists of just a bunch of application modules supplying parameters to the ODBC functions, and the second layer is a quite trivial module (sitting in a file called ODBC32.DLL). The third ODBC layer—the ODBC driver—is the most important and complex part of the ODBC architecture.

ODBC Drivers

There are ODBC drivers for almost any database that exists in the world. Table 5-1 lists all the databases currently supported by ODBC.

Adabas	Btrieve	C-ISAM
CA-Datacom	CA-DB	CA-IDMS
Cincom SUPRA Server	Clipper	dBase
DEC Rdb	DEC RMS	DP4
EDA/SQL	FirstSQL	FOCUS
Gupta SQLBase	HP ALLBASE/SQL	HP IMAGE/SQL
IBM AS/400	IBM DB2	IBM DB2-DDCS/2
IBM DB2/2	IBM DB2/6000	IBM IMS
IBM SQL/DS	IDSII	Informix
Ingres	Integra-SQL	Interbase
MDBS IV	Microsoft Access	Microsoft Excel
Microsoft FoxPro	Model 204	MUMPS
NetWare SQL	Objectivity/DB	Oracle
Paradox	PICK	Progress
Quadbase	R:BASE	Raima
Red Brick Warehouse	RFMII	SAS
SESAM/SQL	Sharebase	SQL Server
System 2000	Tandem Non-stop SQL	Tandem Enscribe
Teradata	Text	TOTAL
UDS/SQL	UFAS	UNIFY
Unisys DMS-1100 and RDMS-1100	UniSQL	VSAM
WATCOM SQL	White Cross Parallel RDBMS	XDB

Table 5-1: Databases supported by ODBC.

Selecting an ODBC Driver

For every database in Table 5-1, there are drivers for different client operating systems and hardware platforms. The drivers are usually developed by the different software companies (vendors). For example, Table 5-2 shows all the ODBC drivers and software development tools that currently exist for SQL Server.

Company Name	Product Name	Client Platforms
DEC	DEC ODBC Driver for MS Windows V1.0	Windows 3.x, Windows NT, Macintosh
Information Builders	EDA/Extender for Microsoft ODBC v. 2.0	Windows 3.x, Windows NT, Macintosh
Independence Technologies	DAL Client for Windows v1.5 DAL Client for Macintosh v1.5	Windows 3.x, Macintosh
MDI	ODS ODBC Driver	Windows 3.x, Windows NT, Macintosh
Microsoft	Microsoft ODBC Database Drivers v. 2.0 Microsoft SQL Server for NT Microsoft SQL Server Programmers Toolkit	Windows 3.x, Windows NT
MDA Computing	OpenLink ODBC (ST) v. 1.1 OpenList ODBC (MT) v. 1.1	Windows 3.x, Windows NT, Macintosh, UNIX, OS/2
Progress Software	Progress DBMS	Windows 3.x
Intersolve	ODBC Pack v. 2.0 for Win	Windows 3.x, Macintosh, Windows NT, Solaris, OS/2 *Not all drivers supported on all platforms
Sybase		Windows 3.x, Windows NT, Macintosh, OS/2, Solaris
Techgnosis	SequeLink v2.5	Windows 3.x, Windows NT, Macintosh, OS/2, UNIX
Visionware	SQL Retriever 3.0	Windows 3.x, Windows NT

Table 5-2: SQL Server ODBC drivers.

Note that in many cases you can choose from several ODBC SQL Server drivers written for a given platform. These drivers may differ by the conformance level (see "ODBC API Conformance Levels" later in this chapter) and, perhaps, some idiosyncrasies (e.g., how they present the *date* data type). To get more detail on a particular driver, contact the vendor. Throughout this book, we used the Microsoft SQL Server 32-bit ODBC Driver version 2.65.

Types of ODBC Drivers

There are three different types of possible ODBC driver implementations: one-tiered, two-tiered, and three-tiered.

The one-tiered implementation, in which the ODBC driver accesses database files directly, is the simplest type. This method is primarily used for the file-server DBMS systems such as dBase, FoxPro, Paradox, and so on (see Figure 5-2).

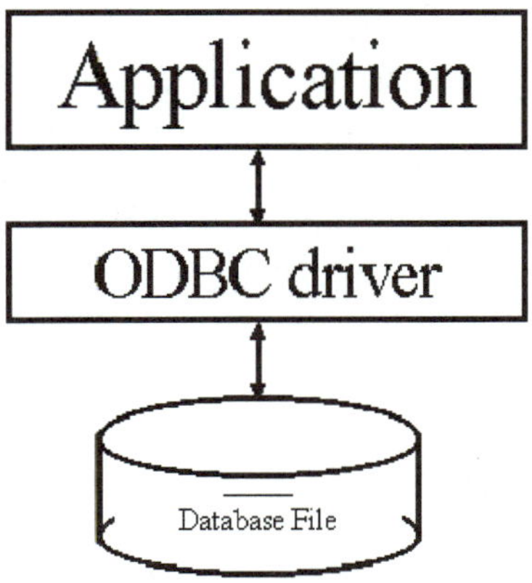

Figure 5-2: The ODBC one-tiered driver.

In the one-tiered implementation, an ODBC driver acts as a database management system; in other words, in order to access, for example, a dBase file via ODBC, you do not need to have the dBase system running on your computer—the ODBC driver will perform functions of the dBase DBMS.

The two-tiered model is a more complicated ODBC driver implementation. In this case, the ODBC driver usually accesses a client/server sort of a database such as SQL Server, Oracle, or Sybase (see Figure 5-3).

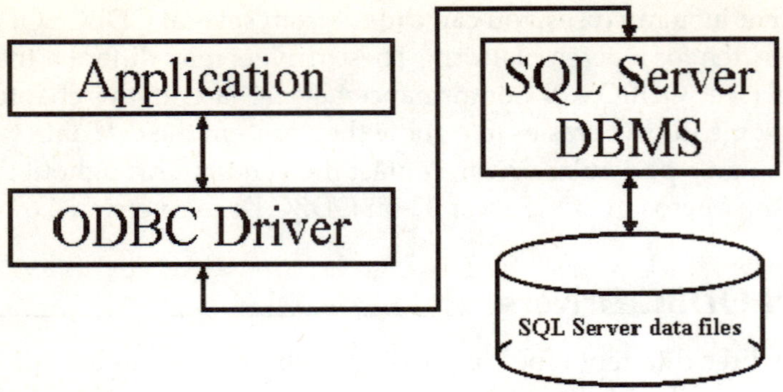

Figure 5-3: The ODBC two-tiered driver accessing an SQL Server database.

The two-tiered driver does not access data files directly but instead communicates with an appropriate DBMS (the SQL Server in this example). As far as SQL Server is concerned, this ODBC driver represents a regular client application in the client/server model. In the big picture, however, this driver is just an interface between the real client and the server.

The last possible type of ODBC driver is a three-tiered driver. In this scenario, the ODBC driver can neither access data files directly nor request data directly from the DBMS because the database that needs to be queried resides on a different and incompatible platform. In this case, a driver has to use a gateway to send a request to DBMS (see Figure 5-4).

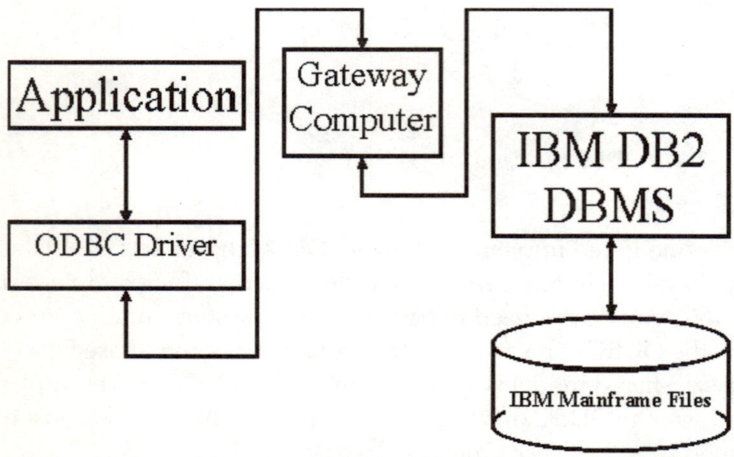

Figure 5-4: The ODBC three-tiered driver; the ODBC driver is accessing an IBM Mainframe DB2 database via a gateway computer.

ODBC API Conformance Levels

An ODBC driver is in conformance with X/Open and SQL Access Group CLI core specifications if it supports the complete set of core functions defined by the specifications. There are two additional sets of extended ODBC functions: Level 1 and Level 2. An ODBC driver may optionally conform to the Level 1 set of functions or to the entire set of API functions, which is called the Level 2 set.

It is important that you choose the right ODBC driver for your client/server application. Consider this: if all you need is a few basic, core ODBC functions, you may prefer to install a simple, core-level conformant driver—a driver that uses less resources in your system and is less likely to cause problems in the multiuser environment. If, on the other hand, your application performs more convoluted tasks (especially if it deals with cursors), you need a more complex driver, possibly a driver that conforms to the Level 2 API.

Table 5-3 contains short descriptions of ODBC functions, including Core/Level 1/Level 2 conformance levels.

Conformance Level	Function Group	Function Name	Description
Core	Connecting to a data source	SQLAllocEnv	Allocates an environment handle. This handle can be used for one or more connections.
		SQLAllocConnect	Allocates a connection handle.
		SQLConnect	Connects to a data source.
	Preparing SQL queries	SQLAllocStmt	Allocates a statement handle.
		SQLPrepare	Prepares an SQL statement for execution.
		SQLSetParam	Allocates memory for a parameter.
		SQLGetCursorName	Returns the cursor name for a specified statement handle.
		SQLSetCursorName	Assigns the name to a cursor.
	Executing SQL queries	SQLExecute	Executes a prepared SQL statement.
		SQLExecDirect	Executes an SQL statement.

Conformance Level	Function Group	Function Name	Description
	Getting results	SQLRowCount	Returns the number of rows affected by an SQL request.
		SQLNumResultCols	Returns the number of columns in the query result.
		SQLDescribeCol	Describes a column in the query result.
		SQLColAttributes	Describes attributes of a column in the query result.
		SQLBindCol	Allocates memory for a result column and specifies the datatype.
		SQLFetch	Returns a result row.
		SQLError	Returns error or status information.
	Terminating a statement	SQLFreeStmt	Terminates statement processing including its cursor and pending results.
		SQLCancel	Cancels an SQL statement.
		SQLTransact	Commits or rolls back a transaction.
	Terminating a connection	SQLDisconnect	Disconnects from a data source.
		SQLFreeConnect	Releases the connection handle.
		SQLFreeEnv	Releases the environment handle.
Level 1	Connecting to a data source	SQLDriverConnect	Connects to a data source using connection string, or requests the connection parameters by displaying connection dialogs for the user.
	Retrieving driver and data source information	SQLGetInfo	Returns information about a driver and data source.
		SQLGetFunctions	Retrieves the list of ODBC functions supported a specific driver.

Conformance Level	Function Group	Function Name	Description
		SQLGetTypeInfo	Returns information about supported datatypes.
	Setting and retrieving drive options	SQLSetConnectOption	Sets a connection option.
		SQLGetConnectOption	Retrieves the value of a connection option.
		SQLSetStmtOption	Sets a statement option.
		SQLGetStmtOption	Retrieves the value of a statement option.
	Submitting requests	SQLParamData	Supplies parameter data.
		SQLPutData	Supplies a data value for a parameter.
	Retrieving results	SQLGetData	Retrieves part or all of one column of one row of a result set.
	Retrieving system information	SQLColumns	Retrieves the list of column names in specified tables.
		SQLSpecialColumns	Retrieves information about columns that uniquely identifies a row in a specified table.
		SQLStatistics	Retrieves statistical information about a table and the list of table indexes.
		SQLTables	Returns the list of table names.
Level 2	Connecting to a data source	SQLBrowseConnect	Similar to SQLDriverConnect, but more flexible.
	Retrieving information about a driver and data source	SQLDataSources	Returns the list of available data sources.
	Preparing SQL requests	SQLParamOptions	Specifies the use of multiple values for parameters.
		SQLSetScrollOptions	Sets options that control cursor scrolling behavior.
	Submitting requests	SQLNativeSql	Returns the converted version of an SQL statement.

➥

Conformance Level	Function Group	Function Name	Description
		SQLDescribeParam	Returns the description for a specific parameter in an SQL statement.
		SQLNumParams	Returns the number of parameters in an SQL statement.
	Retrieving results and information about results	SQLExtendedFetch	Returns multiple rows from a result.
		SQLSetPos	Positions a cursor.
		SQLMoreResults	Processes the next result set if it's available.
	Retrieving system information	SQLColumnPrivileges	Returns a list of columns and their privileges for a table.
		SQLForeignKeys	Returns the names of the columns that form foreign keys.
		SQLPrimaryKeys	Returns the names of the columns that form the primary keys.
		SQLProcedureColumns	Returns information about the specified procedure.
		SQLProcedures	Returns the list of the available procedures.
		SQLTablePrivileges	Returns the list of tables with their privileges.

Table 5-3: Brief descriptions of the ODBC API functions.

Use the SQLGetInfo function to obtain conformance information about a driver. To obtain information about support for a specific function in a driver, an application can call SQLGetFunctions.

ODBC Data Sources

A *data source* is information about a specific database that an application needs to access via ODBC. Data sources are usually set up outside of the applications (although it is possible to set them up "on the fly"). Data sources should contain complete information about the DBMS being accessed, including the

ODBC driver name and version, the network that is used to access the DBMS, the network address of the data source, a description of the data source, and optionally, any additional parameters, depending on the specific ODBC driver.

Using the ODBC Administrator

To set up data sources, use the ODBC Administrator program that is available in the Windows 95/NT4 Control Panel.

To start ODBC Administrator, double-click on its icon. Figure 5-5 shows the main ODBC Administrator window.

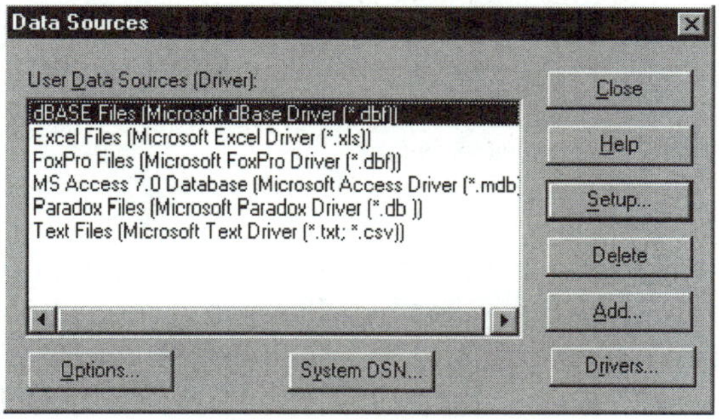

Figure 5-5: The ODBC Administrator main window.

On this screen, you can see all the existing data sources, which are the default data sources created by the ODBC installation program. The left part of each entry is a description of a data source; the right part is the name of an appropriate ODBC driver.

First, check to see if the SQL Server ODBC driver is installed on your system by clicking on the Drivers button.

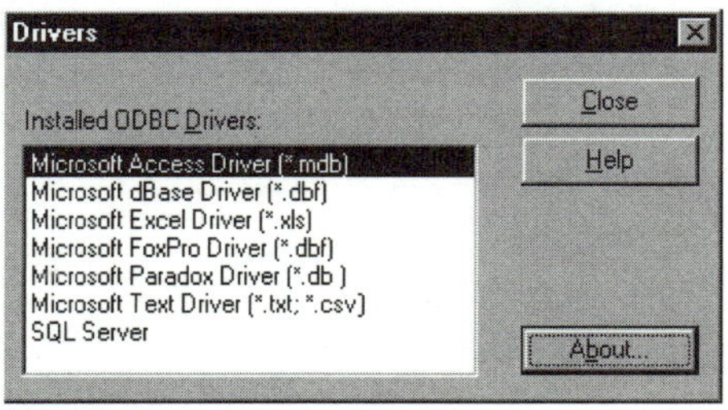

Figure 5-6: The ODBC Drivers window.

The ODBC Drivers window in Figure 5-6 shows an SQL Server ODBC driver. To get more information about this driver (e.g., the vendor and the exact version), highlight the driver name, and click on the About button.

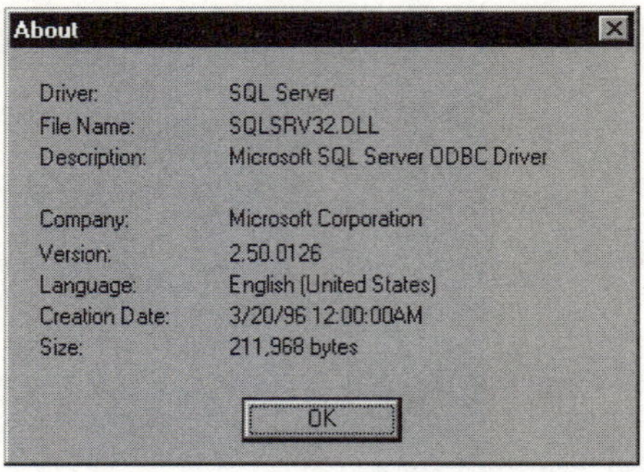

Figure 5-7: ODBC SQL Server Driver About window.

Figure 5-7 shows the SQL Server Driver About window. The information you see in this window may be requested by Microsoft technical support, for example, if you call them with a question or a problem. To return to the main ODBC Administrator window, close the About window, and then close the ODBC Drivers window.

Adding a Data Source

To add an SQL Server data source that points to the SQL Server called MARKETING, click on the Add button in the main ODBC Administrator window, which opens the Add Data Source window (Figure 5-8).

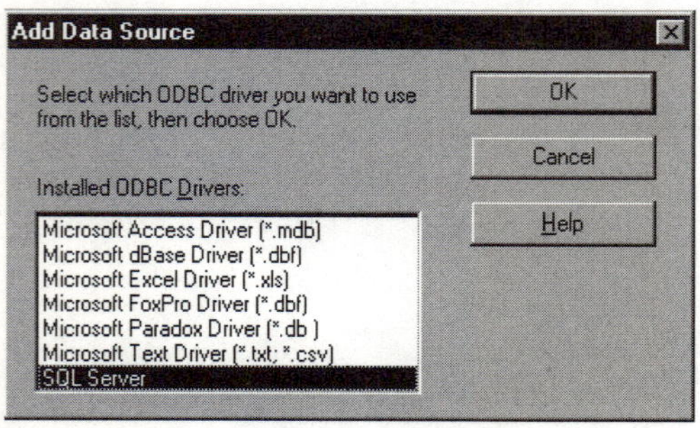

Figure 5-8: The Add Data Source window.

Select SQL Server as your ODBC driver, and click OK. The Driver Setup window opens for you to enter the general and driver-specific parameters (Figure 5-9).

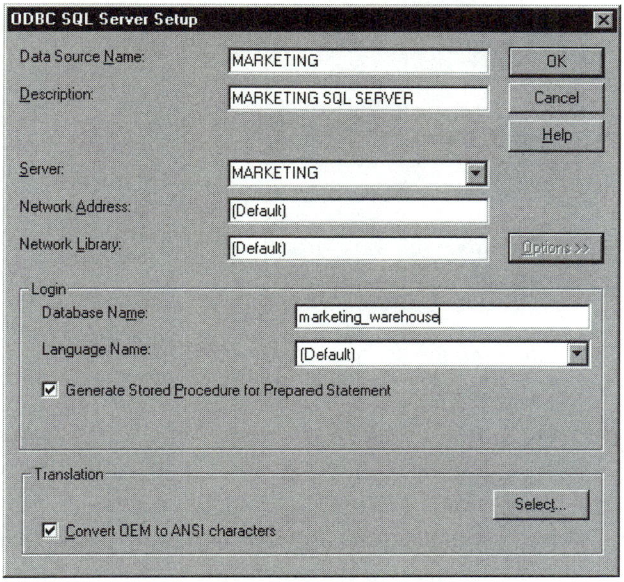

Figure 5-9: The ODBC SQL Server Driver Setup window.

The most important parameters in this dialog are Data Source Name, Server, Network Library, and Database Name:

- **Data Source Name.** A name that will be used in an application for accessing this data source.
- **Server.** Either a name that was specified for the selected network in SQL Setup (see "SQL Setup" in Chapter 4) or an alias assigned by the SQL Server Client Configuration Utility.
- **Network Library.** Leave the default setting to use the network defined by the SQL Server Client Configuration Utility as the default network (see Figure 4-6 in Chapter 4).
- **Database Name.** An SQL Server database that an application will be using when an ODBC connection is established.

The rest of the parameters in the SQL Server Driver Setup dialog can be usually left unchanged.

Click the OK button to go back to the main ODBC Administration Utility window. Note that now the window looks different—a data source called MARKETING has been added to the list of the data sources (Figure 5-10).

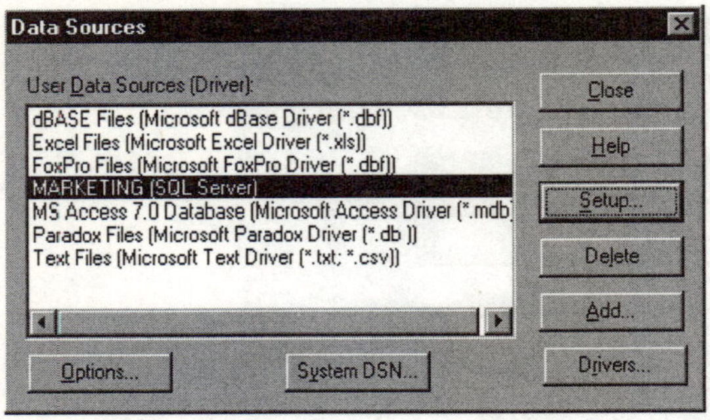

Figure 5-10: A new data source called MARKETING had been added.

Use the System DSN button in the main window to create a system data source (Figure 5-11). A system data source works exactly the same way a regular data source works, except that a system DSN is available to any user on your machine. A regular data source, on the other hand, is only available to the user who has created it. Actually, the only difference between system DSN and a regular DSN is that the information about a regular DSN is kept under the HKEY_USERS folder of the Windows 95/NT4 Registry and the information about a system DSN is kept under the HKEY_LOCAL_MACHINE folder.

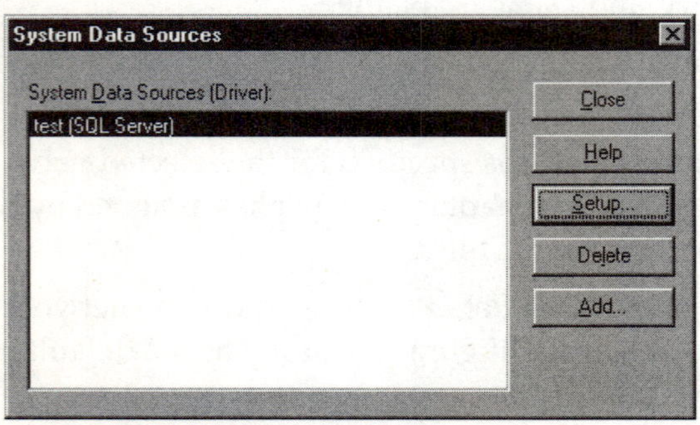

Figure 5-11: The System Data Sources dialog.

Use the Options button on the main window to set up an ODBC trace, which will log all the communication between an application and ODBC into a file (Figure 5-12).

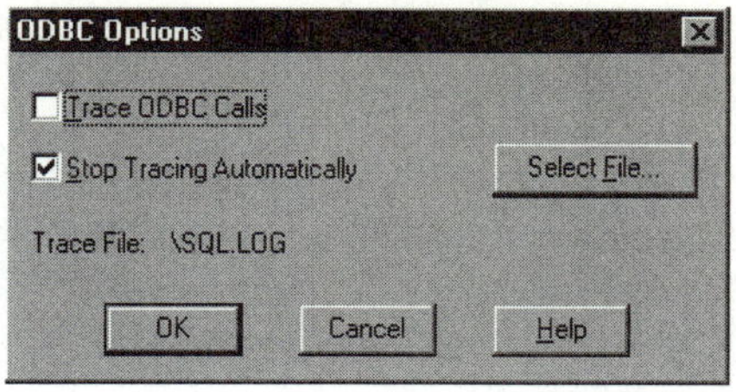

Figure 5-12: The ODBC Options window.

Check the Stop Tracing Automatically check box if you want to log only the current ODBC application and stop logging when the current application terminates ODBC connection. Of course, tracing ODBC API calls is going to slow down your application tremendously as it initiates a huge number of disk I/Os. That is why the warning on Figure 5-13 will be issued if you try to disable the Stop Tracing Automatically option.

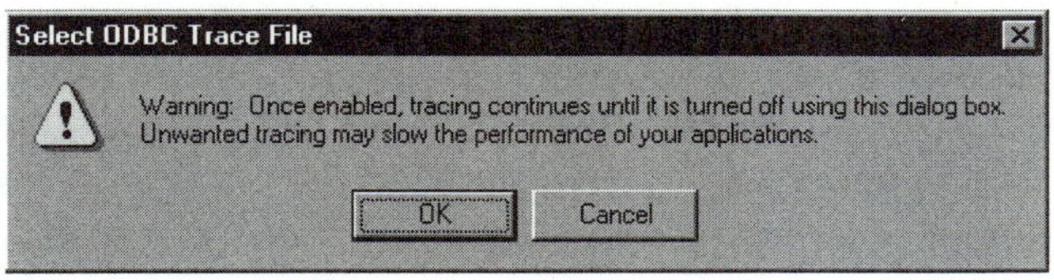

Figure 5-13: The ODBC trace warning.

To examine the composition of an ODBC trace, create a trace file, and print it. Note that it looks pretty cryptic and would not make much sense to a person who is not familiar with ODBC API functions.

The following is a short excerpt from a real ODBC trace file:

```
SQLAllocEnv(phenv00436288);
SQLAllocConnect(henv00436288, phdbc00436AEC);
SQLSetConnectOption(hdbc00436AEC, 103, 00000014);
SQLDriverConnect(hdbc00436AEC, hwnd00000C00, "(null)", -3, szConnStrOut,
255, pcbConnStrOut, 1);
SQLGetInfo(hdbc00436AEC, 9, rgbInfoValue, 2, pcbInfoValue);
SQLGetInfo(hdbc00436AEC, 6, rgbInfoValue, 100, pcbInfoValue);
SQLGetInfo(hdbc00436AEC, 46, rgbInfoValue, 2, pcbInfoValue);
SQLGetInfo(hdbc00436AEC, 23, rgbInfoValue, 2, pcbInfoValue);
SQLGetInfo(hdbc00436AEC, 24, rgbInfoValue, 2, pcbInfoValue);
SQLGetInfo(hdbc00436AEC, 1, rgbInfoValue, 2, pcbInfoValue);
SQLSetConnectOption(hdbc00436AEC, 101, 00000000);
```

```
SQLAllocStmt(hdbc00436AEC, phstmt00438018);
SQLGetStmtOption(hstmt00438018, 0, pvParam);
SQLSetStmtOption(hstmt00438018, 0, 0000003C);
SQLExecDirect(hstmt00438018, "SELECT Config, nValue FROM MSysConf", -3);
SQLError(henv00436288, hdbc00436AEC, hstmt00438018, szSqlState,
pfNativeError, szErrorMsg, 8192, pcbErrorMsg);
SQLError(henv00436288, hdbc00436AEC, hstmt00438018, szSqlState,
pfNativeError, szErrorMsg, 8102, pcbErrorMsg);
SQLFreeStmt(hstmt00438018, 1);
```

In some situations, especially if an application does not have adequate ODBC error trapping, an ODBC trace file may be the best way to debug a problem. Fortunately, Microsoft Access, our front-end application, has its own way to trace ODBC calls.

ODBC Settings for Microsoft Jet Database Engine

To optimize ODBC performance in MS Access, use the *Jet Database Engine* to modify the ODBC configuration parameters in the Windows 95 Registry. The Jet database engine is a software element that actually issues ODBC API functions as a part of Microsoft Access. The Jet database engine is a set of dynamic link libraries (DLLs) functioning as a relational database engine. It handles all database operations, not only for Microsoft Access but also for Visual Basic (see Chapter 3 for more details about the Jet database engine).

The default Jet database engine settings for the ODBC drivers are built in. The Setup program doesn't create an \HKEY_LOCAL_MACHINE\ Software\ Microsoft\ Access\7.0\Jet\3.0\Engines\ODBC Registry key. To override a default setting, you must add the ODBC key and then insert a value for a parameter that you want to override.

To create the new key, open the \HKEY_LOCAL_MACHINE\ Software\ Microsoft\ Access\7.0\Jet\3.0\Engines key in the Registry Editor, and choose Add Key from the Edit menu. In the Key Name box, type **ODBC,** and click OK. The Registry Editor creates the new key as shown on Figure 5-14.

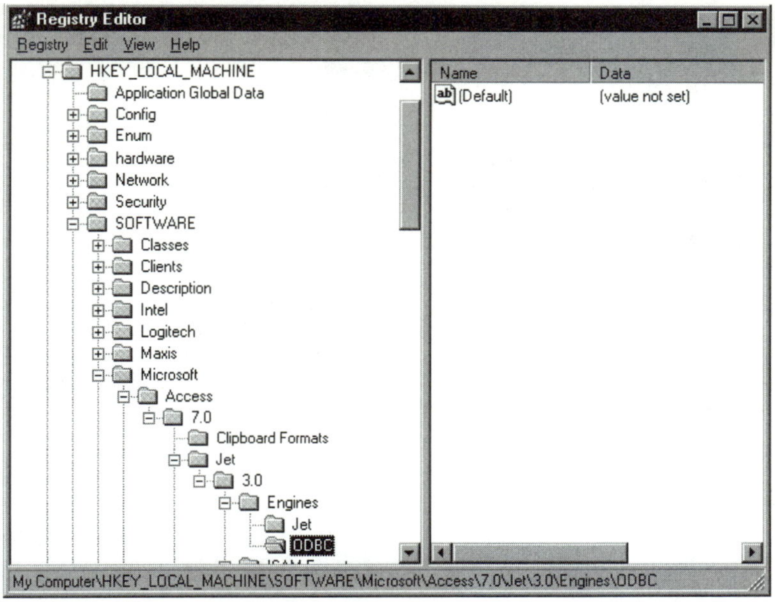

Figure 5-14: The ODBC key created in the Windows 95 Registry.

The following example shows typical settings for the entries in the Jet\3.0\Engines\ODBC folder:

```
LoginTimeout=20
QueryTimeout=60
ConnectionTimeout=600
AsyncRetryInterval=500
AttachCaseSensitive=0
AttachableObjects='TABLE','VIEW','SYSTEM TABLE','ALIAS','SYNONYM'
SnapshotOnly=0
TraceSQLMode=0
TraceODBCAPI=0
DisableAsync=0
JetTryAuth=1
PreparedInsert=0
PreparedUpdate=0
FastRequery=0
```

Use the LoginTimeout parameter to specify the number of seconds a login attempt can wait before timing out. On a slow or heavily utilized network, a low value for this parameter can cause the SQL Server Login dialog to pop up (Figure 5-15). If this occurs, bump this parameter to 60 or more.

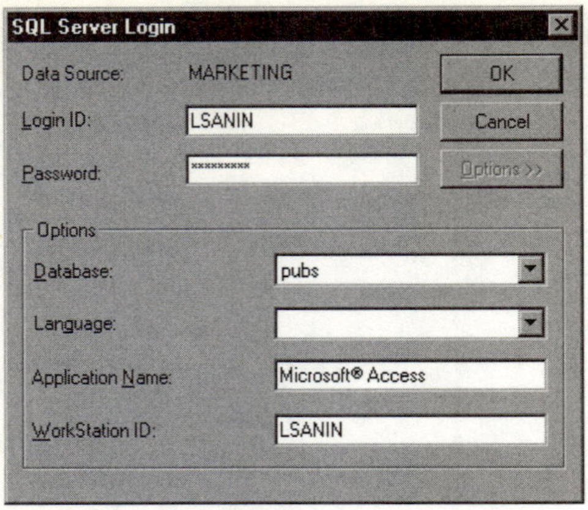

Figure 5-15: The SQL Server Login dialog.

Use the QueryTimeout parameter to interrupt queries when they run longer than the number of seconds specified. The default setting of 60 seconds is probably too low for a real client/server application. Set the QueryTimeout to zero to disable the whole timeout feature. To assign different timeouts on different queries, use the ODBC Timeout query property.

Use the ConnectionTimeout parameter to specify how long idle ODBC connections to the SQL Server should be kept. If the Jet database engine needs to run another SQL Server command during this interval, it can pick up and use an idle connection as opposed to establishing the new one. On a busy network, you may decide to set this parameter higher to reduce network traffic.

Watch for the SnapshotOnly parameter: if it is set to one, it forces all the recordsets open by Access via ODBC to be of a *snapshot* type, which makes them *Read Only*.

Use the TraceODBCAPI and TraceSQLMode parameters to create a trace of SQL statements sent to the SQL database and ODBC API function calls. (These parameters are similar to the Trace ODBC Calls check box in the ODBC Administrator.)

Use the DisableAsync and AsyncRetryInterval parameters to tune up the asynchronous executions of ODBC queries. If it is supported by ODBC driver, asynchronous query execution allows the Jet database engine to initiate an SQL Server query and then switch to some other activity (e.g., start initiating another query or process a form or report). Every time the interval specified by the AsyncRetryInterval parameter expires, the Jet database engine looks to see if any of the asynchronously running queries have finished their processing. Although asynchronous processing has clear advantages, it may also cause some pretty odd adverse effects (e.g., runaway queries, hanging applications, ambiguous ODBC error messages, etc.). Set DisableAsync to one if you experience any these things (or any other mysterious problems) and see if they go away.

To make a connection to the SQL Server, your application uses ODBC functions (such as SQLConnect) and passes your SQL Server login and password as parameters to them. There are several different ways to handle the SQL Server login and password. If an application does not have them saved in a connection string, it will ask you to supply them in the SQL Server Login dialog (Figure 5-15).

Set the JetTryAuth parameter to one to make the Jet assume that your SQL Server login is the same as your Access username and your SQL Server password is the same as your Access password, and try to make connection with SQL Server using these values. If this attempt to make connection fails, the Jet will open the SQL Server Login dialog. If, on the other hand, you know most of your users' Access passwords do not match their SQL Server passwords, set JetTryAuth to zero to avoid a failed SQL Server login attempt.

ODBC SQL Server Driver Error Messages

Remember, any client/server interaction starts with the client program calling an ODBC function. Any and every abnormality that occurs during execution of this function will be reflected in the function's return code. Whether the actual error occurred on the SQL Server, in a network driver, or in an ODBC function itself, the first message that you see in your application is "ODBC—call failed" (see Figure 5-16). In other words, almost any error message that your client/server user sees will be attributed to the ODBC and will be reported to you by users as an ODBC error (even a message such as the one in Figure 5-17 telling you that you have insufficient permissions on the SQL Server). In many other cases, an ODBC driver returns a bunch of messages (Figure 5-18), and then your task is to separate the critical one from the others. Under these circumstances, it is really essential to feel comfortable in dealing with the ODBC error messages.

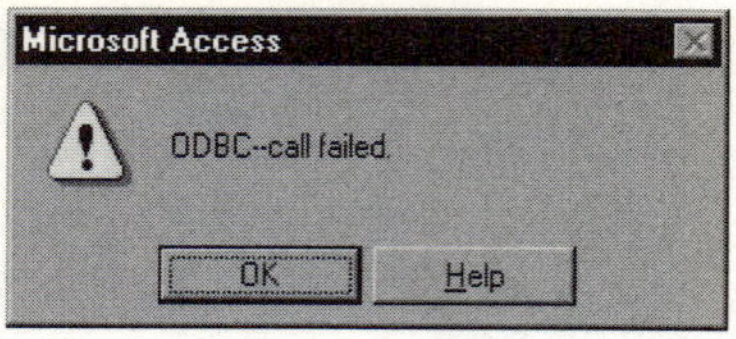

Figure 5-16: The Microsoft Access "ODBC—call failed" message.

Figure 5-17: An SQL Server error returned by ODBC driver.

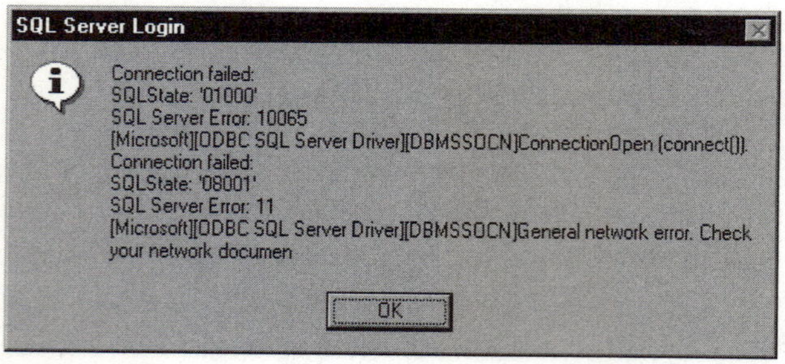

Figure 5-18: A Net Library error returned by ODBC driver.

ODBC API functions always return an *SQL_ERROR* return code when a programming error occurs during execution of an API function, when the network library detects a problem, or when an SQL script generates an error. Error messages or additional status information can be retrieved from ODBC driver. The *SQLError* function retrieves error message information, and it may have to be called several times to retrieve all the messages.

Error Message Format

ODBC SQL Server Driver always returns so-called *native* error code and the corresponding *SQLSTATE* error code.

Native error code can be set to:

- An SQL Server error code, if an error occurred during processing by SQL Server.
- A Net Library error code, if an error occurred in networking software.
- The value zero, if an error occurred in ODBC SQL Server Driver itself.

In a case when an error is detected and returned by SQL Server, the SQLSTATE value is determined by the *native* error. If an appropriate SQLSTATE value does not exist for a native error, SQLSTATE 37000 (syntax error or access violation) will be returned.

The value of SQLSTATE, which is a five-character-long string, can be umË$ by an error handler in an application. Table 5-4 defines all the possible SQLSTATE values.

Value	Meaning
00000	Success.
01002	Disconnect error.
01004	Data truncated.
01006	Privilege not revoked.
01S00	Invalid connection string attribute.
07001	Wrong number of parameters.
07006	Restricted data type attribute violation.
08001	Unable to connect to data source.
08002	Connection in use.
08003	Connection not open.
08004	Data source rejected establishment of connection.
08007	Connection failure during transaction.
08S01	Communication link failure.
21S01	Insert value list does not match column list.
21S02	Degree of derived table does not match column.
22001	String data right truncation.
22003	Numeric value out of range.
22005	Error in assignment.
22008	Datetime field overflow.

Value	Meaning
22012	Division by zero.
22026	length mismatch for the string data,.
23000	Integrity constraint violation.
24000	Invalid cursor state.
25000	Invalid transaction state.
28000	Invalid authorization specification.
34000	Invalid cursor name.
37000	Syntax error or access violation.
3C000	Duplicate cursor name.
40001	Serialization failure.
42000	Syntax error or access violation.
70100	Operation aborted.
IM001	Driver does not support this function.
IM002	Data source name not found and no default driver specified.
IM003	Driver specified by data source name could not be loaded.
IM004	Driver's SQLAllocEnv failed.
IM005	Driver's SQLAllocConnect failed.
IM006	Driver's SQLSetConnect-Option failed.
IM007	No data source specified; dialog prohibited.
IM008	Dialog failed.
IM009	Unable to load translation DLL.
S0001	Base table or view already exists.
S0002	Base table not found.
S0011	Index already exists.
S0012	Index not found.
S0021	Column already exists.
S0022	Column not found.
S1000	General error.
S1001	Memory allocation failure.
S1002	Invalid column number.
S1003	Program type out of range.
S1004	SQL data type out of range.
S1008	Operation canceled.
S1009	Invalid argument value.
S1010	Function sequence error.

Value	Meaning
S1012	Invalid transaction operation code specified.
S1015	No cursor name available.
S1090	Invalid string or buffer length.
S1091	Descriptor type out of range.
S1092	Option type out of range.
S1093	Invalid parameter number.
S1094	Invalid scale value.
S1095	Function type out of range.
S1096	Information type out of range.
S1097	Column type out of range.
S1098	Scope type out of range.
S1099	Nullable type out of range.
S1100	Uniqueness option type out of range.
S1101	Accuracy option type out of range.
S1102	Table type out of range.
S1103	Direction option out of range.
S1106	Fetch type out of range.
S1107	Row value out of range.
S1108	Concurrency option out of range.
S1109	Invalid cursor position; no keyset defined.
S1110	Invalid driver completion.
S1C00	Driver not capable.
S1DE0	No data at execution; values pending.
S1T00	Timeout expired.

Table 5-4: SQLSTATE *values.*

Error messages issued by ODBC include three prefixes and have the following format:

```
[vendor][ODBC_component][data_source]error_message
```

For the Microsoft SQL Server ODBC driver:

- The value of the [*vendor*] prefix is always [Microsoft].
- The values of the [*ODBC_component*] prefix are [ODBC Driver Manager], [ODBC Cursor Library], and [ODBC SQL Server Driver].
- The values of the [*data_source*] prefix are [SQL Server] and [*net_library*].

Working With ODBC Error Messages

A higher level application such as Microsoft Access usually generates its own message first, which just states that an ODBC error was detected (Figure 5-16).

Access then issues the SQLError ODBC function as many times as needed to retrieve all the driver's error and information messages, which it displays in a separate message box (Figures 5-17 and 5-18).

Finally, Access shows the message box in Figure 5-19, confirming that an action, that called the failed ODBC function (in this case Open Table), will not be executed.

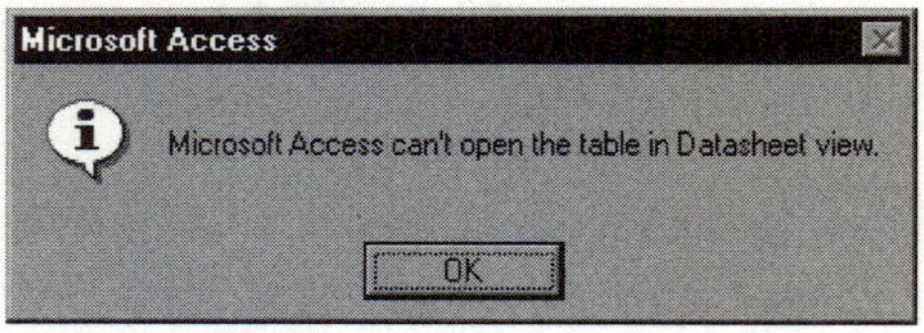

Figure 5-19: The "Microsoft Access can't open the table . . ." message.

Moving On

This concludes an overview of one the most important components of the client/server architecture: the ODBC interface. It started with the definitions of general concepts but also included some pretty specific details and recommendations. Whether you are creating new ODBC data sources, changing ODBC-related parameters in MS Access, or reacting to ODBC error messages, it is important that you feel confident in understanding Open DataBase Connectivity.

In Chapters 6, 7, and 8 of this book, we will show how to link an SQL Server table to an Access application, import an SQL Server table to an Access application, create an SQL Server pass-through query running in the Access environment, and do other neat client/server stuff using ODBC SQL Server Driver and ODBC data sources.

The next chapter is the last introductory chapter in this book. It covers client/server integration with the legacy systems as well as methods of data manipulation in the client/server environment.

chapter 6

Manipulating Data in the Client/Server Architecture

At this point, you are already familiar with Microsoft Access as the front end of the client/server architecture, SQL Server for Windows NT as the back-end database, and ODBC as a mechanism of communicating between them. There is just one more general component to discuss: the data itself. It is almost impossible to imagine a client/server application that has been created and released to production without any data. Even if all the business transactions are supposed to be freshly entered by the users of the new application, there is almost always a considerable amount of supplementary data (e.g., reference tables) that is supposed to exist in the application at the time of production release.

More commonly, though, huge amounts of data are once or regularly loaded into an application from so-called legacy systems (e.g., applications developed for UNIX, Wang, or IBM mainframe computers), from other client/server applications (possibly built on a different relational database system), or from file/server-type databases (such as dBase). Another common practice is to export fragments of data from the client/server applications and store it on user's desktop PCs to be used in their spreadsheets or local desktop databases. This chapter is an introduction to some of the methods of manipulating data in the client/server architecture.

Integration With Mainframe Systems

While more and more companies are looking for ways to take advantage of the client/server architecture, the data accumulated in the old mainframe systems, as well as their processing power, still provides significant business value. Many large and midsize companies still use their mainframe systems for a high-volume data repository and high-intensity data processing. In many cases, data from mainframe databases is then loaded into the client/server environment where it can be accessed, presented, and manipulated much easier. In this chapter, an IBM-mainframe-based MIS—one of the most typical examples of legacy systems—is chosen to conceptually represent all of them. Of course, in other cases a legacy system might be based on UNIX, Wang, UNISYS, or another platform.

The procedure of loading large amounts of data to an SQL Server for Windows NT DBMS can be performed in three steps:

- **Step 1.** Extracting data from a legacy system DBMS into operating system files.
- **Step 2.** Copying/converting these files to the Windows NT platform.
- **Step 3.** Loading data from Windows NT files to SQL Server tables.

While methods of extracting data from a mainframe database (Step 1) depend entirely on the legacy system and its database, the last two steps have a few implementations that are commonly accepted by the data processing industry. Some of them are examined in the following sections.

Copying Data to the Windows NT Platform

If the data only needs to be loaded once a month, once a year, or perhaps just one time only, your best solution may be to use some mutually compatible media (e.g., magnetic tape). Chances are, however, that you have to load it several times a week, or you may even need to selectively capture some data from mainframe application terminal screens. In this case, you may want to consider more advanced techniques of accessing legacy systems.

Terminal Emulation

One of the most basic forms of integration with legacy systems is terminal emulation, which assumes that the legacy program is running on the back-end mainframe machine while the client is only emulating terminal protocols. One of the important features that many terminal emulation packages have is client-side support for protocol-specific script languages. A script language allows you to program certain actions that are usually manually performed at the client terminal. These scripting languages are usually pretty simple; the most commonly used commands in a typical script language are:

- Send a sequence of keystrokes.
- Wait for a certain string of characters to be sent from the host (for instance, the string "READY").
- Basic execution control commands (for example, IF, GOTO, WHILE, and so on).

The IBM mainframe terminal emulation scripting languages range from very primitive interfaces such as High Level Language Application Programming Interface (HLLAPI) and Extended HLLAPI (EHLLAPI) to a quite sophisticated script language called REXX, which was designed and created originally as a general purpose language for systems administration.

Of course, we only mention all these terminal emulation interfaces here in the context of their capabilities to perform file transfer. In fact, most of the script languages are capable of downloading IBM mainframe files to a hard drive of a Windows NT machine.

Before using an IBM mainframe terminal emulation interface program, you usually have to set up a network protocol (for example, TN3270 TCP/IP-based emulation) and define the network-specific parameters (IP address and TCP/IP stack). This setup will allow you to connect to the TSO (Time Sharing Option) or CICS (Customer Information Control System) systems on the IBM mainframe machine.

The established connection will normally work as an emulation of the IBM3270 terminal, allowing you to use the TSO/ISPF development environment as well as to run application-specific CICS transactions. The file transfer option, on which we are focusing in this chapter, is usually an additional and secondary option of the terminal emulation software.

Before using the file transfer option, some parameters usually have to be configured. It is a good idea to force the emulation program to convert files from IBM's EBCDIC to PC's ASCII and to add Cr/Lf (carriage return /line feed) to the end of every record.

Another option that many emulation programs provide is the batch transfer. Use this option to set up a batch of files to be transferred as a single unit. The batch, with the filenames and parameters, can usually be saved and used for later downloads. The more sophisticated emulation programs can also provide a way to start and execute the download batches automatically at a specified time by employing some kind of a macro or scripting language.

FTP Protocol

FTP protocol is another way to transfer files from legacy systems to Windows NT computers. While the TCP/IP protocol with FTP support is quite natural for a UNIX machine, MVS emulation software for an FTP server on an IBM mainframe has also been around for several years. Among a great number of various FTP *client* programs on the market, the one that we use for the demonstration in this chapter is a shareware program called CuteFTP. It can be downloaded from the Internet (http://www.cuteftp.com/) for free.

CuteFTP has a simple database where it keeps all the FTP sites you need. CuteFTP has a subsystem called FTP Site Manager that maintains this database; it is shown in Figure 6-1.

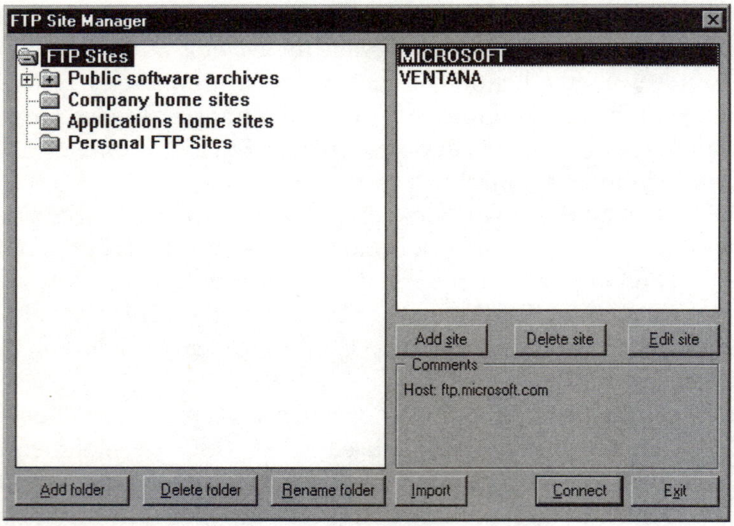

Figure 6-1: CuteFTP's FTP Site Manager.

Enter a new FTP site or edit, delete, or connect to an existing one using the dialog shown in Figure 6-1. Click the Edit Site button to open the FTP Site Edit dialog box (Figure 6-2).

The most important information to enter in the Site Edit dialog is the address (URL, or Uniform Resource Locator) of the FTP site. The address used in this example, ftp.microsoft.com, is a URL pointing to Microsoft's FTP site. Use the Initial Remote Directory text box to specify a directory path to the location of your data on the FTP server (in this case, /SOFTLIB/MSLFILES).

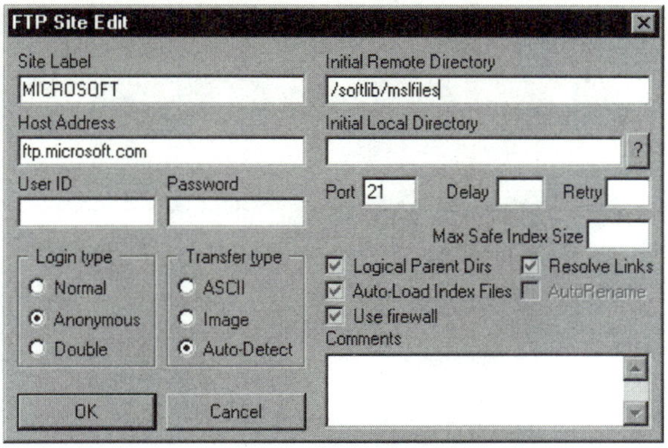

Figure 6-2: CuteFTP's FTP Site Edit dialog.

Another important element of a site's entry is the security information: username and a password. If a site is open to the public, you can usually log in as *anonymous* and use your Internet e-mail address as a password. When the site information has been entered, connect to that site by highlighting the FTP site entry in FTP Site Manager and clicking on the Connect button. Upon successful connection, login messages will be issued (Figure 6-3) and then CuteFTP displays the contents of the selected FTP directory (Figure 6-4).

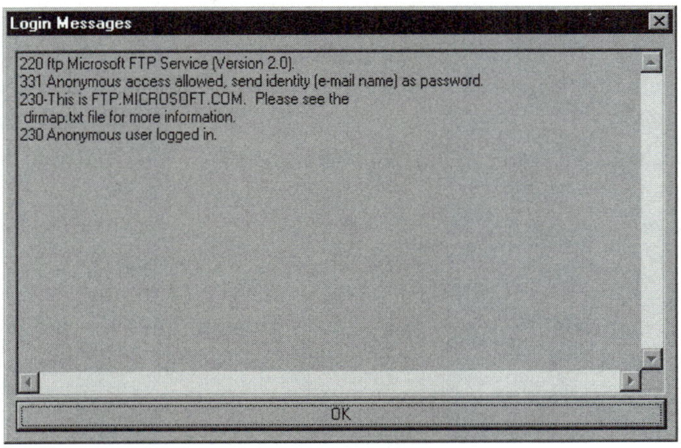

Figure 6-3: CuteFTP's Login Messages screen.

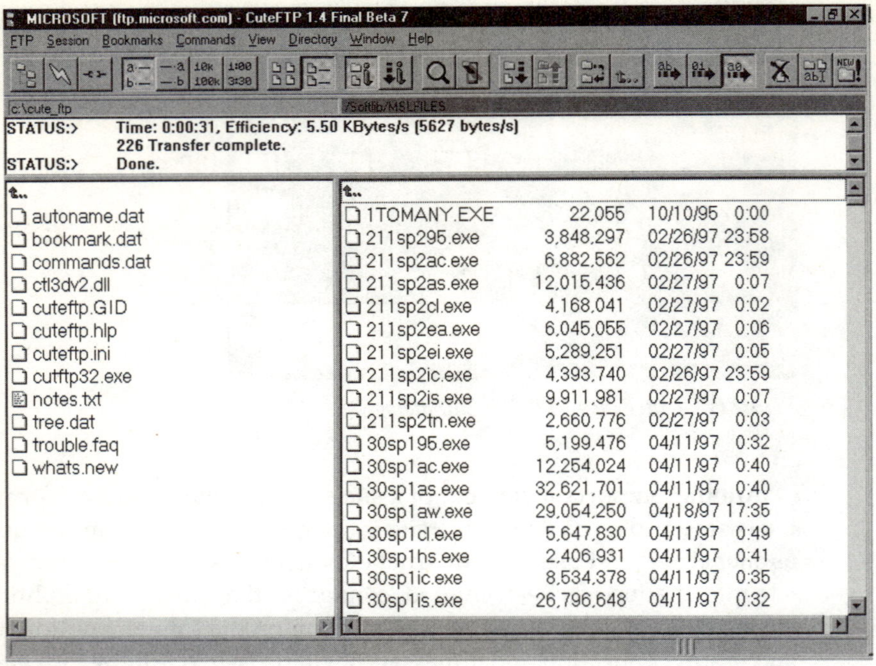

Figure 6-4: CuteFTP's FTP server directory listing.

At this point, you can transfer files either from the FTP server to your PC or from you PC to the FTP server. You can also view, edit, and delete files on the FTP server (subject to the restrictions imposed by the FTP server's security on your user ID).

Select a file and use the right-click menu to select the desirable action (Figure 6-5).

When you are accessing an FTP server, such as ftp.microsoft.com, you do not even have to know which platform this server is built on: it might be run on a UNIX machine, an IBM mainframe with MVS, Windows NT, or any other possible hardware/software configuration (this may not be exactly true because of the different coding systems, such as EBCDIC in IBM mainframes, there may be situations in which you will need to know the server's platform). This hardware and operating system independence is a huge advantage of FTP servers when compared to terminal emulation protocols.

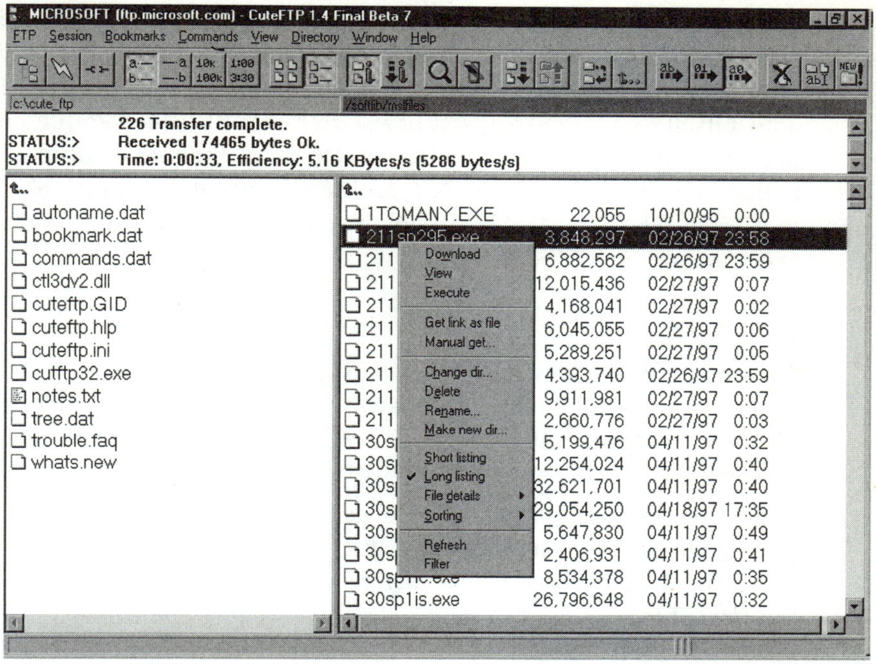

Figure 6-5: CuteFTP's right-click menu.

Other Transfer Options

There are many other ways to copy legacy systems data to the Windows NT server, including some "smart" disk devices that can be connected simultaneously to several different platforms (for example, IBM mainframe and Windows NT) so that every platform can read and process the data as if it were written in the format of this platform (e.g., VTOC for IBM mainframe and NTFS or FAT for Windows NT). The smart disk device performs format conversions on the fly and creates an illusion of the native format for every platform involved in the enterprise.

Loading Data From Windows NT Files to SQL Server Tables

So, data extracted from a legacy database is now loaded to the Windows NT machine's hard drive as a set of ASCII files. Our goal now is to load these extract files into an SQL Server table. The easiest way to do so is to use the Bulk Copy Program provided by Microsoft.

The *Bulk Copy Program* (or *BCP*) is a program that takes a file (which should be an ASCII file in a text format) and loads it into an SQL Server table by using DB Library API functions. The BCP program is very flexible and is able to adjust itself to different formats of a source data file (for example, comma-delimited format, fixed-length format, etc.) and different datatypes in a destination SQL Server table. The BCP program is installed with the SQL Server tools as BCP.EXE in MSSQL\BINN directory. It is a command-line utility executed from the MS-DOS window.

Running BCP

To run BCP, you must have an SQL Server Login with the appropriate permissions on the database tables and views as well as the appropriate NTFS directory/file permissions in Windows NT (if you create, update, or read NTFS files).

The following is a summary of the BCP program syntax:

bcp [[database_name.]owner.]table_name {**in** | **out**} datafile
[**/m** maxerrors] [**/f** formatfile] [**/e** errfile]
[**/F** firstrow] [**/L** lastrow] [**/b** batchsize]
[**/n**] [**/c**] [**/E**]
[**/t** field_term] [**/r** row_term]
[**/i** inputfile] [**/o** outputfile]
/U login_id [**/P** password] [**/S** servername] [**/v**] [**/a** packet_size]

The most important parameters are:

- Fully qualified database/owner/table name.
- In/out parameter (i.e., import/export data).
- SQL Server name (on the default network).
- Format file name.
- Input/Output filename (for import/export operation).
- Login Id and password.

Using a BCP Format File

Use the BCP format file to bring additional flexibility to the program. The BCP format file is used to set up the direct match between a field in the source ASCII file and a column in the corresponding SQL Server table. The following example of a format file illustrates the use of BCP on an ASCII data file. The source file in our example is a comma-delimited ASCII file:

```
172-32-1176,PS3333,1
213-45-8915,BU1032,2
213-46-8915,BU2075,1
238-95-7766,PC1035,1
267-41-2394,BU1111,2
267-41-2394,TC7777,2
274-80-9391,BU7832,1
409-55-7008,BU1032,1
427-17-2319,PC8888,1
472-27-2349,TC7777,3
```

Use the following BCP format file to load the preceding file into the TITLE_AUTHORS table in the pubs database of the SQL Server:

```
6.0
4
1 SQLCHAR 0    11 ","       1       au_id
2 SQLCHAR 0    6  ","       2       title_id
3 SQLCHAR 0    1  "\r\n"    3       au_ord
```

The first line of the BCP format file indicates the version number of the BCP program; the second line specifies the number of fields in the data file. The rest of the file consists of the lines composed in the fixed format. Every line comprises seven columns and explicitly defines location, size, prefix, and a delimiter of a particular source field in the source file as well as the sequential number and a name of a destination column in the SQL Server table.

To create a template for the format file, start the BCP utility and specify the OUT operation as shown in this example:

bcp pubs..titleauthors OUT c:\titleauthors.txt /S<server> /Usa /P<password>

BCP will lead you through the sequence of instructions shown in Figure 6-6. Press enter every time a sentence pops up, thus accepting the default value. BCP creates a format file named, by default, BCP.FMT (although BCP prompts you to type a different name if you choose to). The newly created file can be edited and renamed to create the final version of the BCP format file. Please note that for loading data from an ASCII file to an SQL Server table, the data type of every field should be defined as SQLCHAR.

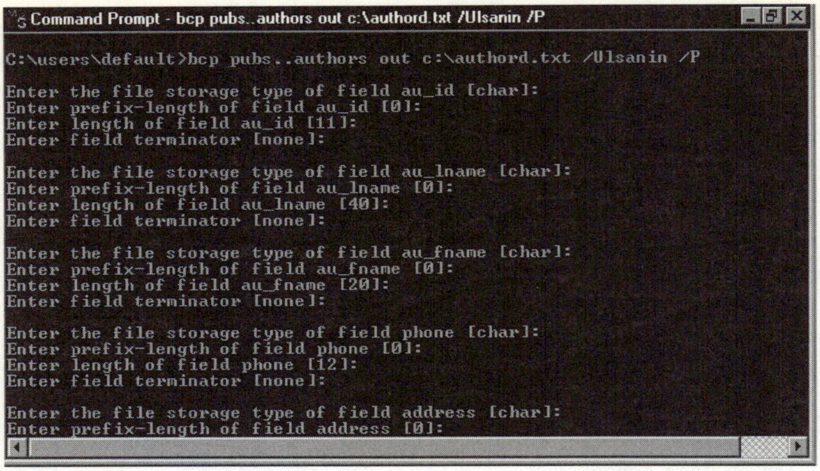

Figure 6-6: BCP creating a template for the format file.

To load data from T_A.TXT to TITLE_AUTHORS SQL Server table in the pubs database, use T_A.FMT format file, as shown in Figure 6-7.

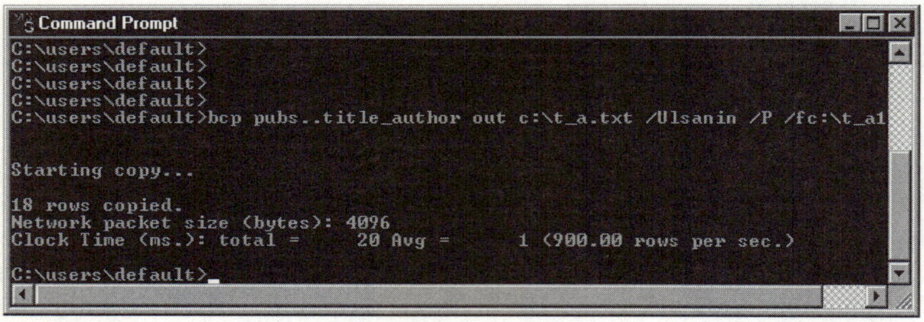

Figure 6-7: Using BCP with the format file to load a table.

If you have a data file that contains more data than you want to load to the table on SQL Server, get rid of the excessive fields by directing them into the *null* field.

Let us assume that in the previous example, field au_id will be filled later by an SQL script, so it has to be skipped in the bulk copy process. The source file, however, has not changed: the first 11 characters of every record are still occupied by the au_id data. The following BCP format file lets us achieve the desirable result:

```
6.0
4
1 SQLCHAR 0    11 ","      0       au_id
2 SQLCHAR 0    6  ","      2       title_id
3 SQLCHAR 0    1  "\r\n"   3       au_ord
```

Note that the only difference between this format file and the one in the previous example is that the sequential number of the destination SQL Server column, au_id, is set to zero, causing the au_id field from the source ASCII file to be skipped.

Slow BCP vs. Fast BCP

When you are loading large amounts of data into SQL Server, one of your primary concerns is the amount of time it takes. SQL Server allows you to save time by performing *fast BCP,* or a nonlogged bulk copy operation. To be able to execute the fast BCP, two conditions must be met:

- The target table has to be located in a database that has its *select into/ bulkcopy* option set to true.
- The target table must have no indexes.

If you are running fast BCP, changes that are made to the target table are not reflected in the database transaction log, and therefore, the full database backup has to be performed after this operation is complete.

Integration With the Client/Server-Type Systems

In some situations, you do not have to go through all these motions (extracting data to a sequential file, transferring the file, BCPing the file into a table) in order to copy data from one database to another. If you are dealing with a client/server database that is using SQL language (e.g., SQL Server, Sybase, or Oracle), you can use some of the SQL Server tools and subsystems, such as SQL Transfer Manager and SQL Server replications. In the easiest case is, both source and target databases are SQL Server for Windows NT. In version 6.5 of SQL Server, you can also transfer data directly from a Sybase source database or replicate data from SQL Server to any ODBC database.

SQL Transfer Manager

Use the SQL Transfer Manager (see Figure 6-8) or, as it's called in SQL Server 6.5, the Database/Object Transfer tool to copy objects from one database to another. Using multiple options on the dialog, you can choose to copy all the objects in the database, selectively copy objects with or without their dependencies, and even copy SQL Server Logins or User Ids.

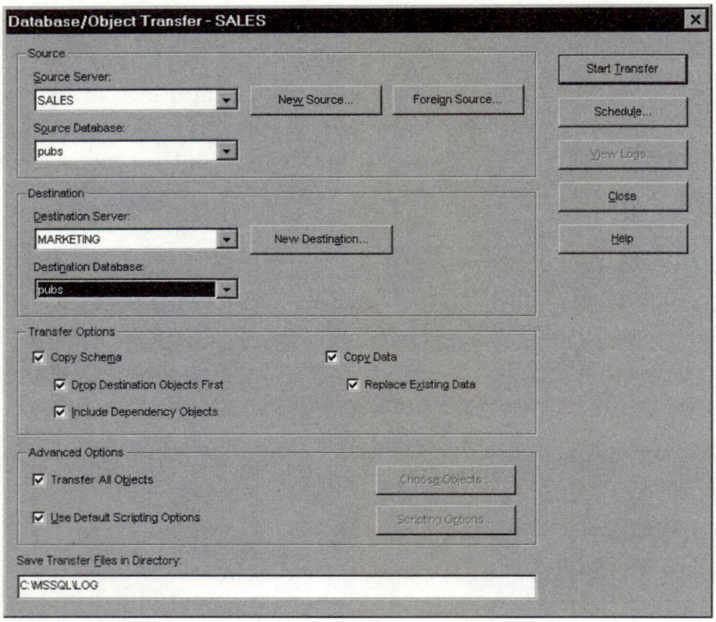

Figure 6-8: The SQL Transfer Manager main dialog.

Use the Transfer Manager's defaults to transfer all the objects. Use the Advanced Options section to change the scripting options (Figure 6-9) and to transfer only selected objects in the database (Figure 6-10). Uncheck Transfer All Objects and Use Default Scripting Options to enable the Choose Objects and the Scripting Options buttons.

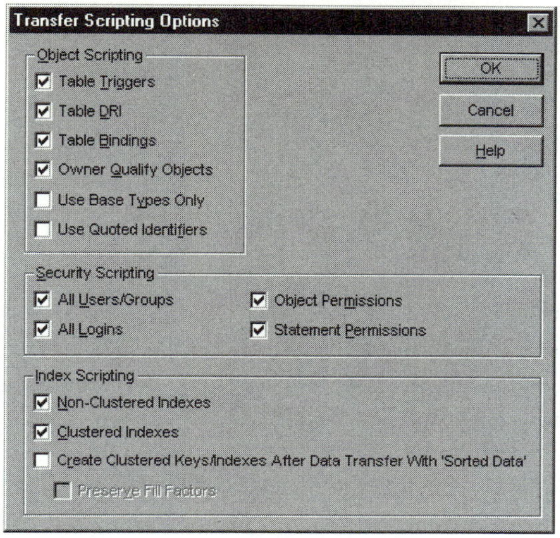

Figure 6-9: Click the Choose Objects button in SQL Transfer Manager's main dialog to get this dialog.

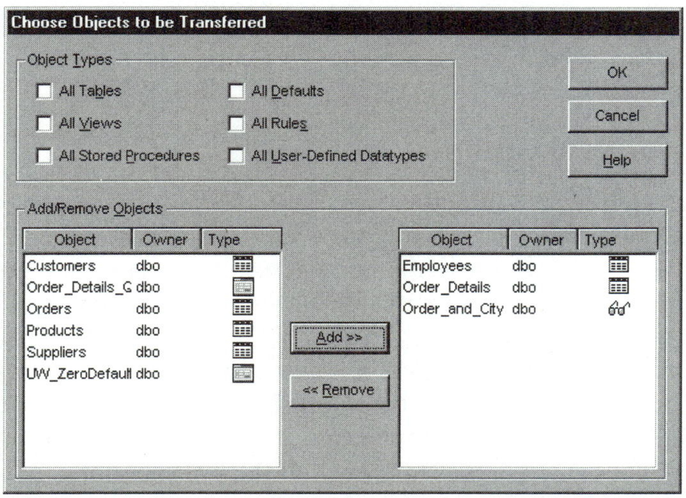

Figure 6-10: Click the Scripting Options button in SQL Transfer Manager's main dialog to get this dialog.

When everything is set up, initiate transfer by clicking on the Start Transfer button in SQL Transfer Manager's main dialog. Alternatively, click on the Schedule button to execute transfer later. In this case SQL Transfer Manager creates a task for the transfer and schedules its execution under the supervision of the SQL Executive (Figure 6-11).

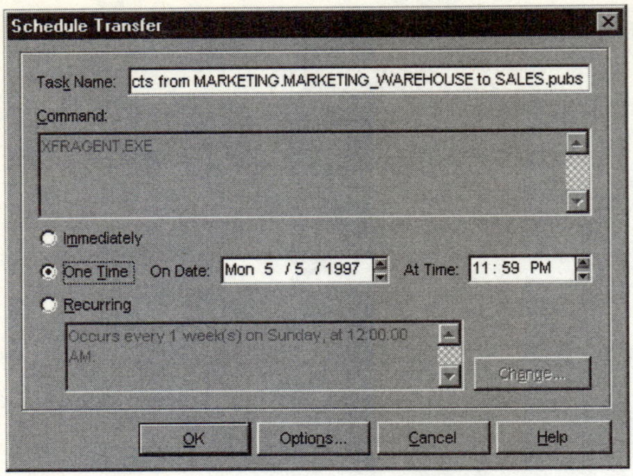

Figure 6-11: SQL Transfer Manager's Schedule Transfer window.

The Transfer Manager creates and executes Transact-SQL scripts to create objects. It uses BCP to transfer the data. An advantage of the Transfer Manager is that it can be used, for example, to fix allocation errors in the database: brand new objects are created; they do not inherit allocation problems of their prototypes. A disadvantage of the Transfer Manager is that it is quite slow, much slower than the database backup and restore.

SQL Server Replications

Replication abilities of SQL Server were first introduced in version 6.0 and received further improvements in version 6.5. Use replications to set up an automated transactions distribution from a source server (called publisher) to destination servers (called subscribers). New in version 6.5 is that a subscriber can now be any ODBC-accessible DBMS.

SQL Server replication is based on the so-called *loose consistency* model (as opposed to a *tight consistency* model). This means that data on a destination server does not have to exactly match the current copy of the source server. The publishing server forwards all the transactions it performs to the subscribers, but it does not synchronize with the subscribers; it does not wait for them to acknowledge that the replicated transactions were posted. The loose consistency model is not ideal. It's a trade-off: you sacrifice guaranteed accuracy while gaining flexibility, much faster response, and the ability to replicate over slow and not always reliable communication links (for example, USA-to-Europe replications).

A server participating in replications can perform one or more of the following functions: publication, distribution, and subscription.

A publication server (*publisher*) contains one or more *publications.* A publication is a set of *articles* that are replicated as a unit. An article is a subset of rows and columns from a single table; it is an elementary unit in the replication phraseology. Publisher uses a database transaction log to replicate; that is, complete transactions are copied from the publisher's SYSLOGS table and sent to a distribution server (*distributor*), which, in turn, transmits them to all the *subscribers.* Subscribers receive replication data in a form of transactions and apply these transactions (or *roll them forward*) in the subscribing database.

A distributor receives transactions performed on the publisher and stores them in the distribution database, where they stay until applied to every subscriber. The distribution server plays the central role in the whole process by running *log reader, synchronization,* and *distribution processes.* All three processes are automatically created by the replication subsystem and run as scheduled tasks of the SQL Executive service.

A *log reader process* retrieves transactions marked for replication from the publisher and saves them into the distribution database.

A *synchronization process* initially brings the new subscribers in sync with the publisher.

Finally, a *distribution process* moves transactions from the distribution database to the subscription servers. This mechanism allows the Publishing server to get rid of the old transactions and continue normal processing even though not all of these old transactions have been replicated. In many cases, however, the same physical machine performs both publisher's and distributor's functions.

SQL Server replications are administered by SQL Enterprise Manager as are almost all the other functions of SQL Server. SQL Setup does not install replication functions with the basic SQL Server configuration; it has to be done later when you decide exactly what role (if any) this server will play. To set up a server as a publisher, select Install Publishing in Replication Configurations under the Server menu option. Use the Install Replication Publishing dialog box (Figure 6-12) to either install the publisher and the distributor in the same server or only the publisher, which uses another server as a remote distributor.

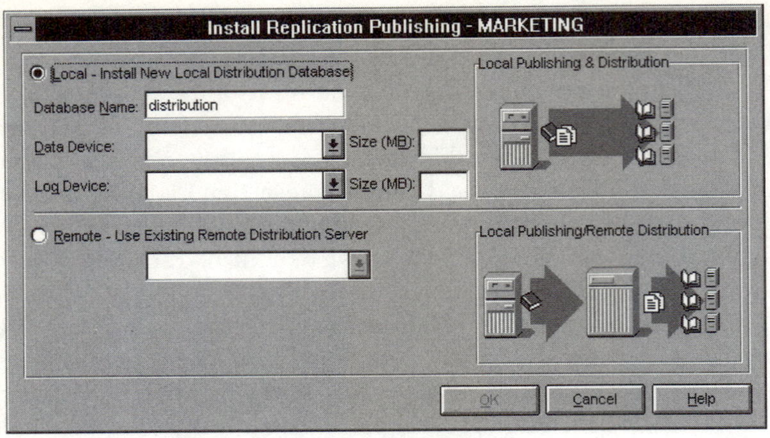

Figure 6-12: The Install Replication Publishing dialog.

To activate the publisher use the Replication-Publishing dialog (Figure 6-13), which can be opened by choosing Publishing from the Server submenu.

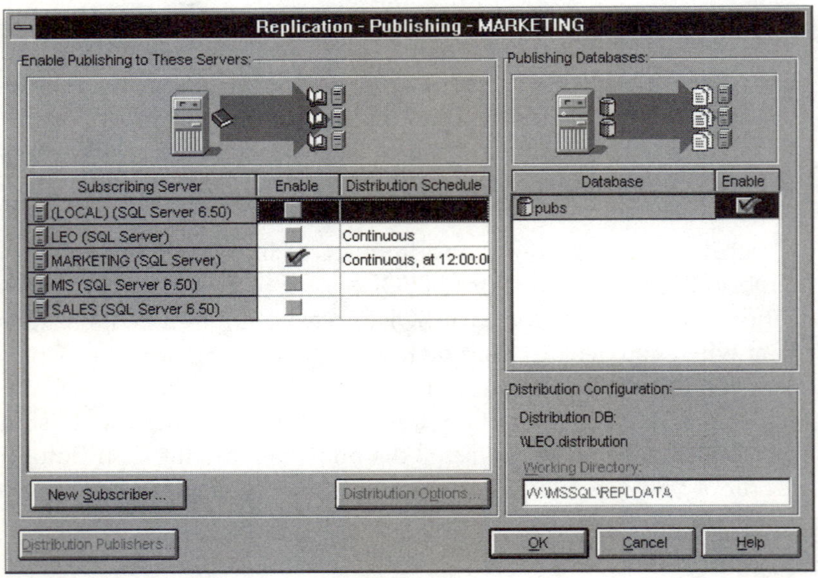

Figure 6-13: The Replication-Publishing dialog.

When the publisher is installed and activated, you can start creating publications. To open the Manage Publications dialog (Figure 6-14), click on "book in a hand" button on the toolbar, or choose Publications from the Manage submenu.

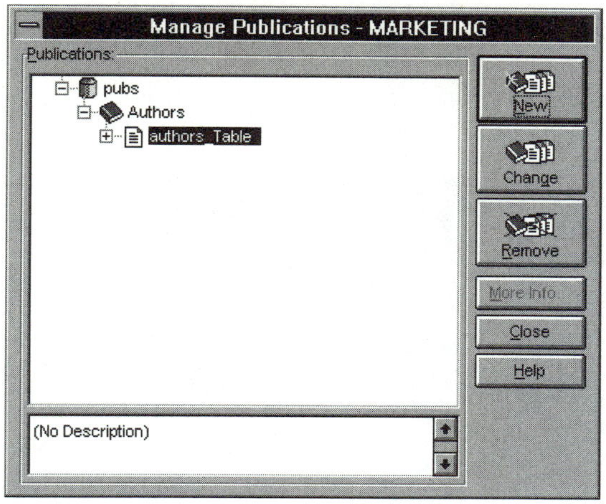

Figure 6-14: The Manage Publications dialog.

The example in Figure 6-14 shows a publication called Authors, which contains the single article called authors_Table. Click on the Change button to edit this publication. The Edit Publications dialog (Figure 6-15) will appear, which you can use to add, delete, and edit articles and set up synchronization method, security restrictions, and other replication properties.

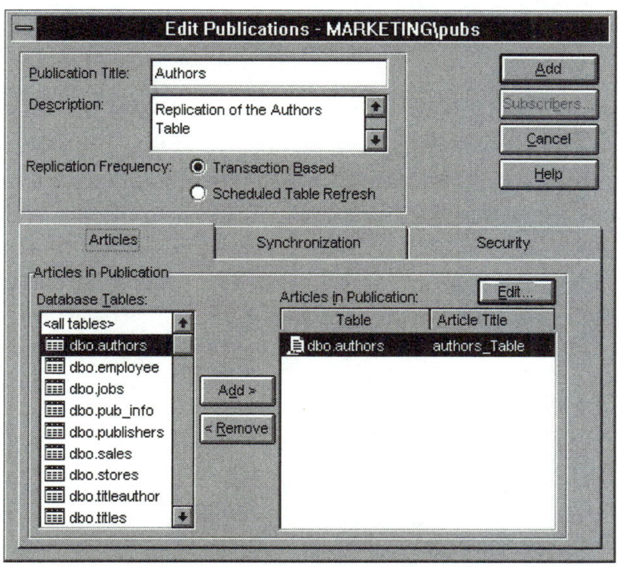

Figure 6-15: The Edit Publications dialog.

Similarly, to install a subscriber, choose Subscribing from the Server submenu. Use the Replication-Subscribing dialog (Figure 6-16) to select publishing servers from which you want to be able to subscribe.

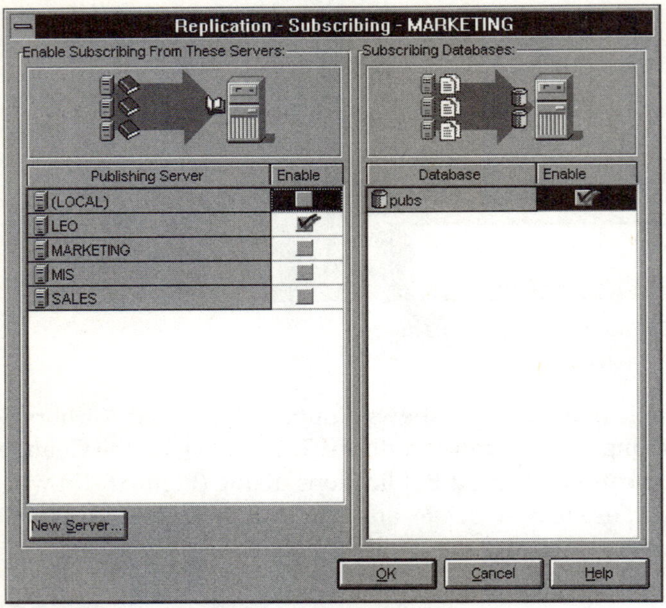

Figure 6-16: The Replication-Subscribing dialog.

After you enabled one or more publishers from which your server can subscribe, select specific publications to be replicated to your server. Click on the "open book" button on the toolbar, and select publications using the Manage Subscriptions dialog (Figure 6-17). This is similar to the way you created publications.

Finally, note how you can immediately identify publishing databases and publications using the Server window of the SQL Enterprise Manager: a publishing database will have a little hand on the icon and all the database's publications can be found in a new folder called Publications (Figure 6-18).

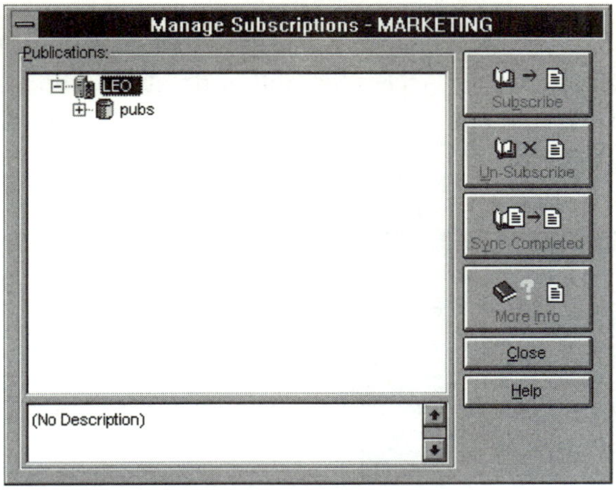

Figure 6-17: The Manage Subscriptions dialog.

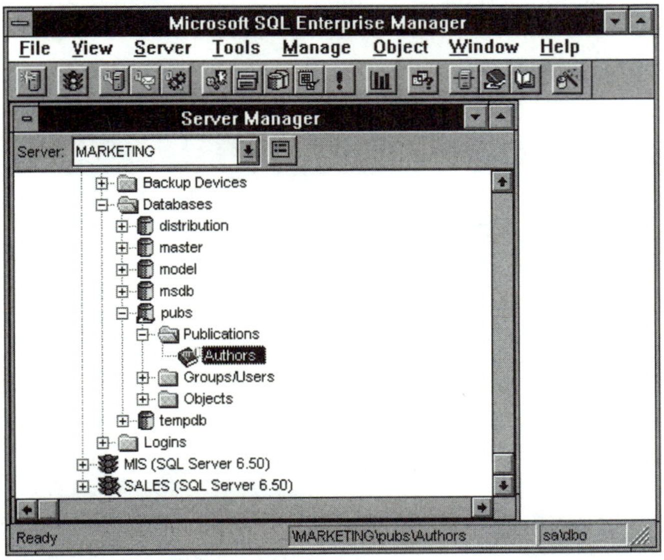

Figure 6-18: The publishing database in the Server window.

Working With Access Data

Microsoft Access has data management capabilities similar to those of SQL Server 6. The functions discussed in this chapter are export, import, and replication.

Exporting Data From Access

To transfer a table with data *from* Access to another database, choose Save As/ Export from the File submenu, and select To an External File or Database in the Save As dialog (Figure 6-19).

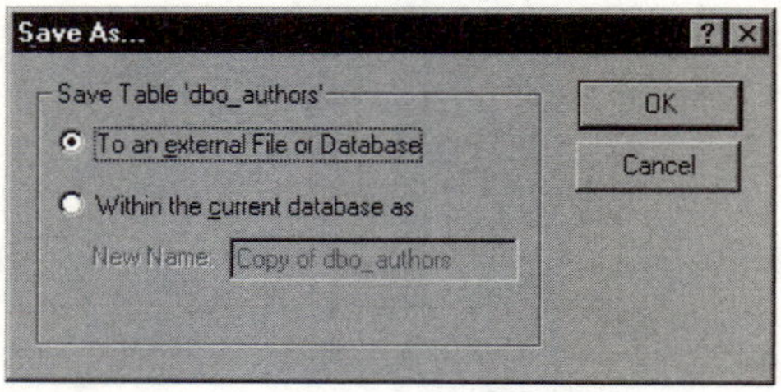

Figure 6-19: MS Access Export—the Save As dialog.

Click OK button to open the Save Table In dialog. Use the Save Table In dialog to choose the database type. Select ODBC Databases to export a table into SQL Server database (Figure 6-20).

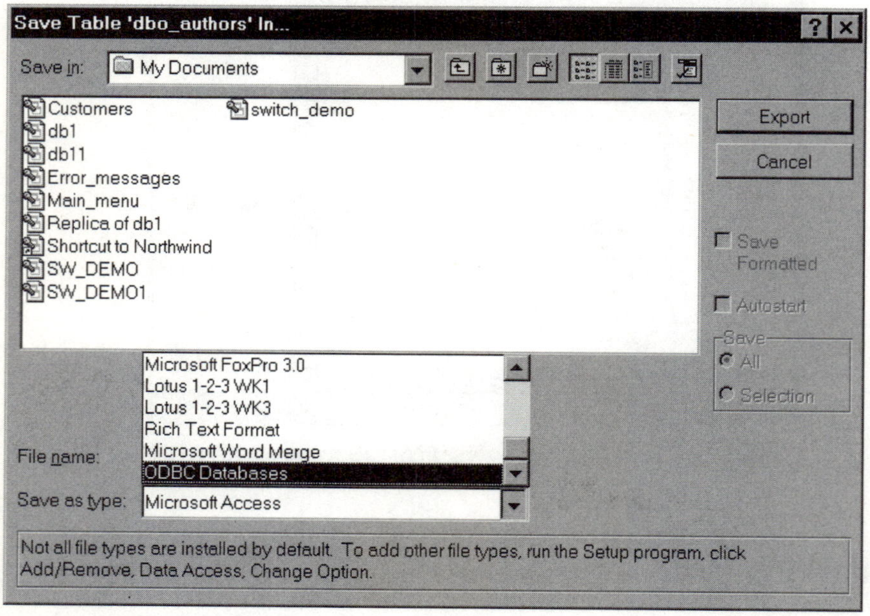

Figure 6-20: MS Access Export—the Save Table In dialog.

At this point Access gives you a chance to change the table name, as shown on Figure 6-21.

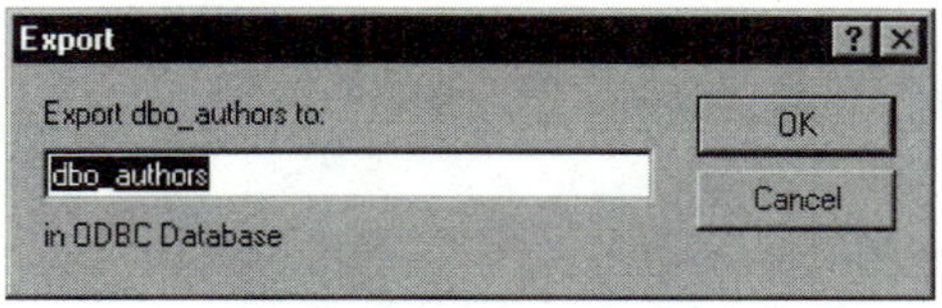

Figure 6-21: MS Access Export—the Export To dialog.

The ODBC driver then leads you through the usual routine of specifying the data source, SQL Login, and password. If you have sufficient permissions on the SQL Server and the table does not exist in the target database, table schema is created, and the data gets copied into it.

Importing Data Into Access

To copy a table from another database to your MS Access application, use the Import function in the Get External Data in the File submenu. Use the Import dialog, shown on Figure 6-22, to select the database type (the ODBC Databases for SQL Server).

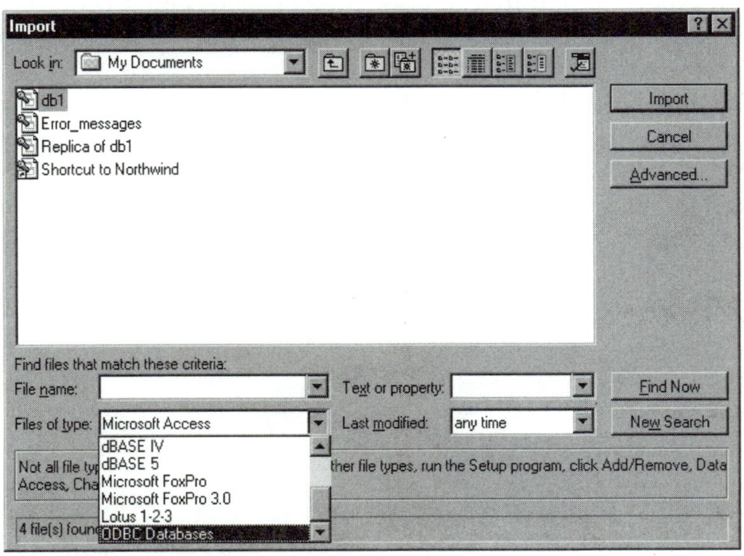

Figure 6-22: The Import dialog.

After specifying the data source and your SQL Server credentials, use the Import Objects dialog to select a table to import from the SQL Server database (Figure 6-23).

Figure 6-23: The Import Objects dialog.

Click the OK button to initiate the import operation. Based on the SQL Server table properties, Access creates a local table and copies all the data from the original SQL Server table into it.

Shortcomings of the Export/Import Functions

Access export/import functions are pretty generic and do not convey any nuances or idiosyncrasies of the source table, not even such fundamental features as primary keys, table indexes, defaults, and so on.

Consider, for example, the Authors table that we just imported from the SQL Server pubs database to our Access database. Properties of this table on the SQL Server are shown in Figure 6-24.

Notice that this table has the primary key on the au_id column and a default value of 'UNKNOWN' on the phone column. This table also has an index on the combination of the au_lname and au_fname columns. Figure 6-25 shows the design view of the same table imported to an Access database.

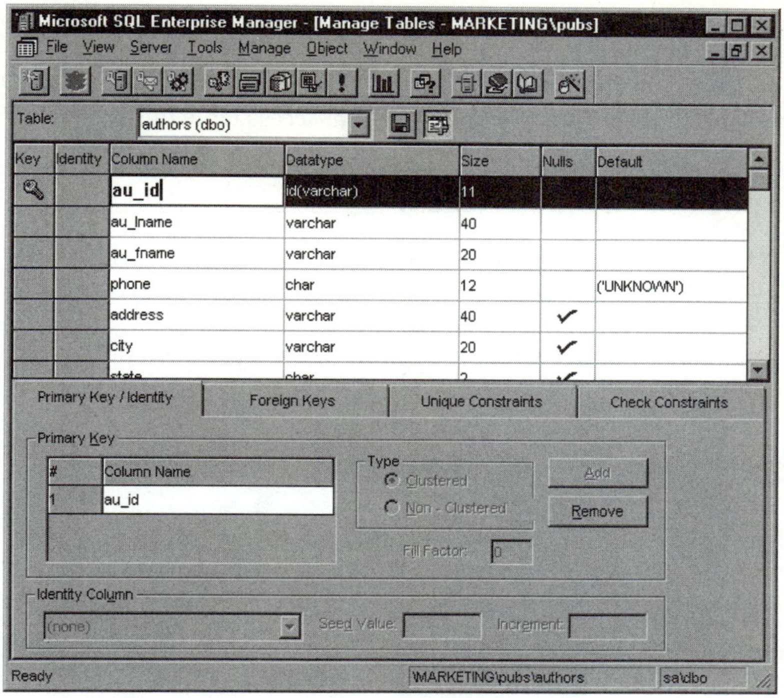

Figure 6-24: Properties of the Authors table on the SQL Server.

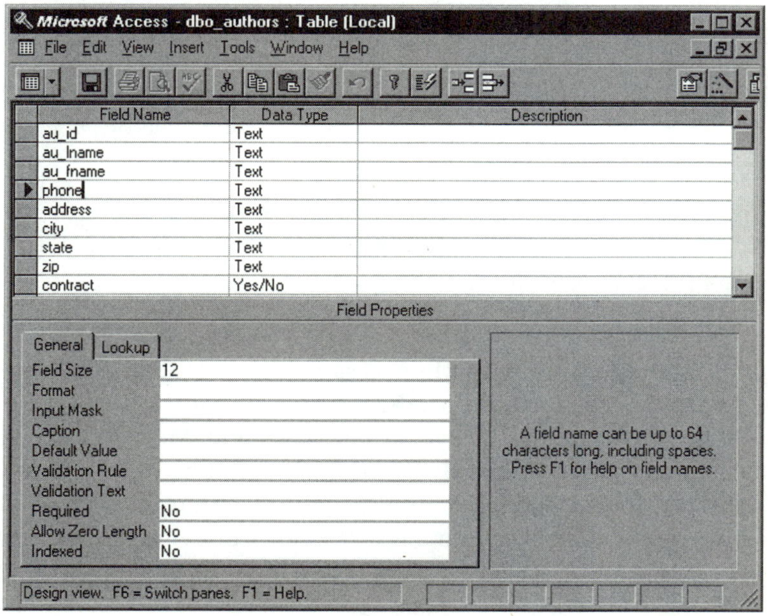

Figure 6-25: Properties of the Authors table imported to an Access database.

Note that the primary key has disappeared, the phone column does not have a default anymore, and (just take my word for it) the index has not been imported either. In the next chapter, we will show how to *link* an SQL Server table rather than import it and *upsize* an Access table rather than export it.

Replicating Data in Access

Access for Windows 95 is capable of performing its own replication functions. Access replications are performed by providing a way to create multiple copies (called *replicas*) of a local Access database (called the *Design Master*) and a way to synchronize all these copies. Access replication options are shown on Figure 6-26.

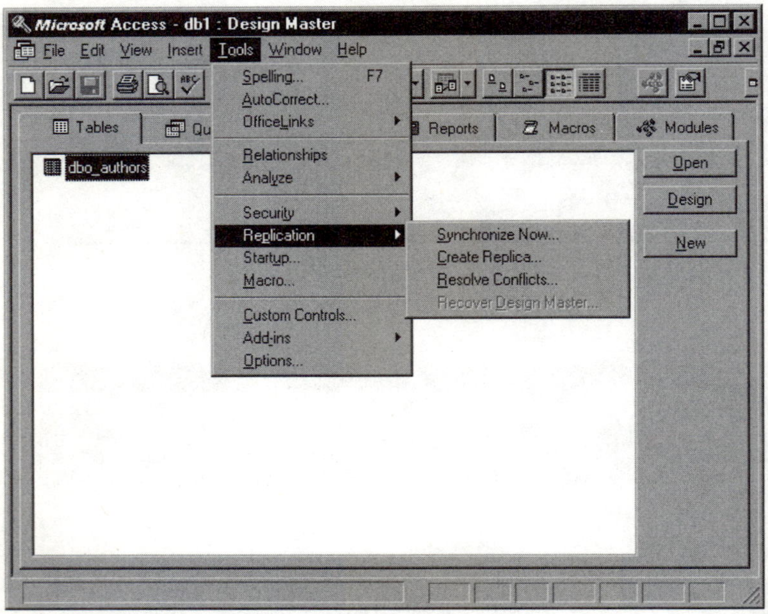

Figure 6-26: The Access Replication menu.

One of the problems with MS Access replication is that if a data element was updated in several replicas, there is no sure way to choose an update that should be propagated to the synchronized version. Microsoft Access replications use some pretty artificial algorithms to select users whose updates are abandoned. Access uses a program called the Conflict Wizard to inform these unfortunate users that their data is lost. Another obvious problem is that the synchronization of the databases is performed only periodically, so that every one of the users works pretty much in the dark, not knowing about the changes made by the others.

These imperfections are inherent flaws of the desktop/file server database architecture. They emphasize the necessity of advancing to the client/server architecture.

Moving On

The feasibility of sharing data between computing platforms in the enterprise, from a desktop PC to the corporate mainframe, is an important part of the client/server design. Although selecting the right procedures for data copying, sharing, and conversions can turn out to be quite a challenging task, there is no lack of methods and approaches. The most commonly used methods (terminal emulation, bulk copy, and replications) have been proven to work and have been successfully implemented in many companies.

Now that we know how to design the client/server's front end, to administer the back end, to evaluate and install ODBC drivers, and to populate the new client/server system with the data, it is time to combine it all. The next chapter discusses the easiest way to create a living and breathing client/server application: by upsizing an existing Access database or by linking SQL Server tables to a new application.

chapter 7

Accessing Data Using Linked Tables

As we discussed in Chapter 1, the client/server architecture requires that data reside mostly on the server and that processing be split between the front and back ends. To use a system based on the client/server model, therefore, you will by necessity have to work with back-end server data from the front-end client application. The SQL Server/Access environment provides several ways by which you can accomplish this.

You can download an SQL Server database file into Access, work with the file, and when you finish, upload the data back into SQL Server through the Import/Export utilities provided by Access, as discussed in the previous chapter. Strictly speaking, however, this is *not* a method that conforms to the client/server model, because if the database file in question is very large or shared among multiple users, this process can become quite cumbersome or even detrimental to the integrity of data in the case of updates by different users.

On the other hand, you can leave data on the server while you work with the data. You can accomplish this by doing one of the following:

- Linking SQL Server tables or views to an Access application.
- Executing stored procedures or pass-through queries on SQL Server tables.

Working with linked tables/views is the focus of this chapter, while stored procedures and pass-through queries will be covered in the next.

In Access, a linked table is in essence the representation of a foreign table, including both its structure and content, in Access format. Ideally, you can perform the same operations on a linked table as you can on local Access tables. To make such a link seem seamless to users is no trivial matter. SQL Server, for example, uses data types that are different from their Access counterparts, and SQL Server and Access each uses its own distinct method to implement relationships. A translator system must be present to make the two systems understand each other. All communication between SQL Server and Access is handled through ODBC (Open Database Connectivity, an interfacing standard described in Chapter 5). It makes, or at least attempts to make, the interface between the two systems seamless.

Of course, there are always complications when two systems converge. In the case of SQL Server and Access, linked tables are not automatically updatable, queries that function well with local tables become sluggish or even break down when run on linked tables/views, and a link needs to be refreshed under some circumstances or else an error occurs. This chapter not only provides the basics on linking tables and working with them but, more importantly, addresses these specific issues with specific solutions and advice. This chapter also discusses in detail a very useful tool that can help you convert local data into linked server data: the Upsizing Wizard.

Linking an SQL Server Table to an Access Application

One of the easiest and most intuitive ways to access data on an SQL Server is to link SQL Server tables to a front-end application such as a Microsoft Access application. Once the links have been established, the Server tables are placed in the Access database window among the local tables and, in most cases, can be used in the same fashion as the local tables: you can build forms and reports based on them; you can run queries on them; and you can add, delete, or alter data in them. Unlike an imported table, a linked table is not actually copied into the Access application; instead, the table resides on SQL Server in its original format.

Whenever you try to use the data in a linked table, Access automatically connects to SQL Server through the ODBC interface and transports data between the Access user interface and SQL Server. The table on the server can be shared among many users. Any changes made to the table by any of the users become available to all, which is very useful in a multiuser environment. There is, however, a price to pay for the increased complexity in a hybrid system: because Access and SQL Server have different data formats and consequently communicate with each other through an additional interfacing system, Access often performs more slowly when working with a linked table than with an Access table of the same content.

Linking to Other Database Programs

SQL Server is not the only system whose objects can be linked to an Access application. Objects from other types of database systems, such as Paradox, FoxPro, or dBase, or from another Access database can be also linked to an Access application. This flexibility in table linking greatly expands the capabilities of Access. In this chapter, however, linking will be discussed solely in the context of Access and SQL Server.

Linking a Table

Before you try to link an SQL Server table, make sure that you have an appropriate SQL Server Login and password that permits you to connect to the target database and at the very least select data from the target table.

To link an SQL Server table or view, open the Access application that will use the SQL table or view. While in the database window, choose File | Get External Data | Link Tables.

In the Link Table dialog, select ODBC Databases from the Files of Type list, and click the Link button (Figure 7-1).

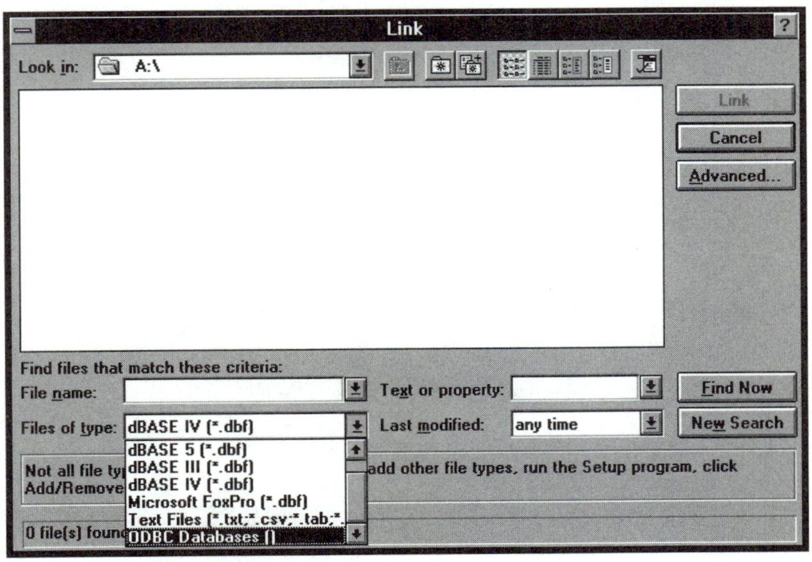

Figure 7-1: The Link Table dialog.

In the SQL Data Sources dialog that appears, select an ODBC data source that points to your SQL Server database, and then click OK (Figure 7-2).

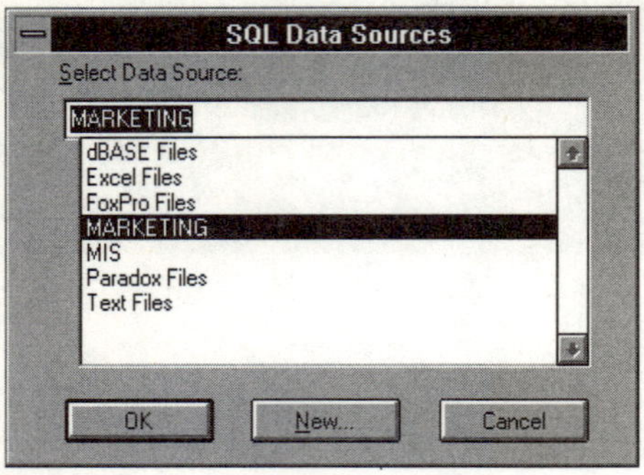

Figure 7-2: The SQL Data Sources dialog.

The SQL Server Login window opens for you to enter your SQL Server login ID and password (Figure 7-3).

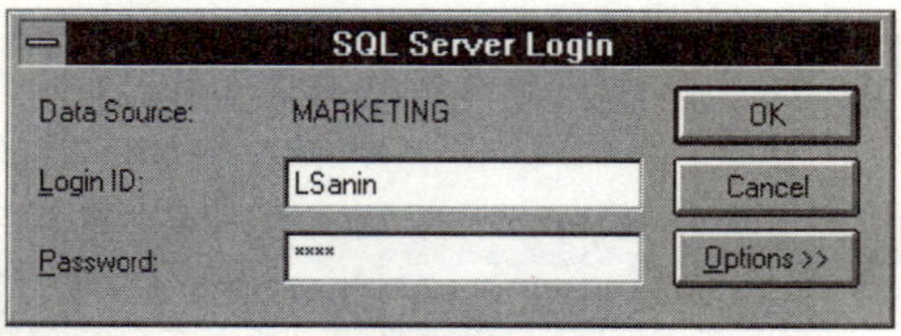

Figure 7-3: The SQL Server Login dialog.

After you log in to SQL Server, the Link Tables dialog appears, in which you can browse a list of SQL Server tables/views available to you (Figure 7-4).

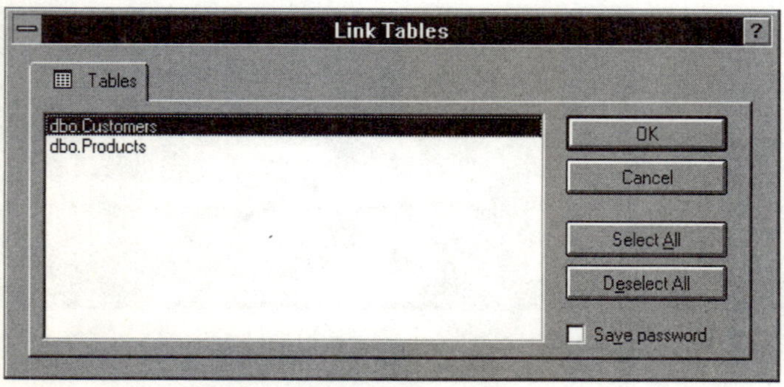

Figure 7-4: The Link Tables dialog.

Note that both tables and views are presented in the Link Tables dialog, and nothing explicitly distinguishes one from the other. You have the option of telling Access to save your login ID and password locally by selecting the Save Password check box. (Saving passwords with a linked table will be discussed in "Saving Passwords With Linked Tables" later in this chapter). Finally, select the table or view you want to link to your Access application to, and click OK.

After a table is linked, Access fetches the data definition of the table or view from SQL Server, translates it into an equivalent Access format, and then stores it locally in the database. The SQL Server table or view is now linked and appears in the database window with other tables. MS Access will automatically connect to SQL Server when you open a linked Server table. Figure 7-5 shows how the linked table looks in the database view.

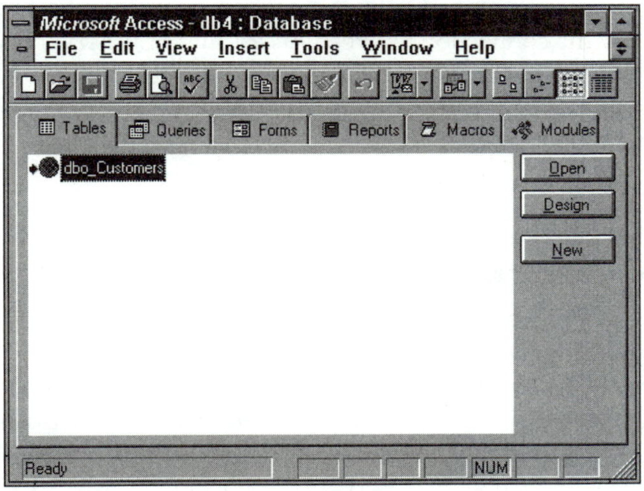

Figure 7-5: A linked table in the database view.

Naming & Deleting Linked Tables

The observant reader must have noticed that in the sample database in Figure 7-5, the prefix *dbo* is added to every SQL Server object name. This occurs because of the way SQL Server names tables/views. In Transact-SQL, the language used by SQL Server, the full name of a table/view in a database must be in the format [*Owner ID*].[*Table Name*], where [*Owner ID*] is the user ID of the owner of the table/view. In the sample database, the owner of all the linked tables/views happens to be the same as the owner of the tables/views' source database, hence the prefix *dbo* (which is short for *d*ata*b*ase *o*wner).

The period in the table name is replaced by an underscore (_) because Access does not allow a period to be a part of a name.

To remove the linked table from your database window, click on a table with the right button on your mouse, and choose Delete from the pop-up menu, or simply highlight the table, and press the Delete key. After you confirm that you really want to remove the table, Access will sever the link to the Server table without deleting the actual SQL Server table.

Saving Passwords With Linked Tables

As mentioned in the preceding section, in the process of linking a table, you have to make a decision on whether or not to store your SQL Server password locally in the ODBC connection string of the linked table in Access. In order to understand the function of the ODBC connection string, you first need to understand how the connection between Access and SQL Server is made. When an Access application is first opened, its connection to its companion SQL Server is *not* automatically established until you initiate an action, such as the following, involving SQL Server:

- Calling a table linked to the server.
- Running a pass-through query that affects data in a Server table.
- Attempting to link to a table/view residing on the Server.

Only after one of these actions is accomplished is the Access application connected to SQL Server.

As an example, let's assume that you are the designer of a database and that the first thing a user does upon opening the database is to call a query that uses a linked SQL Server table. In attempting to fetch data from SQL Server, Access will check to see if an SQL Server user ID and a password are saved locally. If you had saved your SQL Server ID and password while designing the database, Access will send them to the Server and, after authentication by the Server, receive data from the Server. If you had chosen not to save your password, Access will prompt the user of the database for a login ID and password the first time the user connects to the Server. Therefore, by saving your password with a linked table, you allow a user to use the table without ever being prompted for login information to SQL Server.

On the other hand, a user who has permission to read the data in a table can also read the table design and hence your saved SQL Server password, which can be found in the Properties window of the design view of the table (an important exception to this rule will be discussed in Chapter 10, which deals with security issues). In addition, if your login ID and password are saved with the linked table, the end user will in effect log on to SQL Server as you whenever he or she attempts to use the table and, as a result, will have the same permission on the table as you have no matter what level of permission he or she was assigned originally.

Allowing Selective Data Access

When you are developing a multiuser application in which the amount of data a user is allowed to see derives from the user's login ID, no password should be stored with any linked table or view. Take for example a company that does business in all parts of the country. The president of the company should probably be allowed to see all the data in the company's financial database. The manager of the company's northeastern region, however, can be limited to reading only those rows with a REGION value corresponding to the northeastern region.

This kind of selective data access can be implemented on either the client or server level. No matter which level your application security is based on, in order to supply different sets of data to these two different users, the application must somehow be able to distinguish the two users. It can only do this by authenticating a user's *own* password, instead of the developer's or some other user's, against his or her login ID. In this situation, no password should be stored with a linked table's ODBC string.

Preventing the Saving of SQL Passwords in Access

If you are the administrator of an SQL Server database, you may be concerned about the possibility that users can read more data from a linked SQL Server table than they are supposed to because someone else's password has been saved locally with the linked table. Fortunately, you can disallow all those using your SQL Server database to store SQL Server login IDs and passwords locally in the front-end application. This ability applies not only to Microsoft SQL Server but also to the Sybase SQL Server and Oracle database. It forces all users to enter their login IDs and passwords each time they are connected to an SQL database.

To implement this feature, you, as the SQL database administrator, must create a table called MSysConf in the SQL database to which a front-end Access application is linked. When a user connects to the SQL database, Microsoft Access looks for this table in the database and, if it finds it, queries the table. If the values in the table correctly specify that local storing of login IDs and passwords should be disabled, Microsoft Access doesn't store them locally even if the Save Login ID and Password Locally is selected. If the MSysConf table does not exist or does not specify disabling of the feature, users can store login IDs and passwords locally. The SQL database table MSysConf should have the following structure.

Column	Datatype	Nullability	Description
Config	SMALLINT	N	The number of the configuration option.
ChValue	VARCHAR(255)	Y	The text value of the configuration option.
NValue	INTEGER	Y	The value of the configuration option.
Comment	VARCHAR(255)	Y	Comment.

In order to prevent users from storing their passwords with linked tables, you should insert a row into this table with Config=101 and nValue=0. The values in the two other columns do not matter. Permissions on the MSysConf table should be set to SELECT for all the users.

Upsizing an Access Application to the Client/Server Model

It is possible that, in addition to a functioning SQL Server, you already have a working file-server application developed entirely in Microsoft Access. In this case, try to convert the application into the client/server model with SQL Server as the back-end system; it's possible that you'll see system improvements in performance, reliability, and security. First, move local tables and their associated relationships, defaults, indexes, and so on to SQL Server. Then, link the new SQL Server tables back to your Access application with their original names so that your Access queries, forms, and reports will work without any modifications.

If your Access application is not overly complex, you may be able to convert it by utilizing the Upsizing Wizard, which is a valuable add-in application for Access. The Upsizing Wizard can convert and transfer the data and data structure as well as relationships in an existing database into an SQL Server with relative ease. Let's look at the process of upsizing first, and then discuss possible problems.

Pre-Upsizing Checklist

Before we start, do remember that the Upsizing Wizard is not a part of MS Access; it has to be downloaded (or purchased) and installed in your system. You can download the wizard from the Microsoft FTP server free of charge (http://www.microsoft.com/msaccesssupport/content/97downloads.htm#97Wiz).

In addition to an existing MS Access application and SQL Server database, you will need the ODBC SQL Database driver installed on your computer. You'll also need a valid ODBC data source pointing to the SQL Server database you want to upsize your Access application to. (To learn more about ODBC drivers and Data Sources, please read Chapter 5.)

You also need an SQL Server login ID, which allows you to use your SQL database as well as sufficient permissions in that database. The Upsizing Wizard gives you the option to create a new database in the process of upsizing; if you choose to do so, you must also have CREATE DATABASE permissions on SQL Server. To create new database devices for this new database, you have to log in to SQL Server as systems administrator (login ID: sa).

As for the size of your new SQL Server database, Microsoft recommends that you take the size of the MDB file to be upsized and multiply it by two. In order to simplify the upsizing process and avoid unnecessary problems, it is advisable that you create a new SQL Server database by using an SQL Server administrative tool such as the Enterprise Manager and then upsizing an existing Access application into that database.

Upsizing a Table

Open the Access application containing the tables you want to upsize. To start the Upsizing Wizard, choose Tools | Add-ins | Upsize to SQL Server.

Selecting an SQL Server Database & the Access Tables

Select Use existing database in the first screen of the Upsizing Wizard (Figure 7-6) and then click the Next button.

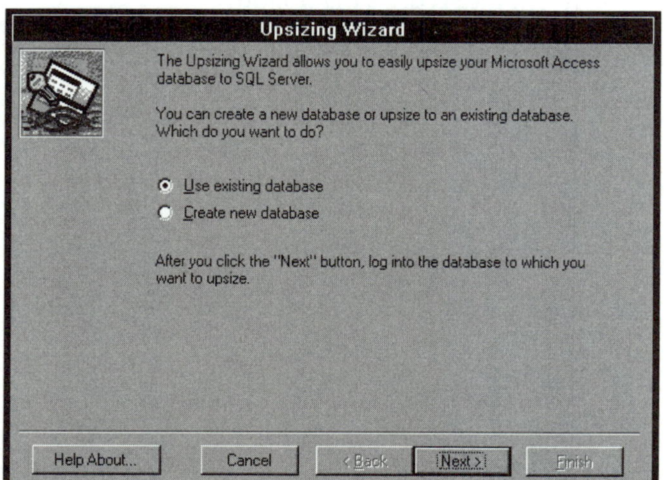

Figure 7-6: The Upsizing Wizard's New Database dialog.

The Upsizing Wizard will prompt you to select an ODBC data source and ask for your SQL Server login ID and password (similar to when you link a table—see earlier sections in this chapter).

Select the local Access table(s) to be upsized to SQL Server from the dialog shown in Figure 7-7. You can select all tables, but sometimes keeping some tables locally helps to achieve significant performance gains.

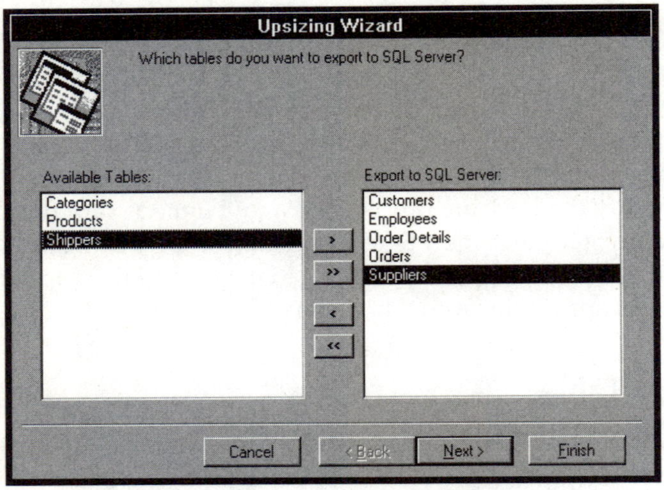

Figure 7-7: The Upsizing Wizard's Select Tables dialog.

Specifying the Upsizing Options

Specify the upsizing options in the next dialog box (Figure 7-8). The upsizing options are described in the sections that follow.

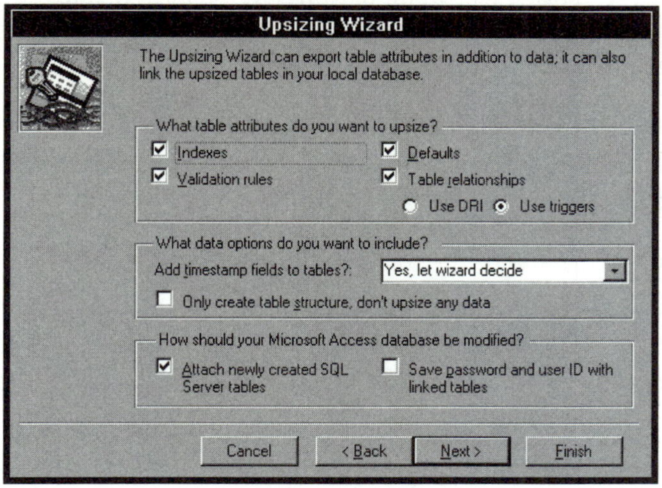

Figure 7-8: The Upsizing Wizard's Upsizing Options dialog.

Indexes

Check the Indexes box to force the Upsizing Wizard to create indexes for the upsized tables based on the indexes for the original Access tables. Each Access primary key will be translated into an SQL Server primary key, which is a unique, clustered index.

Access allows descending sort order for its indexes, but SQL Server does not. Therefore, all Access indexes with descending sort order will not be created on SQL Server.

In Access, a table can be updated without a unique index; however, after being upsized and linked, the table can no longer be updated unless it has a unique index created for it on SQL Server. This point will be elaborated on in "A Linked Table Is Not Updatable Without a Unique Index" later in this chapter.

Defaults

In Access, a default is an integral part of a table definition—you can only specify it in the design view of a table. In SQL Server, on the other hand, a default is an object that can exist independently of any table. Multiple fields in multiple SQL Server tables can efficiently point to the same default if these fields indeed share the same default value.

Check the Defaults box to force the Upsizing Wizard to create a distinct SQL Server default for every Access field that has an associated default value and bind it to the corresponding field in the upsized table even if this field happens to share the same default value with a great many other fields. Checking this box might result in the creation of a large number of defaults that could be replaced by just one.

For the default value of integer zero, however, the Upsizing Wizard will create only one default named W_ZeroDefault no matter how many fields share it or whether the Defaults check box is checked or not. Access Counter fields will have the SQL Server default UW_ZeroDefault bound to them after upsizing; Yes/No fields will automatically have a default of No.

Validation Rules

Check the Validation rules box to transform Access validation rules into SQL Server triggers, with every rule implemented through the use of one or more triggers. A trigger is a special type of stored procedure that is executed only if a specified event occurs.

An SQL Server table can have three triggers associated with it, one for each of the commands that can modify data in the table: UPDATE, INSERT, and DELETE. Each of these triggers is automatically executed when its corresponding command is carried out on the table.

To implement Access validation rules on SQL Server tables, the Upsizing Wizard uses only the UPDATE and INSERT triggers. Just remember that these triggers may also contain appropriate code to emulate the functionality of all validation rules for the same table.

Table Relationships

Relationships between tables are utilized for the sole purpose of enforcing referential integrity. After you specify the relationships between tables in the Access Relationships window, Access automatically enforces referential integrity at the database engine level; you don't have to code anything yourself (see Chapter 2 for more detail on this). SQL Server does not have that ability.

In SQL Server 4, all the referential integrity concepts have to be realized by triggers; SQL Server 6 has a new feature called Declarative Referential Integrity, or DRI (see Chapter 4). It allows you to define primary foreign keys and constraints as part of a table definition. However, DRI does not support cascading updates and deletes. The Upsizing Wizard gives you a choice of using either DRI or triggers to enforce your referential integrity elements for the upsized tables.

If you upsize to SQL Server 4, you have to use triggers, since SQL Server 4 does not support DRI. If you upsize to SQL Server 6 and choose DRI, the Upsizing Wizard will *not* upsize any cascading deletes and updates. In either case, you can safely assume that all existing Access relationships will be upsized if you choose triggers.

The following table shows how various Access features involved in implementing relationships and validation rules are implemented on SQL Server.

Microsoft Access	SQL Server 4.21	SQL Server 6.x
Database	Database	Database
Table	Table	Table
Indexes	Indexes	Indexes
Primary Keys	Nonclustered Unique Index	Nonclustered Unique Index, Primary Key
Field	Field	Field
Default	Default	Default
Table validation rule	Update and Insert triggers	Update and Insert triggers
Field validation rule	Update and Insert triggers	Update and Insert triggers
Field Required property	Update and Insert triggers	Update and Insert triggers
Relations	Update, Insert, and Delete triggers	Triggers or DRI

Timestamp Fields

If you allow the Upsizing Wizard to add timestamp fields to tables, columns of timestamp data type will be created in tables containing floating point-, memo-, or OLE-type fields. Actually, the name *timestamp* is somewhat a misnomer because a timestamp field has nothing to do with time. Every time a row is changed, this timestamp column will be updated to a new, unique, system-assigned value, which allows Access to serialize updates. The following example will illustrate the utilities of timestamp fields.

Let's assume that two users, A and B, simultaneously retrieve into Access the same row from the same SQL Server table. Now that they each have a copy of the original row, they proceed to update different fields in their respective copies. User A finishes first and then saves the updated copy into the SQL Server table. If User B then tries to save his or her own copy into the table, User A's changes will be lost. To prevent this type of conflict from happening, before Access updates any row in a table, it must first ensure that the local copy of the row is *current*, meaning that no change has been made to the original row in the table since the local copy of the row was made. If the original SQL Server table has the timestamp field, Access can accomplish this quite easily by comparing the timestamp field in the local copy against the corresponding timestamp field in the SQL Server table. If they match, then the local copy is current and can be written back into the original; if not, an error message will be given.

We recommend choosing this option in the Upsizing Wizard for two reasons:

- **It improves performance.** Updating records can be tricky in a multi-user environment. Without a timestamp field, in attempting an update on an SQL Server table, Access would have to keep an extra, exact copy of the original row in addition to the copy to be altered. Before the SQL Server table is actually updated, Access would have to compare the unaltered copy of the original row against the corresponding row in the table one field at a time for all the fields in the row. It should be clear that the presence of the timestamp field greatly facilitates the process of checking whether or not a record is current.
- **It improves reliability.** Because of their special nature, floating point-, memo-, or OLE-type fields will not be compared by Access for sameness in the process of checking whether or not records are current. This means that without a timestamp field, Access has no way to tell if any such fields are current at all and that an unintended data overwrite could result. In that respect, a timestamp field in an SQL Server table helps protect the integrity of the data in the table.

Linking Newly Created SQL Server Tables

Check the Linking newly Created SQL Server Tables box to force the Upsizing Wizard to automatically link the newly upsized SQL Server tables back to the Access application that is the source of the tables. The linked SQL Server tables will assume the names of the original local tables, and the local tables will have the suffix _local appended to their original names.

When you are done setting the options, click the Next button.

Completing the Upsizing

On the final screen (Figure 7-9) the wizard allows you to request an Upsizing Report, which gives you all the details on the upsizing process. It is a good practice to create and print this report just in case something in the upsizing process does not go as intended.

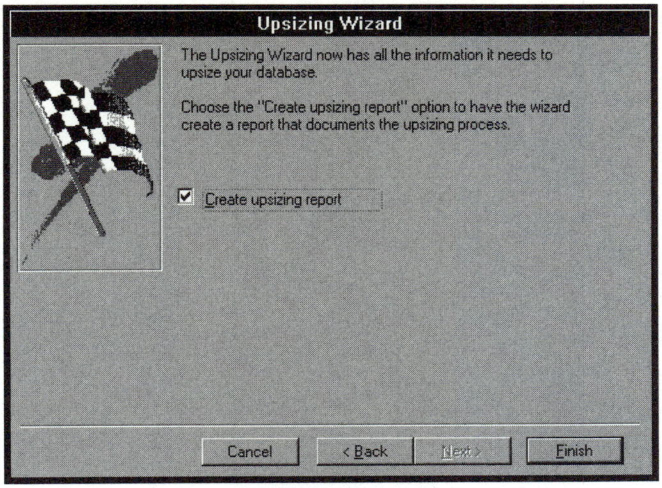

Figure 7-9: The Upsizing Wizard's final screen.

Potential Conversion Problems With Upsizing Tables

While the Upsizing Wizard makes the task of creating a client/server application much easier, incompatibilities that exist between Access and SQL Server may create some pretty tricky situations. The following sections show some potential problems that may occur when upsizing Access applications.

Data Type Conversion

Since SQL Server names its data types differently than Access does, when SQL Server tables are created, data types are translated according to the following table.

Access Data Type	SQL Server Data Type
Yes/No	bit
Number (Byte)	smallint
Number (Integer)	smallint
Number (Long Integer)	int
Number (Single)	real
Number (Double)	float
Currency	money
Date/Time	datetime
Counter	int
Text(n)	varchar(n)
Memo	text
OLE Object	image

Field Names

When re-creating Access tables on SQL Server, the Upsizing Wizard defaults to using the field names in the original Access tables. However, not all Access field names can be used in SQL Server tables. Spaces, along with special characters other than #, $, and _, are not allowed in SQL Server and will be substituted with _. Field names that happen to match SQL Server reserved words will be appended with _. If the Upsizing Wizard does change any field names while upsizing a table, it will add the suffix _remote to the name of the linked table. Then it will create what Microsoft calls an *aliasing query*, a local Access query in which the original field names are mapped to the new SQL Server-compatible names, and give the query the original table's name so that all forms, reports, and queries to point to that aliasing query.

SQL Server Security

The Upsizing Wizard does not copy any security-related user information to SQL Server. Therefore, a user who can run your original stand-alone Access application may not be able to run the client/server version because this user may not be defined in SQL Server yet. For a user who is not yet set up to use SQL Server, your SQL Server administrator must create an SQL Server login ID, create a user ID for this login ID in the appropriate Server database, and grant all the necessary permissions to this user.

When setting up a new user on SQL Server, it is advisable to ask the user to pick the same password for the Server he or she uses for Access. If the parameter TryJetAuth in the Windows 95 Registry database is set to one or omitted, ODBC will try to use his or her Access user name and password to log in to SQL Server every time he or she attempts to connect to the server. If the user has the same login ID and password for both Access and SQL Server, then SQL Server will not prompt the user for login information at all, making the Access-SQL Server interface seem even more seamless to the user. (All this assumes that no password has been saved locally in Access for a linked table/view. See more about the TryJetAuth and other parameters in Chapter 5.)

Remember that in SQL Server you can assign SELECT, UPDATE, INSERT, and DELETE permissions (or any combinations thereof) on tables/views to a user. Generally speaking, it is a good idea to give a user the same permissions in SQL Server as in Access. Consistency can eliminate a great deal of potential confusion down the road.

Beyond the Upsizing Wizard

If your Access application is fairly simple, what has been covered so far may be all you need to create a client/server application out of your stand-alone, file-server Access application. In some cases, however, the Upsizing Wizard just creates a starting point from which you have to manually adjust, optimize, and tune your client/server application. In many cases, if you have complex Access queries that are based on the linked tables, you can significantly improve performance by creating a pass-through SQL Server query instead, which will be the subject of next chapter.

Potential Problem Areas With Linked Tables

Using linked SQL Server tables in an Access application appears to be the most convenient and intuitive way to implement the client/server architecture. On the surface, the linked tables look just like the local Access tables, so an application developer may be tempted to forget that he or she is actually dealing with a very sophisticated logical link. In the next several segments, we will show that a linked table may in fact act quite different than a local table; we will also discuss some potential pitfalls associated with the linked tables.

Idiosyncrasies of Linked Tables

Much of this chapter so far has been devoted to describing how to make linked tables behave like local tables. Now that you have your Access application linked to your SQL Server with your local tables, relationships, defaults, and so on, all successfully upsized and well tuned, you may think you can treat the linked tables as if they were Access tables. Unfortunately, it is not that simple. There are some peculiar aspects of linked tables that can sometimes cause confusion and frustration.

Some Properties of a Linked Table Cannot Be Changed

When you try to open a linked table in design view (in this case it's dbo_Customers), you receive the warning shown in Figure 7-10.

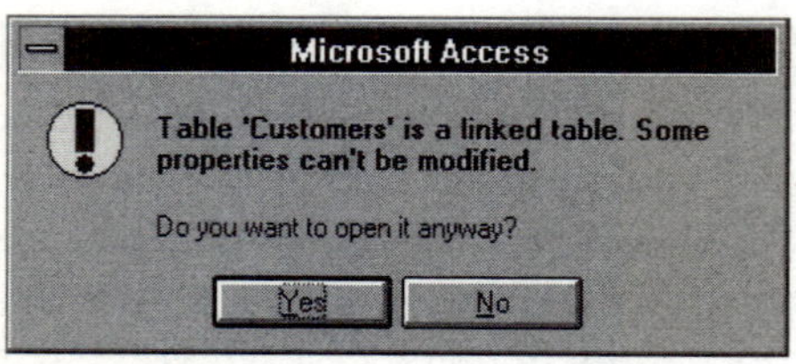

Figure 7-10: The design view linked table warning.

Click the Yes button to see the table design and it properties. You cannot change most of the properties, however. You cannot delete or change:

- Field names, data types, the primary key, or any single-field or multiple-field indexes.
- The ValidationRule, ValidationText, DefaultValue, Required, ZeroLengthString, and FieldSize properties.

You can change:

- A field description or table description.
- The Format, DecimalPlaces, InputMask, and Caption properties.

It makes sense that you can only change "cosmetic" properties on a linked table. Because a linked table resides on SQL Server, Access has no control over it and, moreover, does not even know if it is a table or a view. Access only keeps the linked table's properties in the MDB file and does not automatically detect changes that have been made to the table structure on SQL Server. That is why you have to sometimes to refresh attachment links (more on this later in the chapter).

One additional property that you can (and sometimes need to) change using Access Basic is the ODBC connection string. It looks something like this:

ODBC;DSN=MARKETING_TEST; APP=Microsoft Access;
DATABASE=MARKETING_WAREHOUSE; TABLE=dbo.Customers

The connection string specifies where and how to look for a table. In this case, using ODBC as the interface, go to the ODBC data source MARKETING_TEST in SQL Server database MARKETING_TEST, and link to the table named CUSTOMERS owned by user dbo. When it is time for your application to be rolled into a production environment (as opposed to a test environment used for development), you may have to go through every linked table's ODBC connection string and change the database name to that of your production database (for example, MARKETING_TEST), and you may have to change the ODBC data source name to, say, MARKETING. The following Visual Basic code automatically makes all linked ODBC tables and pass-through queries point to the database MARKETING_WAREHOUSE:

```
Function point_to_MARKETING_WAREHOUSE ()
On Error GoTo Err_point_to_MARKETING_WAREHOUSE
Dim MyDB As Database
Dim I As Integer
   Set MyDB = DBEngine(0)(0)
'The block below goes through all the TableDef objects in the
'TableDefs collection, makes all the linked ODBC tables
'point to the database MARKETING_WAREHOUSE, and then refreshes all the
'attachments for them:
   For I = 0 To MyDB.TableDefs.Count - 1
      If Left(MyDB.TableDefs(I).Connect, 4) = "ODBC" Then
         MyDB.TableDefs(I).Connect = "ODBC;DSN=MARKETING;APP=Microsoft
Access;LANGUAGE=us_english;DATABASE= MARKETING_WAREHOUSE"
         MyDB.TableDefs(I).RefreshLink
      End If
```

```
   Next I
'The block below goes through all the QueryDef objects in the
'QueryDefs collection, makes all the ODBC passthrough queries point
'to MARKETING_WAREHOUSE:
   For I = 0 To MyDB.QueryDefs.Count - 1
      If Left(MyDB.QueryDefs(I).Connect, 4) = "ODBC" Then
         MyDB.QueryDefs(I).Connect = "ODBC;DSN=MARKETING;APP=Microsoft ø
            Access;LANGUAGE=us_english;DATABASE= MARKETING_WAREHOUSE"
      End If
   Next I
Exit_point_to_MARKETING_WAREHOUSE:
    Exit Function
Err_point_to_MARKETING_WAREHOUSE:
    MsgBox Error$
    Resume Exit_point_to MARKETING_WAREHOUSE
End Function
```

Assuming that the SQL Server database MARKETING_WAREHOUSE already contains the same tables and stored procedures to be used by the front-end Access application as MARKETING_TEST, then running the preceding function alone will be sufficient to switch your application into the production environment.

A Linked Table Is Not Updatable Without a Unique Index

Yes, this is how Jet database engine works, and here is why. Before it does anything with a table—be it a select, insert, update, or delete operation—Access must first create a record set of the table. There are three kinds of record sets: dynaset, table, and snap-shot, only the first two of which are updatable sets, and only the dynaset and snap-shot records can be created on a linked table. Therefore, Access can only use a dynaset for updating a linked table. In order to create a dynaset, the Jet database engine needs a unique index on a linked table.

Once the unique index has been established on the table, a dynaset of the table can be generated that consists of the key columns in a table; the non-key columns are fetched in when necessary. If a table you are linking does not have a unique index, Access will prompt you to specify the set of columns that would constitute a unique index (Figure 7-11).

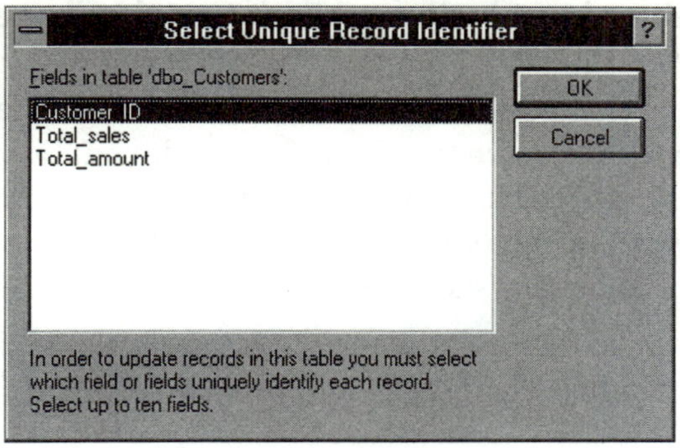

Figure 7-11: The Select Unique Record Identifier dialog.

Highlight columns that you would like to use as a unique index, and click the OK button. Do not select anything, and click the OK button to use a table in the Read Only mode. You can always build a unique index on this table later, as explained in the next paragraph.

Although indexes were listed as one of the properties of a linked table that you cannot change, there is a trick that allows you to build an Access index on a linked SQL Server table. You have to create an action query that executes the CREATE UNIQUE INDEX statement. For example, the query

```
CREATE UNIQUE INDEX index01 ON Employees (SSN)
```

defines a unique index called index01 on the SSN column of the Employees table. Of course, in order to create a unique index, the values in the indexed field or fields must be unique. One major shortcoming of such an index is that it cannot accurately reflect the changing values in a table; if the table is updated by some means other than your Access application (remember that the table still resides on SQL Server and may be accessible to many users), your Access index will not be automatically adjusted and hence will become outdated with respect the to the SQL Server table. Therefore, you will have to rebuild this index as often as possible. To remove this index, execute an action query again, this time with the DROP INDEX statement:

```
DROP INDEX index01 ON Employees
```

Links to SQL Server Tables Must be Refreshed if Certain Changes are Made to the Tables

What happens if someone changes the structure of an SQL Server table linked to your Access application? You have to refresh the attachment link. In other words, you have to ask Access to reexamine the SQL Server table/view and refresh all the properties on the linked table. When the following changes are made, the links will have to be refreshed:

- Actual changes made to the underlying SQL Server table (such as new columns; deleted columns; changes in column name, size, or format; or NULLability).
- Changes involving the table's indexes, such as altering the definition of an index, adding new indexes, or deleting indexes.

Furthermore, from our experience, there are sporadic occasions on which all the links in your database inexplicably fail when you open your database.

Choose File | Add-ins | Linked Table Manager to manually refresh attachments to your linked tables (Figure 7-12).

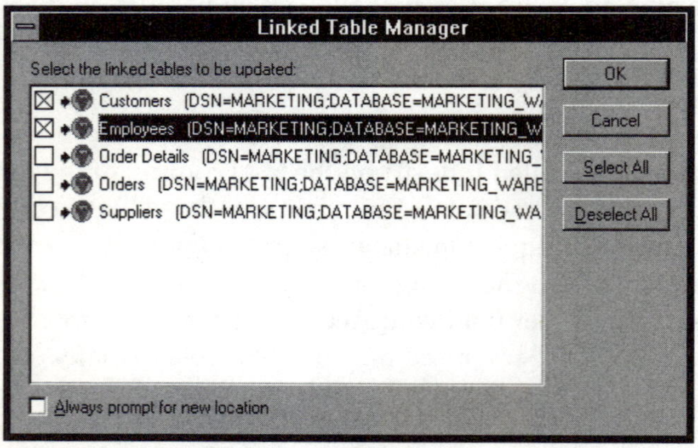

Figure 7-12: The Linked Table Manager.

After you check the tables that you would like to refresh and click OK, Access refreshes the links, and you also get a chance to specify a new location for a table (in case it has been moved to a different database or to a different SQL Server).

Another way to refresh links, though, is to write a function that is called from the error-handling routine in response to an error with an error code of 3247 and a message of "ODBC—linked table definition has changed." Here is a sample function that refreshes links to all tables with ODBC links:

```
Function refresh_links ()
On Error GoTo Err_refresh_links
Dim MyDB As Database
Dim MyTable As TableDef
Dim I As Integer
    Set MyDB = DBEngine(0)(0)
    For I = 0 To MyDB.TableDefs.Count - 1      'Step through all the
TableDef objects in the
 'TableDefs collection.
If Left(MyDB.TableDefs(I).Connect, 4) = "ODBC" Then           'Find linked
tables with ODBC
                 'data sources and...
   MyDB.TableDefs(I).RefreshLink
                 '...refresh their links.
          End If
    Next I
Exit_refresh_links:
    Exit Function
Err_refresh_ links:
    MsgBox Error$
    Resume Exit_refresh_links
End Function
```

Note: If you use the RefreshLink method on a linked table from another Access MDB file, all the user permissions for this table will be copied from the source database.

The Seek Method Does Not Work With Linked Tables

Access Basic provides two methods for searching for records in a table according to some criteria. One is the FindFirst method, which implements a table scan (a straightforward browsing of the table without the aid of any indexes). The other is the Seek method, which searches the table by the index to which the table's index property has been set (for details, see Appendix D, "Visual Basic Language Reference"). The Seek method is preferred because an index search is in most cases much faster than a sequential table scan.

As mentioned in "A Linked Table Is Not Updatable Without a Unique Index" earlier in this chapter, linked tables must be opened as dynaset- or snapshot-type recordset objects. Unfortunately, the Seek method can only be used on table-type recordset objects. Therefore, you cannot use the Seek method on a linked table. This is simply another price you have pay for the convenience of working with linked tables.

When Views Don't Behave Like Tables

From Access, you can link to both tables and views residing on SQL Server. Ideally, tables and views should behave the same as far as the end user is concerned; in fact, when you try to link them to an Access application, you cannot tell tables apart from views in the dialog box containing a list of all the available SQL Server tables and views. However, when you try to use the tables and views, there are some nuances between them that deserve some careful consideration.

Outer Join Errors Involving Views

Let's take a look at an example. Suppose that you have already linked an SQL Server view to an Access application and that the SQL Server view contains an outer join. Suppose further that you construct a query in Access that joins this view with another linked SQL Server table. Figure 7-13 illustrates such an Access query.

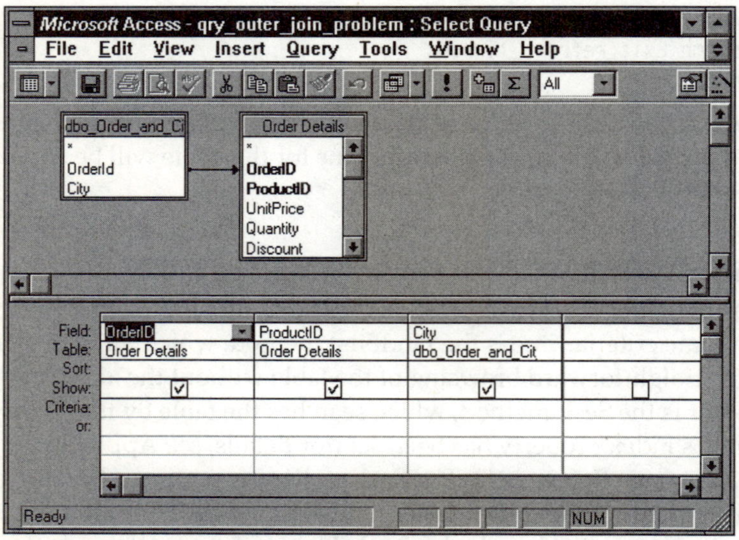

Figure 7-13: An Access query on linked tables.

The following is the SQL equivalent for this query (in Access syntax):

```
SELECT DISTINCTROW [Order_Details].OrderID, [Order_Details].ProductID,
dbo_Order_and_City.City
FROM dbo_Order_and_City LEFT JOIN [Order_Details] ON
dbo_Order_and_City.OrderId = [Order_Details].OrderID;
```

where Order_Details is the SQL Server table, and dbo_Order_and_City is the view, which is defined as:

```
CREATE VIEW Order_and_City AS
select OrderId,City
from Orders,Customers
where Orders.CustomerId*=Customers.CustomerID
```

Notice that in both the Access query and the view definition an outer join is used. Run this Access query to get the error message shown on Figure 7-14.

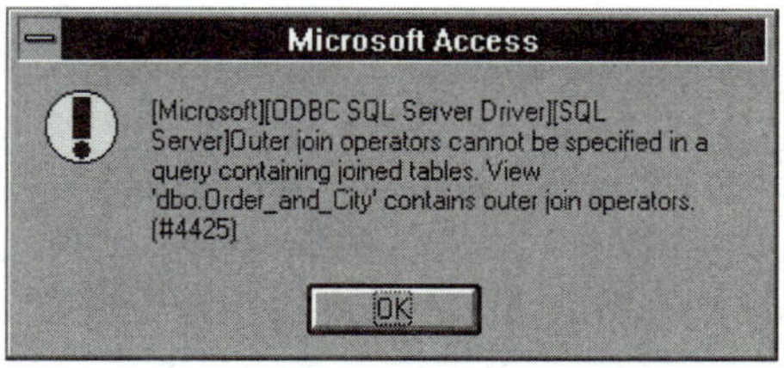

Figure 7-14: An illegal outer-join request error.

So why does this query, which looks perfectly legitimate, fail? When you try to run the query, the Jet database engine sends the query to SQL Server, which in turn combines this query with the Transact-SQL statement defining the view dbo_Test_Contract_Sites. SQL Server then creates a new query with two levels of joins, as illustrated here in Transact-SQL syntax:

```
Select O.OrderID,D.Product.ID,C.City
From Orders O,Customers C,Order_Details D
Where O.CusomerID*=C.CusomerID AND
      O.OrderID*=D.OrderID
```

Although such a join is allowed in Access, Transact-SQL for SQL Server forbids it. Hence the failed Access query.

You can circumvent this problem by using an intermediate table (possibly a temporary table) as a stager between the two joins. The most important thing to remember from this example is that a view is, after all, not a table, and that how it is defined matters in the front-end application.

Why Can't I Sort on Certain Fields?

A view can contain fields that do not exist in its underlying table(s). Take for example the Managers view defined as:

```
create view Managers as
select Last_Name,First_Name,
  Title=
case
  when Position_Code = 5 then "Dept Manager"
  when Position_Code = 6 then "Group Leader"
end
from Employees
where Position_Code = 5 or Position_Code = 6
```

The Title field in the SELECT statement does not come from the Employees table; instead, it is a literal. Go ahead and link this view to an Access application, and construct a report based on this view; then try to sort it by the Title field. You will find that Title does not appear in the Sorting And Grouping dialog box at all.

The root cause for this has to do with how Access interprets the definition of the Title field. Open Managers in design view, and notice that the definition for the Title field is memo—Access considers Title a memo field because the data type of the field is not defined in SQL Server. Since Access cannot sort on memo fields, Title does not show up in the Sorting And Grouping dialog box. If you would still like to sort by Title, you just need to run an intermediate query that converts the literal into text, for instance, with an appropriate length.

Updating Through an SQL View

One restriction on updates through SQL Server views is the rule imposed by the Transact-SQL: if a view includes columns from more than one table, only columns of one underlying table can be updated in one transaction (Figure 7-15).

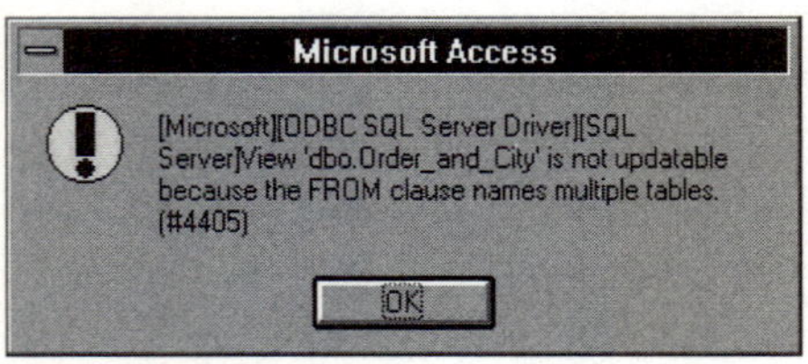

Figure 7-15: The "View is not updatable" message.

Another problem with updating through the views is that an SQL Server view just cannot have an index built on it. Every time you link a view, you find yourself in a situation described in "A Linked Table Is Not Updatable Without a Unique Index" earlier in this chapter.

Performance Problems With Linked Tables

Linked tables have unique properties. Some of them, covered in the last section, may be a little puzzling at the beginning but, once understood, will probably not hamper the normal development process. There are others, though, that can be downright frustrating at times. Some of them do not have clear and direct solutions. To understand and deal with such problems, you need some insight into the inner workings of SQL Server and Access.

Difficulties With Views Containing Queries With Complex Joins

Let's suppose that you have an SQL Server table, used by an HMO, that contains information for its patients and is defined as follows:

```
CREATE TABLE PATIENT_MEDICAL_RECORD
(
PATIENT_LAST_NAME CHAR(30),
PATIENT_FIRST_NAME CHAR (30),
GENERAL_CONDITION_CODE INT,
HEART_CONDITION_CODE INT,
ALLERGY_CODE INT,
VISION_CODE INT,
HEARING_CODE INT,
MOBILITY_CODE INT,
INJURY_CODE INT,
INSURANCE_CODE INT,
HOSPITAL_ID INT,
HOSPITAL_ROOM_TYPE_CODE INT,
PHYSICIAN_ID INT,
SURGEON_ID INT
)
```

The first two columns of the table contain actual patient names, while the rest are merely codes that represent information about the patients. An arbitrary row in the table may look like this:

```
SMITH   JOHN   2   3   1   2   4   2   1   6   3   4   2  4
```

where the numbers are references (foreign keys) to other tables. The meanings of the reference codes are defined in other tables. For example, the HOSPITAL_ID code could be found in the HOSPITALS table, which contains the fields:

```
HOSPITAL_ID
HOSPITAL_NAME
HOSPITAL_ADDRESSB
```

and the SURGEON_ID field could be traced to the SURGEONS table, which consists of the fields:

```
SURGEON_ID
SURGEON_LAST_NAME
SURGEON_FIRST_NAME
SURGEON_SPECIALTY
SURGEON_PAGER_NUMBER
```

and so on.

Let us suppose now that you want to create a report in Access that shows a patient's record. Obviously you would like to see all the reference numbers resolved to something more meaningful so that the record for John Smith will show:

"SMITH" "JOHN" "STABLE" "SATISFACTORY" "NONE" "NORMAL" "NORMAL" "LIMITED" "NONE" "HMO BLUE" "CITY HOSPITAL" "SEMI-PRIVATE" "GEORGE BROWN JR." "NONE"

In order to generate this row, you could create a view that looks like this:

```
CREATE VIEW PATIENT_MEDICAL_RECORD_VIEW AS
SELECT
PATIENT_LAST_NAME,
PATIENT_FIRST_NAME,
GENERAL_CONDITION_NAME,
HEART_CONDITION_NAME,
ALLERGY_NAME,
VISION_NAME,
HEARING_NAME,
MOBILITY_NAME,
INJURY_NAME,
INSURANCE_NAME,
HOSPITAL_NAME,
```

```
HOSPITAL_ROOM_TYPE_NAME,
PHYSICIAN_NAME,
SURGEON_NAME

FROM
PATIENT_MEDICAL_RECORD P,
GENERAL_CONDITIONS G,
HEART_CONDITIONS H,
ALLERGY_TYPES A,
VISION_CONDITIONS V,
HEARING_CONDITIONS HE,
MOBILITY_CONDITIONS M,
INJURY_TYPES I,
INSURANCES INS,
HOSPITALS HO,
HOSPITAL_ROOMS HR,
PHYSICIANS PH,
SURGEONS S
WHERE
P.GENERAL_CONDITION_CODE *= G.GENERAL_CONDITION_CODE
AND P.HEART_CONDITION_CODE *= H.HEART_CONDITION_CODE
AND P.ALLERGY_CODE *= A.ALLERGY_CODE
AND P.VISION_CODE *= V.VISION_CODE
AND P.HEARING_CODE *= HE.HEARING_CODE
AND P.MOBILITY_CODE *= M.MOBILITY_CODE
AND P.INJURY_CODE *= I.INJURY_CODE
AND P.INSURANCE_CODE *= INS.INSURANCE_CODE
AND P.HOSPITAL_ID *= HO.HOSPITAL_ID
AND P.HOSPITAL_ROOM_TYPE_CODE *= HR.HOSPITAL_ROOM_TYPE_CODE
AND P.PHYSICIAN_ID *= PH.PHYSICIAN_ID
AND P.SURGEON_ID *= S.SURGEON_ID
```

Although the definition of this view may look a bit complicated, it is syntactically correct. The notation *= is the equivalent of a LEFT OUTER JOIN in Access parlance and is used to ensure that, even if some references cannot be resolved (for example, a particular value of SURGEON_ID cannot be found in the SURGEONS table), you still see the patient's record in the report.

So far so good. However, as you try to open the view, the SQL Server optimizer attempts to optimize the underlying query. Whenever the SQL Server optimizer sees several joins in a query, it tries to determine the most efficient order in which these joins can be executed. In some cases, the optimizer can greatly reduce the execution time of a complex-join query, but not in this one; the time needed for the optimizer to calculate the optimal join order far exceeds any savings in execution time that such a calculation may generate. In other words, the optimizer takes much longer to run than the query itself. How long does it take to optimize this query? About half a minute. This means that if you run a simple query on the view PATIENT_MEDICAL_RECORD_VIEW:

```
SELECT *
FROM PATIENT_MEDICAL_RECORD_VIEW
WHERE PATIENT_LAST_NAME='SMITH'
```

you will have to wait for half a minute to receive a row. This is clearly unacceptable. Fortunately, in SQL Server you can disable the SQL Server optimizer by using the SET FORCEPLAN statement. In ISQL/W, for instance, the following sequence of SQL statements:

```
SET FORCEPLAN ON
GO
SELECT *
FROM PATIENT_MEDICAL_RECORD_VIEW
WHERE PATIENT_LAST_NAME='SMITH'
GO
```

will return to you the same row within a fraction of a second (assuming that you have created an index for the PATIENT_LAST_NAME field). This code segment can be saved and executed as a stored procedure and must be run *within* SQL Server.

Unfortunately, the preceding solution cannot be applied to views once they are linked to an Access application. Link PATIENT_MEDICAL_RECORD_VIEW to an Access application, and try to obtain a certain patient's record by running a SELECT query on the view. You will discover that there is simply no provision in Access that allows you to disable the SQL Server optimizer for the view. This means that if you want a patient's record, you will have to tolerate a half-minute delay while the optimizer makes the server CPU do meaningless work. If you have a significant number of users running this application, it may eventually bring your server to its knees.

What is the solution to this problem? There is no simple solution. The best one would probably be for Microsoft to improve the optimization algorithms (and we're sure they will sooner or later). Meanwhile, we believe, Microsoft would recommend loading all those reference tables into Access and creating an Access query that joins the base SQL Server table with local Access reference tables. This will work fine except that you would have to now create a process that will reload reference tables into your Access application (or databases) when the reference tables are changed (for example, when a new doctor is hired into the system). It will also be slower than SQL Server view with SET FORCEPLAN ON and is conceptually a step back from the client/server model.

Jet Database Engine Optimizer Can Cause Problems

Jet database engine has its own cost-based optimizer. If you are running a query that joins a local table with a Server table that has only a few rows, the Jet database engine will fetch the entire Server table in and then perform the join locally. If, on the other hand, a Server table has a large amount of data in it, the Jet database engine will try to only fetch rows from that table that satisfy the join condition based on the local table.

This also may cause a problem as more and more data are accumulated in the database. When you have just finished developing an application, the SQL Server tables used in this application may not contain large amounts of data. After the application has been used for some time and the same Server tables have grown in size, the Jet database engine may suddenly elect to adopt different ways of retrieving data from the server, and you can get results you never expected. Consider the following example. Suppose you have an SQL Server table called SALES, which contains information on what type of service is being offered to the customers. It is defined as follows:

```
CREATE TABLE SALES
(
CUSTOMER_ID INT,
SALE_ID INT,
SALE_DATE DATETIME NULL
)
```

If SALE_DATE takes on the value of NULL for a certain SALE_ID, then the service with that SALE_ID is current and has not been finished. This table has an index called SALES_ARCHIVE on the CUSTOMER_ID and SALE_DATE columns.

Suppose you also have a local table called CUSTOMERS with a CUSTOMER_IDs list. Your Access application produces a report on current services offered to these customers. At the beginning, the SALES table was small, and whenever the report was to be generated, the Jet database engine would load the entire SALES table into the Access application and join it locally with the CUSTOMERS table. It worked just fine. After several month of usage, the SALES table has grown significantly, and now the Jet database engine decides to change its algorithm. Instead of loading the entire SALES table, it now sends to the server a query that might look like this:

```
SELECT SALE_ID
FROM SALES
WHERE CUSTOMER_ID = ? AND SALE_DATE IS NULL
```

and it lists all the CUSTOMER_IDs from the local CUSTOMERS table. This query, in turn, will be optimized by the server, and the SQL Server optimizer may decide to use the SALES_ARCHIVE index to retrieve data. The result may surprise you: the query will never return any data! If a column that allows NULLs is part of an index, rows that have NULL value in this column are excluded from the index, and you will never see these rows if you are searching by that index.

Tables Accessed Via Different ODBC Data Sources

Imagine that you need to execute a simple inner join on two large linked SQL Server tables. For example, let us find all the customers who have ordered more than $100,000 worth of our products. This result can be achieved by the Access query shown on Figure 7-16.

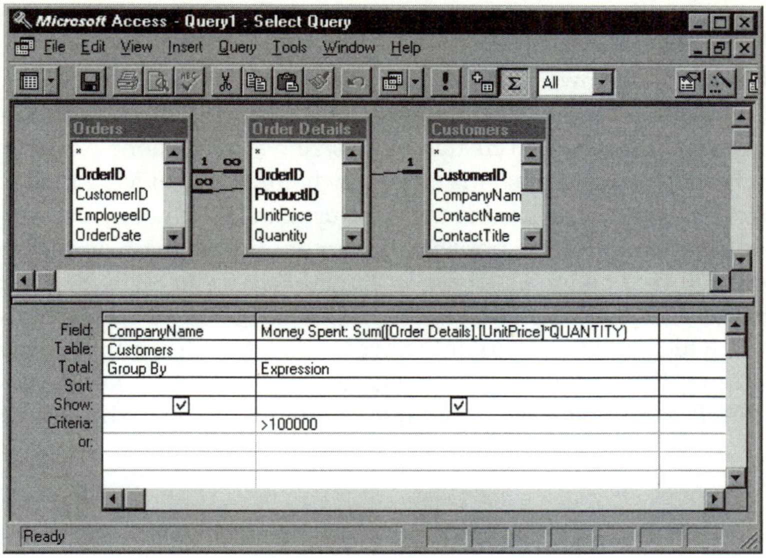

Figure 7-16: An inner join query example.

The following is the corresponding Access SQL statement for this query:

```
SELECT DISTINCTROW Customers.CompanyName,
Sum(Order_Details.UnitPrice*QUANTITY) AS [Money Spent]
FROM (Customers INNER JOIN Orders ON Customers.CustomerID =
Orders.CustomerID) INNER JOIN Order_Details ON Orders.OrderID =
Order_Details.OrderID
GROUP BY Customers.CompanyName
HAVING (((Sum(Order_Details.UnitPrice*QUANTITY))>100000));
```

If all three tables (CUSTOMERS, ORDERS, and ORDER_DETAILS) are SQL Server tables, then the Jet database engine would normally send the whole query to be executed on SQL Server. If sizes of tables involved in the join are in a range of several hundred rows, this query returns results from SQL Server in a few seconds. The picture will be quite different, however, if not all the tables are linked through the same ODBC Data Source. In this case, even if all the tables are located on the same SQL Server (although not necessarily in the same database), Access automatically decides to pull all the data from all three tables into the local machine and join it there. What a difference it makes: now the query runs for several minutes. Obviously, in a situations like this, using linked tables is not really the best possible solution.

Moving On

As this chapter shows, a simple client/server application can be created by linking SQL Server tables and building Access forms, queries, and reports upon them. It can be also created by upsizing a stand-alone Access application. The Upsizing Manager is especially helpful in achieving the latter task. However, the result of linking tables or upsizing may not be the most efficient client/server application possible. If your application has complex queries based on linked tables, Database Jet Engine will try to do its best to optimize them, but in some cases it has to fetch whole SQL Server tables and join them locally, which will most certainly have an adverse effect on performance. In most cases, these problems can be successfully resolved by using pass-through queries. Pass-through MS Access queries are discussed in the next chapter.

chapter 8

Accessing Data Using SQL Pass-Through Queries

There are two ways for Microsoft Access to dynamically access Microsoft SQL Server data. In Chapter 7, we looked at how to access SQL Server data through linked tables in Microsoft Access. This chapter will examine the other means for retrieving and manipulating SQL Server data from Access—pass-through queries.

In Access, every time you do something with a linked SQL Server table (open it in datasheet view, run a SELECT or action query on it, bring up a form or report based on it, and so on), the Microsoft Jet database engine must make data requests in the form of ODBC function calls to SQL Server. The Jet database engine plays the vital role of coordinating operations between Access and SQL Server—it interprets and compiles Access data requests (e.g., a SELECT query), translates them into Transact-SQL statements to be sent to SQL Server (remember that Transact-SQL is a flavor of SQL used by SQL Server and is slightly different than Access SQL), and optimizes the overall performance by determining which processes should take place locally in Access and which should run remotely in SQL Server.

A great strength of the Jet database engine is that it accomplishes this entire process in a transparent manner. In some situations, however, this very same transparency prevents you as a designer from uncovering nonoptimized or even incorrect operations. For example, because of the inherent and subtle differences between Transact-SQL and Access SQL, certain Access queries involving unequal joins between linked SQL Server tables may yield erroneous results. Sometimes, a seemingly innocuous query on a linked table can take an excessively long time because the query contains constructs not understood by SQL Server, which will force the Jet database engine to bring large amounts of SQL Server data to the front end. In such cases, the presence of the Jet database engine actually hinders the precision and efficiency of data operations.

Pass-through queries circumvent the Jet database engine all together. Instead of letting the Jet database engine dictate how Access data requests are to be run in SQL Server, you can send Transact-SQL commands directly to SQL Server through SQL pass-through queries. In Access, building pass-through queries is less intuitive than running queries on linked tables. However, in exchange for some loss of GUI capabilities, you gain greater control and understanding with pass-through queries.

Getting Acquainted With Pass-Through Queries

The essence of every query, conventional or pass-through, is a set of SQL statements. SQL statements instruct a database management system to perform data operations. While you are constructing an ordinary Access query graphically in the design view, Access automatically builds corresponding SQL statements in the background. If you click the SQL view of the same query, you can see these SQL statements. If you make changes directly to the SQL statements (such as adding a field to the selection list), the changes are reflected back to the graphical representation of the query. Note that the version of SQL used in Access is a "dialect" specific to Access.

Pass-through queries are similar to ordinary queries in that SQL also lies at the heart of each query. However, in the Access/SQL Server environment, pass-through queries only take Transact-SQL, which is SQL Server specific. There is no way to build a pass-through query graphically—you have to type all Transact-SQL statements in a pass-through query.

In Microsoft Access, SQL pass-through queries are a feature exclusively reserved for the purpose of remote processing. As its name suggests, a SQL pass-through query in Access passes a set of SQL commands to SQL Server (or any ODBC database server) to be executed. A pass-through query has two main components: a command string written in SQL and an ODBC connection string.

The SQL string may comprise a variety of things: it could contain one or more Transact-SQL statements (SELECT…, UPDATE…, and so on), or it may include a complex procedure involving SQL program flow-control statements (such as IF…THEN), and it could also call compiled programs residing in SQL Server called *stored procedures*.

Access uses the ODBC connection string to identify the data source to which the command string is to be sent. The connection string may also contain user login information for the designated SQL Server (or any ODBC data source).

Why Use Pass-Through Queries?

Pass-through queries perform many of the same functions as ordinary queries that are based on linked SQL Server tables. You can run most SELECT, INSERT, UPDATE, and DELETE queries on SQL Server tables by using either one of the two methods. The main difference between pass-through queries and other queries lies in whether the Jet database engine is involved.

When you run a query based on a linked SQL Server table, several complicated steps take place behind the scene:

1. The Jet database engine parses the SQL string.
2. The Jet database engine compiles the SQL string and determines which parts to send to SQL Server.
3. The Jet database engine creates a Transact-SQL command string and sends it to SQL Server.
4. SQL Server parses and compiles the Transact-SQL command string.
5. SQL Server performs the tasks specified by the command string, returning to the Jet database engine the resultant records, if any.

Pass-through queries, by contrast, contain Transact-SQL statements that are meant to be sent directly to SQL Server for processing; they don't rely on the Jet database engine to compile and interpret them. Using pass-through queries, you can accomplish the same things you can with Transact-SQL statements in utilities that allow you to access SQL Server directly (such as the Enterprise Manager), including:

- SELECT, INSERT, UPDATE, and DELETE queries on SQL Server tables.
- Calling stored procedures.
- Creating indexes on SQL Server tables.
- Performing administrative actions, such as granting/removing user permissions on SQL Server tables, views, and stored procedures.

Pass-through queries offer some advantages over ordinary queries:

- Pass-through queries can use SQL-Server-intrinsic functionality—such as stored procedures and SQL Server intrinsic functions—that have no Microsoft Access equivalent.
- Pass-through queries can log informational messages returned by SQL Server, such as warning and statistics.
- Update, delete, and append pass-through action queries are faster than action queries based on linked SQL Server tables, especially when many records are affected.

Of course, since pass-through queries are sent to SQL Server for processing, they can't use functions unique to Access or custom functions created by designers in Access. They can't operate directly on local Access tables—for example, you can't use them to perform bulk inserts from a local table into a SQL Server table.

Building Pass-Through Queries

Pass-through queries are developed in a slightly different environment than that in which ordinary Access queries are developed. Ordinary Access queries can either be built graphically in design view (Figure 8-1) or, equivalently, explicitly expressed through SQL statements in the SQL view (Figure 8-2).

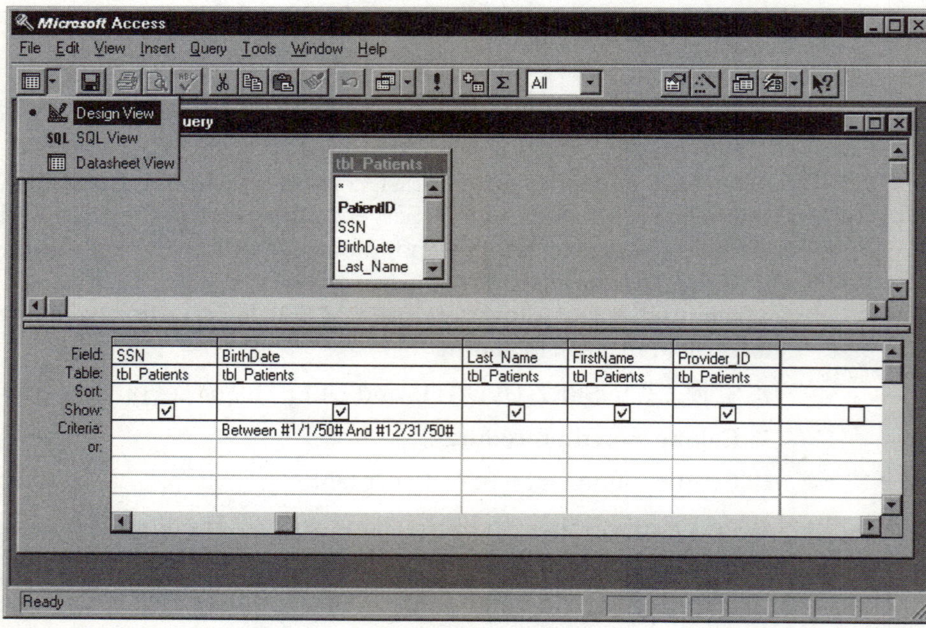

Figure 8-1: An Access query built in the design view.

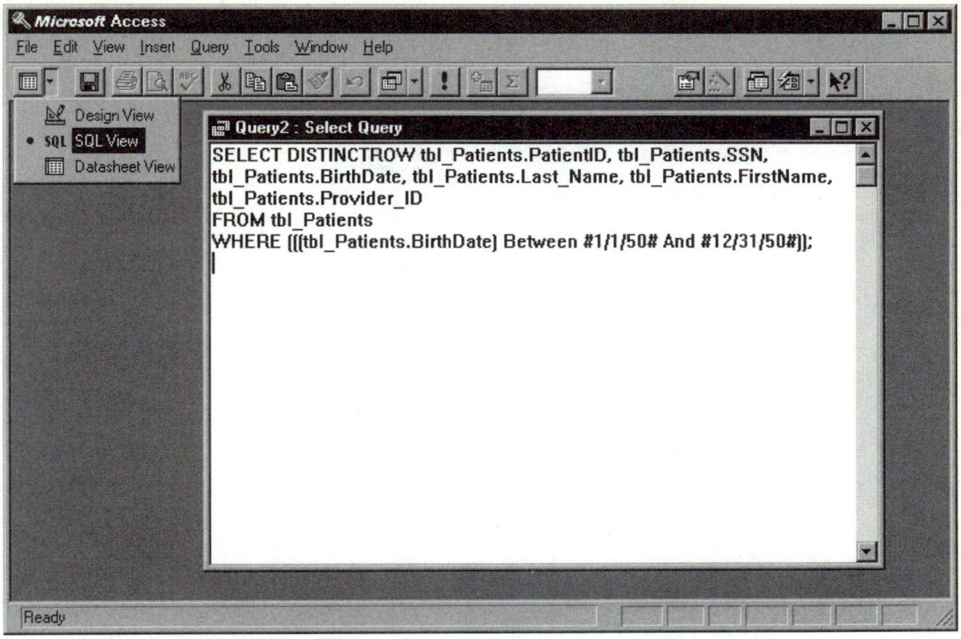

Figure 8-2: The same Access query as shown in Figure 8-1, but expressed through SQL statements in the SQL view. You can only build pass-through queries in the SQL view.

Pass-through queries, by contrast, must always be expressed in Transact-SQL in the SQL view—you can't build them graphically in the design view.

To create a new pass-through query, choose the Queries tab in the Database window, and click the New button. In the subsequent New Query window, pick Design View, and click OK (Figure 8-3).

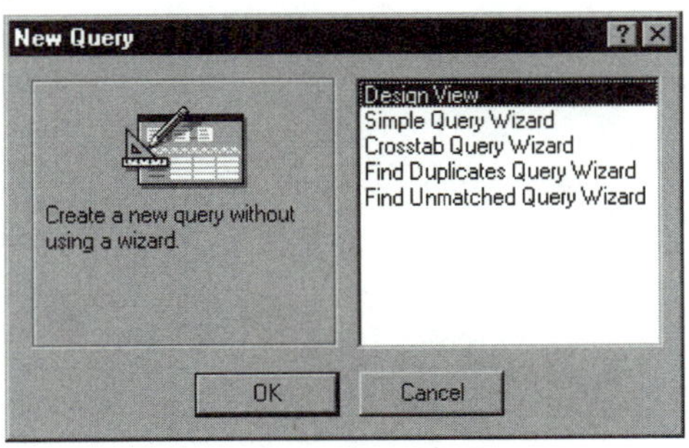

Figure 8-3: The New Query window.

When the Show Table window appears, click Close (Figure 8-4).

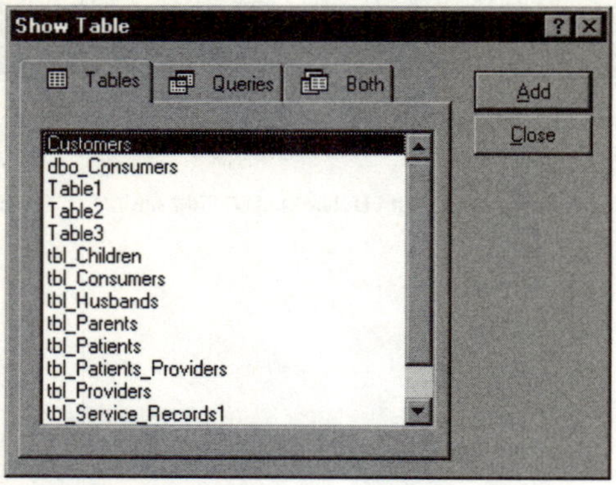

Figure 8-4: The Show Table window.

Now you are in the design view of the new query. At this point, Access still recognizes the query as an ordinary query. To specify it as a pass-through query, choose Query | SQL Specific | Pass-Through from the menu bar, and you are presented with the SQL Pass-Through Query window in the SQL view (Figure 8-5), which is where you develop your pass-through queries. Note that now you have only two possible views of the query: the SQL View and the datasheet view. The design view has been grayed-out and is no longer an option.

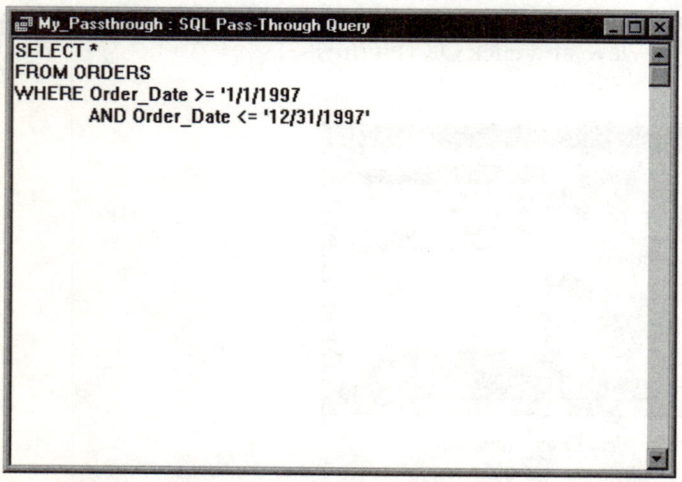

Figure 8-5: The SQL Pass-Through Query window in the SQL view.

Entering SQL Commands

The SQL Pass-Through Query window is where you type in Transact-SQL commands (Figure 8-5 shows a complete Transact-SQL statement entered in this window). You can enter SQL commands here in very much the same way you do in the Query window in the SQL Server Enterprise Manager, discussed in Chapter 4. Appendix C contains reference material on some useful Transact-SQL commands.

When you build a new pass-through query, you are creating a new QueryDef object (see Chapter 3 for a detailed discussion on data access objects and an introduction to Visual Basic). This means that pass-through queries can be created, run, and manipulated in Visual Basic. Two aspects of the SQL commands you enter are extremely important for dealing with pass-through queries in Visual Basic:

- The entire body of SQL statements constitutes one string (e.g., all the content of the SQL Pass-Through Query window in Figure 8-5 is nothing more than a text string). Even though there may be multiple lines and punctuation marks, they are all considered parts of a string because carriage returns, line feeds, and punctuation marks are nothing more than special characters.
- The SQL string in a pass-through query is a property of the query. Remember that each DAO (data access object) has associated with it a set of methods and a set of properties. A QueryDef object, which holds the definition of a query, has a property called SQL. When you enter an SQL command in the SQL Pass-Through Query window, you are actually setting the SQL property.

The first aspect allows you to build a SQL string by concatenating characters in Visual Basic. No matter how complex a query may be, you can always string together bits and pieces of its constituent SQL commands. By breaking up and reassembling SQL commands, you can insert or alter variables, constants, or even syntactic constructs, thereby creating dynamic parameter queries. Much more on this later.

The second aspect means that the content of the SQL property is what gets executed when the query is run. Therefore, in Visual Basic, you can simply set the SQL property to whatever SQL string you have concocted, and the pass-through query becomes an executable procedure. Of course, before you can send the pass-through query away for execution, you have to specify where to send it.

Specifying Query Properties

Unlike local Access queries, pass-through queries have a Properties window that demands a great deal of tweaking because it specifies where to send a pass-through query and how the query is to be run. Without proper care, many errors can originate here.

Open the Properties window of a pass-through query by clicking the Properties button in the SQL view of the query. Figure 8-6 shows the Properties window of a pass-through query.

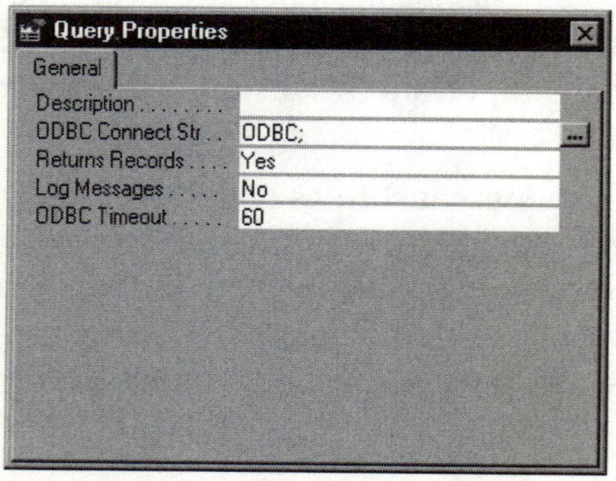

Figure 8-6: The Properties window of a pass-through query. Note that it is very different from that of an ordinary query.

Description

As discussed in Chapter 7, the Description item in the Properties window of a linked table contains the connection information for that table. This is not the case with pass-through queries. You can type in an arbitrary description for the pass-through query or simply ignore it.

ODBC Connect Str

In the ODBC Connection String field, you specify where this pass-through query is to be sent and other pertinent connection information. To do that, place the cursor anywhere in the field, and click the button to the far right of the field (the Build button, as shown in Figure 8-6). The Data Source window (Figure 8-7) pops up.

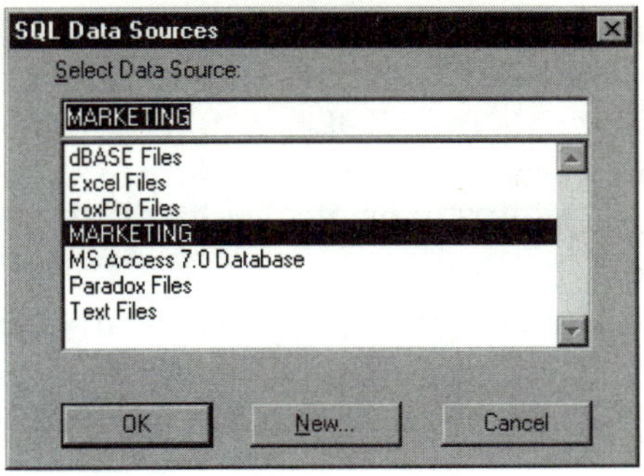

Figure 8-7: The Data Source window.

Select the appropriate data source (in this case, MARKETING), and click OK. If the data source has been set up properly, it should point to a specific SQL Server and a database within that server. Next, the SQL Server Login prompt comes up. Enter your SQL Server login ID and password.

Access then asks you whether you want to save your SQL Server username and password in the connection string.

Generally, if you want the end users of your database to access SQL Server under their own names, you shouldn't save your own SQL Server username and password in the connection string. On the other hand, you can save the SQL Server login ID and password of a user who has a special SQL Server status in the ODBC Connection String property if you want the end users of this pass-through query to have certain otherwise nongranted SQL Server permissions. Just remember that you need to prevent the end users from viewing the design of the query so that they can't see your username and password (see Chapter 10 on how to do this).

When the connection process has been completed, the ODBC Connection String field will look something like this:

```
ODBC; DSN=[data source name];UID=[SQL Server login ID];PWD=[SQL Server
password];DATABASE=[SQL Server database]
```

Of course, you can type this entire string in the ODBC Connection String field manually. When you create a pass-through query on the fly in Visual Basic, you also need to assemble the ODBC connection string without the aid of the dialog boxes by concatenating the various component pieces together in code.

Returns Records

You must specify whether your pass-through query returns any records. If the pass-through query retrieves any data from SQL Server (i.e., rows returned by the SELECT statements), then you should set this property to Yes; if you are passing only action queries (i.e., INSERT, UPDATE, or DELETE statements) to SQL Server, then set this to No.

If you set this property to Yes for an action query that returns no records, an error results when the pass-through query is run. If you set this option to No even though your pass-through query should return records, you won't get any records back.

Log Messages

Setting the Log Messages property to Yes allows you to log all messages returned from the pass-through query in a table. Messages are different from records—they may include, for example, warnings and status messages.

For example, let's say your pass-through query's Returns Records property has been set to No, and the query consists of the following Transact-SQL commands:

```
INSERT INTO TABLE_1
VALUES ('X', 'Y')
PRINT "Insertion Completed"
```

After the INSERT statement, this pass-through query returns the message "Insertion Completed." This message is placed in the [User Name]-00 table when the query is run, where [User Name] is your Access login name. If you don't see the Access login prompt, your username defaults to Admin, and the table is then Admin-00. The next time you run the same query, the message will be placed in another table, Admin-01; the time after that Admin-02; and so on.

ODBC Timeout

Sometimes a pass-through query may hang because of various factors such as network problems and locks on SQL Server tables. To prevent a pass-through query from running indefinitely, you can set its ODBC Timeout property to the amount of time beyond which you want the execution of the query to be terminated.

The number you enter for this option is in seconds. The default is 60. If you want to disable the ODBC Timeout feature (i.e., if you want a query to run indefinitely no matter how long it takes), simply set this option to 0.

Saving & Editing Pass-Through Queries

You can save a pass-through query just like any other query by choosing File | Save As/Export. If you have a new query, the Save As dialog box will allow you to save into the current database only (Figure 8-8). If you are trying to save an existing query after editing it, the Save As dialog box will give you the additional option of saving to an external database or file (Figure 8-9). Of course, you can always choose File | Save from the menu bar (Ctrl+S) to save your query in your current database.

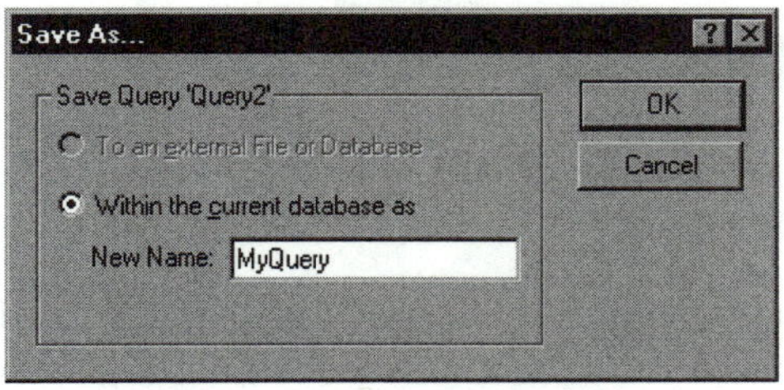

Figure 8-8: A new query can only be saved in the current database.

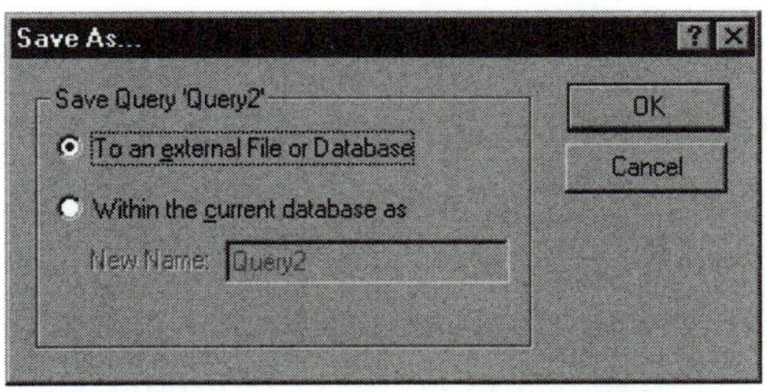

Figure 8-9: A existing query can be saved either in the current database or an outside database.

Once saved, a pass-through query will have an ODBC icon (a globe) in front of its name in the Database window, as shown in Figure 8-10. Pass-through queries that have their Returns Records property set to No have an exclamation mark between the globe icon and their names; pass-through queries that have their Returns Records property set to Yes don't have the exclamation mark.

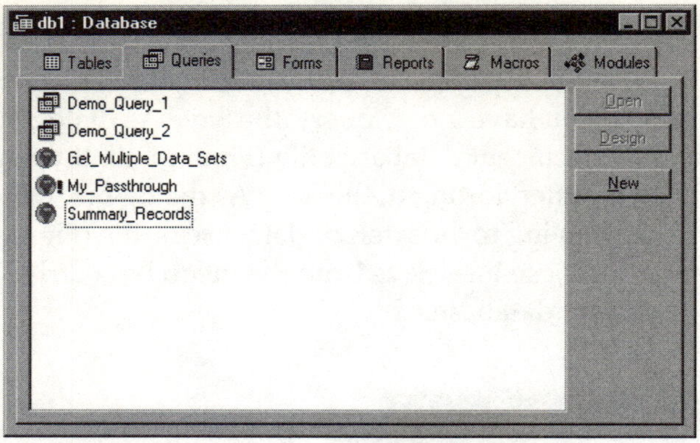

Figure 8-10: Pass-through queries have globe icons in front of them. Those that are set not to return records also have an exclamation mark next to the globe icon.

You can edit an existing pass-through query the same way you edit others: Simply choose the Queries tab in the Database window, highlight the query you want to edit, and click the Design button. You will automatically be presented with the SQL view of the query—remember that there is no design view available for a pass-through query.

Working With Stored Procedures

Using tools such as the SQL Server Enterprise Manager (discussed in Chapter 4), you can write a program in Transact-SQL, compile it, and store it in SQL Server. Such a program is called a stored procedure. Stored procedures are like DOS batch files or UNIX shell programs in that they are often used to lump multiple commands together.

Stored Procedure Examples

A stored procedure may consist of a simple SELECT query. For example, the following Transact-SQL code creates a stored procedure that returns all orders made in 1997:

```
CREATE PROCEDURE Procedure_1 As
SELECT *
FROM ORDERS
WHERE Order_Date >= '1/1/1997'
      AND Order_Date <= '12/31/1997'
```

A stored procedure can consist of multiple Transact-SQL statements. The following procedure first creates a temporary table called #MyTemp, inserts a pair of dates into the temporary table, and then returns records from a join between #MyTemp and the ORDERS table. Functionally, it does exactly the same thing as Procedure_1:

```
CREATE PROCEDURE Procedure_2 As

CREATE TABLE #MyTemp
(
Beginning_Date Datetime NOT NULL,
End_Date Datetime NOT NULL
)

INSERT INTO #MyTemp
VALUES ('1/1/1997','12/31/1997')

SELECT ORDERS.*
FROM ORDERS, #MyTemp
WHERE ORDERS.Order_Date >=
          #MyTemp.Beginning_Date
      AND
      ORDERS.Order_Date <=
          #MyTemp.End_Date
```

Note that in Transact-SQL, all tables whose names begin with # or ## are temporary tables. Temporary tables with # in their names are local tables, meaning that they are automatically dropped after a session is over. In the preceding example, the table #MyTemp exists only during the execution of the stored procedure. Temporary tables beginning with ## are global and available to all connections. A global temporary table is dropped at the end of the last session that uses the table.

A stored procedure can also take variable input parameters. The following procedure has two input variables (all variables names must begin with @ in Transact-SQL):

```
CREATE PROCEDURE Procedure_3 @Start_Date Datetime, @End_Date Datetime As

SELECT ORDERS.*
FROM ORDERS
WHERE ORDERS.Order_Date >=
          @Start_Date
      AND
      ORDERS.Order_Date <=
          @End_Date
```

When run with the two input parameters set to (1/1/1997) and (12/31/1997), this stored procedure produces the same result as Procedure_1 and Procedure_2, namely all orders made in the year 1997.

Calling Stored Procedures From Access

There is only one way to call stored procedures from Microsoft Access: by using pass-through queries. The idea is to embed stored procedure names into the SQL command string of a pass-through query. When the SQL string is sent to a SQL Server database, the stored procedure is executed.

To build a pass-through query that calls a stored procedure, go to the Pass-Through Query window as described earlier. Then instead of entering Transact-SQL statements, simply use the keyword EXECUTE to call stored procedures. For example, Figure 8-11 shows a pass-through query that calls three stored procedures in sequence.

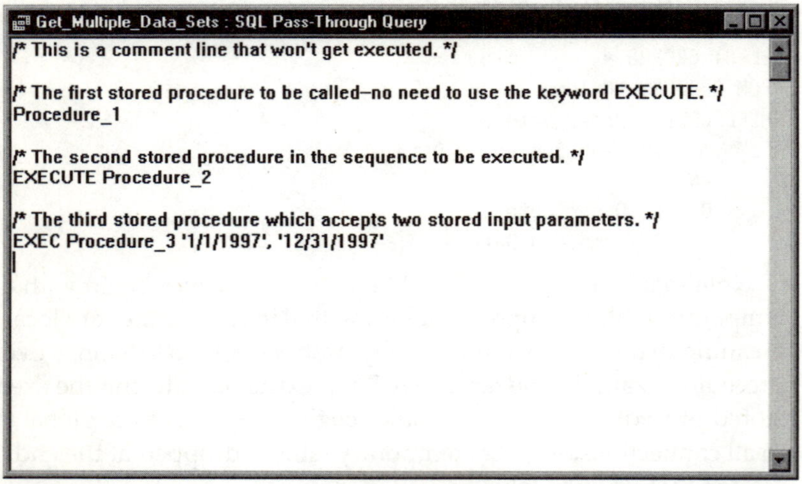

Figure 8-11: A pass-through query that calls three stored procedures.

Note that you don't have to use EXECUTE for the first stored procedure in a sequence of stored procedures or on a single stored procedure. You may also shorten EXECUTE to EXEC. After completing the SQL Server string, you need to go through the items in the Properties window to set the connection string and other properties.

The last stored procedure called in Figure 8-11 accepts two input parameters of DATETIME datatype. You can also explicitly name the parameters in the execution statement:

```
EXEC Procedure_3 @Start_Date='1/1/1997', @End_Date='12/31/1997'
```

where @Start_Date and @End_Date are names under which the input parameters were declared when the stored procedure was created.

You can also have an output parameter that is used in conjunction with a stored procedure. For example, let's say a stored procedure, My_Procedure, accepts two strings as input and returns a single three-character-long string. The following code executes My_Procedure, puts the result in a variable called @OutputParameter, and returns the value of @OutputParameter:

```
DECLARE @OutputParameter CHAR(3)

EXEC My_Procedure 'InputString1', 'InputString2', @OutputParameter OUTPUT

SELECT @OutputParameter
```

Returning Multiple Data Sets

The pass-through query example shown in Figure 8-11 brings up an additional issue: What happens if all three stored procedures called return data and you want to see the results from all three? If you simply run the query, it will produce a datasheet view that includes only the records produced by the first stored procedure.

The only way you can see all of the returned records is to use an INSERT query in Access, which takes the result of the pass-through query and places them in local tables. The SQL view of the local query will look like this:

```
SELECT *
INTO All_Records
FROM Get_Multiple_Data_Sets
```

where Get_Multiple_Data_Sets is the pass-through query that returns several sets of data. When run, this table places the three result sets in three tables: All_Records, All_Records1, and All_Records2, where the numbering of the tables is done automatically by Access. You have to use * because each resultant data set may have different columns.

Processing Pass-Through Queries Dynamically

As powerful as pass-through queries are, they have one prominent weakness—they are incapable of functioning as parameter queries. If you are not yet familiar with parameter queries, Figure 8-12 shows one, where the restriction criteria on the column Customer_ID is not hard-coded when the query is created; instead, it awaits an input when the query is run.

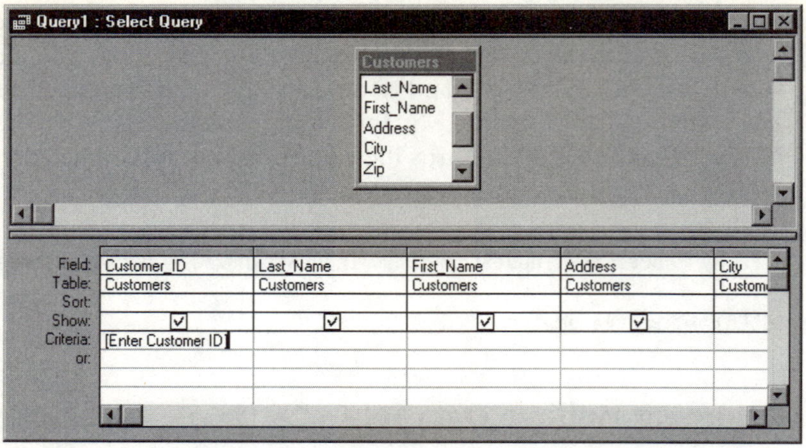

Figure 8-12: A parameter query.

When you run the query in Figure 8-12, you get a prompt box (Figure 8-13) asking you for a value to be used in the query's selection criteria. A query parameter is actually an object subordinate to a QueryDef object and is contained in the Parameters collection under a QueryDef object. Whatever you put between the square brackets (such as Enter Customer ID in Figure 8-12) becomes the name of the Parameter object as well as the text in the parameter prompt dialog box (the Enter Customer ID text field in Figure 8-13). You can't use periods (.) in a parameter because the name of an object can't contain periods in general.

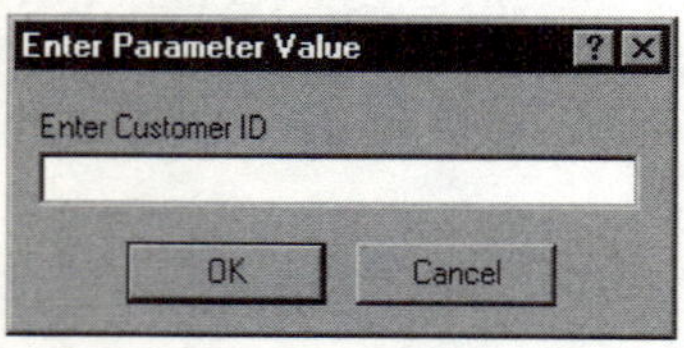

Figure 8-13: The parameter prompt box.

A pass-through query, unfortunately, is not able to prompt you for input parameters. Whatever criteria for SQL statements or input parameters for stored procedures you specify as part of the SQL command string gets sent to SQL Server and executed as is. If you want to change the criteria/input parameter, you have to alter the SQL command string itself. To do so dynamically (i.e., creating or altering queries automatically as part of a process instead of manually), you have to use Visual Basic.

Creating a Pass-Through Query in Visual Basic

The following Visual Basic procedure creates a pass-through query and then opens it in the datasheet view. The commented-out numbers at the ends of lines have been inserted for easy reference when we explain what each line does:

```
Dim MyDB As Database                          '(1)
Dim MyQuery As QueryDef                       '(2)

Set MyDB = CurrentDB()                        '(3)

Set MyQuery = MyDB.CreateQueryDef("Test")     '(4)

MyQuery.Connect = "ODBC;DSN=sql-1;UID=TESTUSER;PWD=MYSQL;DATABASE=MARKETING" '(5)

MyQuery.SQL = "SELECT * FROM Patients"        '(6)

MyQuery.ReturnsRecords = True                 '(7)

DoCmd.OpenQuery "Test"                        '(8)
```

As discussed in Chapter 3, Visual Basic deals with data and Access database objects (such as tables and queries) through DAOs (data access objects). In order for a Visual Basic procedure to be able to reference database objects, DAOs must be first defined and then mapped to actual database objects. Lines (1) and (2) in the preceding procedure declare object variables for the DAOs to be used in the procedure, and line (3) sets the database object to the currently open database.

Line (4) creates a query called "Test" and saves it. This means that if you run the procedure through line (4) and then stop, you will see an ordinary Access query icon called "Test" in the Database window, and the query will be devoid of any real content.

It is important to again distinguish between the QueryDef object MyQuery and the query Test. MyQuery is an object variable, just as x and y are variables in algebra. It's used strictly in Visual Basic code—it only exists during the execution of the procedure that references MyQuery. By contrast, Test is a saved database object. Any QueryDef object variable, including MyQuery, can be mapped to Test through the Set statement. An object variable must have a name, but you can actually create a query with no names (i.e., with a name of ""). We will return to nameless queries later.

Lines (5) through (7) set the properties of the newly created query. It is line (5) that makes it a pass-through query and specifies the connection string. Line (6) is equivalent to typing a SQL command in the SQL Pass-Through Query window, and line (7) makes sure that any valid resultant records will be returned by the query.

Line (8) runs the pass-through query Test and presents the resultant data in the datasheet view. This is the same as double-clicking a query in the Database window. So, we've duplicated the process of creating, saving, and executing a pass-through query in Visual Basic—tasks that were demonstrated in the manual mode earlier in this chapter.

Editing an Existing Pass-Through Query

The preceding example showed you how to create a new pass-through query. Suppose we now want to edit the newly created query "Test" and make it a DELETE query that clears everything from the Patients table in the same database. Here is the modified procedure:

```
Dim MyDB As Database                          '(1)

Dim MyQuery As QueryDef                       '(2)

Set MyDB = CurrentDB()                        '(3)

Set MyQuery = MyDB.QueryDefs("Test")          '(4)

MyQuery.SQL = "DELETE FROM Patients"          '(5)

MyQuery.ReturnsRecords = False                '(6)

MyQuery.Execute                               '(7)
```

Here lines (1) through (3) are identical to those in the preceding example. Since the query Test already exists in the QueryDefs collection of the database, line (4) sets MyQuery to Test instead of creating a new QueryDef object. Lines (5) and (6) change the properties of the query accordingly.

In this context, line (7) is equivalent to:

```
DoCmd.OpenQuery "Test"
```

which simply runs the action query "Test". We specifically point out the Execute method because it can only be used with a QueryDef object that has been defined as an action query. Also, when a nameless query is created on the fly, the Execute method will come in handy.

Dealing With Access-Defined Properties

The Log Messages property of a pass-through query is an Access-defined property and not a Jet-Database-Engine-defined property (see Chapter 3 for details on the distinctions). As a result, in Visual Basic you can't refer to the Log Messages property of a QueryDef object as:

```
[QueryDef Name].Logmessages
```

which is the format reserved for Jet-Database-Engine-defined properties. Instead, because this property belongs in the Properties collection (which is in turn contained in the QueryDef object), you must explicitly refer to the Properties collection of the QueryDef object when you want to reference the Log Messages property. The fastest way to refer to this property is as follows:

```
[QueryDef Name].Properties!Logmessages
```

You can also use the following, slightly slower syntax:

```
[QueryDef Name].Properties("Logmessages")
```

If a pass-through query already exists in a database, you can refer to the Log Messages property using the preceding method. However, if you are creating a pass-through query on the fly in Visual Basic code, before you can reference its Log Messages property for the first time, you must first create it using the CreateProperty method of the QueryDef object. The following Visual Basic code segment initiates the Log Messages property of a QueryDef object (named ExampleQueryDef) to No, and then adds it to the Properties collection of the QueryDef object:

```
Dim MyDB As Database
Dim MyQuery As QueryDef
Dim MyProperty As Property

Set MyDB = CurrentDB()
Set MyQuery = CurrentDB.CreateQueryDef("NewQuery")
Set MyProperty = MyQuery.CreateProperty("logmessages", db_boolean, False)
MyQuery.Properties.Append MyProperty
```

Once this procedure is run, you can proceed to reference the Log Messages property of the query NewQuery. For example, you can change the value of this property with statements like the following:

```
MyQuery.Properties("logmessages") = True
```

Passing Parameters to Pass-Through Queries

As discussed earlier, pass-through queries themselves do not have the capability to prompt you for parametized criteria. We will show an example here that simulates the functionality of a parameter query for a pass-through query.

Suppose there is a stored procedure on SQL Server defined as follows:

```
CREATE PROCEDURE MyProcedure @Patient_ID CHAR(8) As

SELECT Patients.*
FROM Patients
WHERE Patients.Patient_ID = @Patient_ID
```

This stored procedure takes an input parameter @Patient_ID, which is used as a selection criterion in returning records from the Patients table. We want to be able to prompt the user for a patient ID and then run a pass-through query that calls MyProcedure with the user-input patient ID as the input parameter.

The first step is to create and save a pass-through query, call_myprocedure. Then build the connection string, and set the Returns Records property to Yes. Leave the SQL string empty.

The next step is to create an unbound form that looks and functions more or less like the parameter query prompt in Figure 8-13. Such a form is shown in Figure 8-14. The unbound text box in the form is called Input_Parameter.

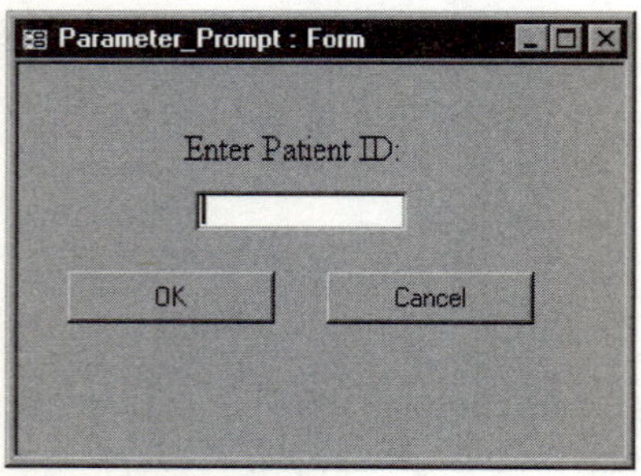

Figure 8-14: The parameter prompt form.

To make it look like a plain prompt box, disable all scroll bars, navigation buttons, and record selectors—you won't need them. You may also want to make it a pop-up window (always stays on top of other Access windows) and modal (has the focus until closed). See Figure 8-15 for the properties setup of the form.

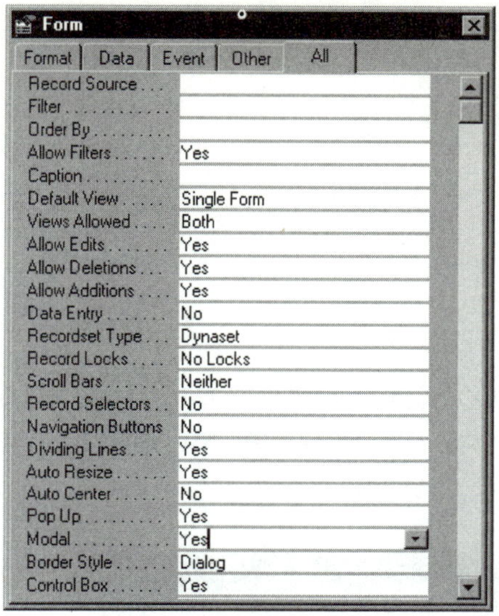

Figure 8-15: The properties setup for the parameter prompt form.

Next, in the design view of the form, bring up the Properties sheet for the OK button. Scroll down the list, place the cursor in the On Click event field (Figure 8-16), and click the Build button at the extreme right of the field.

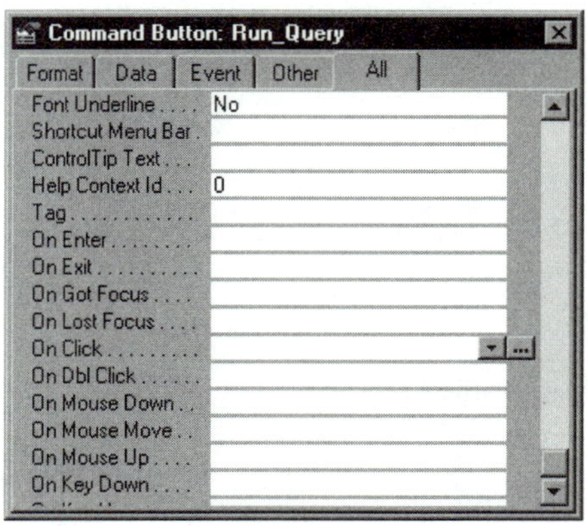

Figure 8-16: The On Click event.

In the subsequent Choose Builder window (Figure 8-17), highlight Code Builder, and click OK.

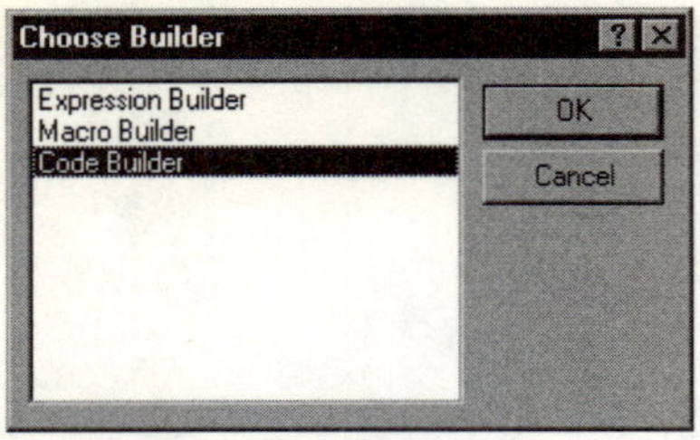

Figure 8-17: The Choose Builder window.

And now you are in the Module window (Figure 8-18). Note that since the button has been named Run_Query, Access automatically names the event procedure Run_Query_Click.

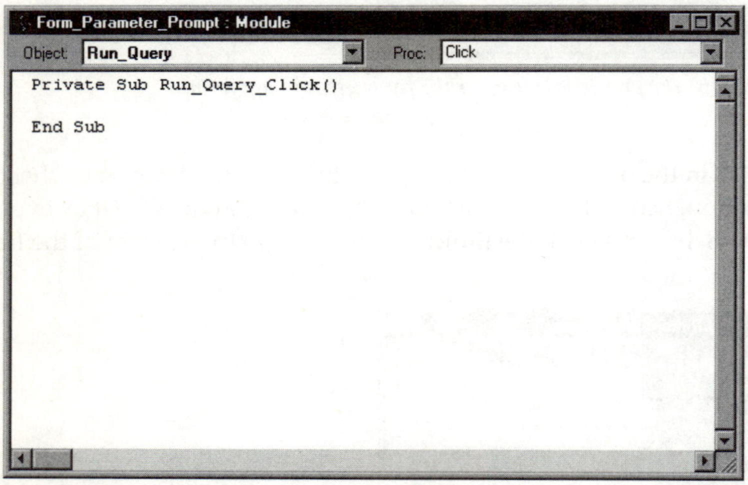

Figure 8-18: The Module window.

In the Module window, enter the following code for the Run_Query_Click procedure:

```
Dim MyDB As Database
Dim MyQuery As QueryDef

Set MyDB = CurrentDB()

Set MyQuery = MyDB.QueryDefs("call_myprocedure")

MyQuery.SQL = "EXEC MyProcedure '" & Me![Input_Parameter] & "'"

DoCmd.OpenQuery "call_myprocedure"
```

The second last line is the key. The idea here is to set the SQL string of the existing query to look something like this:

```
EXEC MyProcedure 'ABCDEFG8'
```

The double quotes and the & operator together help to construct such a string based on the content of the Input_Parameter field in the query prompt form.

So every time you enter a new value in the query prompt form and click OK, the call_myprocedure pass-through query is automatically modified according to the input parameter. With the pass-through query thus altered and, more importantly, saved, you can base queries, reports, and forms on this stored procedure.

Nameless Queries

There is a problem with the preceding method: it requires modifying an existing query and saving the changes. In a multiuser environment, this could lead to conflicts. The following procedure (in place of the preceding) shows how to build a nameless query to avoid the problem:

```
Dim MyDB As Database
Dim MyQuery As QueryDef

Set MyDB = CurrentDB()

Set MyQuery = MyDB.CreateQueryDef("")

MyQuery.Connect = "ODBC;DSN=sql-1;UID=TESTUSER;PWD=MYSQL;DATABASE=MARKETING"

MyQuery.SQL = "EXEC MyProcedure '" & Me![Input_Parameter] & "'"

MyQuery.ReturnsRecords = True
```

In this case, a pass-through QueryDef object is created anew each time the procedure is run. The query is never actually saved, so the Connect and ReturnsRecords properties have to be reset each time. Now there is no longer any problem with multiple users calling the same stored procedure because there won't be any save conflicts.

The downside is that you can't directly base queries, reports, and forms on a nonexistent query. In some cases, you can work around it by using the RecordSet object; sometimes, however, you may have to revert to using named queries.

Transact-SQL vs. Access SQL

Both Transact-SQL and Access SQL conform to the American National Standards Institute's (ANSI) latest relational database language (RDL) standard. This means that they have a great deal in common and can be likened to two dialects of the same language. However, since Transact-SQL and Access SQL are independently developed variants of SQL, there are some small but important differences between them.

When you run Access queries based on linked SQL Server tables, the Jet database engine automatically maps Access SQL statements into Transact-SQL by using the ODBC application programming interface (API), and you don't actually have to write Transact-SQL statements. On the other hand, when you send passthrough queries to SQL Server, you must write all statements in Transact-SQL; otherwise, errors could result. In this section, we will discuss some of the most often encountered differences between Access SQL and Transact-SQL (see Appendix C for detailed information on Transact-SQL).

Statement Syntax

In Access SQL, the SELECT statement usually uses following syntax:

```
SELECT [ALL|DISTINCT|DISTINCTROW] field list
FROM table list
[WHERE selection criteria]
[GROUP BY list of groups]
[HAVING group selection criteria]
[ORDER BY sorting list];
```

Note the semicolon at the end of the statement. Transact-SQL doesn't use a semicolon to denote the end of a statement. This difference also applies to action query statements UPDATE, INSERT, and DELETE.

Join Operators

When two tables are joined in a query, a set of columns from the first table is compared against a corresponding set of columns from the second table. These columns are referred to as *join columns*. Joins that return only the rows whose join columns from both tables completely meet the join conditions are *equal-joins*, or *inner joins*. Joins that return all rows from one of the tables regardless of whether the rows have matching join columns in the other table are *unequal-joins*, or *outer joins*. In essence, outer joins preserve one table in a join. The other table returns values if there is a match between the join columns; otherwise, the other table returns null values.

In a query written in Access SQL, the type of join is specified by one of three join operators used in the FROM clause of the Access SQL statement:

- *Table1* INNER JOIN *Table2*. The query only returns the rows whose join columns are matched.
- *Table1* LEFT JOIN *Table2*. The query preserves all rows from *Table1*.
- *Table1* RIGHT JOIN *Table2*. The query preserves all rows from *Table2*.

In Transact-SQL for SQL Server 6.0, the type of join is specified by one of three join operators that are used in the WHERE clause of the Transact-SQL statement:

- *Table1* = *Table2*. The join only returns the rows whose join columns are matched.
- *Table1* *= *Table2*. The join preserves all rows from *Table1*.
- *Table1* =* *Table2*. The join preserves all rows from *Table2*.

In SQL Server 6.5, both sets of join operators are supported.

Functions

Access SQL and Transact-SQL each use a number of functions not supported by the other. The following are some examples of Access SQL functions that are not defined in Transact-SQL:

- The immediate-if function IIF().
- Aggregate functions such as First(), Last(), Var(), and VarP().
- The IsNull() function, which returns either TRUE or FALSE.

Below are some examples of Transact-SQL functions that are not defined in Access SQL:

- String functions such as Charindex() AND Stuff().
- The IsNull() function, which can return any value of your choice.

Keywords & Operators

Predicates and operators form an integral part of SQL statements. Access SQL and Transact-SQL interpret some of them differently.

DISTINCTROW & DISTINCT

Access SQL supports the keywords DISTINCTROW and DISTINCT, which are used with the SELECT statement. Whereas DISTINCT only applies to fields in the selection list, DISTINCTROW applies to all fields in the underlying table(s) to exclude duplicate rows in the base table(s).

Transact-SQL supports DISTINCT, but not DISTINCTROW.

BETWEEN...AND

The BETWEEN...AND operator is valid only in Access SQL. The following Access SQL statement:

```
SELECT tbl_Orders.*
FROM tbl_Orders
WHERE tbl_Orders.Quantity BETWEEN 1 AND 10
```

can be expressed in Transact-SQL as:

```
SELECT tbl_Orders.*
FROM tbl_Orders
WHERE tbl_Orders.Quantity >= 1
      AND tbl_Orders.Quantity <= 10
```

String Concatenation

In Access SQL, you can concatenate strings with the & operator. In Transact-SQL, you have to use the + operator to concatenate two strings.

Literals

In SQL code, a literal is an item that is interpreted as a value instead of a variable or expression. In some cases, special characters are needed to delimit literals. The table below compares literal delimiters used by Access SQL against those used by Transact-SQL:

Access SQL	Transact-SQL	Data Type of Literal
" " (double quotes)	' ' (single quotes)	String
# # (pound signs)	' ' (single quotes)	Date
(nothing needed)	(nothing needed)	Numbers (integers, long integers, decimals, etc.)

Wildcard Characters

Wildcard characters are used with the LIKE keyword to substitute for any character(s) in a string. For example, the following table lists some Access SQL wildcard characters and their Transact-SQL equivalents:

Access SQL	Transact-SQL	Wildcard Meaning
?	_ (underscore)	Any single character.
*	%	Any text string of zero or more characters.
#	(no equivalent in Transact-SQL)	Any single numeral.

Moving On

Pass-through queries are another extremely important tool for client/server programming with Microsoft Access and Microsoft SQL Server. Pass-through queries allow you to interact with SQL Server more directly than working with linked tables affords. By circumventing the Jet database engine as the middle layer, you can exercise more control over how things are done behind the scenes, which may improve overall system efficiency.

To continue the discussion on efficiency, the next chapter will bring together a wide spectrum of techniques optimizing performance.

chapter 9

Optimization & Tuning

Regardless of whether you have already developed client/server applications or you are just planning to create them, it is impossible to exaggerate the importance of optimizing and tuning them. Inefficient client/server applications will cause frustration and disappointment among the users and will eventually discredit the whole idea of the client/server technology. Even if your applications are efficient enough at the moment, you still have to be aware of optimization and tuning techniques as your application's database and the number of active users grows. Ironically, the better a client/server application works, the more users it attracts, the more new and different ways of utilizing the database it spawns, and consequently, the more difficult it is to keep the response time on the expected level.

In this chapter, optimization and tuning issues are first described in general terms, broken into three main categories: performance gains that can be achieved on the client side alone, optimization and tuning of the server side exclusively, and finally, the client/server communications performance issues. The second part of this chapter introduces some practical techniques of optimization and tuning.

Client-Side Optimization Considerations

Client-side optimization and tuning includes a wide spectrum of actions—from general adjustments to the Windows 95 operating system environment to the tuning of the Jet database engine parameters.

Hardware & Operating System Tuning

Consider these techniques for your hardware and operating system:

- Close unnecessary programs in your system to free up memory; do not waste RAM on unnecessary *terminate and stay resident (TSR)* programs or a RAM drive.
- Get rid of Windows 95 wallpaper to free up memory.
- If necessary, optimize virtual memory settings in Windows 95.
- Consider upgrading your workstation by adding RAM, which improves performance in most cases.
- Take care of you hard drive by periodically checking for the bad sectors and running the defragmentation utility.

General Optimizing & Tuning of Access Applications

Consider the following techniques for Access applications:

- Copy an Access database from the network to your hard drive if you do not need to share it with other users.
- Compact your Access database regularly. Compacting reduces the size of a database, makes all data pages contiguous, and if a primary key is defined for a table, sorts it in the primary key order.
- If your local Access tables contain data that almost never change, create indexes on all the fields and field combinations that are used in queries.

The Jet Optimizer & Performance Issues

The Jet Optimizer creates the "least expensive" (the fastest) way to execute a query; it is based on the statistical information about the underlying tables and queries (e.g., the number of records in every table, table indexes, and so on). The Optimizer uses a fresh set of statistics every time a query is compiled, and a query gets compiled if its "recompile" flag has been set and this is the time for this query to run. The "recompile" flag gets set up when the query gets changed or when the database is compacted.

When you develop and debug your application, you are probably using a small set of test data—perhaps a dozen rows in every table. You then compact the database and distribute it to your production users, who are working with the real data, possibly hundreds of thousands or even millions of rows. Chances are some or all of the execution plans of your queries in the application have now become quite insufficient. Do not forget to recompile all your queries at this point, to give the Optimizer a chance to adjust the execution plans for the new set of data. Not only do you have to do it when you turn your application over to the production users, it has to be done periodically as the number of rows in your tables change or new indexes get created on the tables.

How do you recompile the queries? You can recompact the database; it will set "recompile" flags on all the queries. Note, however, that compacting a database *does not* actually recompile queries; it just sets up the flags. Queries will be *actually* recompiled as they are executed. It takes several seconds to recompile a query, so the first time a user runs the recompacted database, it may feel that it actually *slowed down*!

One of the clearest examples of the need to recompile queries is with a *select* query. When you compile a *select* query, the Optimizer chooses one of two possible strategies: to gather all the data first and then display it, or on the contrary, to start displaying the first-received rows while continuing to retrieve the data. When you develop and test your new application using the small set of data, the Optimizer will probably make a decision to use the first strategy. This decision is represented by a flag whose value will be saved with the compiled query. Later, when the application uses the real production database with possibly millions of records, the value of the saved flag will force the application to employ the same strategy and, consequently, may cause a real disaster by locking your workstation for a long time.

Visual Basic Code Optimization

Visual Basic code is stored in MDB applications either as compiled or as decompiled. An application becomes decompiled when its objects (e.g.; controls, forms, reports, or modules) are modified or created. If an application is renamed, it also becomes decompiled. This means that if you have compacted your application into a new name, the compilation status is reset to decompiled. An application runs more slowly when decompiled because every piece of the code has to be recompiled on the fly as needed. The application also uses more memory than if it was compiled because it has to load both the source code and the compiled code into memory. Decompiled applications, however, use less disk space in MDB files because the compiled code is not saved there. Use the Compile All Modules menu option under Run to compile and the Save All Modules menu option under File to save all the modules in the compiled state.

Another optimization technique for managing modules is to avoid opening too many subroutines and functions simultaneously, especially if they are located in different modules. You can usually save some memory by just rearranging your functions and subroutines between the modules more efficiently.

Optimizing Access Queries

Consider these techniques for access queries:

- Always try to index all the fields used in the query joins and restrictions, especially if tables are not heavily updatable.
- If tables do not change often, create intermediate tables and base your queries, forms, and reports on them.
- An Unmatched Query will be optimized better if designed as an outer join than if it uses NOT IN condition. For example, SELECT DISTINCTROW Categories.CategoryID, Categories.CategoryName, Categories.Description, Categories.Picture FROM Categories LEFT JOIN Products ON Categories.CategoryID = Products.CategoryID WHERE (((Products.CategoryID) Is Null));

  will perform better than:

  SELECT Categories.CategoryID, Categories.CategoryName, Categories.Description, Categories.Picture FROM Categories WHERE Categories.CategoryID NOT IN (SELECT CategoryID FROM Products)
- Do not request more information than you need; if you are using the Query Design view in Access, clear the Show check box for the fields that are only used for the selection criteria.
- Do not use GROUP BY if you do not have to; use as few fields as possible in a GROUP BY clause.
- According to Microsoft, COUNT(*) will be optimized better and will work faster that COUNT([Column Name]) if you need to determine the number of records in a table.
- Do not reserve more space for a field in a table than it needs; use the smallest data type possible. For example, use binary (as opposed to text) type if you only need to store Yes and No.
- A query will run faster if the fields used in a join have the same data types.
- Do not use ORDER BY in a query unless absolutely necessary; especially do not sort by fields without index.

Server-Side Optimization Considerations

Optimize the server side of a client/server application to achieve the most impressive performance gains. This optimization involves both technical (e.g., hardware, systems parameters) and logical (i.e., database design) aspects.

Hardware & Operating System

The most obvious approach to improving SQL Server performance is a hardware upgrade; that is, additional CPUs, more RAM, faster disk arrays, and so on.

Before buying additional hardware, use the Windows NT Performance Monitor to justify the purchase. If, for example, your average CPU utilization is 10-15 percent, adding more CPU power is not going to affect performance in any notable way.

A Windows NT server sitting on a network can be assigned functions of a primary or backup Windows NT Domain Controller. It is not recommended that you assign these functions to the Windows NT server running SQL Server DBMS. It is usually a good idea to relieve this Windows NT server from any unnecessary Windows NT administrative duties.

Use SQL Server configuration parameters to more efficiently utilize your server hardware (see Chapter 4 for more details on the SQL Server configuration parameters). Some of the most important parameters are:

- **Memory.** Specifies the memory amount allocated by Windows NT directly to SQL Server. Among other things, it determines sizes of the data cache and procedure cache. If you allocate too much memory to SQL Server, the virtual memory will be used, causing excessive paging and performance degradation.
- **SMP Concurrency.** Controls the number of CPUs dedicated to SQL Server. Set to -1 for SQL-Server-dedicated SMP support.
- **Set Working Set Size.** Forces Windows NT to allocate physical RAM to SQL Server as opposed to the virtual memory (paging file).
- **Sort Pages.** Specifies amount of memory SQL Server allocates for the sorting procedures.

For the Windows NT file system, Microsoft recommends using the NTFS file system for the SQL Server data devices and the FAT file system for the log devices.

Apply all the necessary service packs from Microsoft to your Windows NT operation system and SQL Server software (currently SP2 for Windows NT and SP2 for SQL Server 6.5).

Database Normalization

The first approach to SQL Server *database* optimization is the reasonable normalization of the logical database, which usually results in a greater number of smaller (narrower) tables. In the initial stages of a project development, it is usually possible to normalize a database by redefining tables, but it may not be a feasible option after the database implementation. At this point, some progress can usually be achieved by selectively normalizing only the large and messy tables. In some cases, table redefinition can still be disguised by creating views that look like the old tables and changing stored procedures to reflect the changes.

Some of the advantages of the database normalization are:

- The database is smaller and more compact since more normalization means less redundancy.
- Indexes are smaller, they make more sense, and more clustered indexes can be created, which makes indexing more efficient.

The greatest *disadvantage* of database normalization is that an average query has more joins, which increases complexity and slows down performance.

Microsoft recommends continuing normalization of SQL Server until the complexity of an average query exceeds four joins.

Indexes

In most cases, amazing performance gains can be achieved by creating the right indexes on tables. There is no universal rule on how to improve SQL Server performance by creating and adjusting table indexes. Many factors may affect your decision on whether to create a particular index on a particular table—among them:

- The current number of rows in a table and its estimated rate of growth.
- The number of columns in the contemplated index.
- The number of indexes that already exist on the table.
- The rate of updates, inserts, and deletes on the table.

Note, by the way, that you can create, drop, and change indexes on tables in a database without compromising the general structure of the database because the indexes are not really a part of the SQL Server data model. These are some general rules to follow:

- Try to create single-column indexes rather than multicolumn ones. When you create a multicolumn index, the effectiveness of your search is limited by the first column. For example, if you have an index on CustomerID+ CustomerCity, and your query performs a search by CustomerCity, this index is useless. In addition, SQL Server only keeps the distribution statistics on the most significant column (CustomerID in our example). See Figure 9-1 for an example of an index distribution page.

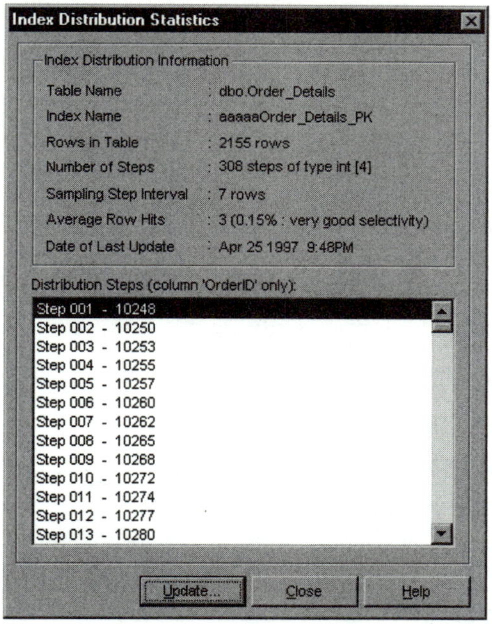

Figure 9-1: The Index Distribution Statistics window.

- Make the most important index a clustered index. The clustered index is especially helpful when a query returns a lot of rows. If an index is defined as a clustered index, then the logical order of the key values is the same as the physical order in which the corresponding rows are stored in the table. A table can contain only one clustered index.
- Examine your most typical queries, your most critical queries, and the longest running queries to determine the columns and the column combinations that are the best candidates for indexing.

- Examine distribution of the values in a column to decide if it makes sense to build an index on this column. If a column only has a few different values, your query might run faster by reading a table sequentially.
- Remember to run UPDATE STATISTICS on a table when a significant share of key values has changed. SQL Server does not automatically maintain the distribution statistics pages; these pages are created with the indexes, and if a significant part of the table's index columns has changed, they can be severely outdated. At the same time, the index distribution pages are the main source for the SQL Server Optimizer to make its decisions.

Query Design

There are some very important points to remember while designing SQL Server pass-through queries, stored procedures used in your client/server application, or even Access queries that will be eventually executed on the SQL Server by the Jet database engine via ODBC:

- Try to write your queries as simply as possible.
- Avoid queries returning large result sets.
- Avoid GROUP BY and ORDER BY.
- In the conditions of WHERE clauses, try to avoid:
  - Using IN and NOT IN conditions.
  - Using expressions, functions, and data conversions.
  - Using local variables.

Optimizing the Client/Server Aspects

Finally, let us examine the most obscure aspects of optimization and tuning: optimization of the items relating to both client and server components. The best way to optimize these items is to evaluate different methods and techniques of accessing data in the client application.

Keep Some Data Locally

Some tables contain data that do not change too often (e.g., state capitals, zip codes, and so on). Keep this data locally, especially if it is used in drop-down lists, combo boxes, subforms, and so on. Store these tables on your local hard drive (see "General Optimizing & Tuning of Access Applications" earlier in this chapter) to significantly reduce the amount of data requested from SQL Server and to decrease network traffic.

Remember that when you open a form, each list box, combo box, subform, and control containing a total requires a separate query. If the queried data is local, performance may be satisfactory; requesting this data from SQL Server, however, may cause long delays when you open a form.

Linked Tables

Most of the performance issues associated with linked tables are discussed in Chapter 7. See that chapter for more information.

One of the worst things that can happen with a query based on linked tables is that the Jet database engine decides to load large SQL Server tables to the workstation and join them locally. Remember that it will most *certainly* happen if tables in a query are linked via different ODBC data sources. Therefore, avoid using more than one ODBC data source in the same application.

Use timestamp fields in linked tables to make updating records more efficient. Timestamp fields are maintained by SQL Server, and their value is increased every time the record is updated. When a table has a timestamp field, Access needs to check only the value of this field to see whether the record has changed since it was last retrieved from the server. If a table does not have a timestamp field, Access has to check every field in the record, thus slowing performance of the UPDATE command.

Access Queries on Linked Tables

Make sure that the whole query gets sent to SQL Server for processing. The Jet database engine always tries to find a way to execute the entire query on the server. There are circumstances, however, in which the Jet database engine has no choice but to bring the raw data to the workstation and then perform operations on this data locally. These situations result in the worst performance nightmares.

Some of the circumstances that could cause this problem are:

- Mixing tables linked via different ODBC data sources in the same query.
- Mixing local and remote tables in the same query.
- Using overcomplicated queries with a lot of sub-queries.
- Using Access-specific operations that have no Transact-SQL equivalent.
- Using Visual Basic functions in a query.
- Using implicit conversions in a query (e.g., mixing text and numeric datatypes).
- Using multiple outer joins in the same query.

When a query needs to have dynamic parameters, it is usually more efficient to create a precompiled and saved query with parameters than to create a dynamic SQL query on the fly in a Visual Basic module.

Pass-Through Queries

Using pass-through queries is generally a good idea from the performance-optimization point of view.

Use SQL pass-through queries to achieve the following performance benefits:

- A pass-through query does not have to be compiled by Access.
- Often a pass-through query calls an SQL-Server-stored procedure. In this case, only the name of a stored procedure (and possibly parameters) gets transmitted over the network, thus reducing the network traffic. Also, a stored procedure is usually precompiled on the server and is kept in the procedure cache.
- A pass-through query can use Transact-SQL-specific commands and functions.
- Updates, deletes, and inserts via pass-through action queries are generally much faster than action queries based on linked tables, especially when many records are affected.

Optimizing ODBC

To tune the ODBC-related parameters of the Jet database engine on the client workstations, use the Windows 95 Registry Editor. For a more detailed description of these parameters, see Chapter 5.

The TryJetAuth parameter, for example, if set to one, forces the Jet database engine to use an Access user name and password to connect to SQL Server. If you know that in most cases Access user name and SQL Server login ID do not match, set TryJetAuth to zero so that you don't waste time on a connection that is inevitably going to fail.

You can optimize another aspect of ODBC performance by adjusting the ConnectionTimeOut parameter: increase its value or set it to zero (no timeout) to keep ODBC idle connections open and ready to be reused.

Optimizing Recordsets

Use MS Access recordsets to acquire data from SQL Server, and keep it ready in the client workstation. Optimize your recordsets by adjusting CacheSize and CacheStart properties of the recordset objects and by using the FillCache method to load data into memory. To release memory on the workstation, set the CacheSize property to zero.

When creating a recordset, do not ask for more data or more functionality than you actually need. For example, do not open a recordset as *dynaset* if you do not need to be able to update records; the *snapshot* type will work just as well, and it will take less resources. If, in addition, you only need to pass through the recordset once, consider opening it as a *Forward-Only* snapshot type to spare even more resources. Moreover, if you realize that a snapshot recordset is sufficient for your purposes, consider using a pass-through query to create it. If you do need to update or insert data, also consider using a pass-through query that calls an SQL-Server-stored procedure—not only will it work faster, it will also add security to your application. See Chapter 10 for more on security.

Create the MSysConf SQL Server table to adjust the rate of server data retrieval (also called *background population*). To achieve faster background population, adjust the values in this table to increase the number of rows of data that are retrieved at one time and to reduce the number of seconds of delays between each retrieval. Sometimes you may notice, however, that the new settings generate too much network traffic—make it lighter by slowing down the background population.

Splitting Access Databases

One of the ways to optimize performance of a large client/server application is to split an Access database into pieces. Use it to achieve some important performance benefits, including:

- Reduced network traffic.
- Better utilization of the workstation's memory by having only a small part of the application loaded at any given time.
- Greatly improved abilities to maintain, fix, and expand the application.

Two different approaches to application splitting are discussed in this section.

Splitting by Separating Tables

If your Access database contains updatable data tables (which makes it half client/server, half file/server), you can advance your applications file/server component to the more client/server-like model by *splitting* it. A split database consists of two MDB files. One database (called the back-end database) contains only the updatable tables and is usually located on a network file server. The other database (the front-end database) contains all the other database objects: queries, forms, reports, macros, modules, and, possibly, tables that do not change for the most part. The front-end database usually resides on a user's local hard drive.

Use the Database Splitter option under Tools and Add-ins to call the Database Splitting Wizard (Figure 9-2).

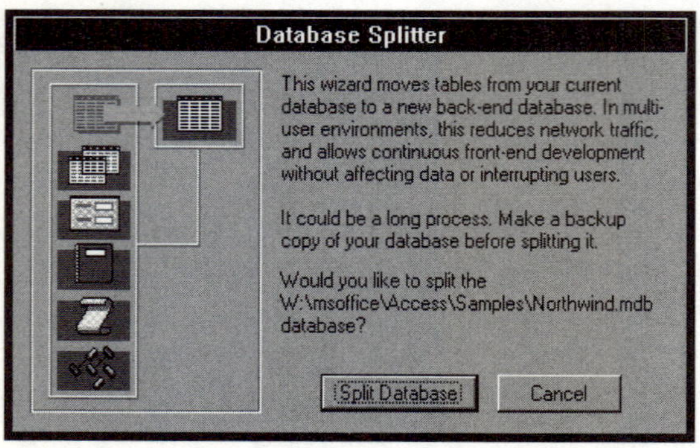

Figure 9-2: The Database Splitter's initial dialog.

Specify the back-end database name and location in the next dialog

(Figure 9-3).

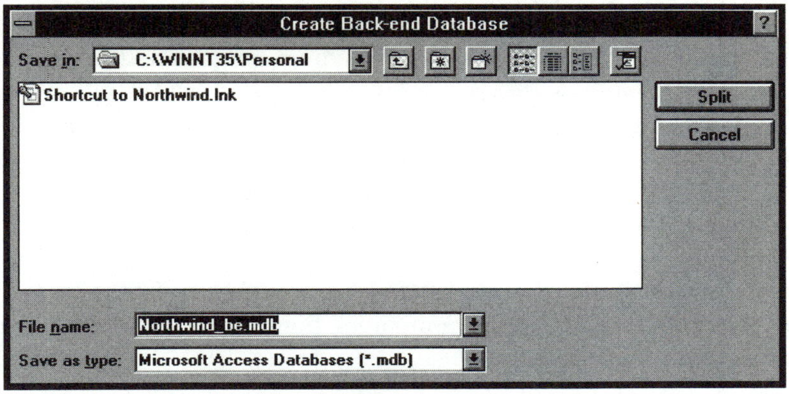

Figure 9-3: The Database Splitter's Create Back-End Database dialog.

The Database Splitting Wizard will now create a new back-end database and copy all the tables into it. The wizard then deletes tables from the original database and creates the same name links to the new back-end database. The wizard's task is now complete.

The performance advantages achieved by splitting a database include:

- Having a personal front-end database allows users to create their own custom reports and queries without affecting other users.
- Network traffic is reduced, and the database objects get loaded to memory at the workstation much faster because they are now located on the local hard disk.
- You can now update your application's objects in the front-end database without having to synchronize these changes with the data in the back-end database.

Splitting by Separating Application Functions

The Database Splitting Utility, described in the previous section, helps to separate Access tables from all the other objects. If you have a large Access database that you want to run in a client/server environment, another way of splitting your Access database is to split it into several smaller subapplication databases.

Imagine a front-end client/server Access application designed for a large group of users and consisting of several different subsystems. For example, a client/server application for a marketing department may consist of a report subsystem, a customer information subsystem, a product information subsystem, and a warehouse information subsystem. These subsystems could have been designed, developed, and supported by different programmers or even by different consulting companies. Some of the problems associated with large Access databases are:

- Trying to join all these "subapplications" together may cause problems—several of the subsystems, for example, may have a form called MENU. Of course, you can rename some of them, but then references to these forms in the Visual Basic code may become incoherent.
- Maintaining a huge application may be quite a challenge: Efforts of different groups of developers to make changes to the application have to be thoroughly synchronized to avoid confusion.
- Large numbers of Access objects (even without the data tables if split by the Database Splitting Utility) can produce a huge MDB file, which is pretty cumbersome to distribute over a network, especially if it has to be copied to every user's local hard drive (as recommended in the previous section). Incidentally, so many things can go wrong in a huge database that it may have to be fixed and redistributed quite often.

Some methods of splitting a large application into several smaller subapplications may have negative side effects, though. Access, unfortunately, does not have any conventional way of switching from one application to another, and as a result, subapplications can not be easily linked together by a connecting application (the Main Menu). This section demonstrates a method of creating such a Main Menu application; all the MDB files discussed here can be found on this book's Companion CD-ROM.

Figure 9-4 shows the Main Menu window for a sample Marketing Department application. The Main Menu application exists as a separate Access database, called MAIN_MENU.MDB.

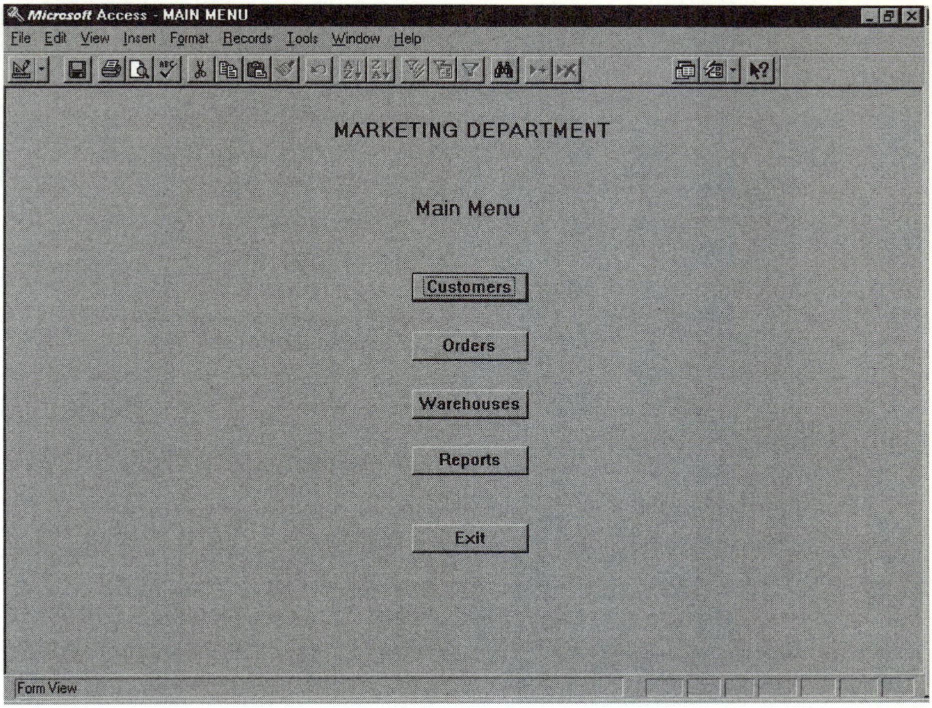

Figure 9-4: The Main Menu window of the Marketing Department application.

Click on the Customers button to call the Customer Information subapplication shown on Figure 9-5. After performing some of the functions of the Customer Information application, click on the To the Main Menu button to switch back to the Main Menu application.

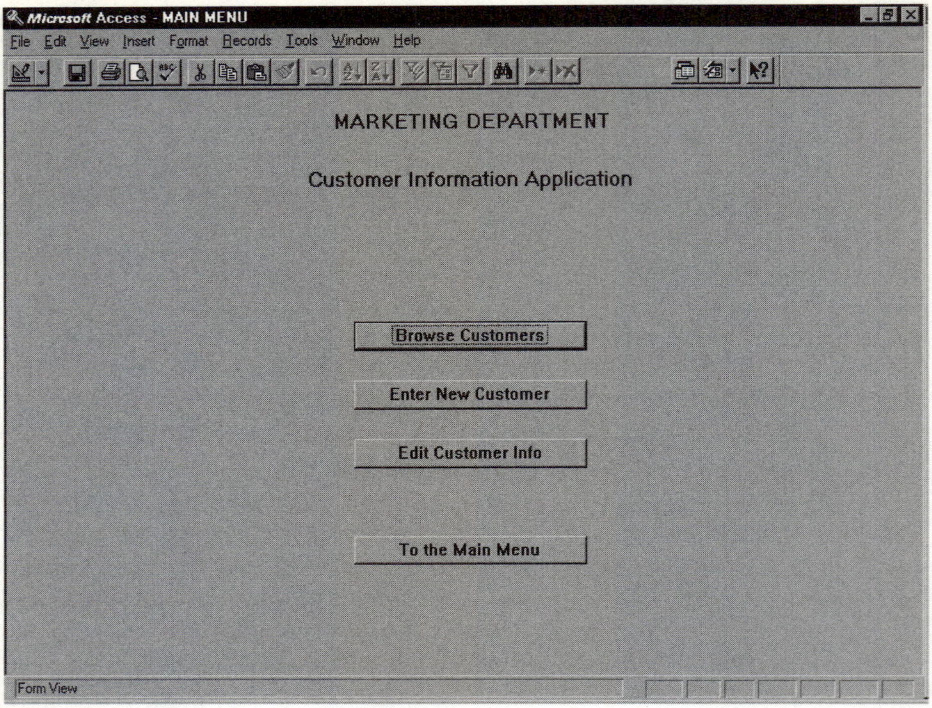

Figure 9-5: The Customer Information subsystem.

To switch from one MDB file to another, these applications use a form called SWITCH. This form does not have any controls; it has a menu attached to it (called SW_MENU) and an OnOpen module that only executes one command (Figures 9-6 and 9-7).

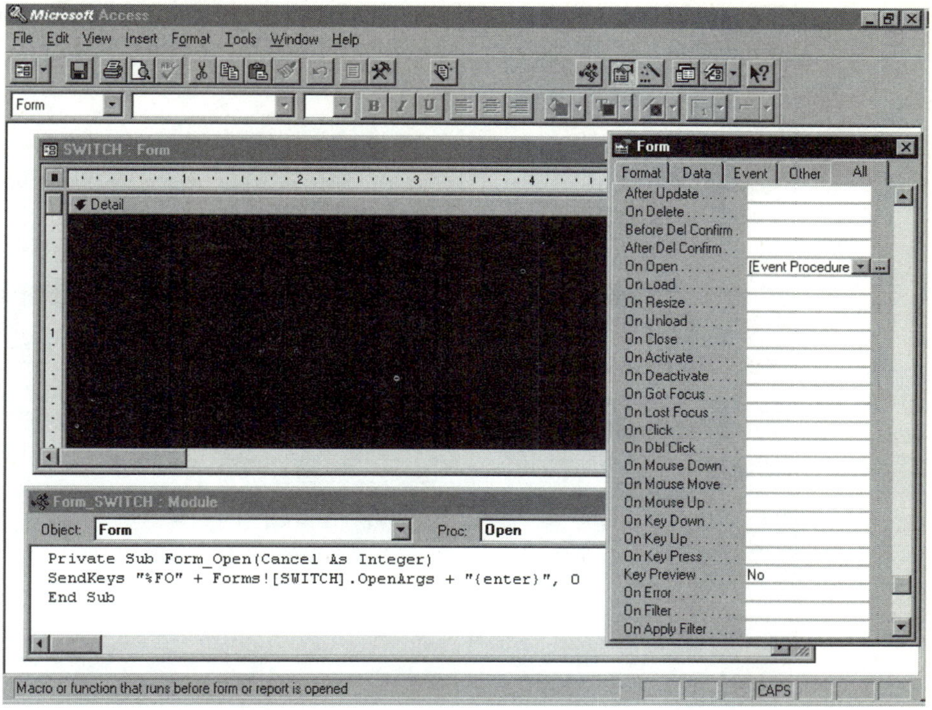

Figure 9-6: The SWITCH form and its OnOpen module.

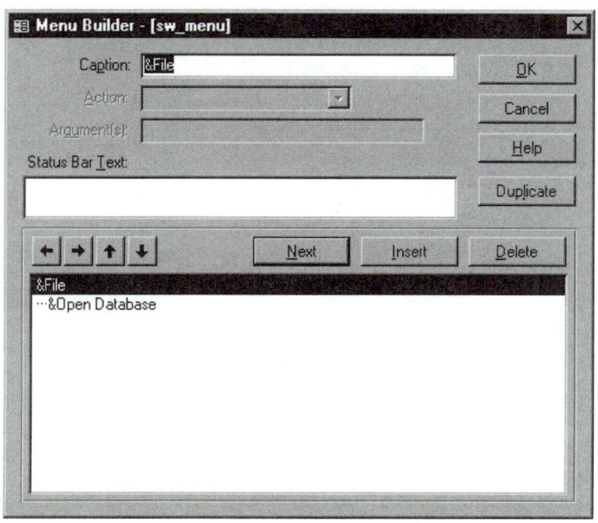

Figure 9-7: The SW_MENU menu, used in the SWITCH form.

When an application opens the SWITCH form, it passes a name of the next application's MDB file as a parameter of the OpenForm command. The OnClick module will then execute the SENDKEY command to imitate the sequence of keys that a user would press to open a database, which includes typing the name of an MDB file. Figure 9-8 illustrates how the OnClick module of the Customer button opens the SWITCH form and passes the name CUSTOMER.MDB as a parameter.

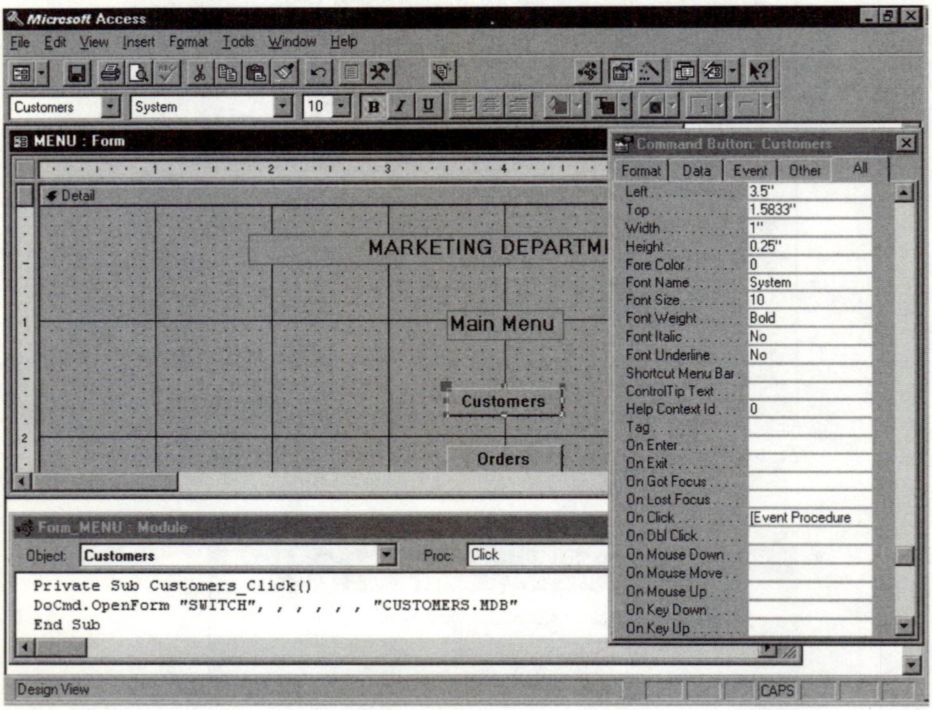

Figure 9-8: The Customer button in the Main Menu application.

When Access jumps back from the Customer subapplication to the Main Menu application, the same OpenForm command is executed in the OnClick module of the To the Main Menu button (Figure 9-9).

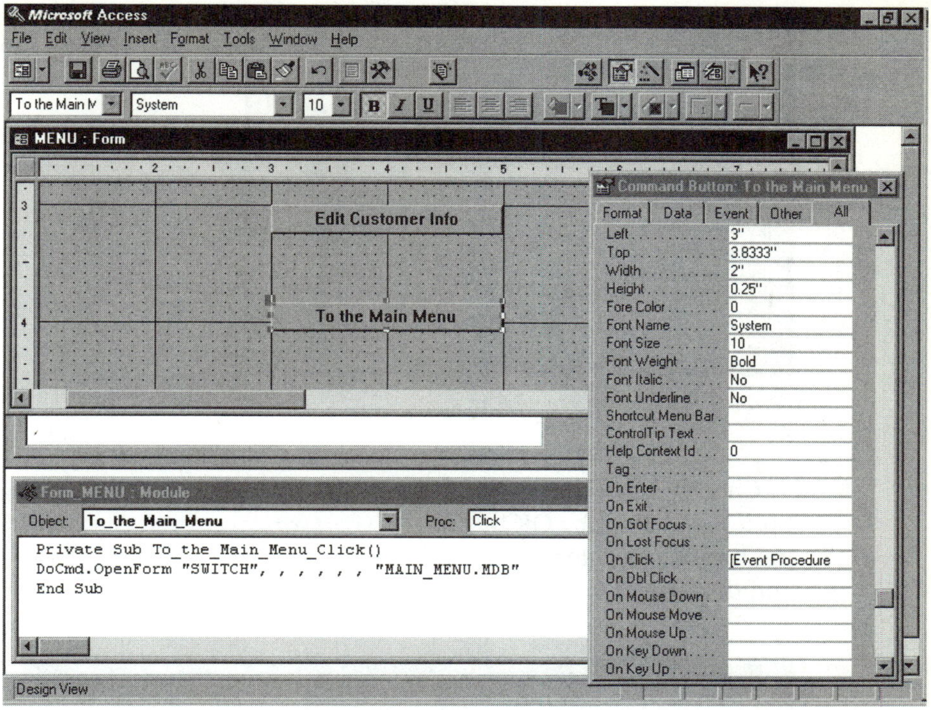

Figure 9-9: The To the Main Menu button in the Customer subsystem.

Using the Performance Analyzer

Use the Performance Analyzer in Access to analyze tables, queries, and forms in your database. The Performance Analyzer is aware of the algorithms used by the Jet database engine Optimizer and accordingly issues recommendations that match the Optimizer's approach.

To run the Performance Analyzer (Figure 9-10), click on the Performance option under the Analyze submenu of the Tools menu.

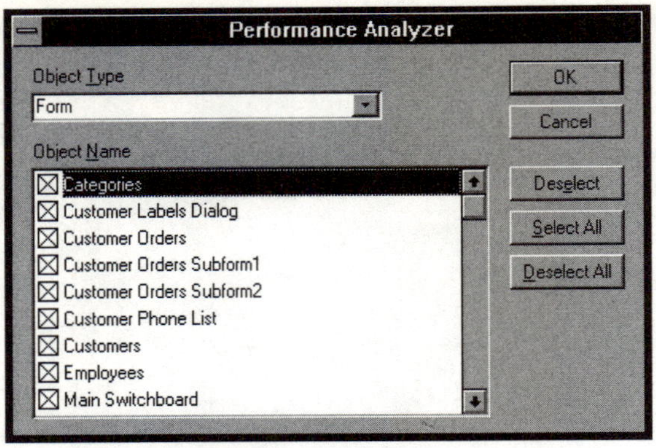

Figure 9-10: The Performance Analyzer.

Choose All from the Object Type drop-down list, click on the Select All button and then the OK button. The Performance Analyzer then starts checking for the possible improvements that can be made to the database objects and displays all of them in the dialog window (Figure 9-11).

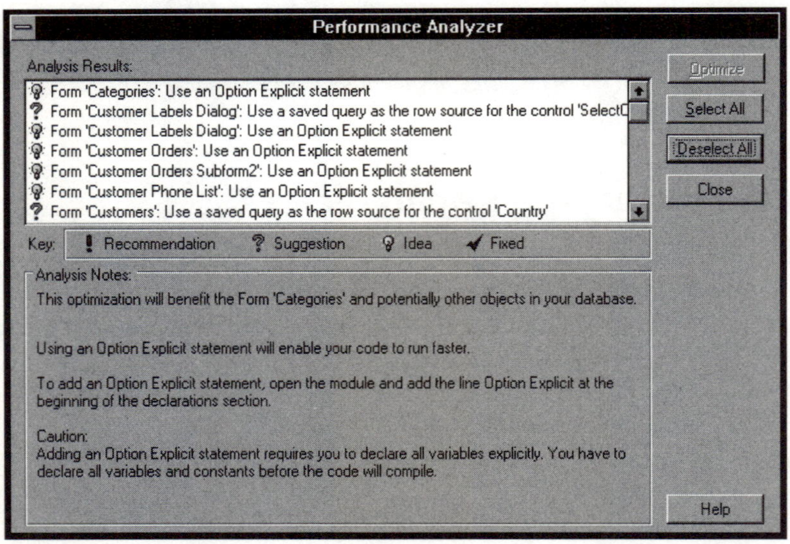

Figure 9-11: Recommendations, suggestions, and ideas from the Performance Analyzer.

Examine the Analysis Notes section of the Performance Analyzer dialog box for the optimization suggestions, and make sure that you understand all the ramifications.

Select those suggestions that you would like to implement, and click the Optimize button. Some of the suggestions may have some adverse side effects, presented to you in the Analysis Notes section. If you still want to implement them, the Performance Analyzer issues another warning (Figure 9-12).

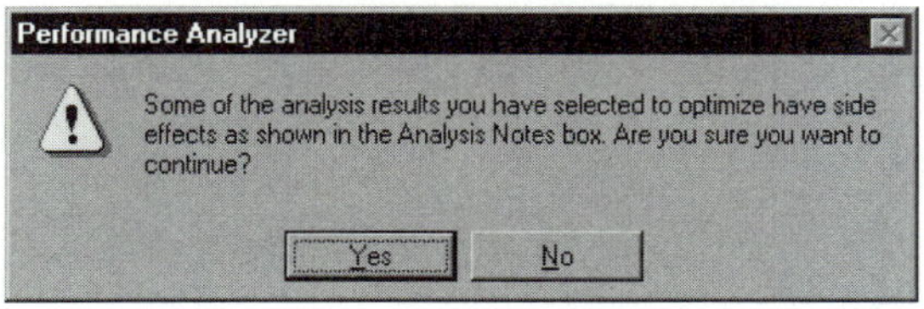

Figure 9-12: The Performance Analyzer's side effects warning.

If you decide to go ahead, the Performance Analyzer then implements its suggestions and marks them as *fixed* in the dialog window.

The SQL Server Database Maintenance Wizard

The Database Maintenance Wizard is a new utility in SQL Server 6.5. Use it to set up and schedule the most important maintenance actions for a selected database. The Database Maintenance Wizard plans and executes many performance-improving actions, including:

- Checking data allocation.
- Checking data and index linkages.
- Updating Optimizer information and reorganizing data and index pages.
- Performing database and transaction log backups.

The Database Maintenance Wizard creates an SQL Executive task that performs these actions at specified daily or weekly intervals. To run the Database Maintenance Wizard, click on the very right button of the SQL Enterprise Manager's toolbar. Select a database to set up for the periodical maintenance from the Target Database drop-down list (Figure 9-13).

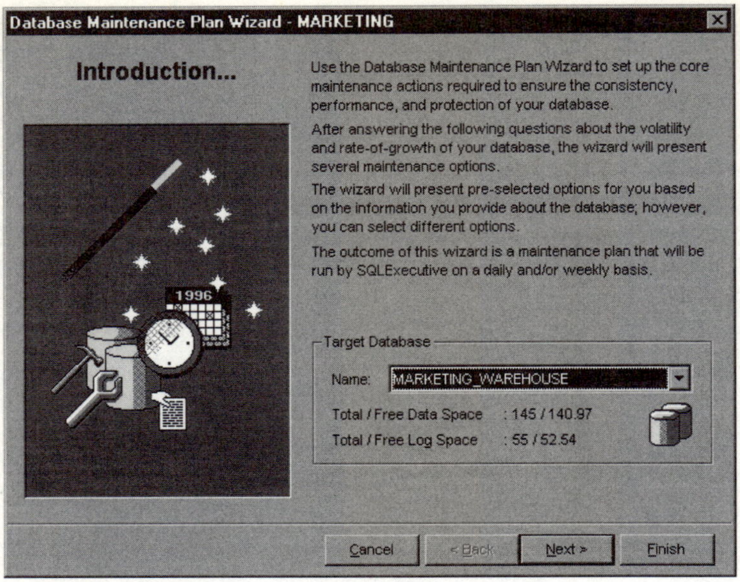

Figure 9-13: The Database Maintenance Wizard's Introduction dialog.

The Database Maintenance Wizard leads you through the sequence of dialog boxes. Use the About the Data in Your Database dialog to give the wizard information about a rate of growth and a rate of updatability of the data in your database (Figure 9-14). The numbers that you enter in this dialog will allow the wizard to determine the most optimal frequency of the maintenance actions for this database.

Use the Data Verification dialog (Figure 9-15) to request the data integrity tests (DBCC functions; see Chapter 4 for more information) to be performed on the database and to set up the frequency of these tests. Keeping your data in a good shape is quite important from the performance-optimization point of view; page allocation problems and inconsistencies in the indexes can cause significant performance problems.

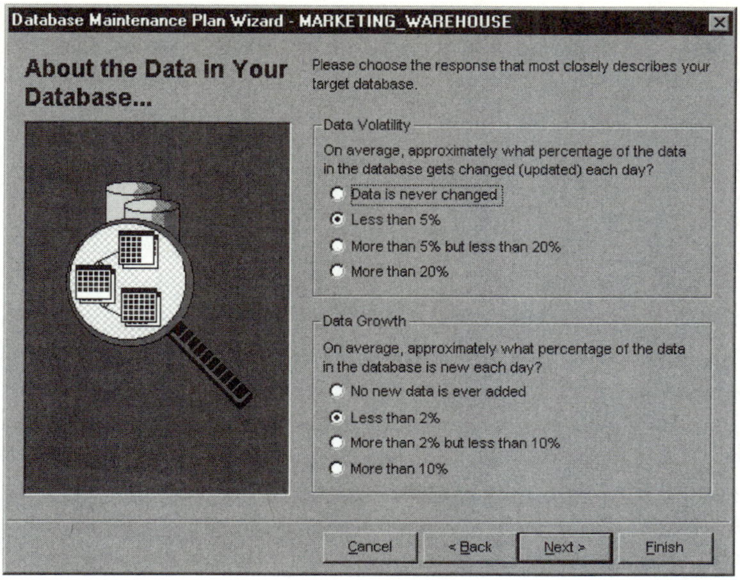

Figure 9-14: The Database Maintenance Wizard's About the Data in Your Database dialog.

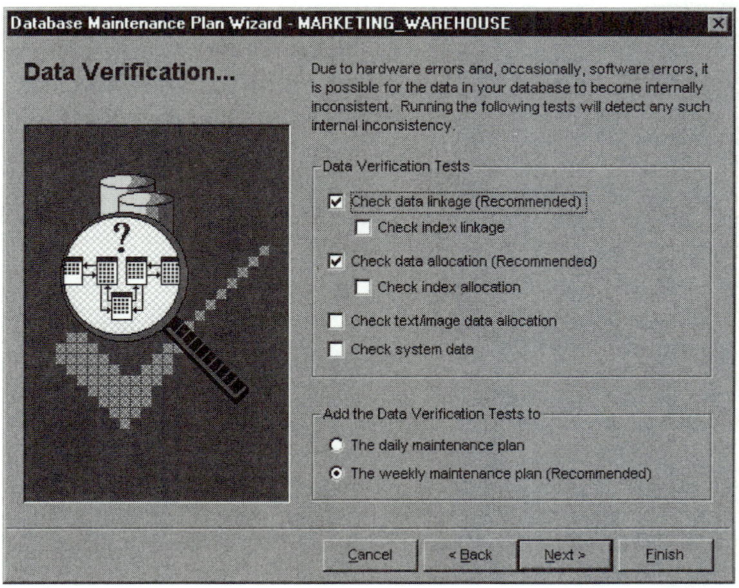

Figure 9-15: The Database Maintenance Wizard's Data Verification dialog.

Use the Data Optimization dialog (Figure 9-16) to force the SQL Server to recalculate the index distribution pages in your database (see earlier in this chapter) and, possibly, to reorganize the data and index pages.

If the rate of growth of your database is high, new extends are allocated to the tables and indexes very often; these new extends may be taken from different areas within the database. Pretty soon your data becomes fragmented; tables and indexes do not occupy contiguous space, which in turn slows down performance, especially for the sequential data access. If you feel that this may be happening in your database, mark the Reorganize Data and Index Pages check box. The data-reorganization procedure takes a significant amount of time and resources, and therefore, the pertinence of this option should be considered carefully in each case. If you do decide to reorganize the data, use the Change Free Space To value in the dialog to change the *fill factor* parameter for the tables and indexes.

Again, the wizard will recommend to you the most optimal frequency for these actions, and it will only recommend those actions that would make sense for this database.

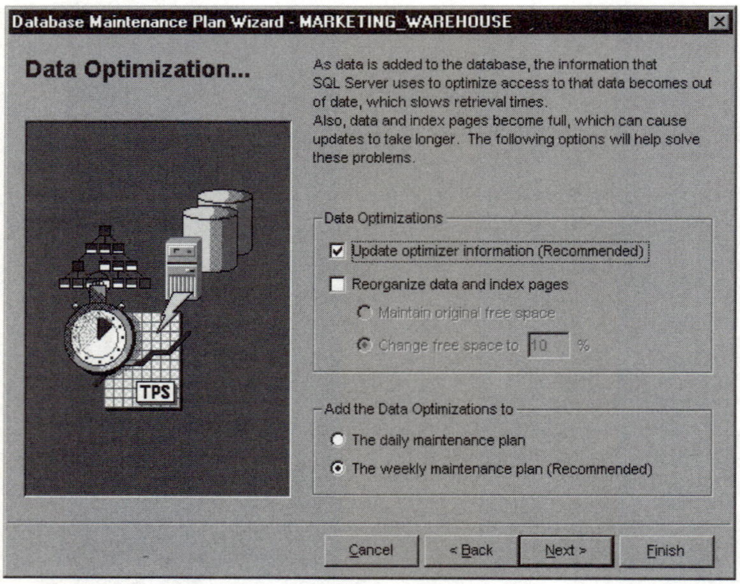

Figure 9-16: The Database Maintenance Wizard's Data Optimization dialog.

Use the next two dialogs to define the parameters of the automatic backups and the intervals between them and to designate the backup tape or disk, directory name, and the backup's media retention period.

Performing regular database backups in the off-peak hours also helps to achieve better performance.

To schedule daily and weekly runs of the maintenance jobs, use the When to Run, Who to Notify dialog of the Database Maintenance Wizard (Figure 9-17). Use When to Run sections to specify the day of the week and the time of day for the weekly and the daily maintenance jobs to run. Use the Filename box to specify the location where the maintenance reports will be created. Finally, use the E-Mail To list box to designate a person to be notified upon completion of a maintenance job.

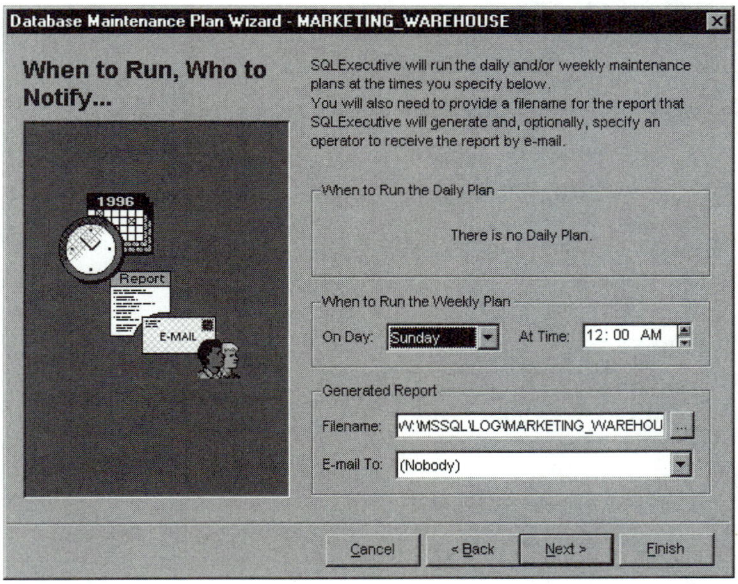

Figure 9-17: The Database Maintenance Wizard's When to Run, Who to Notify dialog.

The Wizard Complete dialog box (Figure 9-18) informs you of the actions that will be taken at the specified time on the daily and weekly schedules.

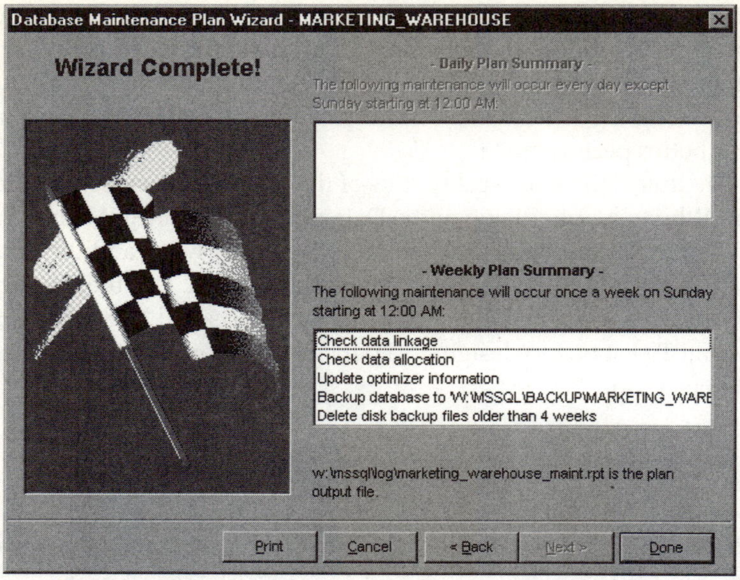

Figure 9-18: The Database Maintenance Wizard's Wizard Complete dialog.

The daily and weekly maintenance jobs created by the Database Maintenance Wizard are, essentially, the SQL-Server-scheduled tasks, managed by the SQL Executive (see Chapter 4 for more details). Use the SQL Executive graphical interface in the SQL Enterprise Manager to view, edit, and delete the maintenance tasks any time after they have been created (Figure 9-19). To re-create the maintenance jobs with different sets of actions, use the Scheduled Tasks dialog to delete the daily and weekly jobs, and then run the Database Maintenance Wizard again.

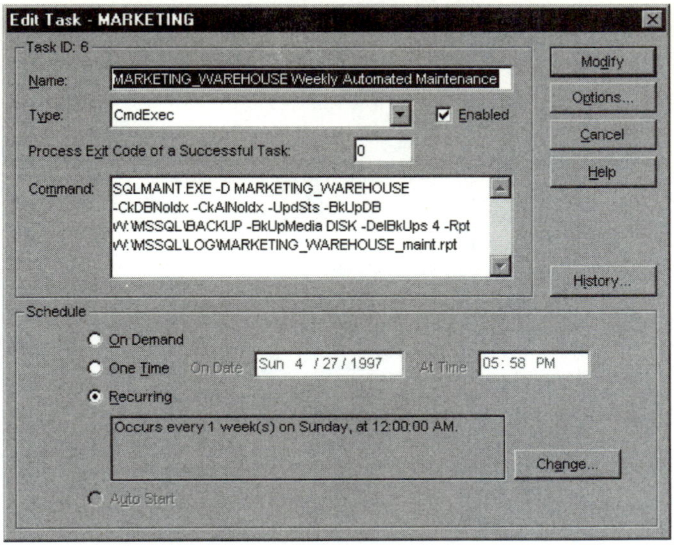

Figure 9-19: The Edit Task dialog of the SQL Executive showing a maintenance job.

Moving On

Both Microsoft Access and SQL Server offer exciting new tools for performance improvements. The Database Splitting Wizard and the Performance Analyzer are new in Access for Windows 95, and the Database Maintenance Wizard is a new tool in SQL Server 6.5. The set of general rules listed in the first half of this chapter can assist you in avoiding the most common pitfalls and achieving some modest performance gains. While the sophisticated tools and general rules certainly help, the key to successful optimization and tuning is hard work, experience, and a great deal of intuition on the part of the application developer, network manager, and the SQL Server database administrator.

The client/server security issues discussed in the next chapter are, in part, related to performance optimization and tuning. If user logins and login permissions are kept, for example, in a separate SQL Server or local Access table and this table joins with every other table in the system to restrict the user's scope of results, it can impose quite heavy performance tariffs on your system.

chapter 10

Security

A database consists of two integral parts: data and an internal structure to organize the data. Securing a database application involves the protection of both the data and the database structure. You need security for several purposes:

- Protecting data from inadvertent damage by end users. In an unsecured database, for example, a user can easily delete the data in a table that is vital to the operation of the database.
- Preventing people from seeing, altering, or duplicating your database design. As a designer, you would probably prefer that your databases not be analyzed and operated on by users. Sometimes, you don't want users to even see your design because there may be something you don't want them to see (such as passwords hard-coded into a connection string).
- Granting selective data access to different users. If you design database systems for an organization, you are likely to encounter sensitive data that's not meant to be seen by everyone in the organization. Each user gets to see a subset of all the data.

There are several types of database security. There is functional security, which determines what operations you can perform with a certain object. For example, you need to grant a user EXECUTE permission on an SQL Server stored procedure before the user can execute the stored procedure. Also, a user needs SELECT, INSERT, GRANT, or UPDATE permission to perform corresponding queries on an Access or SQL Server table.

Then there is selective data security, in which a user has access to only a subset of data in a table. This type of security can be further classified into column-level security and row-level security.

Database security can also be implemented with varying levels of strictness. You can, for example, lock everybody out of your application, which is an easy thing to do but not very useful in most cases. You can allow certain users to do a few things but disallow others to do the same. The hybrid nature of the combined Access/SQL Server system further adds to the complexity.

Security should not be considered as an afterthought in database design. You need to have a fairly clear vision of what your system's security needs are while laying out the blueprint of the system. We will first examine Access and SQL Security separately and then look at the possibilities that we can exploit in the combined environment.

The Microsoft Access Security Model

Microsoft Access is a desktop-oriented DBMS, which means that each computer runs its own session of Access. Since different sessions operate independently, Access does not have an integrated, centralized security scheme such as that provided by SQL Server. You can perform security functions in Access either through the graphical user interface or through Visual Basic.

Share-Level vs. User-Level Security

Microsoft Access for Windows 95 supports both *share-level security* and *user-level security*. This is different from many other desktop DBMSes, which implement only share-level security.

In a share-level security system, each action associated with a database object is directly protected with a password. Anyone who knows the password can perform the action on the object. In some database systems, for example, there is a password for reading a table, and there is a separate password for writing to a table. In Access for Windows 95, the share-level security is implemented in one instance: the password-protection of a database. To give your database a password, choose Tools | Security | Set Database Password from the menu bar in the Database window.

You may want to password-protect your database if, for example, you have a database designed for a small group of users who are allowed to do anything they want once inside the database. In this case, simply assign a password to the database, and then give the password to the users. If you created the database without logging on to Access, then your users won't have to log on to Access, and you can administer the database rather simply—you can just change the password without redistributing the database itself.

In a user-level security system, each action is directly associated with usernames, and each user account is in turn protected by a password—no action is directly protected by a password. For example, the permission to read data from a table is assigned to individual users or groups, and there is no way to impose a password on the read-data action on the table.

The identity of a user is determined when he or she starts Microsoft Access by logging on with a password. Administrators grant specific permissions, such as Read Data or Modify Design, to specific users and groups on specific objects. Different users can have different permissions on the same objects.

For example, let's say you have a merchandise pricing table in which the unit prices for all the products in your company are set. This table may have four levels of permissions:

- The MIS department has ultimate administrative control over the table.
- Managers in the sales department can do anything to the data in the table, including reading, updating, and deleting records. However, they are prevented from removing the table itself from the database.
- Data entry employees in the sales department can enter new records into the table but can't change existing ones (to prevent changes to prices, for instance).
- Everyone else in the company and customers can only read the table.

To implement share-level security in this example, you need to:

1. Create user accounts for those who will be using your system.
2. Establish four group accounts corresponding to the MIS department, the sales managers, sales data entry employees, and all other users.
3. Place each user in one of the four groups.
4. Give the groups appropriate permissions to the table. In this case, the MIS group should have all permissions (including administering the table); the sales managers should have read, write, delete, and update permissions; the sales data entry employees should have read and insert permissions; and the rest of the users will have only read permissions.

In your system, each user presets his or her own password, which Microsoft Access stores in a *workgroup database*. A user logs on to Access by entering his or her own username and a password. Access authenticates the user by comparing this password with the preset password. If they match, Access proceeds to create a new Workspace object under the user's name. The new Workspace object represents a new session of Access (see Chapter 3 for details on data access objects) and contains a Users collection, which corresponds to all user accounts already defined at the time the new Workspace object was created.

Each User object in the Users collection in turn contains a Groups collection, which includes all the groups that the user belongs to (note that a user may belong to multiple groups). Therefore, at the start of a new session, Access has already checked and remembered all the groups to which a user belongs.

Every time the user tries to perform an action on an object, such as running a query, opening a form or table, or modifying a report, Microsoft Access checks to see whether the user or any of the groups to which the user belongs has the necessary permissions. If the required permissions have been granted, Access performs the action. If not, Access informs the user that he or she doesn't have permissions to perform the requested action and does not perform the action.

In Microsoft Access, all the permissions granted to users/groups on objects in a database are stored in the database itself, whereas user/group account information is stored in a separate workgroup database. When a user starts a new session of Access, his or her identity and group membership data is retrieved from the workgroup database and becomes an integral part of the session. After the user opens an application database, the user/group is checked against permissions information contained in system tables within the application database. If you transfer objects from one database to another, their security settings travel with them.

The Security GUI

Microsoft Access provides a convenient graphical user interface (GUI) for managing users/groups and assigning permissions to them. In addition to the ability to set a password on a database, there are three type of security functions you can perform in the Access GUI:

- Assigning user and group permissions.
- Managing user and group accounts.
- Running the user-level Security Wizard

Assigning User & Group Permissions

Choose Tools | Security | User and Group Permissions, and the User and Group Permissions window pops up. If you click on the Permissions tab, you get the screen in Figure 10-1.

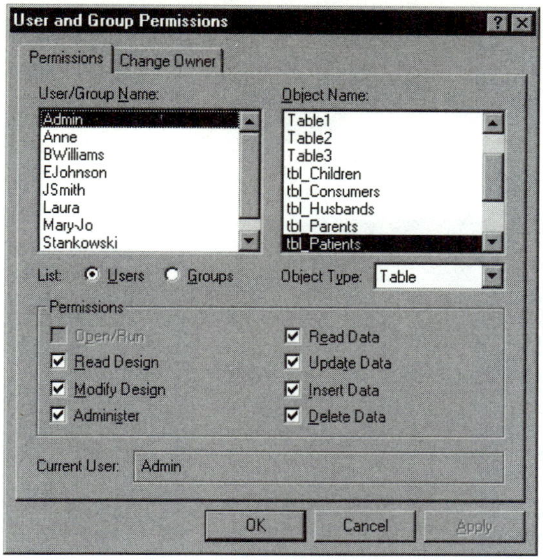

Figure 10-1: The User and Group Permissions window with the Permissions tab chosen.

There are two list boxes in Figure 10-1, which are labeled as User/Group Name and Object Name. You can display either users or groups in the User/Group Name list box by checking one of two option buttons under the list box. You can also choose what type of objects to display in the Object Name list box by selecting an item in the Object Type drop-down box under the Object Name list box. After you highlight a specific user/group and an object from these two list boxes, the permissions check boxes display the permissions granted to the highlighted user/group for the highlighted object; you can change the permissions by checking or unchecking the boxes.

If you click on the Change Owner tab in the User and Group Permissions window, the screen in Figure 10-2 appears.

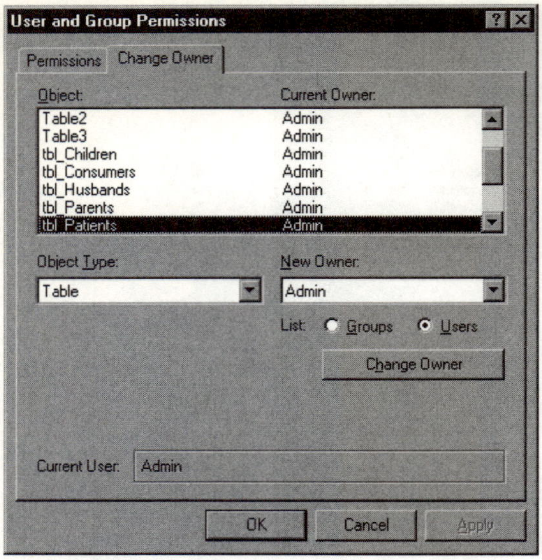

Figure 10-2: The User and Group Permissions window with the Change Owner tab chosen.

The top list box in Figure 10-2 lists the current owners of all objects of the type specified in the Object Type drop-down box. If you choose Database, you get to see the owner of the database—this is the easiest way to find out who created a database. You can change the ownership of an object to either a user or a group by selecting the appropriate radial dial and highlighting a user/group in the New Owner drop-down box.

Managing User & Group Accounts

Choose Tools | Security | User and Group Accounts to reach the User and Group Permissions window. If you click on the Users tab, the screen in Figure 10-3 appears. There are two sections in this screen: User and Group Membership. In the User section, all existing users are listed by their usernames in the drop-down list. Choose a user by highlighting his or her username. You can create/delete a user account or clear a user's password (useful sometimes for application administration) by clicking the appropriate buttons.

After you have chosen a user, the Group Membership section displays the groups to which the user belongs. In Figure 10-3, the username Admin belongs to two groups: Admins (notice the *s*) and Users. To make a user belong to an additional group, highlight the group in the Available Groups list box, and click the Add button; to remove a user from a group, highlight the group in the Member Of list box, and click the Remove button.

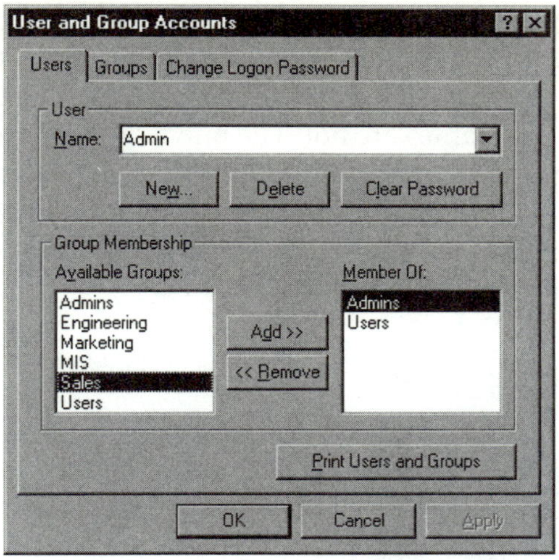

Figure 10-3: The User and Group Accounts window with the Users tab chosen.

If you click the Groups tab in the User and Group Account window, you get the screen in Figure 10-4, which allows you to manage group accounts. User and group accounts actually share the same name space. In other words, if a user already exists with the name Director, then you can't create a new group called Director (for a departmental director's office staff, for example).

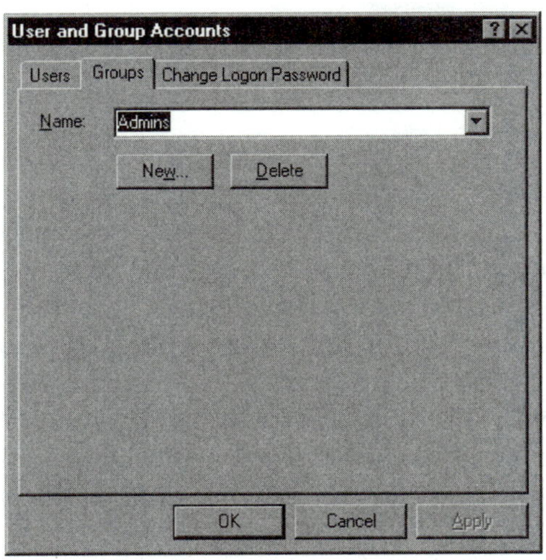

Figure 10-4: The User and Group Accounts window with the Groups tab chosen.

In the User and Group Account window, click the Change Logon Password tab to manage your own password (Figure 10-5). You need to type in your new password twice for Access to accept it. Bear in mind that Access passwords are case sensitive even though usernames are not. The only way you can change a person's password is to log on as that person. In Access, each user is responsible for managing and maintaining his or her own password. There is no way for an administrator to even read the password of a user (on the other hand, an administrator can clear anyone's password).

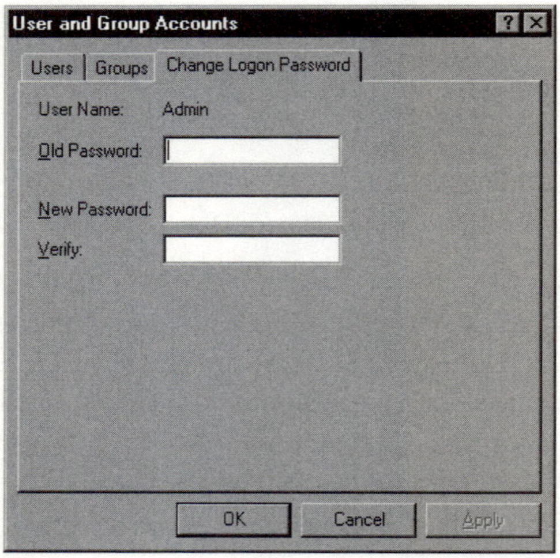

Figure 10-5: The User and Group Accounts window with the Change Logon Password tab chosen.

Running the Security Wizard

By default, an Access database grants permissions on all of its objects to all users through the Users group. The first step in securing a database, therefore, is to remove these all-encompassing permissions. However, manually going through each object-user/group combination and checking the permission boxes in the User and Group Permissions window can be quite laborious and tedious. This is where the Microsoft Access Security Wizard comes in handy. The Security Wizard can give you an extremely restrictive database; it's then up to you loosen up the restrictions and gradually grant permission to select groups and users.

In previous versions of Microsoft Access, the Security Wizard was an add-in application; in Access for Windows 95, the Security Wizard became a standard feature. To secure a database, log on as a user other than Admin who has read permissions on all objects and data in a database. Then open the database and choose Tools | Security | User-Level Security Wizard from the menu bar of the Database window. The Security Wizard window appears (Figure 10-6). Select the types of objects to secure, click OK, and follow the simple instructions in the dialog boxes that follow.

The Security Wizard will create a new, encrypted copy of the original database, export the all objects from the current database, and secure the selected object types by revoking permissions from all accounts other than the user running the wizard. It won't change the current database in any way. It will re-create linked tables and table relationships in the new database as well. It will leave the original copy unmodified.

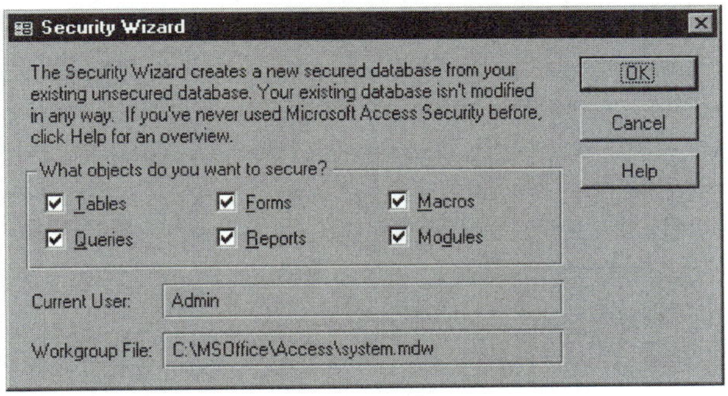

Figure 10-6: The Security Wizard window.

Workgroups

At the center of Access security lies the idea of a *workgroup*. Any kind of security is meaningful only for a clearly defined set of users. For Access, such a set of users is called a workgroup. When a new session of Access starts up, it must specify, or "point to," a workgroup. Unlike SQL Server, which has a fixed set of users, you can start each session of Access with a different workgroup.

An Access workgroup is defined by a *workgroup database*. All user and group information for a workgroup is stored in the workgroup database, which has a default name of SYSTEM.MDW. The workgroup database contains a list of users and groups, user memberships in groups, encrypted logon passwords, and the internal security identifier (SID) for each user and group account. You can make changes to data in the workgroup database through the User and Group Accounts window. A single workgroup database can be used by many application databases.

Creating a New Workgroup

Workgroup databases are created by the *Workgroup Administrator*, which can be started by opening the folder where Microsoft Access is installed (MSOffice\Access is the default folder) and then double-clicking WRKGADM.EXE. (To add the Workgroup Administrator to the Start menu, right-click the taskbar and choose Properties from the pop-up menu. Choose the Start Menu Programs tab, click Add, and then follow the directions in the remaining dialog boxes.) The following are the steps to create a new workgroup:

1. Start the Workgroup Administrator. In the Workgroup Administrator window, click the Create button.
2. In the Workgroup Owner Information window, enter your name, organization, and Workgroup ID (WID). Click OK when you are done. The WID can be any string of 4 to 20 (inclusive) numbers and letters. You should record the name, organization, and WID you enter (all of which are case sensitive) and keep them in a safe place. You would need all three pieces of information in their exact original form to re-create the workgroup in case the original workgroup database were deleted or damaged. If you forget or lose these pieces of information, you can't recover a workgroup database and might lose access to your databases created under the original workgroup.
3. In the Workgroup Information File window, type a name for the new workgroup database, and then click OK. By default, the workgroup database is called SYSTEM.MDW and saved in the folder where Microsoft Access was installed. You can rename the file using any valid filename and save it in a different location by typing a new path or clicking Browse to specify the new path.

When you create a new workgroup, you also automatically join it. The next time you start Access the new workgroup database will be used.

The Default Workgroup

One of the main reasons you may need to create a new workgroup is that the default workgroup may present a security problem. When you install Microsoft Access, the Setup program automatically creates an Access workgroup database based on the name and organization information you supply. Because such information can be easily obtained from the Access Help menu, a hacker can create an identical copy of this workgroup database with himself or herself as an administrator. He or she can then start Access while pointing to this copy of the workgroup database and consequently have permissions to do anything to your databases as an administrator (a member of the Admins group) in the workgroup defined by that copy of workgroup database.

To prevent such a breakdown in security, you need to create a new workgroup database and specify a WID. Only those who know the WID will be able to create a copy of the workgroup information file. A secure WID effectively prevents unauthorized users from duplicating your workgroup database and masquerading as all-powerful administrators to your databases.

Joining a Different Workgroup

Follow these steps to join a different workgroup:

1. With Access closed, start the Workgroup Administrator. In the Workgroup Administrator window, click the Join button.
2. In the Workgroup Information File Information window, enter the full path of the workgroup database for the workgroup you want to join, or click Browse to find the workgroup database. Click OK.

The next time you start Access, this new workgroup will be used. If you want others to join the workgroup defined by this workgroup database, copy the workgroup database to a shared folder, and then have each user run the Workgroup Administrator to join the new workgroup database. Note that this method is equivalent to specifying the location of the workgroup database in the Windows Registry under the key:

```
HKEY_LOCAL_MACHINE\SOFTWARE\Microsoft\Access\7.0\Jet\3.0\Engines\Jet\SystemDB
```

You can also point to a specific workgroup as you open an Access database in a command line by using the command line /Wrkgrp followed by the full path of the workgroup database. For example:

```
C:\MSoffice\Access\MSACCESS.EXE
C:\MyApps\MyTest.mdb /Wrkgrp
C:\Access\System\MyWrkgrp.mdw
```

Password-Protecting a Workgroup

When you start Access using a newly created workgroup database, you are not prompted for a password. This is because a password has not been imposed on the user account Admin, and anyone who starts Access assumes the default username Admin. All permissions in a database granted to the user Admin become applicable to any user who starts Access. To force a login prompt on all users, simply change the password of Admin to something other than null.

Users & Groups

The workgroup database, with a default name of SYSTEM.MDW, contains information about all users in a workgroup as well as the group(s) to which each user belongs. Don't confuse a group with a workgroup—a group (or, more formally, a user group) is a subset of all users in a workgroup. Each user may belong to one or more groups. Each user or group name must be unique. A group may not share the same name as a user because user and group names are stored together in the same system table.

Each user or group has a *security identifier* (SID) associated with it. The SID is a machine-generated, nonreadable binary string that uniquely identifies a user or group. When a user logs on, Access looks in the MSysAccounts table of the workgroup database for a user of the same name. If a user with the same name is found, it compares the password entered in the logon prompt with the password associated with that username in the MSysAccounts table. If the passwords match, Access starts a new session. The SID of the user and the SIDs of all the groups the user belongs to are retrieved and "remembered" by Access throughout the session. SIDs are extremely important for Access security implementation because all permissions on Access objects are assigned to SIDs instead of user or group names.

The SID of a user or group is generated by Access based on the username and personal identifier (PID) you supply when you create a new user or group account. The PID can be any string comprising 4 to 20 numbers and letters and is fed, along with the user or group name, to an encryption program to generate the SID for that user or group account. Functionally, the PID is to a user or group account what the WID is to a workgroup. The same combination of username and PID will result in the same SID. The PID is different from the password, but it helps to keep a user's or group's SID from being duplicated, thus preventing unauthorized users from assuming the SID of another user.

Note that although the username is not case sensitive, the PID is. If you feed in the same username and PID to the encryption program, you will get the same SID. If you ever had to re-create a user's or group's SID (in case a workgroup database were lost or corrupted, for instance), or if you needed to create identical SIDs (identical accounts) in multiple workgroups, you would have to supply an exact copy of the original PID. The PID is useful only when a new user or group account is being created (i.e., when the SID of the account is being created); it's not used for anything else.

A newly created user account doesn't have a password. Either you or the individual user must log on to Access and change the password. Again, the password should be distinguished from the PID. The password simply makes sure that a user attempting to log on to Access is the person he or she claims to be. Passwords have no effect on the user's SID or permissions. Members of the Admins group (described in The Admins Group section) can clear the passwords of all users in a workgroup.

By default, Access first attempts to log on as the user Admin, with a blank password. If this logon fails, the user is presented with the Log On dialog box. If a username and password are specified on the command line (using the /User and /Pwd flags), Access first tries to log on using that username and password. If this logon fails, the user is presented with the Log On dialog box.

Access defines one default user, Admin, and two default groups, Admins and Users. The key thing to remember about the default accounts is that the SID of the Admins group account is unique to each workgroup, but the SIDs of the other two default accounts, the Admin user and the Users group, are identical across all workgroups of Access. Therefore, permissions assigned to the Admins group are secure, but permissions assigned to either the Admin user or Users group are available to anyone with a copy of Microsoft Access.

The Admin User

The name *Admin* is somewhat of a misnomer; the user Admin does not, by default, have any administrative rights in any workgroup. The Admin user is the merely the default user account—when you start Access, Access always first tries to log on as Admin with a blank password. Only when that fails does Access prompt you for another username and password. Therefore, if you can start Access without being prompted for a username and password, then you are actually using the Admin account.

SID Every Access workgroup has an Admin user account, and all Admin accounts in all workgroups have the same SID. Therefore, if the Admin user in your workgroup has any permissions at all to an object in an Access database, then all Admin users from any other workgroup will have the same permissions to that object. Even if the Admin user account in your workgroup has been password-protected, any user with a copy of Microsoft Access can still do what the Admin user in your workgroup can do to your database. This constitutes a serious security breach.

To prevent this problem, you need to make sure that the Admin user has no permissions whatsoever to anything in your secured database. In the User and Group Permissions window, you can accomplish this by manually revoking from the Admin user all the permissions on all objects and then changing the ownership of all objects to something other than the Admin user. Or you can use the Security Wizard to guarantee that the Admin user has no explicit permissions and owns no objects

Default Permissions By default, the Admin account doesn't receive any permissions on new objects. However, users in unsecured environments often log on as Admin and create many objects under the user Admin. As a result, many objects are owned by the Admin user. Because the owner of an object is automatically granted full permissions on this object by default, the Admin user often has full permission to a great many objects. Again, you can use the Security Wizard to easily revoke all such ownership-created permissions.

The Admins Group

Only when a user is in the Admins group (note the *s*) does he or she have administrative rights in a workgroup. A member of the Admins group is a super-user who has the power to create or delete user and group accounts and to clear users' passwords. There must be at least one member of the Admins group at all times.

The Admins group is created when a new workgroup is created. The username, organization, and WID information you supply when you create a new workgroup is fed to an encryption program to generate the SID of the workgroup's Admins group. The SID of the Admins group, in a sense, also identifies the workgroup.

When you create a new workgroup, there is only one user in the workgroup; the user is Admin, who belongs to the Admins and Users groups. You have to create a new user and place this user in the Admins group before you can strip the Admin user of administrative privileges. You can then impose a password on the Admin user to force all future users to log on.

SID Since the Admins group has all-powerful administrative privileges in a workgroup, it's important to make sure the Admins group's SID cannot be easily duplicated. The SID of the Admins group is meant to be created by encrypting three strings: username, company name, and workgroup ID (WID). Unfortunately, the Access Setup program uses only the first two—the username and the company name—as encryption seeds for the Admins group's SID. Because these two strings are available from the Help | About Microsoft Access menu, it is critical that when implementing Access security, you use the Workgroup Administrator to create a new workgroup (with a secret WID, of course) and with it, an Admins group with a secure SID.

Default Permissions When a user starts Microsoft Access while pointing to a workgroup database and then creates a newdatabase, the Admins group of that workgroup is by default given full permissions on all objects in the new database. More importantly, the Admins group's Administer permissions, the right to change permissions, can't be revoked through the Access GUI. Even if you clear the Administer check box in the User and Group Permissions window for the Admins group on an object, the permission remains—a member of the Admins group can always recheck the box.

The Users Group

The Users group is the default group in Access—all users always belong to it. Therefore, any permissions that are assigned explicitly to the Users group are available to all users in Microsoft Access workgroups.

SID The Users group's SID is identical across all Access workgroups. Therefore, if you assign permissions to the Users group on some objects in a database, all users of Access anywhere in the world will have the same permissions on the objects, even if these users belong to different workgroups.

Default Permissions By default, the Users group gets full permissions on all objects at their creation. Since every user of Access is a member of the Users group, any user will be able to access a database if full permissions are granted to the Users group on all objects in the database. This is actually what happens when no security is implemented at all. The easiest way to remove this permission from all objects in a database is to use the Security Wizard, which removes all permissions from the Users group and the Admin user.

CurrentUser Function

The CurrentUser function returns the current user's username. This function comes in handy when you want to log user activities. For example, if you want to keep track of who entered which records in a table, you first need to add an extra text column to the table and name it, for example, User_Name. Then, as a person adds a new record into the table, the CurrentUser function can be invoked to insert the person's username into the User_Name column.

Of course, you should prevent users from accessing the User_Name column. You can do this by using an intermediate query whose RunPermissions property is set to Owner's. This property will be examined in detailed in "Creating Secured Views" later in this chapter.

Ownership

Ownership is an integral part of Access security. The user who creates an object (as identified by his SID, not his username) owns the object. The object's owner can always assign any permissions on the object, even if someone with Administer privileges has revoked his or her explicit permissions on it. This right cannot be revoked; it can only be transferred to another user.

As mentioned earlier, it is extremely important that the Admin user not own any objects. Since the Admin user's SID is identical across all workgroups, anyone who has a copy of Access can do anything to the objects owned by the Admin user.

There are two ways to transfer the ownership of an object. The first is to change the owner in the User and Group Permissions window, which was discussed earlier in this chapter. The second is to re-create the object. This can be done either manually by choosing the File|Save As/Export menu in the Database window or by invoking the Security Wizard. The Security Wizard creates a new secured database with all objects owned by the user who runs the wizard. Note that in order to re-create an object, the person performing the importing/exporting must have Read permission on the object (and its data if the object is a table or query) in the first place.

Permissions

The Microsoft Access security model implements two types of permissions: explicit and implicit. You grant explicit permissions to one user at a time—when they are granted, only that single user is affected. By contrast, implicit permissions are granted to one group at a time—when they are granted, all users who are members of the group get the permissions of the group. If a user is removed from the group, he or she will no longer have the permissions of the group. If a new user is added to the group, he or she will inherit all the permissions assigned to the group. If the permissions of the group are changed, all users in the group are affected.

In this security model, a user may have two different sets of permissions on the same object, one explicit and one implicit. When a user attempts to do something, he or she will get the least restrictive of the two sets of permissions. For example, the user Charlie has no Read Data permissions on the tbl_Sales_Records table. However, Charlie belongs to the group Sales, which has Read Data permission on tbl_Sales_Records. Inheriting the permissions from the Sales group, Charlie will be able to read tbl_Sales_Records even though he has no Read permission granted to himself.

It is considered good practice to use implicit permissions as much as possible—that is, you should try to assign permissions to groups rather than directly to users. After your group permissions are established, they remain relatively constant, and the only administrative task you have is to assign individual users to the appropriate groups as their responsibilities change. It's much easier to maintain permissions for a few groups than for an entire company of users.

In the User and Group Permissions window, you can only see the explicit permissions for a user. To view the implicit permissions, you have to first open the User and Group Accounts window to find out what groups a user belongs to and then go back to the User and Group Permissions window to view the permissions of each group to which the user belongs. Unfortunately, the Access GUI doesn't have a utility that provides summary information on all the permissions, explicit and implicit, that a user has on an object. Through code, however, it's possible to build such a user interface. More to come on this in "Programming Access Security in Visual Basic" later in this chapter.

Right to Change Permissions

By default, the following users have the right to change permissions on an object in an application database:

- Members of the Admins group of the workgroup database in use when the application database was created.
- The owner of the object.
- Anyone who has Administer permissions on the object, either explicitly or implicitly.

These users can grant themselves permissions to perform an action even if they don't have explicit permissions to perform the action. The first two classes of users have the irrevocable right to assign permissions on a given object even if the GUI indicates that those users don't have Administer permissions. This irrevocability is enforced by the Microsoft Access GUI in the first case and by the Microsoft Jet database engine in the second case.

Database-Level Permissions

Database-level permissions are permissions involving the highest-level object: the database object. Microsoft Access for Windows 95 has three database-level permissions: Open/Run, Open Exclusive, and Administer. Here is a look at what each of the database-level permissions does:

- Setting the Open/Run permission allows you to lock unauthorized users out of your database completely. A user who doesn't have this permission simply can't open your database.

- Revoking the Open Exclusive permission prevents users from inadvertently locking each other out of a shared database by opening it exclusively. Microsoft Access for Windows 95 opens databases in shared mode by default. However, if a user who doesn't have the Open Exclusive permission attempts to open a database exclusively, Access will force the database to be opened in a shared mode. The Open Exclusive permission has another utility: a user can compact a database only if he or she has the Open Exclusive permission to the database.
- Removing the Administer permission from a user prevents the user from converting a database to a replicable database and setting the database password.

Permissions on New Objects

You can set the default permissions on all newly created objects in a database. Once this default is set, all future objects will have the same set of permissions. To set permissions for future objects of the same type, open the User and Group Permissions window, and select the user or group for which you want to define default permissions. Choose the object type in the Object Type combo box, and select the <New Object> item in the Object Name list box. Choose the permissions you want the user or group account to inherit for all new objects of that type, and click Apply.

Note that you can prevent users from creating new database objects, tables, and queries by using code to remove permissions on the container object (see "Programming Access Security in Visual Basic" later in this chapter), but you cannot prevent them from creating new forms, reports, macros, or modules.

Creating Secure Views

As introduced in Chapter 2, a view in an RDBMS is a virtual table derived from base tables. In both Access and SQL Server, views are nothing more than SELECT queries. Through views, you can read data from or alter data in the base tables exactly as if you were running queries directly on them. Views are capable of showing only parts of the base tables—either a subset of rows, a subset of columns, or both. This by itself is nothing extraordinary because a user could presumably bypass the views to directly access the entire base tables anyway. What makes views so useful in security implementations is that you can have *secure views*, which can be accessed like ordinary tables but whose underlying base tables are inaccessible to users.

In Access, the key to creating a secure view is a query property called RunPermissions, which is available in the Query Properties window of a query and is a GUI representation of the WITH OWNER ACCESS OPTION clause of the SQL property of the QueryDef object. It can have one of two settings: User's or Owner's. If it is set to User's (the default), the user's permissions on the query's underlying base table will be considered when the query is executed, and nothing unusual happens. If it is set to Owner's, only the query owner's permissions on the query's underlying base table will be considered when the query is executed. So in this case, a user can execute the query even if he or she doesn't have Read permissions on the base table. As long as the query's owner has the proper permissions on the base table, a user can run a secure view without having permissions on its underlying table(s).

Only the owner of a query can save it if the RunPermissions property is set to Owner's. Even members of the Admins group of the workgroup database in use when the application database was created can't save a query created by another user if the RunPermissions property is set to Owner's. It would be a security breach to do so. Note, however, that anyone with Modify Design permissions (including the members of the Admins group) on the query can set the RunPermissions property to User's and successfully save the query. If you need to change the owner of an owner-permission query, first change it to a regular query, then change the owner, and finally change it back to an owner-permission query.

Preventing Users From Viewing Table Designs

You may have noticed that on the Permissions tab in the User and Group Permissions window, if you check the Read Data check box on a table or query, the Read Design permission automatically gets checked; there is no way to check the Read Data check box alone. This is because in order for Access to display a table or query, it needs to know field names and other field properties such as Format, InputMask, and so on. Thus, for a user to read the data in a table or query and display it in the GUI, he or she must also have permissions to read the design of the table or query.

If you don't want your users to see your table or query definitions, you can use owner-permission queries to restrict their access to this information. Here are the steps:

1. Revoke all permissions on the sensitive tables from the users or groups whose access to these tables you want to restrict. For this example, let's call it tbl_MyTable.
2. Create a new SELECT query that includes all the fields from your sensitive table. It can take the form SELECT * FROM tbl_MyTable. For this example, we'll call this query qry_MyQuery.
3. Make sure you or a secure group owns this query. In a multi-developer environment, use the Change Owner tab of the User and Group Permissions window to change the owner of qry_MyQuery to a developer's group. This will allow any developer to modify and save qry_MyQuery.

4. Set the RunPermissions property of qry_MyQuery to Owner's.
5. Grant appropriate data permissions (some or all of Read Design, Read Data, Update Data, Delete Data, and Insert Data permissions) on qry_MyQuery to the users and groups you want to be able to access the data in tbl_MyTable but not view the table's design.

Your users will now be able to read or alter data in tbl_MyTable through qry_MyQuery. However, they won't be able to view the design of the table.

Encryption

Encrypting an Access database means scrambling the MDB file to render its internal content unreadable. If a database isn't encrypted, it's possible for a person to use a file editor (such as Norton Utilities) to read the SID of the database owner or the SID of the Admins group of the workgroup database in use when the MDB file was created. Having obtained the SID, this person could assume ownership of the database and do anything to it. However difficult and improbable this may be, you should bear in mind the possibility.

To encrypt or decrypt a database, close all databases, and then choose Tools | Security | Encrypt/Decrypt Database from the menu bar. The Security Wizard also encrypts a database as part of the process to secure it. Only the owner of an application database or a member of the Admins group of the workgroup database in use when the application database was created can encrypt or decrypt it.

Encryption is not part of Microsoft Access security. It only prevents someone from viewing sensitive systems information contained in a database through the "back door;" it does nothing to protect the database from users accessing it through normal means. Encryption is meaningless without implementing security because anyone can open an unsecured database and do anything to it.

Encryption comes at a cost, too. When Access tries to write new information to a database, it must first try to encrypt it; when it tries to read something from a database, it has to first decrypt it. Because of the extra processing involved in encrypting and decrypting, there is a decrease in performance of roughly 10–15 percent in encrypted databases. It's also very difficult to compress encrypted files using utilities such as PKZIP.

Some Practical Examples

The Access security model can be a little confusing if you've never had to deal with security. The following are some practical examples of security implementation that will help you understand the Access security model even better.

Securing an Existing Database

Suppose you have created an application called MYAPP.MDB without having to log on to Access. As a result, the Admin user owns all the objects in MYAPP.MDB. If you haven't created a secure workgroup, follow these steps to secure MYAPP.MDB:

1. Create a new secure workgroup with the Workgroup Administrator.
2. Start Access. If you are already in Access, exit and restart it. Note that even though you are not prompted for logon information, you are actually logging on to Access as the Admin user because there is no password for the Admin user yet.
3. In the User and Group Accounts window, create a new user account with a username of, say, Myself. Add Myself to the Admins group.
4. Remove the Admin user from the Admins group. You can do so because at least one other user, Myself, is now in the Admins group.
5. Under the Change Logon Password tab in the User and Group Accounts window, set a password for the Admin user. This will force the Log On prompt box to appear the next time you start Access.
6. Exit Access and restart it, logging on as Myself without a password. Once you have started Access, you can change the password for Myself to something other than null.
7. Open MYAPP.MDB.
8. Start the Security Wizard by choosing Tools | Security | User-Level Security Wizard from the menu bar.
9. Select all objects types, click OK, and follow the simple instructions in the dialog boxes. The Security Wizard creates a new, encrypted, and secure copy of the original database. Call this secure database MYAPP_S.MDB.
10. Close MYAPP.MDB and open MYAPP_S.MDB.
11. Create your own users and groups. Assign appropriate permissions to the group accounts, and then add individual users to the appropriate groups.

The new database is now secure. The only people who can access the objects in MYAPP_S.MDB are those you gave permissions to in step 11 and anyone who is a member of the Admins group of the workgroup database in use when you ran the Security Wizard.

If you want to secure your application under an existing secure workgroup instead of a new workgroup, then join the existing workgroup using the Workgroup Administrator and repeat steps 7 through 12 above. Of course, in order to do so, you must be already defined as a member of the existing workgroup.

Securing a New Database

By setting default permissions on newly new objects, you can secure a new database right from the beginning without having to run the Security Wizard later. First, you need to join a secure workgroup. Next, log on to Access as someone other than Admin, and start a new database.

Create appropriate groups, and put your users into these groups. For each category of objects in the new database (tables, queries, forms, reports, macros, and modules), you can set permissions on new objects to user groups; all objects in the category created in the future will inherit such permissions. For example, if you grant Open/Run permission on <New Forms> to the MyGroup group, then all future forms will have the same default permission as they are created.

Unsecuring a Secured Database

If you have followed the steps under "Securing an Existing Database," MYAPP_S.MDB is now tightly locked up, inaccessible to anyone hasn't been granted appropriate permissions. The Myself user is the owner of the database and all of the objects in it. The Admins group of the workgroup database in effect when you ran the Security Wizard has permissions to change permissions on any object in the database.

Now you want to make the database open to all users of Microsoft Access. Since the SID of the Users group is identical across all workgroups, by giving permissions on an object to the Users group, you unsecure that object for all users. (You could achieve the same result by granting permissions on an object to the Admin user; however, this would require users trying to access the unsecured database to be in a workgroup whose Admin user account is not protected by a secure password.) To unsecure the database, follow these steps:

1. Start Microsoft Access, logging on as someone who has Administer permissions on all the objects in MYAPP_S.MDB (in this case, myself).
2. Open MYAPP_S.MDB.
3. Give the Users group full permissions on all objects in the database.

Your database is now completely unsecured. Anyone who has a copy of Microsoft Access has full permissions on all the objects in MYAPP_S.MDB.

Securing Your Database Without Forcing Users to Log On

You can implement security without forcing the users to log on. The idea is to secure your database, grant limited permissions to the Admin user only, and clear the Admin user's password. All users will then share the Admin user account and be able to access your database without logging on to Access. The price you pay for the simplicity of the system is that you can't grant different permissions to different classes of users. To secure a database without forcing users to log on, follow these steps:

1. Log on to Access as a member of the Admins group in a secure workgroup. The Admin user must be removed from the Admins group.
2. Open a database, and secure it using the Security Wizard.
3. Assign appropriate permissions on the database objects only to the Admin user.
4. Clear the password from the Admin user. Users will be able to open your database without logging on and will be able to perform all actions for which the Admin user has permissions.

The problem now is that you can't log on to Access as anyone other than the Admin user when you start Access normally. Because the Admin user is not in the Admins group, you can't perform administrative duties such as managing user and group accounts. To log on as someone other than the Admin user (the Myself user in this case), you need to use the /User and /Pwd command-line options to edit the command-line argument of the Microsoft Access Program Manager icon to include the Myself user's username and password. When you start Microsoft Access using this icon, even though you don't see the Log On dialog box, you will be logged on as Myself and will be able to perform administrative duties.

To complete the security setup on your database, there is an additional bit of work to do: If you keep this icon on your computer, you have to physically secure your computer to prevent someone from seeing the command line.

Preventing Administrators From Accessing Your Objects

Let's say you work at the corporate headquarters of a big company and have developed a client/server application using Access and SQL Server. Now you need to distribute the Access front-end database to other divisions of the company that are in remote locations. Each division has its own Access administrator who performs such duties as managing user and group accounts. To protect your database, you don't want anyone, including the remote administrators, to be able to have administrative privileges to your database; at the same time, you prefer to let the remote administrators perform administrative functions within their respective divisions.

To grant remote administrators the ability to manage user accounts without allowing them to alter your database, you need to secure the database while pointing to one workgroup and operate the database while pointing to another workgroup. The key idea here is to make the SID of the Admins group at a remote site different from the SID of the Admins group of the workgroup used when you secure your database. Follow these steps to implement this idea:

1. Using the Workgroup Administrator, create a secure workgroup database named MYWGP.MDW, which you will use to secure your database.
2. Start Access while pointing to MYWGP.MDW. Secure the database using the Security Wizard.
3. Based on the different levels of permissions you will want your remote users to have, create corresponding groups. Record the exact names and PIDs of these groups (note that the PIDs are case sensitive). You will need these strings later.
4. Grant the necessary permissions, such Read Data and Open/Run, to these groups. Make sure you don't grant any Administer permissions to the groups.
5. Use the Workgroup Administrator to create a new workgroup database that you will distribute with your application. Call it THEIRWGP.MDW. Make sure you use *different* strings for the name, company name, and WID than the ones you used for MYWGP.MDW.
6. Start Access under THEIRWGP.MDW, and re-create the exact same group that now exists in MYWGP.MDW, using the same names and PIDs.
7. Create a user account for your remote administrator to use, and add him or her to the Admins group of THEIRWGP.MDW. For this example, let the username of the administrator be Elaine.
8. While still pointing to THEIRWGP.MDW, impose a password on the Admin user, and remove the Admin user from the Admins group. So now Elaine is the sole administrator of the THEIRWGP.MDW workgroup.
9. Distribute THEIRWGP.MDW with your application. Remind your remote users to join THEIRWGP.MDW before starting the application.

Under THEIRWGP.MDW at her remote site, Elaine will now be able to create new user accounts, reset passwords, and add users to the groups that you have already created. The ordinary groups (groups other than the Admins group) in THEIRWGP.MDW will inherit the same permissions to the objects in your database as the groups in MYWGP.MDW because, as the result of step 6, the SIDs of the ordinary groups in MYWGP.MDW are identical to the SIDs of the ordinary groups THEIRWGP.MDW.

However, because of step 5, the SIDs of the Admins group in the two workgroups are different. Since the database was originally secured under MYWGP.MDW, not THEIRWGP.MDW, the Admins group in MYWGP.MDW has administrative privileges over all the objects in the database. The Admins group of THEIRWGP.MDW, on the other hand, does not have such privileges. So while Elaine can manage user and group accounts within the THEIRWGP.MDW workgroup, she can't alter any of the objects in your database.

Programming Access Security in Visual Basic

All security functions that can be done in the Access GUI can also be performed programmatically in Visual Basic. Some security functions that can't be performed in the Access GUI can be done in Visual Basic, too.

Users & Groups

As discussed in Chapter 3, when you start a new Access session, a Users collection and a Groups collection are established under the new Workspace object.

The Users collection under the Workspace object contains User objects, which represent all the users defined in the currently used workgroup database. Each User object in turn contains a Groups collection, which includes all the groups to which that user belongs. Don't confuse the Groups collection under the Workspace object with the Groups collection under a User object. For example, the following code segment lists all the group names in a workgroup:

```
For I = 0 To DBEngine.Workspaces(0).Groups.Count - 1
   Debug.Print DBEngine.Workspaces(0).Groups(I).Name
Next I
```

while the following code segment displays all the groups that the Admin user belongs to:

```
For I = 0 To DBEngine.Workspaces(0).Users("Admin").Groups.Count - 1
  Debug.Print DBEngine.Workspaces(0).Users("Admin").Groups(I).Name
Next I
```

The Groups collection under the Workspace object contains Group objects, which represent all the groups defined in the currently used workgroup database. Each Group object in turn contains a Users collection, which includes all the users who belong to that group. Don't confuse the Users collection under the Workspace object with the Users collection under a Group object. For example, the following code segment lists all the usernames in a workgroup:

```
For I = 0 To DBEngine.Workspaces(0).Users.Count - 1
  Debug.Print DBEngine.Workspaces(0).Users(I).Name
Next I
```

while the following code segment displays all the users who belong to the Admins group:

```
For I = 0 To DBEngine.Workspaces(0).Groups("Admins").Users.Count - 1
  Debug.Print DBEngine.Workspaces(0).Groups("Admins").Users(I).Name
Next I
```

Listing All the Users in Each Group

In the Access GUI, you can easily find out all the groups that a person belongs to. However, there is no utility that lists all the users in each group. The last code segment from the preceding section can be modified to list all the users in each group as defined by the currently used workgroup:

```
Function Users_By_Group()

Dim I As Integer, j As Integer
Dim MyWS As Workspace

Set MyWS = DBEngine.Workspaces(0)

For I = 0 To MyWS.Groups.Count - 1
  Debug.Print MyWS.Groups(I).Name
  For j = 0 To MyWS.Groups(I).Users.Count-1
    Debug.Print "  " & MyWS.Groups(I).Users(j).Name
  Next j
Next I

End Function
```

Creating & Deleting Users

The following code segment creates a user named Bob, with a password of MyPWD, and saves it in the currently used workgroup database:

```
Dim MyWS As Workspace
Dim MyUser As User

Set MyWS = DBEngine.Workspaces(0)
Set MyUser = MyWS.CreateUser("Bob", "MyPID", "MyPWD")
MyWS.Users.Append MyUser
```

The following code segment deletes Bob's user account:

```
Dim MyWS As Workspace

Set MyWS = DBEngine.Workspaces(0)
MyWS.Users.Delete "Bob"
```

Although it's easier for you to create or delete a single-user account in the Access GUI, there may be times when you need to create or delete users in very large numbers. In such cases, you can use the above code segments in looping structures to process multiple user accounts.

Starting New Workspaces

As discussed earlier, creating a Workspace object corresponds to logging on to Access to start a new sessions. Using the CreateWorkSpace method, it's possible to write code that starts a new Access session. In fact, a person running your code can log onto Access under a different username and perform functions under that username.

For example, the following code segment creates a nameless workspace for a user named Bob who has a password of MyPWD, changes the password for a user named Jane from JanePWD1 to JanePWD2, and then logs out by closing the workspace.

```
Dim MyWS As Workspace
Dim MyUser As User
Set MyWS = DBEngine.CreateWorkspace("", "Bob", "MyPWD")
Set MyUser = MyWS.Users("Jane")
MyUser.NewPassword "JanePWD1", "JanePWD2"
MyWS.Close
```

Note that the new session is valid only in code and doesn't interfere with the first session. Also, if you allow your users to run this type of code, you must make sure that they cannot see the design of the code since the password is imbedded in the code.

Containers & Documents

Most permissions in Access are assigned to Document objects or Container objects. There are two types of Container objects: those defined by Microsoft Access and those defined by the Jet database engine. The Containers collection encompasses both types.

The Jet database engine Container objects include:

Container Name	Contains Information About
Databases	Containing databases
Tables	Saved tables and queries
Relationships	Saved relationships

The following four Container objects are defined by Microsoft Access:

Container Name	Contains Information About
Forms	Saved forms
Modules	Saved modules
Reports	Saved reports
Scripts	Saved macros

Each Container object contains a Documents collection. For example, a table or query is a Document object in the Documents collection of the Tables container.

Permissions

In Visual Basic, in order to assign permission on a Container or Document object to a user or group, you need to do the following:

1. Set the UserName property of the Container or Document object to the name of the name of the user or group account to which you want to assign permissions.
2. Set the Permissions property of the Container or Document object.

The Permissions property is a long integer. Different permissions are assigned by setting or resetting specific bits or groups of bits of that long integer. So you set the Permissions property by combining the value of the original

Permissions property and predefined security constants with the bit-wise operators And and Or. For example, let MyDoc be a Document object that corresponds to a table. The following code assigns Read permission on the table:

```
MyDoc.Permissions = MyDoc.Permissions Or DB_SEC_RETRIEVEDATA
```

By contrast, the following code revokes Read permission from the table:

```
MyDoc.Permissions = MyDoc.Permissions And  (Not DB_SEC_RETRIEVEDATA)
```

Since the security constants are so important in object permissions, we will examine them in some detail. Although you could obtain and use the actual values of the constants, it's considered good practice to reference the predefined constants instead using the actual values. Note that the definitions of these constants may change with new versions of Access. The definitions are listed below because some of them may encompass other constants. Here are the definitions of security constants that apply to all objects:

```
'Common Security Constants
Global Const DB_SEC_NOACCESS = &H0&
Global Const DB_SEC_FULLACCESS = &HFFFFF&

Global Const DB_SEC_DELETE = &H10000&
Global Const DB_SEC_READSEC = &H20000&
Global Const DB_SEC_WRITESEC = &H40000&
Global Const DB_SEC_WRITEOWNER = &H80000&
```

Following are the descriptions of these common constants:

- DB_SEC_NOACCESS revokes all permissions to an object from a user or group.
- DB_SEC_FULLACCESS grants all access to an object. However, it doesn't grant permission to grant permissions.
- DB_SEC_DELETE is associated with deleting a document object.
- DB_SEC_READSEC is the permission to read permission. The owner of an object explicitly has this permission.
- DB_SEC_WRITESEC is the permission to set permissions. The owner of an object has this by default.
- DB_SEC_WRITEOWNER is the permission to change the owner of an object (by setting the Owner property of the appropriate Container or Document object).

Tables & Queries Permissions

Tables and queries are both stored in the Tables container, so from here on, *tables* will refer to both tables and queries in the context of security. The following are definitions of table security constants:

```
Global Const DB_SEC_READDEF = &H4&
Global Const DB_SEC_WRITEDEF = &H8& Or DB_SEC_READDEF Or DB_SEC_DELETE
Global Const DB_SEC_RETRIEVEDATA = &H10& Or DB_SEC_READDEF
Global Const DB_SEC_INSERTDATA = &H20&
Global Const DB_SEC_REPLACEDATA = &H40&
Global Const DB_SEC_DELETEDATA = &H80&
```

- DB_SEC_READDEF is permission to read the definition of a table.
- DB_SEC_WRITEDEF is permission to modify the definition of a table.
- DB_SEC_RETREIVEDATA is equivalent to Read permission on a table. It is defined to include READDEF permission. This makes sense: Access needs to know what fields there are in a table before it can retrieve values in those fields.
- DB_SEC_INSERTDATA is Insert (or Append) permission on a table.
- DB_SEC_DELETEDATA is Delete permission on a table.
- DB_SEC_REPLACEDATA is Update (or Modify) permission on a table.

Forms, Reports, Macros & Modules Permissions

Forms, reports, macros, and modules are defined by Access, instead of by the Jet database engine. There are only three types of permissions that apply to each category: Read, Write, and Execute. The following are the definitions of their security constants:

```
'Form and Report Constants:
Global Const DB_SEC_FRMRPT_READDEF = &H4&
Global Const DB_SEC_FRMRPT_WRITEDEF = &H8& Or DB_SEC_FRMRPT_READDEF Or
DB_SEC_DELETE
Global Const DB_SEC_FRMRPT_EXECUTE = &H100&

'Macro Constants:
Global Const DB_SEC_MAC_READDEF = &HA&
Global Const DB_SEC_MAC_WRITEDEF = &H6& Or DB_SEC_DELETE
Global Const DB_SEC_MAC_EXECUTE = &H8&

'Module Constants:
Global Const DB_SEC_MOD_READDEF = &H2&
Global Const DB_SEC_MOD_WRITEDEF = &H4& Or DB_SEC_MOD_READDEF Or
DB_SEC_DELETE
```

- EXECUTE is permission to open/run the object.
- READDEF is permission to see an object's design in design mode.
- WRITEDEF is permission to alter an object's design.

Database Permissions

The Database object itself doesn't have permissions. Instead, the permissions for the whole database are inherited from the lone document in the Database container named MSysDb. Some of the security constants that apply to this document are:

- DB_SEC_DBOPEN is permission to open a given database.
- DB_SEC_DBEXCLUSIVE is permission to open a given database exclusively. Of course, you need DB_SEC_DBOPEN to open a database in the first place.
- DB_SEC_DBADMIN is permission to administer a database (i.e., to convert it into a replicable database or to set a database password).
- DB_SEC_DBCREATE is permission to create a database. Because this permission is related to a user's account, it is stored in the workgroup database. It is not available in the Access GUI; you can access it only through Visual Basic code. The following code revokes the user Joe's permission to create new database under the currently used workgroup database:

```
Dim MyDB As DATABASE, MyCont As Container
Dim MySys As String

MySys = "c:\msoffice\access\system.mdw"

Set MyDB = DBEngine.Workspaces(0).OpenDatabase(MySys)
Set MyCont = MyDB.Containers("Databases")

MyCont.UserName = "Joe"
MyCont.Permissions = MyCont.Permissions And Not DB_SEC_DBCREATE
```

Containers Permissions

Permissions that are applicable to Container objects are:

- DB_SEC_READCONTROL.
- DB_SEC_WRITEDAC.
- DB_SEC_WRITEOWNER.
- DB_SEC_CREATE.

Container objects have an Inherit property. If you set the Inherit property of a Container object to True and then set a permission on the container, then all new documents created in that container will inherit this permission. This is equivalent to setting permissions on new objects in the Access GUI.

Security Examples

The following are some practical examples of programming Access security in Visual Basic code. All the examples assume the following declarations:

Check Explicit Read Permission on a Table

This example shows how you can check if a particular user has explicit Read permission on an object:

```
Dim MyDoc As Document, MyCont As Container
Dim MyDB As DATABASE

Set MyDB = CurrentDb()
Set MyDoc = MyDB.Containers!Tables.Documents("Orders")
MyDoc.UserName = "Joe"

If (MyDoc.Permissions And DB_SEC_RETRIEVEDATA) Then
   MsgBox "Joe has explicit Read permission on Orders."
Else
   MsgBox "Joe has no explicit Read permission on Orders."
End If
```

This code checks if the user Joe has been granted Read permission on the Orders table and displays a message on the status of the permission. The expression:

```
MyDoc.Permissions And DB_SEC_RETRIEVEDATA
```

is a bit-wise operation that yields a value of TRUE if the part of the Permissions value that corresponds to Read permission matches its counterpart in DB_SEC_RETRIVEDATA.

Note that this code segment only checks the explicit Read permission granted to Joe directly. It doesn't check Joe's permissions inherited from the groups he belongs to.

List Explicit & Implicit Read Permission on a Table

This example illustrates how you can obtain both explicit and implicit permissions on an object for each user defined in the currently used workgroup database:

```
Dim MyWS As Workspace, MyDB As Database
Dim MyDoc As Document
Dim MyUser As String

Set MyWS = DBEngine.Workspaces(0)
Set MyDB = CurrentDb()
'Set the document you want to look at:
Set MyDoc = MyDB.Containers("Tables").Documents("Orders")

For J = 0 To MyWS.Users.Count - 1

   'Check explicit permissions
   MyDoc.UserName = MyWS.Users(J).Name
   If (MyDoc.Permissions And DB_SEC_RETRIEVEDATA) Then
     Debug.Print MyWS.Users(J).Name & " can read " & MyDoc.Name
   End If

   'Check implicit permissions
   For I = 0 To MyWS.Users(J).Groups.Count - 1
      MyDoc.UserName = MyWS.Users(J).Groups(I).Name
      If (MyDoc.Permissions And DB_SEC_RETRIEVEDATA) Then
         Debug.Print MyWS.Users(J).Name & " can read " & MyDoc.Name & "
through the group " & MyWS.Users(J).Groups(I).Name
      End If
   Next I

Next J
```

This code segment first examines the table Orders. It loops through all the user accounts defined in the currently used workgroup database. For each user, it first lists any explicit Read permission on the Orders table granted to the user. Then it goes through all the groups to which a user belongs. For each group in which the user is a member, it lists any Read permission on the Orders table granted to the group. It displays the result in the Debug window.

Grant Read Permission on a Table to a User

This example shows how you can grant Read permission on a table to a user:

```
Dim MyDoc As Document
Dim MyDB As DATABASE

Set MyDB = CurrentDb()
Set MyDoc = MyDB.Containers!Tables.Documents("Orders")
MyDoc.UserName = "Joe"

MyDoc.Permissions = MyDoc.Permissions Or DB_SEC_RETRIEVEDAT
```

This example gives Read permission on the Orders table to the user Joe. Note that you can add permissions to the Permissions property of a Document or Container object by using the Or operator to combine the existing Permissions property with predefined security constants.

Revoke Execute Permission on a Form From a Group

This example shows how you can remove Execute permission on a form from a group:

```
Dim MyDoc As Document
Dim MyDB As Database

Set MyDB = CurrentDb()
Set MyDoc = MyDB.Containers!Forms.Documents("frm_Orders")
MyDoc.UserName = "Joe"

MyDoc.Permissions = MyDoc.Permissions And Not DB_SEC_FRMRPT_EXECUTE
```

This example revokes Execute permission on the form frm_Orders from the user Joe. Note that the Container object in this case is Forms.

Preventing A Group From Saving New Tables & Queries

You have created a secure Access application that only authorized users can access. After a while, you realize that your database seems to be rapidly growing in size because your users have been saving new tables and queries into the database. This example shows how you can prevent a group from saving new tables and queries in a database.

```
Dim MyCont As Container
Dim MyDB As DATABASE

Set MyDB = CurrentDb()
Set MyCont = MyDB.Containers!Tables
MyCont.UserName = "Users"

MyCont.Permissions = MyCont.Permissions And Not DB_SEC_CREATE
```

After this code segment is run, the Users group will not be able to create new tables and queries. Note that DB_SEC_CREATE is a permission of the Tables container and not of a permission of any Table document.

SQL Server Security

Like Microsoft Access, SQL Server implements user-level security. Each user logs on to SQL Server under his or her own login ID and password. SQL Server then looks up the group to which the user belongs. Permissions on objects are assigned to users and groups.

Compared with Access security, SQL Server security is relatively straightforward. Each instance of SQL Server provides its own independent, integrated security—you don't have to deal with multiple workgroups and external workgroup information files. It is more robust and tamper-proof; it is also easier to administer because of its centralized nature. On the other hand, it is also more rigid than Access security, as will be discussed later.

There are several possible configurations for implementing SQL Server security. In the Windows NT environment, you can combine NT security with SQL Server security by using one set of login IDs and passwords. This is called *integrated security*. Since we are only interested in using SQL Server in conjunction with Access for Windows 95, we will discuss only standard SQL Server security, which uses SQL Server's own login validation process and bypasses Windows NT security.

Login IDs

A *login ID*, or simply *login*, is a unique name used to identify a user on SQL Server. To access SQL Server, a user must have a valid login ID. Each login ID is mapped to a machine-generated unique number called *system user ID* (SUID), which serves as SQL Server's internal identifier for a user.

Several parameters are associated with a login ID, which you specify when you create a login ID. The parameters include the following:

- The password for the login ID. The default is NULL.
- The default language.
- The default database, which is the database that the user is connected to immediately after logging in to SQL Server.
- The databases to which the login ID will be permitted access.
- A username (or alias) and, optionally, a group for each database to which the login ID is permitted access.

Two login IDs are automatically created when SQL Server is installed on your computer—SA and PROBE:

- SA stands for systems administrator. SA is the super-user of SQL Server who can do everything permitted by SQL Server.

- PROBE is a special login ID created by the SQL Server Setup program. It's useful only for some administration functions that are seldom related to users.

Database Users

Unlike in Access, having a login ID is not sufficient for a user to access a SQL Server database. You must assign a *database username* to a user's login ID before the user can access a database. The username can be one created uniquely for that login ID, or it can be mapped to several login IDs. In other words, several users may share the same username in an SQL Server database.

Users must be belong to at least one, at most two, groups. An SQL Server group is conceptually very similar to an Access group. A group is a collection of users and is a convenient way to provide common permissions to those users. You can specify which group(s) a user belongs to when you create the user in a database. There is a built-in group, called Public, that users belong to by default.

A user who creates a database becomes the database owner (DBO) and has full privileges for that database. A user who creates a database object (for example, a table or a view) becomes the database object owner and has full privileges for that object.

Usernames

A user's login ID is associated with each instance of SQL Server as a whole; a *database username*, on the other hand, is only known to an SQL Server database. A database is assigned to a login ID for the purpose of allowing a user to have access to a database. Each username is mapped to a machine-generated unique number called *user ID* (UID), which is internal to each database and serves as the user's identifier inside the database. A database username is often simply referred to as a *user*. The abilities a user has within a database depend on the permissions granted to the username and the permissions granted to any groups to which the username belongs.

In order for a user to become a database user, he or she must already have a login ID on SQL Server. If you add a new user to a database without specifying a username, the username is automatically the same as the login ID. Since usernames are distinct from login IDs, it's possible to accommodate different users with the same username in different databases. For example, a user Elaine in one database won't interfere with another user Elaine in another database, even though the two users have different login IDs.

Users who have access to a database need additional permissions to access objects inside the database. These permissions can be granted by the database owner or the owners of individual database objects.

Aliases

An *alias* is a database username that is shared by several login IDs. An alias allows you to treat more than one person as the same user inside a database, giving all of them the same permissions. For example, you can assign several users to the alias of the database owner (DBO) so that they will all have DBO permission.

Since an alias is a special type of database username, you can create an alias in the same way as you do an ordinary database username. To give a user an alias, simply assign a login ID to an existing database username instead of creating a unique username specifically for that login ID. A login ID that can be assigned to only one alias automatically belongs to the group(s) that the alias belongs to. If a user is already authorized to use a database, you must drop the username for that login ID before you can assign an alias to it.

Groups

In SQL Server, a group refers to set of users defined in a database. The users of a group automatically inherit the database permissions granted to the group. Therefore, groups allow permissions to be granted to and revoked from multiple people at the same time, thus greatly simplifying the management of a large number of database users who share common requirements. When you create users, you can add them to appropriate groups.

Every database has a built-in group, public. Each user automatically belongs to public and can be added to one other group. Note that this is very different from Access, in which a user may belong to as many as groups as there are in a workgroup. You cannot remove a user from the public group.

When you drop a group, all users in that group are automatically removed from the group. However, dropping a group does not drop its users. Users who were members of the dropped group are still valid users in the database and members of the public group.

Owners

Within each SQL Server database, there are two types of owners: the *database owner* and *database object owners*.

Database Owner The database owner (DBO) is the creator of a database. The systems administrator must grant special permissions to a user before the user can create a database. The DBO has full privileges inside the database that he or she owns. The DBO can:

- Control user access to the database.
- Grant or revoke permissions within the database.

- Create and remove groups.
- Manage group memberships.

Just like other users, a database owner logs in to SQL Server by using an assigned login ID. In his or her own database, the user is recognized as DBO; in other databases, the database owner is known by his or her database username, which may or may not be the same as his or her login ID.

When SQL Server is installed, the systems administrator is the database owner of the master database. The systems administrator is also treated as database owner of any databases he or she uses. In each database, only one login ID can be DBO, although several login IDs can be aliased to DBO.

Database Object Owner Database objects include tables, indexes, views, defaults, triggers, rules, and procedures. The user who creates a database object is the *database object owner*. In order for a user to be able to create a particular type of object, the database owner must first grant him or her permissions to do so.

The owner of a database object is automatically granted full permissions on it. A database object owner must explicitly grant permissions to other users before they can access the object.

Unlike in Access, there is no way to transfer the ownership of objects in SQL Server. In Access, when you delete a user account, an object originally owned by this user stays unaffected except in one respect: under the Change Owners tab of the User and Group Permissions window, the owner of the object becomes <Unknown>. In SQL Server, however, if a database object owner must be dropped from a database, the owned objects must first be dropped.

Permissions

There are two types of permissions in SQL Server security: *object permissions* and *statement permissions*.

Object Permissions

Object permissions regulate the use of certain SQL statements on certain database objects. They can only be granted and revoked by the owner of the object. The object permissions are listed in Table 10-1.

Statement	Object
SELECT	Table, view, columns
UPDATE	Table, view, columns
INSERT	Table, view
DELETE	Table, view
REFERENCE	Table
EXECUTE	Stored procedure

Table 10-1: The object permissions in SQL Server.

To grant or revoke object permissions, use SQL Enterprise Manager or the GRANT and REVOKE statements.

Statement Permissions

Statement permissions are tied to SQL statements and not to specific objects. Within an SQL Server database, statement permissions can be granted only by the SA or the database owner. Statement permissions are not transferable across databases. Statement permissions are applicable to the following statements:

- CREATE DATABASE.
- CREATE DEFAULT.
- CREATE PROCEDURE.
- CREATE RULE.
- CREATE TABLE.
- CREATE VIEW.
- DUMP DATABASE.
- DUMP TRANSACTION.

You can use the SQL Enterprise Manager or the GRANT/REVOKE statements to grant or revoke statement permissions.

Views & Stored Procedures

A user can be granted permission on a view or on a stored procedure even if he or she doesn't have permissions on objects that the view or procedure references. This is extremely important for the implementation of column-level security, which will be discussed later.

Views

Views are by design well suited for the implementation of selective data access, that is, accessing a subset of a table. Through a view, users can query and modify only the data they can see. The following scenarios exist:

- Accessing only those rows that meet certain criteria.
- Accessing a restricted number of columns.
- Accessing a restricted number of rows for a restricted number of columns from a table.
- Presenting only summary information from a table.

You can grant or revoke permissions on a view with the same method you use to grant or revoke permissions on tables.

Stored Procedures

The one relevant permission for stored procedures is EXECUTE. A user with permission to execute a stored procedure can do so even if he or she doesn't have permissions on tables or views referenced by the stored procedure.

EXECUTE can be granted or revoked by using the SQL Enterprise Manager or the GRANT/REVOKE statements.

Ownership Chains

In SQL Server, views can be based on other views and/or tables. Procedures can be based on other procedures, views, and/or tables. These dependencies constitute an *ownership chain*.

Often the entire chain is owned by the same user and resides in the same database. When a user opens a view or runs a stored procedure whose underlying objects are all owned by himself or herself and reside in the same database, then SQL Server doesn't check permissions on any of the underlying objects. In this case, only the permissions on the top-level view or stored procedure are checked to maximize efficiency.

For example, let's say there is a view, View1, which selects records from a base table, Table1. Both Table1 and View1 are owned by the same user, Albert, who grants SELECT permission on View1 to another user, Elaine. When Elaine tries to run View1, SQL Server only checks whether Elaine has permission to read from View1. Since Albert has given her this permission, SQL Server allows her to run View1 regardless of whether Elaine has permission to read from Table1.

However, if the ownership chain of a procedure or view is broken–that is, if not all the objects in the chain are owned by the same user–SQL Server checks permissions on each object in the chain whose next higher link is owned by a different user plus, of course, the top object. This rule allows the owner of an object to exercise control over who can access the object.

For example, let's say the following situation exists:

- Albert owns View4, which is based on View3.
- Silvia owns View3, which is based on View 2.
- Albert owns View2, which is based on View1.
- Albert owns View1, which is based on Table1.
- Albert owns Table1.

When Elaine tries to run View4, SQL Server checks whether she has permissions on View4, View3, and View2. It doesn't check View1 and Table1 because they are owned by the same owner as View2.

Combined Access/SQL Server Security

Microsoft Access and SQL Server constitute two distinct pieces in a combined client/server environment. Therefore, security for a hybrid database application entails protecting both the Access front-end MDB file and the data residing on SQL Server.

As you have seen earlier, Access security and SQL Server security have their own strengths and weaknesses. In general, data security should mostly be performed at the server level using SQL Server logins/passwords because of the high degree of protection SQL Server offers. In some cases, however, Access security techniques can be used to hide SQL Server login IDs and passwords. The primary function of Access security in a client/server application is to protect the front-end MDB file.

Protecting the Front End

As the front-end component in a client/server application, Access shields SQL Server from direct user interaction and provides transparent access to SQL Server data. Not surprisingly, the Access front end is most vulnerable to user damage—accidental or deliberate.

To protect an Access MDB file, several measures can be taken that offer varying degrees of protection. One is thoroughly securing an Access database using methods described earlier in the chapter, assigning different permissions on every object in the database to appropriate Access users/groups. Another possibility is to implement little real security on a database and then hide everything away from well-meaning and not-too-curious users. Variations based on these two extremes are all viable possibilities.

To implement the keep-everything-out-of-sight strategy, create a macro called AUTOEXEC that performs the following upon starting up the Access database:

- Opens a form that serves as the main menu to your application.
- Hides the Database window.
- Hides all built-in toolbars. Shows custom toolbars when necessary.
- Replaces the custom menu bar with either a blank one or one with very limited choices that won't lead a user to "explore" your database.
- Disables the F11 key in a macro called AutoKeys.

If you want to open the database without running the AutoExec macro, press the Shift key while opening the database. If your user doesn't know or use this action, he or she simply won't be able to get to the objects in the database.

Column-Level Security Strategies

Column level security is a type of selective data access in which a user has permissions to read or alter some, but not all, columns of a table. The easiest way to implement column-level security is to use SQL Server views. These are the steps:

1. Create a view that selects the columns you want from a table.
2. Grant permissions to the view.
3. Revoke all permissions from the view's underlying table.
4. Link the view to your Access front end. If the view is to be updated, create a unique index on the linked view (see Chapter 7).

If you want to accomplish the same thing in Access by using an intermediate Access query based on a linked SQL Server table, you need to follow these steps:

1. In the SQL Server Enterprise Manager, grant appropriate permissions on the SQL Server table of interest to all your users.
2. Link the SQL Server table to your front-end Access application. In Access, revoke all permissions on the linked table from those users who are not allowed to view the entire table.
3. Create a new SELECT query in Access that includes the fields of your choice from the linked SQL Server table.
4. Make sure you own this query.
5. Set the RunPermissions property of the query to Owner's.

6. In Access, grant appropriate permissions (some or all of Read Design, Read Data, Update Data, Delete Data, and Insert Data permissions) on the query to the users and groups who should be able to access the data in the linked SQL Server table.

Your users will now be able to read or alter data in the linked SQL Server table through the local Access query. From within your Access application, they won't be able to see the table itself. However, this approach has significant shortcomings:

- It is more complicated than the first method because you have to worry about two sets of user permissions, one on SQL Server and the other in Access.
- Your users are not truly prevented from viewing the entire SQL Server table—and this is a fatal flaw. It's true they can't directly open it from your Access application; however, they can always link to it from another Access database (remember that your users have to have SQL Server permissions to the SQL Server table—when a user runs the query, it's his or her SQL Server login and password that get sent to SQL Server by the Jet database engine instead of your own).

Therefore, implementing column-level security through the use of SQL Server views is clearly superior to implementing column-level security through linked tables.

Row-Level Security Strategies

Row-level security allows users access to only some of the rows in a table. There are many ways you can accomplish this, which we will consider in turn in the following subsections.

Simple Restrictions

Conceptually, this is the easiest method for implementing row-level security. For example, the following example returns all orders that have not been shipped:

```
Create View Unshipped_Orders As
SELECT *
FROM Orders
WHERE Shipped_Flag = 'N'
```

Of course, you have to grant READ permission on this view to the group PUBLIC and then revoke Read permissions on the Orders table from PUBLIC. After you create this view in SQL Server, you can simply link it to your Access database and use it as a table.

Let's take a look at another example. A table contains overtime/absence records of employees in a company. There is a field in the table called Employee_Login. When a record is submitted, that field is filled with an employee's SQL login name. Now you want each employee to be able to see only his or her own records. To do this, make the following view:

```
Create View Your_Time_Sheet As
SELECT *
FROM Employee_Time
WHERE Employee_Login = USER_NAME()
```

where USER_NAME() is a very useful SQL Server system function that returns the username of the user currently accessing data through the view. Of course, you have to grant READ permission on this view to the group PUBLIC and then revoke READ permission on the Orders table from the group PUBLIC.

Employing Security Lookup Tables

Let's take the time sheet example one step further. Say there is another field in the table called Department, which shows the department that an employee is in. The secretary in each department needs to see all the records from his or her own department. One way to do this is to create a security lookup table listing each secretary's username along with his or her department. This security lookup table, Security_Lookup, may look like this:

Secretary_Login	Department_Code
jsmith	1
susanwilliams	2
johnson	3
bill	4

You have to make sure that everyone has READ permission on the Security_Lookup table. Now you can create a view, Your_Departmental_Time_Sheet, that implements the security lookup:

```
Create View Your_Departmental_Time_Sheet As
SELECT T1.*
FROM Employee_Time T1, Security_Lookup T2
WHERE T1.Department = T2.Department_Code
      T2.Secretary_Login = USER_NAME()
```

Embedding Security Information in SQL Server Database Username

The preceding example involves the joining of two tables, which may slow down the performance somewhat if the lookup table is large. An alternative method is to take advantage of a user's database username. For example, every employee in a company, EGI, has access to the same SQL Server database. Their usernames are all of the same form, EGI_X_username, where X represents the department an employee is in. You can set usernames in the SYSUSERS table in a database.

With username properly set, you can create a modified version of Your_Departmental_Time_Sheet as follows without a lookup table:

```
Create View Your_Departmental_Time_Sheet As
SELECT *
FROM Employee_Time
WHERE Secretary_Login =  SUBSTRING(USER_NAME(),1,5)
```

Again, you have to grant READ permission on this view to the group PUBLIC and then revoke READ permission on the Orders table from the group PUBLIC. You can link this view to your Access database and use it as a table.

Complex Security Hierarchy in Username

In previous examples, security divisions are at the same level: each user can read from a department but can't read records from multiple departments, for example. To allow certain users, say employees of the personnel department, to access multiple security divisions on the same level, you need a security hierarchy. Using the username method, you can format usernames as EGI_X_Y, where X is still the one-digit department code, and Y can be either P (personnel) or O (other).

If you want to allow users from the personnel department to have a choice of selecting one or more departments, then the best way to do it is through a combination of Access and SQL Server operations. The following are the steps:

1. Link the Employee_Time table to an Access database.
2. Write an Access query based on the linked table Employee_Time. Call it Select_Employee_Time.
3. In Access, write a pass-through query, sql_username, which retrieves a user's SQL username. Its SQL Command string should simply be SELECT USER_NAME().

4. Write a Visual Basic procedure that runs sql_username, retrieves the SQL Server database username, and extracts security information from the SQL username. If Y=O, then this procedure returns X; if Y=P, this procedure prompts the user for any department code or lets the user enter the wildcard character * for all departments and then returns the input value.
5. Use this procedure as argument to the LIKE operator in the criterion grid of the Department column of the query Select_Employee_Time.

Summary

The fact that security issues in the Access/SQL Server environment are discussed in the last chapter of this book by no means implies that they are less important than the other topics. On the contrary, security is among the first things you have to consider in the planning stages of an application because it will affect how you structure your database.

Fortunately, with the possibilities provided by the client/server environment, you have a vast repertoire of techniques from which to find a balanced security setup. Hopefully, you have gained a firsthand feel for the variety and subtlety of security implementations in the Access/SQL Server environment.

appendix A

About the Companion CD-ROM

The Companion CD-ROM included with your copy *of Client Server Programming with Access & SQL Server* contains author source files and valuable software. The author source files are found in the Resources folder.

Navigating the CD-ROM

To find out more about the CD-ROM and its contents, please open the "README.HTM" file in your favorite browser. You will see a small menu offering several links.

Listing of Author Files

File	Description
MKT_DUMP.DAT	SQL Server database dump that has to be loaded into the reader's Server to be able to run most of the following examples. Database should be called MARKETING_WAREHOUSE and its size should be at least 100M. See Chapter 4 for information on how to load a file into an SQL Server database. Two ODBC data sources, MARKETING and MARKETING1 pointing to this database, are also required.

File	Description
ERR_TAB.MDB	Code example on creating a table with Access error messages (Appendix B).
JOINFRMT.MDB	Illustrates the differences in the two formats of the SQL Server SELECT statement (Chapter 8).
FRCEPLAN.MDB	Illustrates the problem with the SQL Server optimizer (Chapter 7)
RFSH_DS.MDB	Example of the "Refresh all the table links" function (Chapter 7).
SECURITY.MDB	Illustrates the Explicit and Implicit security permissions in Access (Chapter 10).
MKT_MENU.MDB and MKT_CUST.MDB	These two files together illustrate the technique of splitting an Access application into separate .MDB files and opening one .MDB file from another (Chapter 9). Copy these two files into your C:\TEMP directory. If your are using Access 97, convert both .MDB files to Access 97 format.
DIFF_DS.MDB	Illustrates performance degradation caused by using two different ODBC data sources (Chapter 9).
CHNG_DS.MDB	Code example for changing ODBC data source throughout the whole application (Chapter 7).
TEMP_QRY.MDB	Code example for creating temporary query on the fly (Chapter 8).
TOOLBAR.MDB	Code example for hiding/showing toolbars and the status bar (Chapter 10).
VIEW_QRY.MDB	Illustrates a problem with using outer join in Access query based on an SQL Server view that contains an outer join itself (Chapter 7).

Software on the CD-ROM

File	Description
CuteFTP	CuteFTP is a Windows-based Internet application that allows novice users to utilize the capabilities of FTP without having to know all the details of the protocol itself. It simplifies FTP by offering a user-friendly, graphical interface instead of cumbersome command-line utility. Visit http://www.cuteftp.com for more information.
Desktop DBA	Platinum Technologies' Desktop DBA is a Windows-based, multi-server data administration and migration tool for Oracle, Sybase, Microsoft SQL Server, and Informix databases. One of these must be installed in order for this program to run. Database objects, including tables, indexes, and keys, can be created and altered,

File	Description
	without knowing the complex SQL involved. Tedious, repetitive tasks are made simple. This product needs a password to be activated. The password is HAQFIJ2J5RJEJ8ITPIJIQU, and the serial number is 000000000000000. Note: Before installing this program, read the dspx22ig.pdf file in the Dsktpdba folder for more information. (If you don't already have a copy of Acrobat Reader to view the .pdf file, double-click on the Ar32e30.exe file to install a copy.)
SQLBench	SQLBench is a multi-platform load testing tool which is designed to predict the reliability of client-server applications before or after they are programmed/deployed. SQLBench produces simulations, standard TPC or custom benchmarks and test data for Client/Server databases. SQLBench works in the design phase and does not require a completed application. SQLBench can model an unlimited number of virtual users, up to 300 virtual users on one NT workstation. The versatile Test Data Generator supports 14 built-in and any user-defined random functions. Wizards and plug-in benchmarks make SQLBench the most cost-effective tool for database application testing. For information on how to use SQLBench see the ManualV4.doc on this CD-ROM.
SQL Spy	This is a time limited version of Platinum Technologies' SQL-Spy: a Windows-based, real-time performance monitoring, event definition, and notification tool for distributed database servers. It can simultaneously track numerous heterogeneous databases (Oracle, SYBASE SQL Server, Microsoft SQL Server, Informix, and DB2 common server) from a single desktop console. (One of these servers must be installed in order for this program to run.) By providing bar charts, graphs, and other graphical displays, it enables DBAs to quickly evaluate system status and database activities. In addition, SQL-Spy can automatically perform appropriate user-defined and/or predefined actions when certain activity thresholds are reached. It offers users over 250 pre-defined events and allows them to create an unlimited number of user-defined events and script files. Winner of ENT Magazine's Reader's Choice Award, 1996, this program needs a password to be activated. The password is 3Q1IY2J5RJBJ5ITPIJIQU and the serial number is 000000000000000. Note: Before installing this program, read the ddbs40ig.pdf file for more information. (If you don't already have a copy of Acrobat Reader to view the .pdf file, double-click on the Ar32e30.exe file to install a copy.)

Technical Support

Technical support is available for installation-related problems only. The technical support office is open from 8:00 A.M. to 6:00 P.M. Monday through Friday and can be reached via the following methods:

- Phone: (919) 544-9404 extension 81.
- Faxback Answer System: (919) 544-9404 extension 85.
- E-mail: help@vmedia.com.
- FAX: (919) 544-9472.
- World Wide Web: **http://www.vmedia.com/support.**
- America Online: keyword *Ventana.*

Limits of Liability & Disclaimer of Warranty

The authors and publisher of this book have used their best efforts in preparing the CD-ROM and the programs contained in it. These efforts include the development, research, and testing of the theories and programs to determine their effectiveness. The authors and publisher make no warranty of any kind expressed or implied, with regard to these programs or the documentation contained in this book.

The authors and publisher shall not be liable in the event of incidental or consequential damages in connection with, or arising out of, the furnishing, performance, or use of the programs, associated instructions, and/or claims of productivity gains.

Some of the software on this CD-ROM is shareware; there may be additional charges (owed to the software authors/makers) incurred for their registration and continued use. See individual program's README or VREADME.TXT files for more information.

appendix B

Access Run-Time Errors

The Run-Time errors occur when an Access application is running. Use the On Error statement to trap the errors and error handling procedures to process them. If the On Error statement is not used, Access will open a dialog box indicating error code and the short error description. After you click OK button on the dialog box, application will be interrupted.

Use the ERR_TAB.MDB Access application on the Companion CD-ROM to generate and examine an Access table containing error codes and messages. The ErrorTable in this application is created by the Visual Basic code that calls the Error() function to generate error messages for the specified error codes.

3 Return without GoSub

Description For some reason, Access does not detect this problem at compile time, so it causes run-time error.

Cause/Solution *A matching GoSub statement can not be found for the Return statement in your program.*

➤ Insert GoSub statement.

5 Invalid procedure call

Description The procedure call can not be completed.

Cause/Solution *A procedure argument exceeds the maximum value. For example, the argument of the Sin function is greater or equal to 2,147,483,648.*

➤ Check the procedure argument for the valid values.

Procedure is not valid on the current platform. For example, some procedures may only be valid for the Macintosh and cause this error if called from an Access application running under Windows.

➤ Check to see if a procedure is valid on your platform.

6 Overflow

Description This error occurs when you are trying to assign a value that exceeds the maximum.

Cause/Solution *The result is too large for the type of variable used in a expression.*

➤ Change the datatype for the variable.

The value assigned to a property exceeds the maximum value that this property can accept.

➤ Assign the valid value to the property.

7 Out of memory

Description This error occurs when memory required for an operation can not be allocated.

Cause/Solution *Too many Windows applications open.*

➤ Get rid of all the unnecessary applications.

An extremely large Access module.

➤ Break a large module into several smaller modules.

Your system does not meet requirements for running Access.

➤ Upgrade your system's hardware.

You operating system has inefficient virtual memory settings.

➤ Adjust your virtual memory settings in Windows.

There is not enough space for the Public variables.

➤ Get rid of unused and unnecessary Public variables.

9 Subscript out of range

Description This error occurs when a value of an array subscript used in an expression is out of the array's boundaries.

Cause/Solution *The value of the subscript is smaller then the minimum or larger than the maximum specified in the array declaration.*

➤ Check the declaration of the array to find out its upper and lower limits. To dynamically detect these values, use the UBound and LBound functions.

The array was declared without specifying the index range. For example, the following code causes this error:

```
Dim Last_Names() As String
Last_Names(8) = "Smith"
```

➤ You can not assign values to an array with unspecified array ranges until you explicitly specify the number of elements.

The expression contains a nonexistent collection member. For example, the expression:

```
MyDB.TableDefs(23).RefreshLink
```

will cause an error if you have less than 23 tables in your application.

➤ Use a variation of this code instead:

```
For I = 0 To MyDB.TableDefs.Count - 1   'Step through all the
TableDef objects in the
 'TableDefs collection.
  If Left(MyDB.TableDefs(I).Connect, 4)="ODBC" Then
        MyDB.TableDefs(I).RefreshLink
     REFRESHED = REFRESHED + 1
   End If
NEXT I
```

10 This array is fixed or temporarily locked

Description This error is caused by an attempt to redimension an array that is temporarily or permanently locked. Access can temporarily lock arrays even if they are specifically declared as dynamic.

Cause/Solution *An attempt to redimension a fixed-size array. For example, in the following code, the fixed array Last_Names is passed to the procedure More_Customers as array Names, and More_Customers tries to redimension it:*

```
Dim Last_Name(100) As String
   More_Customers Last_Name()
End Sub

Sub More_Customers(Names() As String)
   ReDim Names(500)
   . . .
End Sub
```

➤ To avoid this problem, make the original array dynamic by declaring it without specifying the number of elements:

```
  Dim Last_Name() As String
  More_Customers Last_Name()
End Sub

Sub More_Customers(Names() As String)
  ReDim Names(500)
  . . .
End Sub
```

An attempt to redimension a dynamic array, when one of the array's elements has been passed as an argument to a procedure. Consider, for example, the following code:

```
Dim Last_Names() As String
   . . .
Sub More_Customers()
   ReDim Last_Names (500) As String
   Active_Customers Last_Names (90)
End Sub

Sub Active_Customers(Name As String)
   ReDim Last_Names (200) As String
End Sub
```

➤ The execution of this code will cause an error. Procedure Active_Customers is trying to redimension the dynamic Last_Names array while accepting its element number 90 as a parameter. Access temporarily locks this array to prevent the situation where the parameter loses its value and perhaps even its location in memory.

An attempt to change a value to a Variant variable containing an array, which is currently locked. Consider the following example:

```
Names = Array("Smith","Jones","Brown")
For Each I In Names
   Names = "Jackson"
Next I
```

➤ In this example, the variable Names is locked as it controls the For...Each loop. Use the For...Next instead.

11 Division by zero

Description This error is caused by division by zero.

Cause/Solution *An expression contains a division operation and the value of the divisor is zero.*

➤ In many cases, this situation is caused by the misspelling of a variable. A misspelled name is considered an implicit declaration of a numeric variable that is initially set to zero. If it is not a misspelling, check the value of the divider and make sure that it is not zero.

13 Type mismatch

Description This error caused by an attempt to perform an impossible data conversion.

Cause/Solution *An attempt to convert a value to the wrong type. Consider the following example:*

```
dim Last_Name as Integer
Last_Name = "Smith"
```

➤ This will obviously cause an error. Conversions can be easily made, however, between compatible data types. Use a Variant datatype to accept any value.

An attempt to assign an object to a data variable or pass it as a parameter to a procedure that expects a data value.

➤ Fix the erroneous assignment.

An attempt to use a module or project name where a data value or an object property is expected; for example:

```
Debug.Print <Module Name>
```

➤ Fix the erroneous expression.

An attempt to convert vbError variable to a Date variable or use it with the traditional error handling.

➤ Use an explicit conversion.

An attempt to print a Variant containing an array (using Print # statement).

➤ Use a variation of this code to print an array:

```
For I=1 to 10
 print #1 Last_Name(I)
Next I
```

14 Out of string space

Description This error is caused by incorrect manipulations of the extra long String variables. The maximum string length value can be different for the different operating systems and for the different versions of Access.

Cause/Solution *The following code may cause an "Out of string space" error:*

```
Last_Name = "Smith"
For I = 1 To 100
   Last_Name = Last_Name + Last_Name
Next I
```

Use this code to avoid the problem:

```
Last_Name = " "
John_Smith = "Smith"
For I = 1 To 101
   Last_Name = Last_Name + John_Smith
Next I
```

An attempt to allocate a long string when a workstation does not have sufficient amount of memory.

➤ Close unused applications; remove unnecessary TSRs, device drivers, and so on; upgrade the hardware on your workstation.

16 Expression too complex

Description This error is caused by an excessive number of "sub-expressions" in an expression, and it varies among platforms. For Windows 95, you can have up to eight levels of nested floating-point expressions.

Cause/Solution *An attempt to run a floating-point expression containing too many nested sub-expressions.*

➤ Break the complex expression into several simple expressions as necessary.

17 Can't perform requested operation

Description The requested operation can not be performed in the current state of the project.

Cause/Solution *An attempt to perform an operation that would invalidate the current state of Access.*

➤ Run the operation after changing the current status. For example, stop execution of the currently running code.

An attempt was made to programmatically modify the module that is currently running.

➤ Again, you have to stop the currently running module, make all the necessary corrections and additions, and then restart the module. You can programmatically modify the code that is not currently running, though.

18 User interrupt occurred

Description This is not really an error; the execution of an application was interrupted by a user.

Cause/Solution *A user pressed Ctrl+Break.*

➤ Use Run | Continue or press F5 to continue execution. This interruption can be handled by an On Error statement.

20 Resume without error

Description A Resume statement can only be executed inside an error-handling program.

Cause/Solution *An attempt to execute a Resume statement outside of an error-handling program.*

➤ Get rid of the erroneous statement.

An attempt to execute a Resume statement within an error-handling program when an error did not occur.

➤ Check a label of the error-handling procedure and the GOTO statements within all the procedures. Make sure the label of the error-handling procedure is specified only in On Error GOTO statements.

28 Out of stack space

Description Access and other computer systems use a working area allocated in memory (stack) to pass parameters between procedures, functions, and subroutines for local variables as well as for other internal functions. Additional space is allocated to the stack as necessary.

Cause/Solution *An attempt to call too many nested procedures, functions, or subroutines.*

➤ Reduce the number of nested calls.

An attempt to allocate more space for the local variables than is available.

➤ Move some local variables to the global level. Use the keyword *Static* to move variables into the static memory pool. Declare the procedure Static to make all the variables static.

An attempt to allocate too much space for the fixed-length strings.

➤ Redefine some of your fixed-length strings as variable-length strings or, as in the previous case, declare them at the module level.

An attempt to make too many nested DoEvents function calls.

➤ Use the Tools | Calls menu option to view the active procedures and limit the number of the nested function calls.

Cascading sequence of events causes recursive calls of an event procedure.

➤ Again, use the Tools | Calls menu option to view the active calls and then fix erroneous logic in the application.

35 Sub, function, or property not defined

Description A Sub, function, or property procedure that you call from within your code must be defined first.

Cause/Solution *Misspelled sub, function, or procedure name.*

➤ Check the spelling and correct it.

An attempt to call a procedure from another project without explicitly adding a reference to that project in the References dialog box.

➤ To add a reference, use the Tools | References menu option to open the References dialog box. Then find the name of the project containing the procedure you want to call. Use the Browse button to search for the desirable project. Check the box to the left of the project name, and click OK.

An attempt to call a procedure that is not within the scope of the calling procedure.

➤ If you are calling a procedure from a different module, do not declare it as Private. If a procedure is called from another project, the Option Private Module must not be in effect.

An attempt to call a routine declared as a dynamic-link library (DLL) routine while it is not in the specified DLL file.

➤ Check the routine name spelling. Check the version of the DLL file. Delete or rename all the old versions of the DLL file found in your system.

47 Too many DLL application clients

Description A dynamic link library (DLL) can only be accessed by 50 simultaneous host applications.

Cause/Solution *An attempt to access the Visual Basic DLL library while it is already being accessed by 50 other applications that are Visual Basic hosts.*

➤ Close some of the open Visual Basic applications accessing the DLL library.

48 Error in loading DLL

Description Visual Basic detected an error while trying to load a DDL.

Cause/Solution *An attempt to load a file that is not in the DLL format.*

➤ Get the right DLL file.

An attempt to load a DLL file that is not compatible with the current version of Windows.

➤ Get the right DLL file.

An attempt to load a DLL file that references another DLL file that can not be found.

➤ Get all the necessary DLL files.

One of the DLL files is not in a directory specified by the PATH command in your operating system and therefore can not be found.

➤ Move all the DLL files to a referenced directory.

49 Bad DLL calling convention

Description This error is caused by an attempt to pass the wrong number of arguments, arguments of the wrong type, or arguments of the wrong calling convention to a DLL routine.

Cause/Solution *An attempt to pass the wrong type of arguments to a routine in a DLL.*

➤ Check types of arguments expected by the routine, and make sure that you pass the right types of arguments.

An attempt to pass the wrong number of arguments to a routine in a DLL.

➤ Check the number of arguments expected by the routine, and make sure that you pass the right number of arguments.

An attempt to pass parameters to a routine in a DLL not using the Pascal calling convention.

➤ Check the calling convention expected by the routine, and if it expects arguments by value, make sure that ByVal is specified.

51 Internal error

Description Unless this is the user-generated error, it is the undefined Visual Basic error, internal malfunction.

Cause/Solution *Visual Basic experiences an internal malfunction.*

➤ Make sure that this is not a user-generated error, and contact Microsoft Product Support Services.

52 Bad filename or number

Description Visual Basic may detect this error when it tries to access an external file.

Cause/Solution *A Visual Basic statement (e.g., WRITE #, INPUT #, PRINT #) refers to a file that is not open.*

➤ Open the file. If the file was open, it can be closed by the Close statement without arguments.

A Visual Basic statement refers to a file out of the range of file numbers (1511).

➤ Fix your code so that it does not specify the wrong file number. If the file numbers are generated by a program, consider using a statement checking for the legitimacy of the generated number.

A Visual Basic statement refers to a file whose name is not valid.

➤ Make sure that the filename conforms to the conventions of your operating system. For example, in Windows 3.1, you can only use eight-letter names with three-letter extensions.

53 File not found

Description Visual Basic could not find the external file specified in a procedure.

Cause/Solution *An attempt to specify an nonexisting filename in a statement (e.g., Kill or Open).*

➤ Check the spelling.

An attempt has been made to call a procedure in a DLL, but the library file specified in the Lib clause of the Declare statement does not exist.

➤ Check the spelling.

An attempt to reference a nonexisting project.

➤ Check the spelling.

54 Bad file mode

Description This error can be caused by opening an external file in the wrong mode.

Cause/Solution *An attempt to use Put or Get statements for a file opened as sequential.*

➤ Put and Get can be only applied to files opened for Random or Binary access. Change the file mode in the OPEN command.

An attempt to use the Print # statement for a file opened for an access mode other than Output or Append.

➤ Change the file mode in the OPEN command, or use a statement other than PRINT #.

An attempt to use the INPUT # statement for a file not open for Input access.

➤ Change the file mode to INPUT in the OPEN command, or use a statement other that INPUT #.

An attempt to write to a read-only file.

➤ Change the read/write file mode.

55 File already open

Description This error is caused by an attempt to open a file that was already open and has not been closed. This attempt will only cause an error in certain circumstances.

Cause/Solution *An attempt to open a file in sequential-output mode for a file that is already open.*

➤ Close the file before opening it again.

An attempt to execute a file-manipulation statement (e.g., Kill, SetAttr, or Name) for a file that has been open.

➤ Close the file before executing the statement.

57 Device I/O error

Description This error can be caused by the malfunctioning of external devices or by their incompatibilities.

Cause/Solution *An input/output error occurred while your program was accessing an external device.*

➤ Make sure that the device operates properly, repair or replace it, and repeat the operation.

58 File already exists

Description This error can be caused by attempting to create a file with a filename that already exists.

Cause/Solution *An attempt to create a new file or rename a file to a name that is identical to a filename that already exists.*

➤ Specify a unique name for the new file, or delete or rename the old file.

An attempt to use the Save As command to save a currently loaded project, while the project name already exists.

➤ Change the project name, or replace the old project.

59 Bad record length

Description This error can be caused by an attempt to write a record with the wrong length to an external file.

Cause/Solution *An attempt to execute the PUT command with a total record length that does not match the length specified in the corresponding Open statement.*

➤ Correct the variables in the PUT command, or change the LEN parameter of the OPEN command to match the right record length.

An attempt to use a variable-length string as the variable in a Put statement.

➤ If the output file is opened for random access, the two-byte descriptor is always added to a variable-length string, and therefore, the string's length must be reduced by two bytes.

An attempt to use a Variant as the variable in a Put statement.

➤ Variant datatype also requires a two-byte descriptor. If a Variant contains a variable-length string, there will be a four-byte descriptor. All these descriptors are considered part of the record length specified in the LEN parameter of the OPEN statement.

61 Disk full

Description This error is caused by the lack of space on the specific disk drive.

Cause/Solution *An attempt to complete a Print #, Write #, or Close operation while there is not enough space on the disk.*

➤ Delete unnecessary and temporary files.

An attempt to create files while there is not enough space on the disk.

➤ Delete unnecessary and temporary files.

62 Input past end of file

Description This error is caused by an attempt to read a file past the end-of-file position.

Cause/Solution *An attempt to execute an INPUT # or LINE INPUT # statement for a file in which the end-of-file condition has been reached.*

➤ Use the EOF function to detect the end-of-file condition. Do not execute any of the reading commands after the end-of-file condition has been reached.

63 Bad record number

Description This error is caused by an incorrect attempt to access a file.

Cause/Solution *An attempt to execute a Put or Get statement when the record number is zero or less than zero.*

➤ Check the spelling for the variable with the record number. If the variable is misspelled, it is implicitly defined and set to zero. If the spelling is correct, check the calculations that could cause this variable to be zero or less than zero.

67 Too many files

Description This error occurs when the number of open files in your operating system exceeds the maximum number of open files allowed.

Cause/Solution *An attempt to create a file in the root directory (in the MS-DOS operating system) when the total number of files in the root directory exceeds the maximum (usually 512).*

➤ Delete unnecessary files in the root directory, or change your program so that it uses a subdirectory.

An attempt to open a file (in the MS-DOS operating system) when the total number of open files in the system exceeds the number specified by the parameter FILES= in your CONFIG.SYS file.

➤ Increase the number specified by the parameter FILES= in your CONFIG.SYS file, and reboot your computer.

An attempt to open more that 40 files while running on a Macintosh machine.

➤ Do not open unnecessary files, close files as soon as you are finished working with them, or use a utility to modify the MaxFiles parameter of the boot block.

68 Device unavailable

Description This error is caused when you are trying to access a device that is not online.

Cause/Solution *An attempt to access a device that is not online.*

➤ Check the connection and power cables used by the device.

An attempt to access a network device after the network connection has been broken.

➤ Restore the network connection.

70 Permission denied

Description This error is caused by an attempt to write to a write-protected disk or file.

Cause/Solution *An attempt to open a write-protected file for sequential Output or Append.*

➤ Reset the Read-Only file attribute, or do not try to write to this file.

An attempt to open a file on a disk that is write-protected for sequential Output or Append.

➤ Make the disk write-enabled, copy the file to another disk, or do not try to write into this file.

An attempt to open a file for sequential Output or Append while a file is locked by another process.

➤ Cancel the process that locks the file, or wait until it closes the file.

An attempt to open the Windows 95 Registry without adequate permissions.

➤ Ask the systems administrator to give you the necessary permissions.

71 Disk not ready

Description This error occurs when a disk drive that you are trying to access returns the "device is not ready" signal.

Cause/Solution *An attempt to access a disk drive that does not have a disk in it.*

➤ Insert a disk into the drive.

An attempt to access a disk drive while the door of the drive is open.

➤ Close the drive door.

74 Can't rename with different drive

Description This error occurs when you are trying to rename a file to a different drive.

Cause/Solution *An attempt to move a file to a different drive using the Name statement.*

➤ Use the FileCopy statement to copy the file to another drive, and then use the Kill statement to delete the old file.

75 Path/File access error

Description This error occurs when you specify the wrong PATH in the file-access operation (e.g., Open, MkDir, ChDir, or RmDir).

Cause/Solution *An attempt to use a relative path while in a different current directory.*

➤ Use a fully qualified (absolute) path.

An attempt to save a file that would replace an existing read-only file.

➤ Reset the Read-Only attribute of the target file, or use a different filename.

76 Path not found

Description This error is caused by the wrong PATH for the file-access commands.

Cause/Solution *An attempt to execute a file-access operation (e.g., Open, MkDir, ChDir, or RmDir) with the PATH that does not exist.*

➤ Specify the right path.

91 Object variable or With block variable not set

Description This error is caused by referencing an object or With block variable that has not been assigned a value.

Cause/Solution *An attempted to reference an object variable that has not been initialized yet by a valid object.*

➤ Set the object variable to the right value. For example, use the Set statement to initialize Rset as a recordset in the following code:

```
Dim RSet As Recordset 'Create object variable.
Set RSet = DB.OpenRecordset("Orders")
Count = RSet.RecordCount
```

An attempt to use an object variable that has been set to Nothing, as in the following example:

```
Set RSet = Nothing
Count = RSet.RecordCount
```

➤ Again, use the Set statement to set the object value.

An attempt to use an object whose value has not been set because the object library in which it is described has not been selected in the References dialog box.

➤ Select the object library in the Add References dialog box.

An attempt to execute the GOTO statement with a label inside a With block.

➤ Change the GOTO destination label.

An attempt to specify a line inside a With block by using the Set Next Statement.

➤ Initialize the With block by executing the With statement.

92 For loop not initialized

Description This error occurs when a loop counter is not initialized.

Cause/Solution *An attempt to get inside a For...Next loop by the GOTO command.*

➤ Do not pass control to a label inside a For…Next loop.

93 Invalid pattern string

Description This error is caused by specifying the wrong pattern string in the Like operation of a search.

Cause/Solution *An attempt to use the wrong pattern string in the Like operation.*

➤ Check the syntax.

94 Invalid use of Null

Description This error is caused by the invalid use of a Variant subtype variable that contains no valid data.

Cause/Solution *An attempt to obtain the value of a Variant variable or an expression that is Null. For example:*

```
Max_Names = Null
For I = 1 To Max_Names
   . . .
Next I
```

➤ Assign a valid value to the variable.

325 Invalid format in resource file

Description This error occurs when you are trying to access a resource file that does not have a valid format.

Cause/Solution *An attempt to access a resource file that does not have a valid format or a specific resource in the file does not have a valid format.*

➤ Get the right resource file.

380 Invalid property value

Description This error is caused by an attempt to assign a wrong value to a property.

Cause/Solution *An attempt to assign an inappropriate value to a property.*

➤ Assign the right value to the property.

423 Property or method not found

Description This error is caused by using an undefined object property or method.

Cause/Solution *An attempt to refer to an undefined method or property of an object.*

➤ Check the spelling. See Visual Basic Help for the valid methods and properties.

424 Object required

Description This error caused by using invalid references to properties and methods for an object.

Cause/Solution *An attempt to refer to an object property or method without an object qualifier.*

➤ Use the explicit qualifier for referencing the property or the method.

An attempt to refer to an object property or method with a qualifier that is not recognized as an object.

➤ Check the spelling. If the spelling is correct, check to see if the object exists and if it is within the visibility scope of your program.

An attempt to refer to the Variant variable as an object when its value was not initialized using the SET command.

➤ Always assign a reference to an object with the Set statement.

429 OLE Automation server can't create object

Description This error is caused by creating objects and not performing all the required preparations for the classes and DLL libraries.

Cause/Solution *An attempt to create an object of a class that is not registered in your system.*

➤ Use the object's application or its setup program to create or correct the information in the Registry.

An attempt to create an object when a DLL required by the object does not exist or is corrupted and can not be used.

➤ Make sure all the necessary DLLs are available. If a corrupted DLL or an older version of a DLL exists on your hard drive, Visual Basic might pick it up instead of the correct DLL. Delete or rename the old DLLs.

An attempt to create an object when it is available, but the object is a licensed OLE object and cannot verify the availability of the license necessary to create an instance.

➤ Reinstall the object's applications.

An attempt to use the GetObject for a class created with Visual Basic.

➤ Do not use GetObject to obtain a reference to a class created with Visual Basic.

An attempt to access an object that can not be accessed at this time.

➤ The object might be temporarily locked to prevent a deadlock. Try to access it later.

430 Class doesn't support OLE Automation

Description This error is caused by using an object that does not support an OLE Automation interface.

Cause/Solution *An attempt to specify a class in the GetObject or CreateObject function that has not exposed a programmability interface.*

➤ Check to see if the application is able to use OLE Automation with this class of object.

432 Filename or class name not found during OLE Automation operation

Description This error is caused by specifying an invalid filename or class name for the GetObject function.

Cause/Solution *An attempt to specify an invalid name of a file or a class in the GetObject function.*

➤ Use the correct names.

438 Object doesn't support this property or method

Description This error is caused by using a property or a method not supported by the object.

Cause/Solution *An attempt to specify a method or property that does not exist for this OLE automation object.*

➤ Use only properties and methods that are valid for the particular object.

440 OLE Automation error

Description This error is reported by Visual Basic when specific OLE Automation errors occur.

Cause/Solution *An error occurred in an object's application.*

➤ Check the properties of the Err object to obtain more information about the error.

443 OLE Automation object does not have a default value

Description This error is caused by specifying an object name without a property or method when the object does not have a default member.

Cause/Solution *An attempt to point to a default property or method for an object when the default member for the specified object can not be determined.*

➤ Do not use the object name without a property. Explicitly specify the property or method.

445 Object doesn't support this action

Description This error is caused by using an unsupported action for an object.

Cause/Solution *An attempt to reference a method or property that is not supported by this object.*

➤ Check the spelling. Check the object's documentation.

446 Object doesn't support named arguments

Description This error is caused by using named arguments not supported by an object.

Cause/Solution *An attempt to access an object whose methods do not support named arguments.*

➤ Use positional notation instead.

447 Object doesn't support current locale setting

Description This error caused by a locale setting that is not supported by an object.

Cause/Solution *An attempt to access an object that does not support the locale setting for the current project.*

➤ Check the object's documentation and your locale settings to find the inconsistencies. Change you locale settings.

One of the national language support dynamic link libraries is out of date.

➤ Install the right version of the DLL; rename or delete the old, outdated DLLs on your hard drive.

448 Named argument not found

Description This error is caused by a named argument that does not appear in the procedure definition.

Cause/Solution *An attempt to use a named argument in a procedure that is not defined to accept an argument by that name.*

➤ Check the spelling.

449 Argument not optional

Description This error is caused by omitting an argument that is not optional.

Cause/Solution *An attempt to omit an argument in a procedure or function call.*

➤ Pass all the required arguments to the function or procedure.

450 Wrong number of arguments

Description This error is caused by passing the wrong number of arguments to a procedure.

Cause/Solution *In a call to a procedure, an attempt to pass a certain number of arguments that does not match the number of required arguments for the procedure.*

➤ Check the number of required arguments for the procedure.

An attempt to specify an index for a control that is not part of a control array.

➤ Remove the index specification in the function call; use the INDEX property of a control instead.

An attempt to assign a value to a Read-Only property.

➤ Check to see if a property is Read-Only, and if it is, do not try to assign a value to it.

451 Object not a collection

Description This error is caused by applying certain properties, methods, or operations to a Non-Collection object.

Cause/Solution *An attempt to specify to an object that is not a collection, an operation, or property that can be only applied to collections.*

➤ Check the spelling.

452 Invalid ordinal

Description This error is caused by a call to a dynamic link library using the #num syntax.

Cause/Solution *An attempt to use a nonnumeric expression as a num-value.*

➤ Use a valid number.

An attempt to use a number that does not specify any function in the DLL.

➤ Use a valid number.

Error in the DLL file procedure.

➤ Do not call this procedure.

453 Specified DLL function not found

Description This error occurs when the specified function is not found in a DLL file.

Cause/Solution *An attempt to specify an invalid ordinal in the function declaration.*

➤ Check the spelling.

Old version of the DLL file.

➤ Install the right version, and rename or delete all the old DLL files with the same name from your hard drive directories.

454 Code resource not found

Description Only for the Macintosh platform; this error is caused by unavailability of a code resource.

Cause/Solution *An attempt to make a call to a procedure in a code resource while the code resource is not available.*

➤ Check the spelling. Check the availability of the resource.

455 Code resource lock error

Description Only for the Macintosh platform; Locking error.

Cause/Solution *An invalid attempt to lock the resource.*

➤ Check for an error returned by HLock .

456 Get and Put cannot be used with arrays in Variants

Description This error is caused by using the file access statements Get and Put with Variants containing arrays.

Cause/Solution *An attempt to use Get and Put with a Variant variable containing an array.*

➤ Copy array elements from a Variant to an array, or transfer the elements one by one within a loop.

457 This key is already associated with an element of this collection

Description This error is caused by specifying a key string (for the Add method) that matches a key that already exists in the system.

Cause/Solution *An attempt to specify for a collection member a key string that already identifies another member of the collection.*

➤ Use a different key string.

481 Invalid picture

Description This error is caused by an invalid picture format.

Cause/Solution *An attempt to assign a file that is not a valid picture file to a Picture property or a Picture object.*

➤ Use a supported picture format.

appendix C

Transact-SQL Reference

The Transact-SQL Reference appendix illustrates the most commonly used Transact-SQL statements. Description of each statement includes:

- Syntax.
- Arguments.
- Statement permissions.
- Remarks.
- Examples.

Only Transact-SQL statements mentioned in the book and those that are necessary for creating basic SQL queries were selected for this appendix.

For each Transact-SQL statement described in this appendix, the features that are new to SQL Server 6.5 are emphasized.

CREATE INDEX

Description Use this statement to create an index on a table. This statement provides an additional list of references to the keys in the base table (or rearranges the base table in the order of the keys), which allows the Optimizer to increase efficiency for queries.

The Primary Key index is created not by the CREATE INDEX statement but by using the Primary Key constraint in the CREATE TABLE or ALTER TABLE statements.

Syntax

```
CREATE [UNIQUE] [CLUSTERED | NONCLUSTERED] INDEX index_name
    ON [[database.]owner.]table_name (column_name [, column_name]...)
[WITH
    [PAD_INDEX, ]
    [[,] FILLFACTOR = fillfactor]
    [[,] IGNORE_DUP_KEY]
    [[,] SORTED_DATA | SORTED_DATA_REORG]
    [[,] IGNORE_DUP_ROW | ALLOW_DUP_ROW]]
[ON segment_name]
```

Arguments

UNIQUE

Creates a unique index—duplicate key values are not allowed. For a unique index, UPDATE and INSERT statements will fail when you are trying to create a row with the index's key values that already exist in the table.

If the base table already has duplicate values, the CREATE INDEX statement with the UNIQUE argument will fail.

CLUSTERED

The CREATE INDEX statement with this argument will sort rows in the base table in the key order. If CLUSTERED is not specified, NONCLUSTERED is in effect. By definition, only one clustered index can exist for a particular table.

NONCLUSTERED

Creates an index that does not change the physical order of the rows in the base table. It allocates a set of pages that contains pointers to the data rows; the pointers are arranged in the order of the key columns. There can be up to 249 nonclustered indexes for any particular table.

index_name

The name of an index that is to be created.

table_name

The name of the base table.

column_name

List of the column names that make up the index key.

Limitations: up to 16 columns per key; up to 256 bytes of the combined lengths of the columns.

PAD_INDEX
If specified, indicates that the FILLFACTOR argument should be applied to the index node pages (higher levels of an index) as well as to the leaf pages in the index.

FILLFACTOR
Specifies the percentage of space in every index page that should be left free (in anticipation of the future INSERTs and UPDATEs) when creating the index.

Note: The FILLFACTOR argument is considered *only* during the index creation.

Valid values: 0 to 100. If set to 100, no buffer space will be left. If any updates and/or inserts are performed on the base table and the FILLFACTOR is set up at 100 percent, page splits (allocation of the new page and moving part of data to this page) are likely to happen quite often, thus causing performance degradation. On the other hand, if the FILLFACTOR value is low, the index pages are not fully filled and some extra space in the database will be used, especially if this is the clustered index.

IGNORE_DUP_KEY
If specified, causes the duplicate rows to be ignored while allowing valid INSERTs and UPDATEs to complete when inserting or updating multiple rows. If IGNORE_DUP_KEY is not specified, all the changes, including the valid ones, will be rolled back. This argument affects the index behavior *after* the index has been created; you still will not be able to create a unique index on a table that has duplicate key values.

Note: If IGNORE_DUP_KEY is specified and an update is disallowed because of a duplicate value, the row that you are trying to update will be deleted from the table.

SORTED_DATA
The SORTED_DATA argument allows you to save some time when building a clustered index on a table that is known to have its rows already sorted in the right order. If the SORTED_DATA argument is specified, SQL Server will not sort the table, but it will verify if the table is really sorted, and if inconsistency has been detected, the CREATE INDEX statement fails.

SORTED_DATA_REORG
The SORTED_DATA_REORG argument has the same effect as the SORTED_DATA argument. In addition, the SORTED_DATA_REORG argument causes the physical table to be reorganized, thus reapplying the FILLFACTOR argument and defragmenting the table.

IGNORE_DUP_ROW

Only for a nonunique clustered index. If specified:

- **When creating index.** The duplicate rows are deleted, a warning is issued, and the index is created.
- **When updating or inserting into the table.** Nonunique inserts are not performed and nonunique updates cause deletion of the updated rows.

ALLOW_DUP_ROW

Only for nonunique clustered indexes. If specified, SQL Server gives no special consideration to the duplicates.

ON segment_name

Indicates a segment in a database where the index is to be created. Normally, a database has *data*, *log*, and *system* segments. By default, the index is created on the *data* segment. In addition, user-defined segments can be created in a database and a new index (only a nonclustered index, of course) can be created on one of these segments.

Remarks

- There are limitations on the column types on which indexes can be created: text, image, and bit columns can not participate in an index key.
- Creation of a clustered index requires an amount of free space in a database that is equals to about 120 percent of the table size. No additional space required if the SORTED_DATA argument is specified.
- Use the sp_helpindex system stored procedure to get information on all the indexes of a table.

Permission Permissions for the CREATE INDEX statement defaults to the table owner, and it can not be GRANTED/REVOKED.

Example Create a unique clustered index, ORDERID_INDEX, on the ORDERID column of the ORDERS table. This CREATE INDEX statement includes the IGNORE_DUP_KEY argument so that in a mass UPDATE or INSERT statement, only those rows that do not violate uniqueness will be updated or inserted.

```
CREATE UNIQUE CLUSTERED INDEX orderid_index
    ON orders (orderid)
    WITH IGNORE_DUP_KEY
```

CREATE TABLE

Description Use this statement to create a new table in an SQL Server database. While creating a table in SQL Server 6, you can also define primary, foreign, unique, default, and check constraints.

Syntax

```
CREATE TABLE table_name
(
    {col_name column_properties[constraint [constraint [...constraint]]]
    | [[, ] constraint]}
        [[, ] {next_col_name | next_constraint}
)
[ON segment_name]
```

Arguments

table_name
The name of a table to be created. The table name defines whether the table will be permanent, local temporary, or global temporary. A local temporary table can only be accessed from within the session that created the table, while a global temporary table can be accessed from any session and exists as long as the session that created the table is open. Prefix the table name with a single pound sign to create a local temporary table and with a double pound sign to create a global temporary table. Any other name will create a permanent table.

col_name
Name of a column in the table.

column_properties
Defines the datatype, null values, and identity values for the column.
Note: The IDENTITY property implicitly defines the NOT NULL property value.

Constraint
Is one of the following:
PRIMARY KEY:
[CONSTRAINT *constraint_name*]
PRIMARY KEY [CLUSTERED | NONCLUSTERED]
(*col_name* [, *col_name2* [..., *col_name16*]])
[ON *segment_name*]
UNIQUE:
[CONSTRAINT *constraint_name*]
UNIQUE [CLUSTERED | NONCLUSTERED]
(*col_name* [, *col_name2* [..., *col_name16*]])
[ON *segment_name*]

FOREIGN KEY:
[CONSTRAINT *constraint_name*]
[FOREIGN KEY (*col_name* [, *col_name2* [..., *col_name16*]])]
REFERENCES [*owner*.]*ref_table* [(*ref_col* [, *ref_col2*
[..., *ref_col16*]])]
DEFAULT:
[CONSTRAINT *constraint_name*]
DEFAULT {*constant_expression* | *niladic-function* | NULL}
[FOR *col_name*]
CHECK:
[CONSTRAINT *constraint_name*]
CHECK [NOT FOR REPLICATION] (*expression*)

constraint_name
If not specified, will be generated by the system. You can specify any valid name that does not start with a pound sign.

PRIMARY KEY [CLUSTERED | NONCLUSTERED]
All the columns participating in the PRIMARY KEY must be defined as NOT NULL. SQL Server creates a unique index (clustered by default) on the primary key set of columns to enforce integrity of the relation. There can be only one PRIMARY KEY constraint for one table.

UNIQUE [CLUSTERED | NONCLUSTERED]
Enforces uniqueness for a set of columns. SQL Server builds a unique index for every UNIQUE constraint; the index is nonclustered by default.

[FOREIGN KEY (col_name [, col_name2 [..., col_name16]])]
REFERENCES [owner.]ref_table [(ref_col [, ref_col2 [..., ref_col16]])]
Enforces referential integrity. Every time a column specified in the FOREIGN KEY clause is assigned a value, this value must exist in the table defined in the REFERENCE clause. Columns from the REFERENCE clause must have a PRIMARY KEY or UNIQUE constraint defined on them.

Note: To create a FOREIGN KEY constraint, you must have SELECT or REFERENCES permission on the referenced columns.

Note: FOREIGN KEY constraints are not enforced on temporary tables.

DEFAULT constant_expression | niladic-function | NULL
Specifies the default value for the column. This value will be assigned to the column when an INSERT command is executed on the table and a value for the column is not explicitly supplied.

Note: DEFAULT constraints can not be created on *timestamp* columns or columns that have IDENTITY property.

Niladic-function is one of the following systems functions:

- USER.
- CURRENT_USER.
- SESSION_USER.
- SYSTEM_USER.
- CURRENT_TIMESTAMP.

CHECK (expression)
Imposes limitations on the values for a column.

NOT FOR REPLICATION
Voids the specified CHECK constraint for changes caused by the replication's distribution process.

ON segment_name
If specified for the created table, places the table on the named segment. If specified for a constraint, places an index (created by the constraint) on the named segment. If it is a clustered index, the whole table will be created on the named segment.

Remarks The following limitations are applied to SQL Server tables:

- Maximum of 2 billion tables per database.
- Maximum of 250 columns per table.
- Maximum of 1,962 bytes per table row.

Use the sp_help and sp_helpconstraint system stored procedures to obtain information about a table, columns, and constraints.

Permission Any valid user of the database who has CREATE TABLE permission in this database (granted by the DBO).

Example This example creates a table called publishers:

```
CREATE TABLE publishers
(
pub_id  char(4) NOT NULL
        CONSTRAINT UPKCL_pubind
                PRIMARY KEY CLUSTERED
        CHECK (pub_id IN ('1389', '0736',
            '0877', '1622', '1756')
            OR pub_id LIKE '99[0-9][0-9]'),
```

```
pub_name        varchar(40)     NULL,
city            varchar(20)     NULL,
state       char(2)      NULL,
country     varchar(30)     NULL
        DEFAULT('USA')
)
```

DBCC UPDATEUSAGE

Description One of the functions of DBCC (Database Consistency Check) statement. Use it to examine the sysindexes table and to correct discrepancies in this table.

Syntax

```
DBCC UPDATEUSAGE ({0 | database_name} [, table_name [, index_id]])
[WITH COUNT_ROWS]
```

Arguments ***UPDATEUSAGE ({0 | database_name} [, table_name [, index_id]])***

This ODBC function examines, reports, and corrects inaccuracies in the sysindexes table. The columns of the sysindexes table that are examined and corrected are *used*, *reserved*, and *dpages*; the rows that are examined represent clustered indexes on user's and system tables (values of the *type* column: U and S).

WITH COUNT_ROWS

Forces ODBC to update entries in sysindexes with the recalculated actual number of rows in the corresponding tables. This only applies to rows with values of the *index_id* column equal to 0 or 1. Specifying this parameter can significantly decrease performance.

Remarks DBCC UPDATEUSAGE acquires a shared lock on the table that is being processed, so if you specify *syslogs* table, you have to set the database into the *single user* mode.

DBCC UPDATEUSAGE displays information about corrections made to the sysindexes table. If there are no inaccuracies in sysindexes, DBCC UPDATEUSAGE does not display anything.

Permission DBCC UPDATEUSAGE can be run by the SA or DBO only.

Example This example corrects all of the page and row counts in the sysindexes table for all the indexes on the ORDERS table.

```
DBCC UPDATEUSAGE (MARKETING_WAREHOUSE, ORDERS) WITH COUNT_ROWS
```

DUMP TABLE

Description This option of the DUMP statement initiates the backup of an individual table. This function is new in SQL Server 6.5.

Syntax

```
DUMP TABLE [[database.]owner.]table_name
    TO dump_device [, dump_device2 [..., dump_device32]]
[WITH options]
```

Arguments ***[[database.]owner.]table_name***
Specifies a table name for the dump operation.

dump_device ={dump_device_name | @dump_device_namevar}
| {DISK | TAPE | FLOPPY | PIPE} =
{'temp_dump_device' | @temp_dump_device_var}
[VOLUME = {volid | @volid_var}]
Specifies destination of the dump file. It can be coded as a name of a previously created dump device or as directly specifying a destination hard drive, tape drive, floppy drive, or a network pipe name.

options
Specifies one or more of the following additional parameters:

- ***UNLOAD / NOUNLOAD.*** Unload/Not Unload the tape after backup is complete.
- ***INIT/NOINIT.*** Overwrite/Append the disk or tape file.
- ***SKIP/NOSKIP.*** Skip/Read the tape headers.
- ***EXPIREDATE = date | @date_var or.***
- ***RETAINDAYS = days | @days_var.*** Specify Expiration Date/ Retention Period.
- ***STATS= percentage.*** Show statistics of the dump progress in percentage increments.

Remarks New operation in SQL Server 6.5. Use it to back up individual tables instead of the whole database, thus saving time and system resources. It also provides a much easier and better way to restore a table in a case of accidental loss of data in the table.

Note: Loading an individual table into a database may cause inconsistencies in the FOREIGN KEY constraint. It must be performed only in emergency recovery.

Permission You must have SELECT permission for the table that you intend to dump.

Example This example creates the TABLE_DUMP dump device and then dumps the ORDERS table to the TABLE_DUMP disk:

```
sp_addumpdevice 'disk',' TABLE_DUMP', 'c:\DUMPS\TABLE_DUMP.DAT'
DUMP TABLE ORDERS TO TABLE_DUMP WITH STATS
```

GRANT

Description Use this statement to grant access and statement permissions to database users.

Syntax To grant permission to access database objects:

```
GRANT {ALL [PRIVILEGES][column_list] | permission_list [column_list]}
    ON {table_name [(column_list)]
     | view_name [(column_list)]
     | stored_procedure_name}
    TO {PUBLIC | name_list }
    [WITH GRANT OPTION]
```

To grant permission to execute specific SQL statements in the current database:

```
GRANT {ALL | statement_list}
    TO { PUBLIC | name_list}
```

Arguments ***ALL***

Use it to grant to the grantee all the access or statement permission that you (the grantor) have.

Note: Only systems administrators can use ALL while granting statement permissions.

permission_list

A list that includes one or more of the following access options:

- SELECT.
- REFERENCES.
- UPDATE.
- INSERT.
- DELETE.
- EXECUTE.

Only SELECT, REFERENCES, and UPDATE permissions can be granted while assigning permissions on columns.

Only SELECT, INSERT, DELETE, and UPDATE permissions can be granted while assigning permissions on a view.

Only SELECT, INSERT, DELETE, REFERENCES, and UPDATE permissions can be granted while assigning permissions on a table.

Only EXECUTE permission can be granted while assigning permissions on a stored procedure.

table_name
The name of a table in the current database.

column_list
A list of column names in the specified table.

view_name
The name of a view in the current database.

stored_procedure_name
The name of a stored procedure in the current database.

PUBLIC
The specified permissions assigned to all the users in the database.

name_list
A list of names of users/groups in the current database.

WITH GRANT OPTION
Gives the grantee the ability to be a grantor of the specified permission.

statement_list
A list that includes one or more of the following statements:

- CREATE DATABASE.
- CREATE DEFAULT.
- CREATE PROCEDURE.
- CREATE RULE.
- CREATE TABLE.
- CREATE VIEW.
- DUMP DATABASE.
- DUMP TRANSACTION.

Remarks Use the WITH GRANT OPTION argument (which is new in SQL Server 6.5) to designate a local DBA for every group of users.

To execute an UPDATE statement, a user may need SELECT permission in addition to the UPDATE permission.

Example This example grants permission to select from the ORDER_DETAILS table and permission to update the DISCOUNT column in this table to a group called MARKETING_MANAGERS:

```
GRANT SELECT, UPDATE(discount) ON order_details TO marketing_managers
```

INSERT

Description Populates a local table with default values, constants, values returned from a SELECT statement, or results returned from a procedure.

Syntax

```
INSERT [INTO]
    {table_name | view_name} [(column_list)]
{DEFAULT VALUES | VALUES (values_list) | select_statement}
```

or

```
INSERT [INTO]
{table_name | view_name} [(column_list)]
    EXECute { procedure_name | @procedure_name_var}
    [[@parameter_name=] {value | @variable [OUTPUT] | DEFAULT}
    [, [@parameter_name =] {value | @variable [OUTPUT] | DEFAULT}]...]
```

Arguments

table_name
The name of a table in a database.

column_list
A list of one or more columns in the specified table. You can omit a column list if you are inserting values into *all* the columns in the table. In this case, inserted values have to be in the order in which they appear in the CREATE TABLE statement.

DEFAULT VALUES
Use this parameter to insert the default values into all columns. If the column does not have a default value, SQL Server will try to insert the NULL value in the column. If the NULL value is not allowed for this column, SQL Server will generate an error.

values_list
A comma-delimited list of constant expressions or a keyword DEFAULT. Every element of the list represents a value that will be assigned to a corresponding column from the column list. If DEFAULT is specified, the default value will be assigned to a column.

select_statement
A SELECT statement that returns the values into the corresponding columns.

procedure_name
The name of a stored procedure. The name can be qualified to point to a stored procedure in a different database.

@procedure_name_var
The name of a local variable containing the name of a stored procedure.

@parameter_name
The name of a parameter for the specified stored procedure.

Value
The value for a specified parameter.

@variable
The variable that contains a parameter value.

OUTPUT
Indicates the OUTPUT parameter of the stored procedure.

DEFAULT
The default value that is used for the parameter value.

Remarks The INSERT statement adds new rows to a table. Inserting a row with the INSERT statement involves activation of almost all of the table's properties: primary key, foreign key constraints, defaults, unique constraints, and insert triggers. Violation of one or several of these constraints can make the INSERT statement fail. The "procedure" format of the INSERT statement can be used to run procedures on *remote* systems and store the returned information in a local table.

Permission Permission for the INSERT statement is granted to the table owner, who can transfer it to other users.

Example This example shows an INSERT into the Shippers table in the MARKETING_WAREHOUSE database. This command inserts constant values:

```
INSERT Shippers (CompanyName, Phone)
    VALUES('UPS', '1-800-555-3214')
```

The following example illustrates an option of inserting data into a table by selecting it from another table:

```
INSERT Shippers (CompanyName, Phone)
SELECT CompanyName, Phone from Yellow_Pages
       WHERE CompanyType='SHIPPER'
```

The following example retrieves information from a remote database and places it into the local employees table:

```
INSERT INTO employees
EXECUTE HR_SERVER.HR_DATABASE.DBO.EMPL_PROCEDURE
```

LOAD TABLE

Description This option of the LOAD statement loads a backup copy of a table into a database. This function is new in SQL Server 6.5.

Syntax To load a table:

```
LOAD TABLE [[database.]owner.]table_name
    FROM dump_device [, dump_device2 [..., dump_device32]]
[WITH options]
```

Arguments ***table_name***
The name of a table to be restored.

dump_device_name | @dump_device_name_var
Specifies a predefined dump device or a direct reference to a disk, tape, or a network pipe name. See similar argument in the DUMP TABLE command earlier in this appendix.

Options
One or more of the following:

- **UNLOAD/ NOUNLOAD.** Specify UNLOAD to force the tape to be automatically rewound and unloaded when the operation is finished.
- **SKIP/ NOSKIP.** Specify SKIP to force SQL Server not to read the tape headers.

- **FILE = fileno.** Specify the sequential number of the backup file on the tape.
- **APPEND.** Specify APPEND to load the backup data to the table in addition to the data that already exist in the table.
- **SOURCE = source_name.** Specify the name of the source table if the names of the source table and the table in the database are different.
- **STATS = percentage.** Show statistics of the dump progress in percentage increments.

Remarks The new LOAD TABLE function of the LOAD statement adds flexibility to the DUMP/LOAD operation. If a table participates in relationships with other tables, however, loading it individually into a database can cause inconsistency in the foreign key constraints and therefore is not recommended in a non-emergency situation.

The table that is being loaded is locked by an EXCLUSIVE lock for the entire time so that it can not be changed during the load. The same is true about an individual table dump (see DUMP TABLE earlier in this appendix).

Note: Always load a table from a table dump (as opposed to an entire database dump) because during a database dump, individual tables do not get locked (consistency is achieved by applying transaction log).

The LOAD TABLE operation bypasses the table's triggers, rules, defaults, and declarative referential integrity (FOREIGN KEY, CHECK, PRIMARY KEY), and it is not logged.

Note: Since the LOAD TABLE operation is not logged, the entire database dump has to be performed after the operation.

The LOAD TABLE operation can not be permitted on:

- Tables with the text columns.
- Tables with indexes.
- Tables that are set up for publishing.
- Tables that were dumped on a different hardware platform.

Permission The INSERT permission on a table must be granted to the user who performs this operation. In addition, the database must have **SELECT INTO/BULK COPY** option set to true.

Example The following example appends the **EMPLOYEE** table from the disk file HR_DUMP to the HR table:

```
LOAD TABLE HR FROM HR_DUMP WITH SOURCE='EMPLOYEE', APPEND
```

REVOKE

Description Use this statement to revoke access and statement permissions from the database users. The CASCADE option is new in SQL Server 6.5.

Syntax

```
REVOKE [GRANT OPTION FOR]
    {ALL [PRIVILEGES] | permission_list } [(column_list)]
    ON { table_name [(column_list)]
    | view_name [(column_list)]
    | stored_procedure_name | extended_stored_procedure_name}
    FROM {PUBLIC | name_list}
    [CASCADE]
```

To revoke statement permissions:

```
REVOKE {ALL | statement_list}
    FROM {PUBLIC | name_list}
```

Arguments

GRANT OPTION FOR
Use this argument to revoke the ability to grant permission to other users (reverses the WITH GRANT OPTION argument of the GRANT statement).

ALL
Use this argument to revoke all access or statement permissions from users.

permission_list
Use this to specify permissions to revoke (same as in the GRANT statement earlier).

table_name
The name of a table to which the access permissions apply.

column_list
The list of column names to which the access permissions apply.

view_name
The name of a view to which the access permissions apply.

stored_procedure_name or ***extended_stored_procedure_name***
The name of a stored procedure to which the access permissions apply.

PUBLIC
Use the PUBLIC argument to revoke the specified permissions from all the users in the database.

name_list
The list of user/group names, comma-delimited.

CASCADE
Use CASCADE to revoke WITH GRANT privileges that were granted by the specified user (or a list of users/groups).

statement_list
The list of statements to be revoked.

Remarks Use the CASCADE option to revoke the grantable permissions from the specified user and from all the users to whom the specified users granted permissions. This option allows you to effectively control the work performed by local DBAs in your company.

Example

```
REVOKE SELECT, UPDATE(discount) ON order_details FROM marketing_managers
```

SELECT

Description Use the SELECT statement to retrieve rows from the tables in SQL Server databases.

Syntax

```
SELECT [ALL | DISTINCT] select_list
    INTO [new_table_name]
[FROM table_name [, table_name2 [..., table_name16]]
[WHERE clause]
[GROUP BY clause]
[HAVING clause]
[ORDER BY clause]
[COMPUTE clause]
[FOR BROWSE]]
```

Arguments ***ALL/DISTINCT***
Use ALL to return all the rows, including duplicates, or use DISTINCT to return only unique rows.

select_list
The list of columns to retrieve. You can specify one of the following:

- **Asterisk (*).** Specify asterisk to retrieve all the columns of the tables that are specified in the FROM clause. Columns will be listed in the CREATE TABLE order.
- **A list of column names.** Specify the columns that you want to retrieve in the order of your choice. You can also specify column headings.

- **An expression.** Any valid SQL Server expression.
- **IDENTITYCOL keyword.** Used to specify an IDENTITY column.
- **Local or global variable.** Used to include a value of a local or a global variable in the result.
- **Local variable assignment.** Used to assign a value to a local or a global variable in a form @variable=expression.

INTO new_table_name

The name of a new table that will be created with the set of columns from the select_list; the new table will include the rows that satisfy conditions in the WHERE clause.

FROM

Use the FROM clause to specify the tables, subqueries (also called *derived tables*), and views (optionally with the aliases) used in the SELECT statement. The FROM clause also allows you to specify the Optimizer hints (e.g., the locking method or the index to be used for a particular table). In SQL Server 6.5, you can also specify a table join in the FROM clause using the following format:

```
<table_name> <join specification> <table_name> [ON <conditions>]
```

where the join specification can be one of the following:

- **CROSS JOIN.** The cross-product of two tables (each row from one table is matched with every row in another table). No conditions must be specified for the CROSS JOIN.
- **[INNER] JOIN.** Returns all the matching rows; unmatched rows are dropped.
- **LEFT [OUTER] JOIN.** Returns all the rows from the left table with the matching rows from the right table; returns NULL if the matching rows could not be found in the right table.
- **RIGHT [OUTER] JOIN.** Returns all the rows from the right table with the matching rows from the left table; returns NULL if the matching rows could not be found in the left table.
- **FULL [OUTER] JOIN.** Includes only those rows from both tables that do not match the criteria; the corresponding columns for another table are set to NULL.

WHERE search_conditions

Use the WHERE clause to specify the conditions that rows returned in the result have to meet.

The LIKE operator (used in conditions) has an ESCAPE option in SQL Server 6.5, which allows wildcard characters to be searched for in strings.

GROUP BY clause

Use the GROUP BY clause to break the whole table into groups that will be used to calculate aggregate functions.

SQL Server 6.5 has two additional arguments used with the GROUP BY clause:

- **WITH CUBE.** Used to produce the super-aggregate rows, which are calculated on the whole result set.
- **WITH ROLLUP.** Used to calculate the more complicated "set-within-another-set" aggregate functions.

HAVING clause

Use the HAVING clause to specify additional conditions for the aggregate functions in the SELECT statement. The HAVING clause restricts the rows returned by the query but does not affect the calculations of the aggregate functions.

ORDER BY clause

Use the ORDER BY clause to specify the sort order of the returned columns.

COMPUTE clause

Use the COMPUTE clause to specify the row-aggregate functions for the SELECT statement.

FOR BROWSE

Use FOR BROWSE to indicate that updates will be allowed while in client applications that use DB-Library.

Remarks Even though SQL Server 6.5 introduces the new syntax for the join specifications, the old *= and =* outer join syntax is still supported (but you cannot mix both in the same statement). Unfortunately, the new format does not always return the same results that the old format does (please run the JOINFRMT.MDB application on the Companion CD-ROM for more details).

A SELECT statement that serves as a derived table in the FROM clause cannot contain INTO, ORDER BY, or COMPUTE clauses.

Permission The owner of the table gets the SELECT permission on the table when the table is created. The table owner can then grant the SELECT permission to other users. For the INTO clause, you need the CREATE TABLE permission in the destination database and the SELECT INTO/BULK COPY option set in the database.

Example The following example executes a join of three tables:

```
SELECT
Customers.CompanyName,
Orders.OrderID,
Order_Details.ProductID,
Sum(UnitPrice*Quantity) AS "Extended Price"

FROM (Customers INNER JOIN Orders ON Customers.CustomerID =
Orders.CustomerID) INNER JOIN Order_Details ON Orders.OrderID =
Order_Details.OrderID

GROUP BY Customers.CompanyName, Orders.OrderID, Order_Details.ProductID
```

Result:

Company Name	Order ID	Product	Extended Price
Alfreds Futterkiste	10643	28	$684.00
Alfreds Futterkiste	10643	39	$378.00
Alfreds Futterkiste	10643	46	$24.00
Alfreds Futterkiste	10692	63	$878.00
Alfreds Futterkiste	10702	3	$60.00
Alfreds Futterkiste	10702	76	$270.00
Alfreds Futterkiste	10835	59	$825.00
Alfreds Futterkiste	10835	77	$26.00
Alfreds Futterkiste	10952	6	$400.00
Alfreds Futterkiste	10952	28	$91.20
Alfreds Futterkiste	11011	58	$530.00
Alfreds Futterkiste	11011	71	$430.00
Ana Trujillo Emparedados y helados	10308	69	$28.80
Ana Trujillo Emparedados y helados	10308	70	$60.00
Ana Trujillo Emparedados y helados	10625	14	$69.75
Ana Trujillo Emparedados y helados	10625	42	$70.00
Ana Trujillo Emparedados y helados	10625	60	$340.00
Ana Trujillo Emparedados y helados	10759	32	$320.00

UPDATE

Description Use the UPDATE statement to change data in existing rows.

Syntax

```
UPDATE {table_name | view_name}
SET [{table_name | view_name}]
    {column_list
    | variable_list
    | variable_and_column_list}
```

```
        [, {column_list2
            | variable_list2
            | variable_and_column_list2}
            ... [, {column_listN
                    | variable_listN
                    | variable_and_column_listN}]]
[FROM {table_name1 | view_name1}[(optimizer_hints)]
    [, {table_name2 | view_name2}[(optimizer_hints)]
    [..., {table_name16 | view_name16}[(optimizer_hints)]]]]
[WHERE clause]
```

Arguments

table_name / view_name
The name of the table or view in which rows will be updated.

column_name
The name of a column to be updated.

column_list / variable_list / variable_and_column_list / expression
The name of a column, local or global variable, constant, function, or an expression consisting of these elements.

WHERE {search_conditions / CURRENT OF cursor_name}
Use the search_conditions parameter to define a set of the columns to be updated. Use the CURRENT OF cursor_name coding to update the current row within a cursor.

FROM
Use the FROM clause to specify the tables used in the UPDATE statement in addition to the table being updated. The FROM clause lists the tables, views, aliases, and Optimizer hints the same way they are listed in the SELECT statement.

Remarks If two different tables have the same column names, these names should be fully qualified in the UPDATE statement.

If you update via a view that is based on a join of several tables, columns in more than one table can not be updated in the same UPDATE command.

Example The following example increases the discount amount by 10 percent for the ProductId=32 when the ordered quantity is greater that 10:

```
UPDATE ORDER_DETAILS SET Discount=Discount*1.1
WHERE ProductId=32 and Quantity>10
```

appendix D

Visual Basic Language Reference

In this appendix, you will find some of the most commonly used Visual Basic language references concerning statements, objects, and built-in functions.

Statements

Visual Basic statements are used in a program code to perform various operations. Usually one statement is coded on one line; several statements can be included on one line if they are separated by a colon. The following segments briefly describe the most commonly used Visual Basic statements grouped by general functionality.

Branch Statements

These Visual Basic statements are used to pass control to a specified line within a program.

GoSub...Return Statements

`GoSub LineLabel`
Passes control to a line specified by the LineLabel parameter.

`Return`
Returns control to the line immediately following GoSub.

GoTo LineLabel Statement

```
GoTo LineLabel
```

Passes control to a line specified by the LineLabel parameter.

On Error Statement

```
On Error GoTo LineLabel
```

Specifies an error-handling routine.

```
On Error Resume Next
```

Instructs Access to pass control to the next statement when an error occurs.

```
On Error GoTo 0
```

Disables error-handling procedures.

On...GoSub Statement

```
On expression GoSub destinationlist
```

Passes control to a LineLabel from the *destinationlist* defined by the value of *expression*.

On...GoTo Statement

```
On expression GoTo destinationlist
```

Passes control to a LineLabel from the *destinationlist* defined by the value of *expression*.

Pause & Exit Statements

These Visual Basic statements are used to pause or stop execution of a program or a function.

End Statement

```
End [Function | If | Property | Select | Sub | Type | With]
```

End a block of code.

Exit Statement

```
Exit {Do | For | Function | Property | Sub}
```

Exits a Loop, Function, Sub, or Property.

Stop Statement

```
Stop
```

Stops code execution.

Loop Statements

These Visual Basic statements are used to repeatedly execute a group of statements.

Do...Loop Statement

```
Do [{While | Until} condition]

[statements]

[Exit Do]

[statements]

Loop
```

Executes *statements* repeatedly.

For...Next Statement

```
For counter = start To end [Step step]

[statements]

[Exit For]

[statements]

Next [counter]
```

Executes statements repeatedly until value of the *counter* reaches *end*.

For Each...Next Statement

```
For Each element In group

[statements]

[Exit For]

[statements]

Next [element]
```

Executes *statements* repeatedly for each element in an array or collection.

While...Wend Statement

```
While condition
[statements]
Wend
```

Executes *statements* repeatedly while the *condition* is True.

With Statement

```
With object
[statements]
End With
```

Executes *statements* on the specified *object*.

Conditional Execution Statements

These Visual Basic statements are used to conditionally execute a group of statements.

If...Then...Else Statement

```
If condition Then statements [Else elsestatements]
```

or

```
If condition Then
[statements]
[ElseIf condition-n Then
[elseifstatements]] . . .
[Else
[elsestatements]]
End If
```

Executes *statements* or *elsestatements* (if any) depending on the value of *condition*.

Select Case Statement

```
Select Case testexpression
[Case expressionlist-n
    [statements-n]] . . .
[Case Else
    [elsestatements]]
End Select
```

Executes one of the *statements-n*, depending on the value of the *testexpression*.

Procedure Statements

These Visual Basic statements are used to define and call functions and subroutines.

Call Statement

```
[Call] name [argumentlist]
```
Calls function or procedures.

Function Statement

```
[Public | Private] [Static] Function name [(arglist)] [As type]
    [statements]
    [name = expression]
    [Exit Function]
    [statements]
    [name = expression]
End Function
```
Declares a Function procedure.

Sub Statement

```
[Private | Public] [Static] Sub name [(arglist)]
    [statements]
    [Exit Sub]
    [statements]
End Sub
```
Declares a Sub procedure.

Objects & Collections

One of the important features of Visual Basic is its ability to reference different objects and collections. Microsoft Access objects and collections establish a framework that allows Visual Basic code to create and manipulate components of the user interface and the database system. Visual Basic code can examine and modify objects' and collections' properties and execute their methods in order to manipulate them. The following sections describe two main categories of objects used in a typical Access application: Microsoft Access objects and Data Access objects.

Microsoft Access Objects

Object	Description
Application	Represents the current Access application.
Form	Represents a Form.
Report	Represents a Report.
Control	Represents a control on a form or report.
Screen	Represents a form, report, or control that currently has the focus.
DoCmd	Represents an action of Access.

Data Access Objects (DAO)

Object	Description
Container	Stores information about other objects.
Database	Represents an open database.
DBEngine	The Jet database engine.
Document	Stores information about one instance of a type of object.
Error	Stores information about errors.
Field	Represents a table column.
Group	Represents a group of users.
Index	Represents a table index.
Parameter	Represents a parameter for a query.
Property	Represents a property.
QueryDef	Represents a query definition.
Recordset	Represents a set of records.
Relation	Represents a tables/queries relationship.
TableDef	Represents a table definition.
User	Represents a user account.
Workspace	Represents a Jet database engine session.

Example of Object's Properties & Methods

To better understand the concepts of objects, properties, and methods, examine the Group object, which represents a group of user accounts in a secure workgroup environment.

Properties

The Group object has the following two properties:

- The Name property contains a name of the group.
- The PID property contains the so-called personal identificator for the group. This property cannot be viewed.

Method

The Group object has only one method: CreateUser. Use this method to create a new user in a group represented by the Group object.

Syntax

Set <user variable> = <group object>. CreateUser([name[, pid [, password]]])

Parameter	Description
name	Identifies a name of the new User object.
pid	Specifies the personal identification (PID) value for a user account.
password	Specifies password for the new user.

The following code example shows a NewUser function that creates a new user in an existing group with a name, PID, password, and a group name passed as function parameters:

```
Function NewUser (uname As String, upid As String, upassword As String,
groupname As String)
  Dim Us As User
  Dim Ws As WorkSpace
  Dim Gr As Group
  Set Ws = dbengine.workspaces(0)
  Set Gr = WS.groups(groupname)
  Set Us = Gr.CreateUser(uname, upid, upassword)
  Gr.users.Append Us
  Gr.users.Refresh
End Function
```

Functions

Visual Basic has dozens of different built-in functions. In this appendix, we included four major groups of functions: date and time functions, string functions, math functions, and functions dealing with files and directories.

Date & Time Functions

Function names	Description
Date, Now, Time	Returns current date and time.
DateSerial, DateValue	Performs conversion to date.
TimeSerial, TimeValue	Performs conversion to time.
Date, Time	Returns date and time.
Timer	Returns number of seconds since midnight.
DateAdd, DateDiff, DatePart	Performs calculations with dates.

String Functions

Function names	Description
StrComp	Compares strings.
Format, LCase, UCase	Performs conversion to lower-/uppercase.
Space, String	Creates strings.
Len	Signifies string length.
Format	Formats a string.
LSet, RSet	Justifies a string.
InStr, Left, LTrim, Mid, Right, RTrim, Trim	Performs manipulations on strings.
Option Compare	Sets comparison algorithms.
Asc, Chr	Works with characters.
StrConv	Converts strings.

Math Functions

Function names	Description
Abs	Returns absolute value of a number.
Atn	Returns arctangent of a number.
Cos	Returns cosin of an angle.
Exp	Returns exponent of a number.
Fix, Int	Returns integer part of a number.
Log	Returns natural logarithm.
Rnd	Rounds a number.
Sgn	Returns sign of a number.
Sin	Returns sine of a angle.
Sqr	Returns square root of a number.
Tan	Returns tangent of an angle.

Files & Directories Functions

Function names	Description
ChDir	Changes the directory.
ChDrive	Changes the drive.
FileCopy	Copies a file.
MkDir	Makes a directory.
RmDir	Removes a directory.
CurDir	Returns the current path.
GetAttr	Returns file attributes.
Dir	Returns a filename.
FileDateTime	Returns a file date/time stamp.
FileLen	Returns file length.
Name	Renames a file or directory.
SetAttr	Sets a file attribute.

Index

D

E

F

G

H

I

J

K

L

M

N

O

P

Q

R

S

T

U

V

W

X

VENTANA

Official Netscape Enterprise Server 3 Book

Richard Cravens
$49.99, 480 pages, part #: 1-56604-664-5

- Detailed examination of web-site security issues and benefits.
- Complete coverage of installation, configuration and maintenance, along with troubleshooting tips.
- Shows how to enrich web sites with multimedia and interactivity.

CD-ROM contains sample HTML editors, HTML references, current Netscape plug-ins.

For Windows NT & UNIX • Intermediate to Advanced

Official Netscape Technologies Developer's Guide

Luke Duncan, Sean Michaels
$39.99, 352 pages, part #: 1-56604-749-8

- Guide to the most critical ONE SDKs and APIs—CORBA/IIOP, IFC, plug-ins and server-side JavaScript.
- Overview of Internet/intranet application development with IFC.
- Example plug-in project to integrate multiple aspects of Netscape ONE.

All Platforms • Intermediate to Advanced

VENTANA

Official Netscape SuiteSpot Book

$49.99, 640 pages, illustrated, part #: 1-56604-502-9

Integrate your intranet with Netscape's power tools! Here's all you need to set up, configure and manage an intranet using any or all five Netscape SuiteSpot servers. With thorough coverage of each server, you'll learn to choose the SuiteSpot servers that best fit your needs. Follow step-by-steps to maximize the myriad advanced features and build an integrated intranet with SuiteSpot. Or get to know its features and benefits before you invest.

Official Netscape ONE Book

$49.99, 500 pages, illustrated, part #: 1-56604-632-7

Your ONE-Stop Reference for Internet/intranet Solutions. Netscape's Open Network Environment (ONE) provides the tools and technology for developing versatile applications with cross-platform functionality. This in-depth guide helps you harness ONE to create integrated Web solutions that balance ease of use with economy of resources—both financial and human. Learn to master the basic tools, streamline development with Internet Foundations Classes (IFC) and much more. The CD-ROM features all the code examples from the book; complete step-by-step plug-in example.

VENTANA

Novell IntranetWare: The Comprehensive Guide

Mark R. Bell, Heath Ramsey
$54.99, 1152 pages, illustrated, part #: 666-1

The latest Network Operating System (NOS) from Novell enables you to add all the functionality of Internet technologies to your internal network and open it to global resources in the bargain. Learn how to start from scratch with IntranetWare—or make the smooth transition from an existing Novell LAN or WAN—to build a powerful, versatile system that's easy to administer. More readable than typical networking study guides and packed with real-life examples.

Platform-independent • Intermediate to Advanced

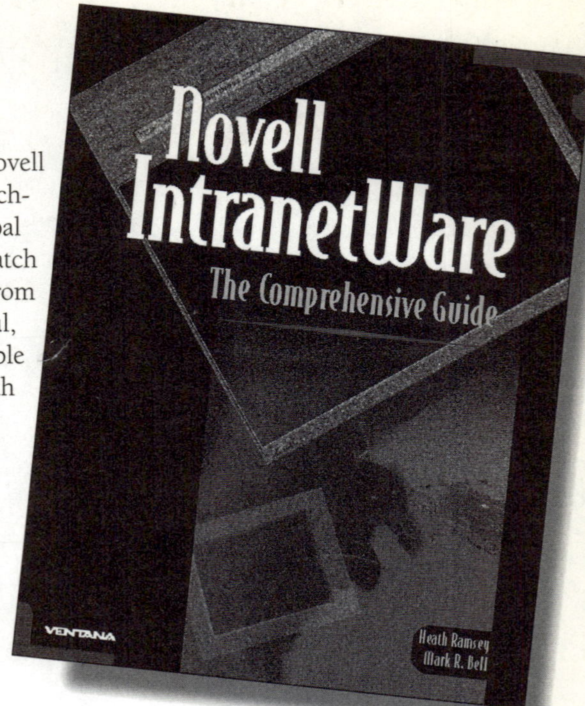

ActiveX Development With Visual Basic 5

Evangelos Petroutsos
$49.99, 600 pages, illustrated, part #: 648-3

Developing ActiveX controls is just the beginning! This advanced guide takes VB programmers into the wider world of ActiveX, as it applies to the desktop, intranets, the Internet and more. Also covers VBScript.

CD-ROM: Extensive collection of ActiveX controls; shareware, links and source code for examples.

For Windows 95/NT, Macintosh
Intermediate to Advanced